Play

Therapy

WITH ADULTS

Play
Therapy
WITH ADULTS

Edited by **Charles E. Schaefer**

John Wiley & Sons, Inc.

βS

Library of Congress Cataloging-in-Publication Data:

Play therapy with adults / editor, Charles E. Schaefer.
     p. cm.
   Includes bibliographical references and index.
   ISBN 0-471-13959-9 (cloth : alk. paper)
    1. Recreational therapy. 2. Play therapy. I. Schaefer, Charles E.

   RC489.R4 P56 2002
   615.8′5153—dc21

                            2002029618

Printed in the United States of America.

10 9 8 7 6 5 4 3 2 1

1/7/05

To the inner child in every adult

Contents

Preface

Adults need to play. We are working creatures, we are bonding creatures, and we are playing creatures.

—John R. Kelly, Sociologist

Philosophers from Plato to Sartre have observed that people are most human, whole, free, and creative when they play. In the Western world there has been a growing recognition that the need to play is not a trivial or childish pursuit but remains a powerful, positive force throughout our lives. Prominent mental health professionals, such as Martin Seligman and Lenore Terr, have recently pointed out that the three prime pillars of mental health are love, work, and play. Each of these three great realms of human behavior are interwoven, enrich one another, and contribute to psychological and physical health.

In the twentieth century, play therapy has emerged as a field unto itself that is being successfully applied not only with children, but with adolescents and adults as well. Insights into the healing powers of play are being discovered by investigators from such diverse fields as anthropology, child development, psychology, psychiatry, physical education, ethology, theology, and a growing number of other disciplines. The study of play and playfulness is part of a trend in our culture toward realizing the importance of "right brain" sources of human activity.

The purpose of this book is to present in one volume the diverse approaches and clinical strategies employed by play therapists with adult populations. To provide authoritative and up-to-date information, I asked pioneers and innovators in the field to write an original chapter on their area of expertise. The contributors not only offer compelling reasons for using play in adult therapy, but give specific, "hot to" strategies for incorporating play in therapy sessions. They describe the use of role play, verbal play (humor), doll play, sandplay, and game play modalities, as well as applications with both young adults and the elderly.

Interdisciplinary in approach, eclectic in theory, and comprehensive in scope, this state-of-the-art handbook should prove to be an essential resource in the field. Hopefully, this book will encourage beginning and experienced clinicians from all disciplines to make greater use of fun, fantasy, and playful activities to enliven and enrich their therapeutic interactions. Given the fear and darkness the world has known since September 11, 2001, we should not hesitate to brighten spirits and relieve suffering through play and laughter.

CHARLES E. SCHAEFER

Contributors

Kate Amatruda, MA, LMF, ISST
International Society for Sandplay
    Therapy
Psychotherapist/Private Practice
Novato, California

Adam Blatner, MD
Writer, Teacher
Georgetown, Texas

**Christine Caldwell, PhD, LPC,
    ADTR**
Associate Professor
Somatic Psychology Department
Naropa University
Boulder, Colorado

David Cantor, JD, FLFT
Staff Therapist
Rimmon Pond Counseling Center
Seymour, Connecticut

Mally Ehrenfeld, PhD, RN
Head, Department of Nursing
Tel Aviv University
Tel Aviv, Israel

Harriet S. Friedman, MA, MFT
C. G. Jung Institute
Los Angeles, California

Laura W. Hutchison, MA
Center for Humanistic Studies
Detroit, Michigan

Miller James, PhD, RDT
Institutes for the Arts in
    Psychotherapy
New York, New York

David Read Johnson, PhD, RDT
Institutes for the Arts in
    Psychotherapy
New York, New York

Jennifer Kendall, PsyD
Private Practice
Lancaster, California

Robert J. Landy, PhD
Professor and Director
Drama Therapy Program
New York University
New York, New York

Herbert M. Lefcourt, PhD
Professor of Psychology
Department of Psychology
University of Waterloo
Waterloo, Ontario, Canada

Kathleen S. Mayers, PhD
Las Vegas, Nevada

Rie Rogers Mitchell, PhD, ABPP
Professor and Chair
Educational Psychology and
    Counseling
California State University
Northridge, California

Joseph Richman, PhD
Professor Emeritus
Albert Einstein College of Medicine
Bronx, New York

Charles E. Schaefer, PhD, RPT-S
Professor
Psychology Department
Fairleigh Dickinson University
Teaneck, New Jersey

Marian Kaplun Shapiro, EdD
Licensed Psychologist
Lexington, Massachusetts

Ann Smith, MA, RDT
Institutes for the Arts in
    Psychotherapy
New York, New York

Steven M. Sultanoff, PhD
Clinical Psychologist
Adjunct Professor
Pepperdine University
Malibu, California
Staff Psychologist
Cognitive Therapy Center
Costa Mesa, California

**Dottie Ward-Wimmer, RN, MA,
    RPT-S**
William Wendt Center for Loss and
    Healing
Washington, District of Columbia

Daniel J. Wiener, PhD, LMFT
Professor
Marriage and Family Program
Central Connecticut State University
New Britain, Connecticut

Chapter 1 ────────────────────────────────

INTRODUCTION: THE HEALING POTENTIAL OF ADULTS AT PLAY

Dottie Ward-Wimmer

Susanna looked quite amazed. With an edge of anger and incredulity in her voice, she said, "You want me to play with this stuff? Well, I'm not going to."

The therapist explained that there were no expectations, and they could work in whatever way felt most comfortable to her. She sat stiffly on the couch and they began by just talking.

It wasn't long before curiosity won out. Over time, games were tried, art projects explored, and, eventually, the sand proved irresistible.

One day she took a great deal of time creating a scene using only three "neutral" objects. Then, sitting with her head resting on the edge of the tray, she gazed into it, tears falling silently.

When the session was over, she sighed, smiled, and quietly left. There was simply nothing to be said. Words would have been an intrusion.

The next morning, the therapist found a message on her voice mail. It was Susanna. "Thank you for letting me figure it out. I'll see you next week."

Play therapy is, indeed, a powerful tool for adults. Susanna had become stuck in her traditional talk therapy and was referred by her therapist who was "desperate" to help her unlock the deeply rooted and seemingly unspeakable feelings. Her therapist was right in referring rather than labeling Susanna *resistant,* for hope did find its way into her heart through the use of play.

PLAY AND PSYCHOLOGICAL ADJUSTMENT

Play, joy, and spontaneity are rooted in all of our hearts. Infants, driven by curiosity in their quest for survival, playfully explore with their entire bodies the universe

1

around them that is then translated into an inner world. Manipulation of the relationship between this inner self and the external world is a primary tool for growth. For adults, play continues as an important vehicle because it fosters numerous adaptive behaviors including creativity, role rehearsal, and mind/body integration.

Creativity

Carl Jung once said, "The small boy (himself) is still around, and possesses a creative life which I lack. But how can I make my way to it?" (Jung, 1965, p. 174). He subsequently learned that a key to unlocking his creative potential was to engage in the constructive play he had particularly enjoyed as a child.

Frey (1983) describes four categories of children's play: physical, manipulative, symbolic, and games. Adult activities in each of these categories hold enormous creative potential. In her book *Your Child's Growing Mind*, Dr. Jane Healy (1994) discusses techniques for creative people. These include play, humor, dramatizing, moving, imagining, listening, expressing, originating, and incubating. These qualities, too, are an intrinsic part of growth and are found in the literature on play therapy for adults.

Role Rehearsal

In their play, animals practice survival skills by engaging in play fighting and hunt and pounce games. We humans aren't so different. Children bandage imaginary hurts; spend hours pretending to cook, shop, travel, and go to school; and be everything from a firefighter to ballet dancer. They enact funerals, weddings, births, and literally all of life's milestones as they practice adaptive behaviors and grown-up roles.

Adults do the same thing, although in much subtler ways. How many of us have thought about or even had conversations aloud with ourselves in anticipation of a talk with someone else? How long do we stand in front of our mirrors trying on outfits, swaying to imagined music to be sure of how it (or I) will look? How often do we sit in awe at the circus and wish we could ride the elephants, too? And of course, there is the old favorite Halloween when, at last, we're allowed to play dress up!

Mind-Body Integration

Play is a wholistic experience in that it invites our total being into the process. Starting at the top: It uses both hemispheres of our brain. The left, analytical, side is essential in deciding what to do next, which strategies get us the win, and how it can be verbalized. The right, artistic, side allows us to enjoy the experience of turning the shapes of the clouds into magical creations. Moreover, the value and impact of beta-endorphins on our overall sense of well-being is well known.

Moving down into the body, we can look at other major systems. When we are laughing, singing, moving about happily, or simply engrossed in a pleasant diversion (i.e., play), we tend to take fuller breaths, thus getting a better oxygen exchange. When our digestive process relaxes, we reduce the chances of gastrointestinal disorder-not to mention the easing of cardiac tension. General muscle tension is eased, as well, when we play, which reduces fatigue and generalized body aches and stiffness.

THE COMPETITIVE NATURE OF PLAY

Children are no longer given old pots and wooden spoons, but instead are offered electronic drums that blink brightly colored lights. The infant's natural joy-filled kicking is now a means to an end as his or her movements trigger lights and sounds. And so, it begins the notion that results matter. By the time the child is in preschool, he or she has begun to learn the basics of competition and the importance of external approval.

It is easy to see how our ability to play freely for play's sake has gotten lost amidst our societal need to excel. Sandlot games have been replaced with highly organized football, baseball, and soccer leagues. Too often, kids need to "try out" because it's really about winning, not just playing. Underdogs are seen occasionally in movies such as *Bad News Bears, The Little Giants,* and *Rudy.* Yet, even then, their ultimate win is the core of the happy ending.

The roots of today's national mania with competitive sports may lie in our Victorian ancestors who believed that most amusements were frivolous and seductive by nature. As early as the mid 1800s, vigorous physical activity was being suggested as a way of offsetting the pleasures of the modern world (Rader, 1996). Thus began organized sports.

For better and worse, the organization of sports has changed the way we look at play in American culture. Play had historically been a reflection of the child's and adult's needs to experiment. It reflected the ethnic flavor of the group's roots, yet universal truths rang true. The *Counting Out* game of Trinidad (Nelson & Glass, 1992) parallels the *Wonder Ball* sung and played in the United States. The *Child is Down* (Nelson & Glass, 1992), about sleeping and suddenly waking, played in Sweden, is much like *Ring Around the Rosie,* a song we all know that has its roots in the streets of London. Dice and a variety of hoops and balls have been found in archeological digs all over the globe.

Traditional dances celebrating life events and reflecting the feelings of a culture are seen around the world. These are primarily adult activities with children as the learners. Anyone who has ever attended a traditional Greek wedding has probably been drawn into the joy and abandon of one of the many circle dances. Native American culture is also rich with ceremonial dancing. All across America today, a host of new and old traditional dances ranging from the chicken dance to country-western line dancing can be found.

That people of all ages have always played is clearly a historical fact. What is new is how we, in this culture, perceive and use it. In New Guinea, children play games in which neither side wins. The game ends when the two sides achieve equality. Japanese play focuses on group importance and interdependence rather than independence and self-expression. Native American children did not view "cheating" negatively. It was simply a creative trickster part of the game. That attitude changed after exposure to Euro-American culture (Rettig, 1995).

As our competitive society places rigid performance demands on us, childhood creativity is too often lost. In the need to score well on standardized tests, our inner drive to color outside the lines must be kept in check. Color-coordinated uniforms have replaced tee shirts and old shorts. Games must have a proven educational value and enjoyment must be kept in proper perspective. A woman was recently dismissed from her bowling team because she was having too much fun. Although she maintained a good average, it was felt that she wasn't taking her game seriously! That may be more telling about the core of our attitude toward play than the recent Little League scandal in which a father lied about his son's age in order to allow him to be on a winning team.

Small wonder that by the time we reach adulthood, we've lost touch with our ability to be loose and creative without worrying about what the other person is doing. There is a great line in the movie, *The Sure Thing* (1985), in which the heroine, in response to an accusation that she is uptight and repressed, defends herself by saying, "I am as spontaneous as anyone. I simply believe that spontaneity has its time and place."

INCORPORATING PLAY INTO ADULT THERAPY

Play can increase our self-esteem. It invites access to states of well-being and calm as well as silliness and joy. When relaxed in play, we often have an increased capacity for empathy and intimacy. Play is affirming. Diana Fosha (2000) describes joy and emotional pain among the affective markers of healing. Play becomes a natural and gentle environment in which the inner landscape can safely be explored in any language. The results are easy to see.

Stress Release

We are, generally, a nation of adults who must relearn the art of playfulness. Actually, most folks are quite willing. They just need permission.

> The staff gathered, notebooks in hand, for its regular staff meeting. The group knew the speaker on the agenda, and they expected an in-service; but what they got was two hours of pure fun.
>
> The director of the agency had arranged (unbeknownst to her staff) for a play shop as a holiday gift. The table was cleared and teams were formed (everybody won). Markers, sparkles, and stickers were used to decorate goody bags for carrying the prizes (candy bars, erasers, and other such treasures) and snack foods (nothing too healthful) appeared. The games had *no* educational value whatsoever, but their healing potential was undeniable. It was amazing to watch these professional caregivers emerge into creative, spontaneous, silly, and often quite loud playmates.

Business leaders are discovering the power of play to refresh, nurture, and reduce stress. Organizational development professionals often work with staff in playful ways to invite the most genuine, rather than narrow, cognitive responses. In major corporations across America, gyms are being made available because the physical release of stress is now understood. In most stressful jobs from business executive to therapist, the interview includes at least one question on self-care. Perhaps top executives have always known this, which explains the importance of golf in business relationships.

Business awareness notwithstanding, playfulness remains a competitive art form. However, competition in the hands of a play therapist can be turned to an advantage. When caught up in a contest, our other defenses are often down; and inner truth can, and often does, emerge.

> The game was simple. See who could make the longest list of answers (there were no right or wrong) to some ordinary questions.
>
> "What things would you find at a party?"
> "How many flavors of ice cream can you name?"
> "How do you feel when someone you love dies?"
>
> The "contestants" were so wrapped up in winning that filters were dropped and feelings that had never been expressed poured onto their papers. Even the guilt-provoking word *relieved* found its way into the open. Some didn't even

realize what they had said and so discovered some feelings they had never admitted to themselves before. Others knew what was on their minds and the hurried competition had allowed it to slip out. All of them discovered they were not alone; others had felt the same things.

Mastery

Competition, as powerful as it is, is not the only thing that invites play. Adults, like children, have a need to experience mastery. The ego is implicitly nurtured by the absence of failure. Play is the most natural tool because, in a therapeutic context, it is impossible to do wrong. As we saw with Susanna, having one's creativity witnessed and simply accepted invites the emergent self. "It is in playing and only in playing that the individual child or adult is able to be creative and to use the whole personality, and it is only in being creative the individual discovers the self" (Winnicott, 1971, p. 54).

They were just absently kneading the clay as they talked. She lined up four nondescript objects to prove that she was not at all creative.

Together they mused about the objects and the number four. A powerful memory emerged of an event that had happened when she was four years old. Through the clay, it found voice and the beginning of healing. The objects were kept in a special box and, from time to time, brought out to help piece together the puzzle of her past. The objects, though technically nondescript, clearly spoke the language of her heart.

Play Assessment

Therapy requires assessment, which is sometimes a fairly straightforward process. At other times, it can be elusive. This becomes even more complicated when the therapy and the client are to be eyed under the floodlights of a courtroom.

She was from a foreign land and was seeking asylum based on years of repeated abuse during her adolescence. Several court psychiatrists had said it was impossible to prove her allegations, and she would be deported. Fortunately for her, a savvy law student knew about play therapy and sought a consultation.

Over the course of three visits, several techniques were used. The woman she drew when invited to draw a person had a lovely smiling face but no hands or feet. Her sand tray was filled with themes of female helplessness, abandonment, and fear. And, although of average intelligence, it took her three times as long as an average seven-year-old to put together a puzzle that she had made as a metaphor for healing after trauma.

While the discrete allegations couldn't be proven, there was sufficient "play assessment" evidence of psychic trauma to convince the immigration attorney to drop the move for deportation and allow her to remain in the country. She is now in therapy in a sexual abuse clinic and is on her way to a peaceful life.

Communication: Speaking the Unspeakable

She had been in nonplay therapy for over a year. Haunted with nightmares and overwhelmed with anxiety attacks, she could do little more than scribble the hideous thoughts onto paper, then lock them safely in envelopes to be stored in the therapist's office.

Eventually, she was able to write some of the thoughts into brief stories about someone else. Then, in a carefully planned extended session, two playback performers were invited in. The client and the therapist sat at the far end of the room. The client read the first story aloud.

The actors played it out and sat down on the floor. As though they were alone in the room, the client and therapist talked and, when she was ready, the client asked to read another story. Again, it was simply acted out at the other end of the room. It was projection personified. Merciful and powerful, it gave unspeakable truth enough distance to be safely witnessed without being relived.

Perhaps the most interesting point of this story is that the playback was initiated by the client who had seen it done as a public performance piece and felt that somehow it might help her. At first, it was the therapist who was resistant. But, because she was also committed to helping her client heal, she did the necessary legwork to learn about the technique and invite it into the session. This proves once again that the client often knows what he or she needs, and it is our job to respectfully follow even when that means stretching.

Insight

He couldn't explain why this time was different. After all, he had worked at the city morgue for years. It was his job to retrieve the bodies, and so he had been to many gruesome scenes. But this was different—he couldn't stop pacing, and he WOULD NOT talk about it. He also made it clear that he was "not about to draw any pictures!"

After looking around the room for a while, he decided to throw clay (the therapist had a wall in the office for this purpose). For a long time, they were silent, simply throwing. The therapist followed the rhythm and intensity of his throwing. Eventually, he started to talk about how good it felt just to throw something. They remained in parallel conversation, making little eye contact. As they continued throwing, the story unfolded, each time bringing another detail of the specific event and important side issues clearer into focus.

After about 45 minutes, he simply looked at the therapist and said, "Oh my God!" Then he sat and wept. Not just because of the story, but rather because he was so relieved to discover that he wasn't "crazy." As he threw and retold the story, he had found the answer. He was simply an ordinary man who had been caught in a complex convergence of extraordinary circumstances.

Combined Powers

Most of these stories illustrate combinations of the therapeutic powers of play therapy. All play by its nature invites mastery. Physical motion invites release; creativity nurtures insight. Play and its therapeutic value reminds us of the old song "Dem Bones," which says "the head bone's connected to the neck bones," and so on. Play, whether with games, puppets, drums, clay, sports, motion, drawing, drama, dolls, sand, or whatever else is available, invites a cascade of positive effects.

There are endless possibilities for the use of play therapy with adults. Traumatologists have been using various play techniques for both debriefings and therapy for many years (Pynoos & Nader 1988; Shelby & Tredinnick, 1995). Marian Shapiro (1988) describes the use of hypno-play therapy as a technique that uses age regression in combination with play therapy. This results in ego reformation rather than just ego enhancement.

It must be remembered that play exists side by side with talk therapy. Play is not a means to get someone to "talk about it." Like children, adults can heal in the metaphor. Susanna is one example: Her therapist had, in fact, no idea what Susanna had "figured out" as she sat crying by her sand tray. It never emerged in subsequent sessions and, apparently, it never needed to. Exploring what happened may not be essential. Play therapists must be mindful of when and where to interject cognitive conversations.

The client couldn't find the right words and the therapist just couldn't "get it." They were both getting frustrated until finally they decided to dance. Using pieces of colored cloth and spontaneous dance moves, the client showed how she felt. Then the therapist repeated the move over and over until she "got it." It was fun, it was clear, and it allowed for a complete communication that could not be achieved with words.

That is the power and beauty of play. It is as much an art as it is a science.

THE PLAY THERAPIST AND THE PLAY ENVIRONMENT

We must be playful because we cannot expect our clients to go anywhere that we won't. But, playfulness is not necessarily a universal trait. A Playfulness Scale for Adults developed by Schaefer and Greenberg (1997) lists five factors: is fun-loving, has a sense of humor, enjoys silliness, is informal, and is whimsical. It may be useful to take a self-inventory before embarking on this kind of work.

A play therapist must be comfortable with metaphor and silence as well as words. He or she must have a courageous and trusting heart because the therapeutic use of play with adults is new territory. Like the therapist who tried out playback, we must be willing to listen to our clients and invite their wisdom into the healing plan. Playing with adults as they struggle with unseen issues is like walking in a minefield. We must be brave and very careful. Even so, it is well worth the effort. (Remember that the next time you're vacuuming sand and cleaning paint brushes.)

It is utterly wonderful work because it brings an enormous depth to the process. Often, when talking, we see only the "now" while hearing about the "then." Engrossed in play, however, the "then" comes fully into the room. Look into the eyes of a person smashing clay and you see the moment and truth of the pain, not just the memory. It is awesome.

Such power demands an appropriate environment. It must invite playfulness, but not appear childish for, above all, we must be respectful. One might carve out a corner of the playroom and make it the grown-up area with a small sofa or comfortable chairs. That is not to say that some people wouldn't sit happily on the floor, but many need to find their way there more slowly. We must also be mindful that certain toys may trigger traumatic memories, so we need to have a neutral space until we know the issues.

If you are starting in an already adult office, it may be a bit easier to accumulate the toys and games in one area of the room. Adequate soundproofing is needed because play often becomes quite exuberant, and many adults can become embarrassed by their capacity for abandon. And, you don't want to intimidate whoever is in the waiting room.

CONCLUSION

There is a story about soldiers lining opposing trenches during World War I. It was Christmas Eve and all shooting had stopped. Throughout that night and during Christmas day, first tentatively and then with greater enthusiasm, men came out of the bunkers. Carols were sung and a spontaneous soccer game broke out among the opposing soldiers to fill the hours of the truce.

Myth or miracle—either is a tribute to the power of play and the hope of the human spirit.

Play is a natural and enduring behavior in adults. It has healing powers for the mind and spirit that we are only beginning to appreciate and learn to use. The results of integrating play into our psychotherapeutic practice with adults are becoming clear and measurable. This volume lists a wide array of approaches and techniques, but they are just the beginning. It is now up to our clients and us to till this fertile and compassionate soil.

It was her first day of work as a counselor. She knew she had chosen well when she saw hanging on the wall in the office an embroidered quote attributed to C. Jung. It read, "Learn your theories as best you can, but lay them aside when you touch the miracle of the human soul."

With Jung's permission, perhaps we might add something:

Learn your theories as best you can, but lay them aside when you touch the miracle of the human soul. *Lay them aside and play!*

REFERENCES

The Bad News Bears. (1976). Culver City, CA: Paramount Studios.

Fosha, D. (2000). Meta-therapeutic processes and the affects of transformation: Affirmation and the healing affects. *Journal of Psychotherapy Integration, 10*(1), 71–97.

Frey, D. E. (1983). The use of play with adults. In K. O'Conner & C. Schaefer (Eds.), *Handbook of play therapy. Volume II: Advances and innovations* (pp. 189–205). New York: Wiley.

Healy, J. M. (1994). *Your child's growing mind.* New York: Doubleday.

Jung, C. G. (1965). *Memories, dreams and reflections.* New York: Vintage Books.

The Little Giants. (1994). Hollywood, CA: Warner Bros.

Nelson, W. E., & Glass, H. B. (1992). *International playtime.* Fearon Teacher Aids.

Pynoos, R. S., & Nader, K. (1988). Children who witness the sexual assault of their mothers. *Journal of the American Academy of Child and Adolescent Psychiatry, 27,* 567–572.

Rader, B. G. (1996). *American sports: From the age of folk games to the age of televised sports.* Lincoln: University of Nebraska.

Rettig, M. (1995, Winter). Play and cultural diversity. *Journal of Educational Issue of Language Minority Students, 15,* 93–106.

Rudy. (1993). Sydney, NSW: TriStar Pictures, Columbia TriStar Home Entertainment.

Schaefer, C., & Greenberg, R. (1997). Measurement of playfulness: A neglected therapist variable. *International Journal of Play Therapy, 6*(2), 21–31.

Shapiro, M. (1988, July). Hypno-play therapy with adults: Theory, method and practice. *American Journal of Clinical Hypnosis, 31*(1), 1–11.

Shelby, J., & Tredinnick, M. (1995, May/June). Crisis intervention with survivors of natural disaster: Lessons from Hurricane Andrew. *Journal of Counseling and Development, 73,* 491–497.

The Sure Thing. (1985). Los Angeles, CA: Embassy Film Associates.

Winnicott, D. W. (1971). *Playing and reality.* London: Tavistock.

PART I

DRAMATIC ROLE PLAY

Chapter 2

DRAMA THERAPY WITH ADULTS

Robert J. Landy

As I begin to write this chapter, it is several weeks after September 11, 2001, the day the terrorists struck the heart of America, killing some 3,000 innocent civilians and fomenting fear among millions. When asked in the ensuing days and weeks to attempt to make sense of these terrible events from the point of view of drama, generally, and drama therapy, specifically, I likened the effects of the attacks to breaking through the imaginary fourth wall in the theatre, separating audience from actor. If this were to happen, I reasoned, audiences would feel threatened and unsafe, as if the Romans in the ancient coliseums suddenly turned the lions loose on the spectators. When the tallest buildings in the grandest of cities crumbled like a giant erector set, those who took their safety for granted were shaken to the core. In violating the necessary and predictable separation of fantasy and everyday reality, the terrorists left many in America scrambling for ways to make sense of the trauma and move on. As the weeks passed and the inevitable political and military actions were taken, Americans were retraumatized with acts of bio-terrorism and threats of even greater attacks.

As a drama therapist prepared to counsel a range of adult clients, I envisioned proceeding dramatically. I would encourage my clients to play out their fears indirectly, to couch their stories in fictional terms, to express themselves nonverbally through sound and movement, to take on and play out the roles of various figures associated with the trauma. I would respond to my colleague, David Read Johnson (2000), who urges drama therapists to help clients play the unplayable. But when I first met with people who had just witnessed the attack and collapse of the Twin Towers, who had fled their downtown apartments in panic, who had lost contact with loved ones they feared had perished, there was a need to engage directly, to simply allow the stories to be told, unmediated by any obvious therapeutic intervention. The reality was dramatic enough. The play would come later.

With the events and aftermath of September 11 as a backdrop, I discuss several applications of drama therapy to adults. Throughout my discussion, I also suggest that during moments of crisis and trauma, drama therapy as a playful, indirect path to healing needs to be modified so that individuals can more directly tell their stories to empathetic listeners. To begin, we look at the development of a relatively young field with very ancient roots.

HISTORICAL BACKGROUND

It is generally assumed (see Kirby, 1975; and Brockett, 1999) that theatre originated many thousands of years ago as ritual activity performed for religious and healing purposes. The earliest actors were shamans (see Cole, 1975) who performed their ritual dances, songs, and stories to help restore balance and health to wounded individuals and to threatened communities who needed assurance that they would defeat their enemies, bear children, harvest food, and make peace with the spirit world. In the ancient Greek city of Epidauros, the hospital was built next to the great amphitheater, and there is evidence that the patients' treatment included the performance of roles in the Greek chorus.

As Western forms of theatre evolved from small celebrations in honor of the gods to performances for thousands of spectators, its focus changed from healing to entertainment. Over the centuries, with a developing literature and performance aesthetic, the theatre came to be known as a place where spectators could either reflect on the realities and confusions of everyday life or escape from them, indulging in the sensuous pleasures of the play. Throughout this history, some ignoble and notable figures have attempted to revive the essential therapeutic purposes of performance. The Marquis de Sade is one who, in eighteenth century France as an inmate of the institution at Charendon, directed mental patients in therapeutic dramas.

The best-known figure was the psychiatrist J. L. Moreno, a contemporary of Freud in turn-of-the-century Vienna. Moreno turned away from Freud's talking cure, insisting that a more powerful method of psychological healing can come from a dramatic enactment of intrapsychic and socially based problems. Moreno immigrated to the United States in the 1920s, where he established an institute and continued a long and prolific career. Moreno's innovative approaches to dramatic healing, which he called *psychodrama* and *sociodrama,* provided a model for other individuals who would discover more ways to help individuals and communities find balance through forms of enactment.

Dramatic approaches to healing were not unknown in the work of American psychologists in the middle of the twentieth century. Henry Murray employed a variety of role-playing approaches during World War II for the Office of Strategic Services to assess the qualities of potential army officers (see McReynolds &

DeVoge, 1977). Eric Homburger Erikson employed an early form of projective play, asking young men to enact their problems with miniature objects on a table top. This dramatic approach was part of Henry Murray's (1938) experimental personality studies at Harvard in the 1930s. George Kelly (1955) practiced a form of fixed role therapy, encouraging his clients to reconfigure problematic roles in the safety of the consulting room and to practice them in the same way that an actor rehearses a part in a play.

As a discipline in its own right, drama therapy emerged in several places throughout the 1960s and 1970s. In England, influenced by Peter Slade's experimentation in child drama, drama therapy emerged in the work of Sue Jennings with disabled children and Marion Lindkvist with populations of elderly clients and mentally ill adults. In Europe, influenced by the ideas of Evreinov (1927), Assagioli (1965), Moreno (1946), and the Gestalt psychologists, experimentation began in Germany with the work of Petzold (1973) and in the Netherlands with the development of undergraduate courses in drama and related creative arts therapies.

In the United States, a number of practitioners, initially unknown to each other, began work in New York, New Haven, Pittsburgh, and San Francisco. They included Gertrud Schattner and Robert Landy, David Read Johnson, Eleanor Irwin, and Renée Emunah. These and others worked with children, adolescents, adults, and elderly populations who had experienced a range of problems including identity and mood disorders, addiction, posttraumatic stress disorder, mental illness, and developmental disability.

In both Europe and the United States, a diversity of approaches mirrored the diversity of practitioners. Some, like Irwin (2000), remained grounded in psychodynamic theory and methodology. Others, like Schattner, Johnson, and Emunah, began their work with theatre games, popularized by Viola Spolin. Landy and Jennings, with strong roots in the theatre, developed theatrically based approaches, working with both texts and improvisation.

As the profession developed throughout the end of the twentieth century and into the new millennium, these and others solidified specific theoretical and treatment strategies. Examples include Johnson's play approach called Developmental Transformations; Emunah's eclectic approach incorporating dramatic play, ritual performance, and psychodrama, called the Five Phase Integrative Model; and Landy's theatrical and sociological approach, called Role Theory and the Role Method. In the anthology *Current Approaches in Drama Therapy* (Lewis & Johnson, 2000), 16 separate approaches are documented in the United States alone.

THERAPEUTIC RATIONALE

A central assumption shared by most drama therapists is that performance, the act of taking on a role and telling a story in role, is inherently healing. One explanation is that the act of role-taking marks a separation from everyday reality, thereby creating a safe distance between actor and role. When a young girl takes on the demeanor and voice of her mother and assures her teddy bear at bedtime that there is nothing to be afraid of in the dark, she is using the distance provided by the role of mother to reassure herself. In drama therapy, this natural, unselfconscious process of healing is consciously applied to therapeutic treatment.

In theory, the distance provided by the taking on of a role allows actors in everyday life to tell their stories safely, as the stories are not about them. To be more precise, the stories are simultaneously about them and *not* about them. Healing through drama occurs in the transitional space between me (the actor) and not me (the role). Bettelheim (1976), among others, has argued persuasively that the fiction of fairy tales allows children the safety they need to participate in a story that isn't directly about them but that recapitulates real themes in their lives and provides some sense of resolution. The archetypal psychologist Hillman (1983) refers to stories as *healing fictions,* emphasizing their therapeutic values.

Many action psychotherapists such as Jung (1971), Moreno (1946), and Perls (1972), as well as expressive therapists such as McNiff (1992) and Knill, Barba, and Fuchs (1995) have argued that verbal language alone is not sufficient in helping people work though embedded problems. They urge therapists to work also with images generated through sound and movement, painting and poetry, role playing, and story making. Johnson (2000) extends these ideas further, arguing that healing occurs not only through a playful encounter with images, but also and most essentially through a face-to-face encounter with perpetrators of a person's distress, symbolized by the therapist who playfully and provocatively engages with the client.

Although there are a number of theories circulating throughout the drama therapy literature, I focus primarily on one—that of role theory—as a way to further articulate the healing potential of performance. Role theory (see Landy, 1993, 2000) offers a view of the personality as a constellation of roles, called the *role system,* which is determined by a number of biological, psychological, social, and cultural factors. Roles within the system naturally exist in relationship to their counterparts with which they seek balance. As the role system develops, however, and the individual is exposed to a number of internal and external changes and challenges, the natural balance is disturbed and one or more roles tend to expand or contract. In the extreme, certain roles dominate the role system, like that of the fundamentalist who needs to shut down contradictory tendencies in order to embrace one fundamental principle. Subsequently, other roles recede. For example, for the fundamentalist to remain fully attached to the one role, he or she needs to deny the existence of other more questioning ones, such as critic, intellectual, ambivalent one, or rebel.

Like Jung, Landy (1993) argues that roles are essentially archetypal, recapitulating certain universal qualities recognizable to most human beings. In fact, he offers a Taxonomy of Roles (Landy, 1993), a system of repeated role types found throughout the history of Western dramatic literature. Landy argues that there is a correspondence between these dramatically based roles and those that regularly recur in drama therapy. Further, mirroring the thesis of sociologist Erving Goffman (1959), he argues that the roles in the taxonomy can be observed readily in everyday life.

At the heart of role theory in drama therapy is the intrapsychic model of role-counterrole-guide, which informs Landy's approach to practice. *Role* is a predictable set of thoughts, feelings, and behaviors that is recognizable as one aspect, rather than the totality of a person's existence. Applying the metaphor of world as stage and people as actors, role becomes a part that we play in our everyday lives. In speaking about roles from a drama therapy perspective, we see that they are prototypical, embodying universal qualities rather than stereotypical ones. According to Landy (1993), roles can be specified based on their unique qualities, functions, and styles of enactment.

Counterrole is another side of a role. It may be the opposite, as mother is to father, or it may simply be another aspect of father. The counterrole can be a dark, shadowy side of father, such as avenger, or it can be a light and playful part, such as clown. In keeping with role theory, the two parts of the model exist in a dialectical relationship, even as they strive toward balance. The imbalance between the two provides a healthy way for people to be able to reason effectively, sorting through conflicting thoughts, and to empathize with others, accepting multiple points of view.

When a single role becomes too large in a person's psyche, obscuring its relationship to a counterrole, the individual often experiences imbalance and, in some cases, distress. If I am too much the father or too much the victim or too much the clown, I risk losing my sense of balance. Returning to the example of the fundamentalist, this role can be seen in terms of a person who has lost his or her counterrole and is thus locked into a rigid way of thinking and behaving.

The third part of the model is the *guide*. This is the part that functions to integrate the role and counterrole. On an external level, the guide is an effective helper and/or nurturer—a parent, older sibling, elder, teacher, therapist, or leader. When the guide is positive and reliable, it is internalized and becomes a figure that helps individuals live well among their contradictory tendencies. The internal guide helps maintain order. When people become too much the fundamentalist in their thinking, the guide helps them locate an appropriate counterrole to restore balance. The wisdom of the guide facilitates a shift of consciousness from the thought that to live the moral life, people must destroy their enemies, to the thought that to live the moral life, people must make peace with their internal demons.

At the heart of role theory is the notion of *balance*. The drama therapist aims to help clients live within and among their contradictory tendencies. On one level, balance is conceptualized as the interrelationship of affect and cognition. The imbalanced person can be understood as either underdistanced, where an overflooding of affect leads to an experience of vulnerability and lack of containment, or overdistanced, where an extreme rationality blocks the free flow of feeling (see Landy, 1983, 1994, 1996a). The balanced person is characterized by aesthetic distance, a confluence of feeling and reflective thought, the ability to feel intelligently and to think feelingly.

As mentioned, balance is conceptualized in role theory through the model of role-counterrole-guide, where the external guide leads the individual on a search for balance and, once internalized, provides a means for the individual to effectively live among opposing tendencies.

RESEARCH SUPPORT

Drama therapy is a young field and one that, for the most part, produces more practitioners than researchers. Given its arts base, drama therapy presents a specific research challenge. Can or should an arts-based discipline be subject to the same methodological inquiry as its neighbors in the more purely psychologically based healing disciplines? Shaun McNiff (1998) argues persuasively for a new kind of research that is integral to the art-making process itself. Such an approach is modeled after the creative process as exemplified in the work of, for example, Peter Brook (1978), who sees his theatrical creations as research not only into a particular text, but also into its larger context, whether spiritual, political, or psychological.

There have been attempts to apply empirical research methodologies to drama therapy (see Landy, 1984; Rosenberg, 1999), with some promising, though inconclusive, results. However, the primary research approaches tend to be descriptive, theoretical, and qualitatively based. The richest research literature in drama therapy continues to be expressed through case study. When the clinical cases are grounded rigorously in theory, as readily seen in the work of Emunah (1994, 2000), Johnson (1988, 2000), and Landy (1993, 1996b, 2001), among others, the work takes on a complexity and clarity.

Some of the most powerful research in recent years is in the area of assessment. Working with Johnson's dramatic role-playing test, researchers have examined its efficacy with a number of different populations (see James & Johnson, 1997; Johnson, 1988). Landy's two instruments, Tell-A-Story and Role Profiles, are also yielding valuable research evidence as to efficacy and reliability (see Landy, 2001; Seitz, 2000; Tangorra, 1997; Tranchida, 2000).

IMPLEMENTATION

There are a number of practical approaches to drama therapy. As mentioned, 16 of the most prominent have been described in the book *Current Approaches to Drama Therapy* (Lewis & Johnson, 2000). These include psychoanalytic drama therapy, role theory and role method, the integrative five-phase model, developmental transformations, narradrama, developmental themes, psychodrama, sociodrama, ritual theatre therapy, the Stop-Gap method, recovery and individuation two-stage model, playback theatre, prison therapeutic communities, the Enact method, Omega transpersonal drama therapy, and family dynamic play. In this section, I focus on role method, derived from role theory.

The model of role-counterrole-guide informs the role method, which proceeds through a series of eight steps. When working through the role method, the drama therapist helps clients locate the figures of role and counterrole and discover a guide figure that can move the two toward integration. The steps of the role method follow:

1. Invoking the role.
2. Naming the role.
3. Playing out/working through the role.
4. Exploring relationships of role to counterrole and guide.
5. Reflecting on the role play: discovering role qualities, functions, and styles inherent in the role.
6. Relating the fictional role to everyday life.
7. Integrating roles to create a functional role system.
8. Social modeling: discovering ways that clients' behavior in role affects others in their social environments.

The first two steps of the role method provide a warm-up to the action. In general, drama therapists begin a group or individual session with a warm-up. The purpose of the warm-up is twofold. First, it helps to move the individual into a creative, playful state, loosening up the body, engaging the imagination, and establishing connections among group members. Second, it helps each individual invoke or locate a role. Once the roles are present, the drama therapist asks clients to name them. When the roles are named, the warm-up period is complete, and the clients are ready to move to the next stage of enactment.

There are many kinds of warm-up activities used by drama therapists. Some draw upon theatre games, where, for example, individuals in a circle create and transform movements and sounds. Many drama therapists use name games. One example involves a ball toss where the thrower calls out the name of the catcher, who does the same as the ball and the names circulate from person to person.

Consistent with role theory, I might ask individuals to tell stories, either reality- or fantasy-based, then identify and name the characters. Many times, I use a physical warm-up. I begin by asking individuals to move around the room comfortably, checking their bodies for tension and letting it go. I then ask them to focus on one part of their body and to let a movement extend from a knee, for example. Throughout, I encourage the group to play with the movement and then to find a character suggested by the movement. As we proceed, I ask the group to name the characters and to interact with others in their roles. Finally, I freeze the group and ask each individual to give a monologue in role, specifying age, gender, occupation or action, and a wish for the future.

Often the warm-up ends at this point, and the group is ready to move to the third stage of playing out/working through the role. However, some groups may be ready to do more in the warm-up, involving not only role, but also counterrole and guide. With such a group, I proceed by freezing them in role and asking them to slowly transform their bodies into a character on the other side of the role—a counterrole. They do this slowly by shifting their bodies and finding other body parts that can hold the counterrole. Once they have made the shift, they begin to move around the room again, interacting with others in their counterroles. As before, I ask them to name their counterroles and speak in monologue.

And finally, I again freeze the group and have them slowly move into the guide role. Once it is found, they repeat the process as before, naming and deepening their sense of the guide. At the conclusion of this process, I ask individuals to find one of the roles and sculpt it with their bodies, then slowly transform from one to the other, experiencing the shifts in their bodies. This experience ends as all are asked to embody the guide role and, as guide, to hold the role and counterrole, one in each hand, and to bring them toward their bodies, symbolically incorporating them.

At this point, the group is generally prepared to move to steps three and four, the enactment part of the session. The drama therapist might look for a single protagonist who would choose members of the group to play his or her roles. As an example, a woman named Ruth, having identified in the warm-up her initial role as lover, agreed to work on her issues. The drama therapist asked Ruth to embody the lover and then to de-role and choose a member of the group to sculpt in the role of lover. The figure of the lover was further explored as Ruth spoke to the lover, then gave her a series of directions to which she responded in movement. Finally, Ruth interacted with the lover through movement.

Ruth was then asked to choose another in the group and to sculpt her as the counterrole. When asked to name the counterrole, Ruth replied, "avenger." As before, Ruth spoke to the avenger. Next, she directed the avenger in movement. As she worked, Ruth realized that she was experiencing considerable anger and wanted the avenger to strike out at an unidentified enemy. The therapist facilitated this action, enrolling an empty chair as an enemy (a counterrole of the counterrole), and then asked Ruth to direct the avenger and lover to move together. Finally, Ruth engaged in the action, interacting with the lover and avenger/enemy.

In Ruth's work, a third figure, which she called God, the spiritual principle, emerged. In working with this figure, Ruth came to see it as a guide, the only one that could integrate the roles of lover and avenger/enemy.

The drama therapist might also choose to work with the entire group, exploring common issues and concerns through selected roles. As an example, in one session the group was completing its warm-up when one group member arrived late. Some people were angry and demanded that she leave. Others felt equally strong about wanting her to stay. The drama therapist asked the group to specify a role for the latecomer. After several suggestions, all agreed on the name—*intruder*. The group worked with the role of the intruder in relationship to its counterrole, which they called the *in-crowd*. Individuals composed fictional stories about intruders breaking into established communities. The group chose to dramatize one story about an exuberant but iconoclastic man who intrudes on a conventional island culture. Through working with this figure, the group learned that the intruder can actually become a guide.

During steps five through seven, an individual and/or the full group reflects on the enactment, attempting to make sense of it. Following the previous examples, the drama therapist led the group into a discussion of Ruth's roles of lover, avenger/enemy, and God, both as archetypal concepts and as parts of Ruth's intrapsychic life. Through the discussion, Ruth looked for ways to integrate the part of her that is loving with the part that seeks revenge. To temper the part of her that felt most vengeful, Ruth turned to her spiritual guide, the figure of God, which she thought she had left behind in her childhood. In their discussion, members of the group naturally related Ruth's story to that of the recent terrorist attacks. Many openly expressed their anger and need for revenge, which felt hard to reconcile with their avowed peaceful natures. Out of the discussion came a need for a spiritual principle to contain the anger many felt toward the terrorists. Group members supported Ruth and told their own personal stories of love and loss and fantasies of revenge, of uncontrolled sadness, and of spiritual comfort.

In the second example, the full group examined its struggles with conformity and control. In viewing the connection between the intruder and the in-crowd, the group moved toward a greater understanding of its dynamics, even rethinking the concept of *intrusion,* transforming it from a negative burden to a positive guide that, though irritating, can lead the way to a more open environment.

Through the enacted dramas and the reflections on the role dynamics, groups move toward a greater sense of balance and integration. Individuals in drama therapy go through the same process with a similar goal of balance in mind, beginning with an identification and naming of roles, followed by an enactment, and ending with a reflection on the role play.

Social modeling is the last stage of the role method. Generally, this stage occurs outside the therapy group. It occurs when individuals have experienced a change, a new sense of balance and integration among their roles. They then become positive role models for others—not only in the therapy group, but also in the family, workplace, and community. As Ruth became better able to make peace with her need for revenge, she provided a way for others confronting terror to do the same.

The role method is not necessarily linear. Some clients are unable to invoke a role. Some are unable to tell a story. Others have so much to say that their role systems are overflowing with complex figures. Some begin therapy with a guide figure intact; others, with a missing guide.

In working through the role method, the drama therapist needs to be flexible enough to begin at the functional level of the individual or group. For those who can fluidly make the transition between reality and imagination, the method often proceeds chronologically, from invocation of role to social modeling, from warm-up to enactment to reflection. For those traumatized by an event like that of September 11, the sense of order breaks down. One understanding of trauma from the point of view of the role method is that the three parts have become separated, leading to imbalance on many levels of body, mind, and spirit. In this and indeed all cases, the drama therapist needs to be prepared to help clients locate significant role and counterrole figures that have the potential to seek balance with the aid of an effective guide. If an internal guide is missing, the drama therapist must be willing to stand in as long as it takes for the client to internalize that most critical healing figure.

CASE EXAMPLES

The first people I treated in the immediate aftermath of September 11 were at the very least frightened and bewildered; many were traumatized. Because my office is near Ground Zero, some of my clients actually witnessed the planes hit the World Trade Center and the subsequent collapse of the buildings. Some witnessed more grisly scenes—people in high floors of the towers leaping out windows to their deaths, workers covered in white dust, running uptown. One client evacuated her building just two blocks away, running for her life. Several were unable to contact their loved ones who worked in the buildings. One lost her husband. Others lost family members and friends.

As I met with these people, I learned that most were clear as to external counterrole figures, pointing to the terrorists who commandeered the planes into the Twin Towers, the Pentagon, and a field in Pennsylvania, and to Osama Bin Laden and his terrorist network, Al Qaeda. Many, however, felt less clear as to guide figures. Experiencing confusion, disorientation, and loss of control, they told me of feeling disconnected from parents, teachers, religious leaders, and even God.

The role I witnessed most clearly in their presence was that of victim. These people were in crisis, and they needed containment. It was not time to play, to invite them to find a role in their bodies, or to toss a ball. It was not time to enter a fictional, once-upon-a-time frame and make up a story. It was time to listen and to witness.

As listener and witness, I felt I could most effectively embody the qualities of the guide. As such, my goal was to help the clients find ways to tell their stories. It was a struggle for me at first to maintain the mantle of the guide because I had experienced my own sense of helplessness and horror as the towers fell when I was approaching downtown New York. Yet, thrust in the role of counselor and therapist, with a clear mission, I found a way to play my roles with conviction. The more I played guide roles for others, the more I was able to guide myself. Mine was not a story of evil villains and heroes, of terrorists and rescue workers; mine was a story of trauma and recovery, of depression and expression.

And so I listened to the stories—uncritically, quietly. Some were heartbreaking and needed to be told repeatedly. A woman lost both her adult children and had to take on the burden of raising her two young grandchildren. A father lost his job and couldn't sleep, fearing he would not be able to care for his family. A woman needed to fly to a foreign country for her brother's wedding but could not get on the plane. Others had children who acted out aggressively in school, stopped eating, wet their beds, or had trouble breathing.

Some told stories of how the events transformed their lives, provoking a new sense of vitality. One man, chronically depressed and alienated, told of making his way down to Ground Zero. His story was one of resourcefulness as he managed to penetrate the various checkpoints and befriend policemen and firefighters. As if in a dream, he found himself on a bucket brigade, 48 hours after the tragedy, working through the night with rescue workers from around the world. Feeling more fully alive than ever before, he witnessed the most amazing spectacle he could ever imagine. The massive destruction of lives and land presented an awesome vision of apocalypse. In addition, for a short time, he had a profound mission and human connection that he feared would be lost when he left. When he did finally leave, knowing that he would never be allowed to come back, he could not get one person to return his phone calls.

As I listened to the stories, I made an assumption: At some point, many of the clients would be ready to play, to move their stories into a more risky, complex realm. The readiness would depend on several factors. First, they would need to feel safe. Second, they would need to feel connected, at least to me, as guide, or to others in the group. Finally, they would need to feel that their stories have been heard and witnessed. One new group that had met just once before September 11 reconvened three days after the terrorist attacks. Each person had the need to tell his or her story. Many experienced a feeling of safety and connection, and a sense that they had been witnessed. One week later, they felt ready to play.

The group began with a discussion of how children were dealing with the tragedy. Several wanted to explore this concern dramatically and playfully. Jean, a leader in the group, cast herself as a kindergarten teacher. Four others took on the roles of children. The qualities they presented were fun-loving and playful. Jean, as teacher, told the children that many emotions have arisen since the events of September 11 and that emotions are very important to talk about. She asked them to enact happy feelings, which they did by laughing. Then she asked them to portray anger. They stomped their feet and made loud grunting noises. When she asked them to show sadness, they cried and frowned.

The teacher continued: "What event made everyone go through all of those emotions?" They said that planes had hit some buildings. One student thought it was a spaceship. The teacher encouraged them to play out their responses. In preparing for this, she asked: "Who wants to show me what the buildings looked like?" Two students stood side by side, their bodies rigid. The other two students became very excited about being the airplanes. They zoomed and swooshed all around the room, with arms out to the sides as wings.

The teacher asked: "Okay, then what happened?" One child ran into a building and immediately fell down and rolled around the floor. A second hit the building, squatted down, and jumped up high in the air with a loud Ka-Boom, then lay down on the floor. After a few moments, the teacher said: "Oh no! You guys are all on the floor! How are you going to get up? Who can help you get up and clean up this mess?" One child said that a fireman could help. The teacher told them all to be firemen and help each other up and clean up the mess. They did so. One of the students acted as if she had a water hose. It was a big hose and she couldn't hold it alone. So, all the children came over and grabbed a piece of the hose and they worked together to extinguish the fire. One student took on the role of an ambulance and made a sound like a siren. The other children carried stretchers. Then one child stopped and said, "Wait! Not everybody was rescued. Some people died." The play stopped.

The teacher persisted: "It's true. Some people did die." The children said that it made them feel sad. They hugged themselves and pretended to cry. The teacher continued: "A lot of people feel sad right now. Can you think of something that you did with your family to make yourself feel better?" One child said that they lit candles at the firehouse. The teacher invited them to get out candles and she approached each one, pretending to light the pretend candles.

Finally, they all sat down close together and closed their eyes. The teacher asked them to say a silent prayer or to think about hope and peace.

After de-roling, the group reflected on their play. The reflective process continued over the ensuing weeks. Jean, who played the teacher, was particularly articulate in specifying how the play hastened her healing around the traumatic events of September 11:

It affected me quite a bit. I have carried this presentation around with me. The innocent play of the children seemed to lay it all out before me in such a simplistic way that now I could deal with my own confusions. The role of the firemen and the people lighting candles represented hope and peace. The airplanes were the destroyers and the roles of the buildings, the destroyed. Throughout the piece, the struggle between power or control and loss of power or control was evident. The buildings started out in control, strong and rigid. Then the airplanes took control and the buildings lost all of their power. Then the firemen regained control and began to work to make it better. However, that control was diminished by the idea that not everyone could be saved. They have no control over the loss of life. For someone in a life-saving profession, that can be very difficult to swallow. Then, finally, control was regained by doing something about the sadness and lighting a candle and speaking to a higher power. I have gone back and forth between those same struggles myself, wanting to help, and not being able to. I felt that praying and lighting candles was so insignificant at first until this presentation made me realize that my frustration was stemming from a loss of control, and lighting candles and praying does help me gain a little of that control back. Every single candle makes a difference. The light of the candles is what helped the rescue workers keep going. In that way, I did contribute. In that way, I did take on the role of the peacemaker. Seeing the children get such pleasure out of playing the destroyer, the airplanes, was frightening at first. But, it makes sense. Children probably felt so out of control during this whole experience. The feeling of control was probably very good for them. It's sort of funny but I received quite a bit of healing. I walked away from the room that day with a new outlook on the events of September 11. I realized that I can pick myself up and keep going as long as I hold in mind the image of those children. I keep focusing on the role of the teacher, the one who is in control, yet also allows herself to feel emotion. We are all going to feel destroyed at one time or another. It is good to know that there are always things that we can do to make ourselves feel better. When we feel out of control, we just need to find something that gives us a little bit of control back and to remember that it is okay to not be able to do it alone. It is okay to need family and friends right now to help me stand up and "hold my hose."

During the play, the group worked through the stages of the role method, from invoking and naming the critical roles in the drama, playing them out, discovering counterroles and guide roles, and, finally, reflecting on their role play. Some, like Jean, have experienced a new sense of balance and have become role models for others.

The next example is of work with an individual whom I call Roger. For several weeks after September 11, Roger, a 50-year-old man with a history of mood and anxiety disorders, came in with images of destruction and war. On our first meeting, he told me: "As a child I was bitten by a fish and from then on it was jihad." He posed the question to me: "Why did the World Trade Towers fall?" and answered it himself: "Because they were too tall." He compared them to the biblical Tower of Babel that signified the pride of men who believed they could find a direct path to God.

Unlike many clients, Roger, whom I had worked with for two years, was ready to work projectively and playfully. From a discussion about religious fundamentalism two weeks after September 11, he wanted to dramatize an encounter with God through sand play. I keep a sand tray in my office below shelves of miniature objects representing animals, nature, and people in various actions and roles. He chose a Frankenstein figure to represent God. He picked a pregnant, naked woman with her hands on her belly and named her the Holy Mother. He chose a small baby to stand between Frankenstein and the Holy Mother. He also chose Indians with spears to wound God.

Roger set these figures up in the sand tray and told a story. God, the Holy Mother, and the baby fly away on a voyage and fall down "like the World Trade Center." Frankenstein/God resurrects and flies up, in search of the Holy Mother. The baby tells him: "You are a monster without her." Through a series of battles, mock deaths, and resurrections, all three fall down in the end. Roger reflects on the scene: "There are no survivors. We have to find the Holy Mother."

For Roger, God is a wounded figure in search of a female counterpart that is both holy and sexual. The baby figure, both born and unborn, stands as a guide to unite man and woman and to transform the evil, represented by the monster, into good, represented by God.

Two months after the two planes crashed into the World Trade Center, another plane crashed in Queens, an apparent accident, killing all passengers and retraumatizing many in the city. Roger came in the day after the crash and told me he was afraid he was about to eat a lot of sand. I thought he was referring to our previous work in sand play or even to the survivors whose mouths were full of dust after the collapse of the towers. Not certain, I asked him to tell me more about the sand, and he responded: "It's from the sandman." I then asked him to take on the role of the sandman and he spoke: "I am the sandman. I give my sand to Roger so that he can sleep. I need lots of sand, more than he can use, like the blood that was collected on September 11 and had to be thrown away. Now I'm going to be without a job. My work is to pour the sand into the machinery to slow down the machine and cause sleep. Some people say it's scary business, but it saves Roger. When he's asleep, he's like Rip Van Winkle. After 25 years, he's waking up. It's time for him. It's time for him to wake up."

When I asked Roger what happened 25 years ago, he recalled an episode in his life that led to his own "crash." The episode occurred when he was working in a large, elegant restaurant. On a cold, snowy night in December, his father appeared at the restaurant unannounced and began walking through the main dining room, searching for his son. At the time, his father was mentally ill and had walked away from a hospital where he was being treated for a major psychiatric illness. Roger watched from a distance behind the bar, as his father wandered from table to table intensely scanning the faces of guests and employees. Humiliated, Roger grabbed him by the arm and walked him outside. There Roger screamed at his father and told him never to come back again. A passing car stopped and a man asked, "Is everything okay?" Roger's father replied, "Yeah, it's just a father and a son."

After their harsh words, Roger's father offered to drive him home in his car. Roger got in and was horrified by the mess—prescription pills, papers, and garbage were everywhere. The father was having trouble driving and Roger was frightened. Then his father turned on the radio and the heater and Roger felt more comfortable. He was being driven home safely by his father. Having finished the story, Roger looked up at me and said, "I want to be driven home by you."

It was time to play, and I wondered how we should do it. As the moment felt so quiet and meditative, I suggested that Roger meditate on the image of a car ride with me. He liked my idea but added his own. He wanted me to meditate on the same image. I agreed. Over a period of a year, Roger had asked me a number of times to meditate briefly with him at the beginning of a session. Following our meditations, he would tell me what he saw and, if asked, I would share with him some of my images. The ritual of meditation became part of our warm-up, a place to invoke and name roles, a place to connect not only in the transference, but also as two grounded human beings, full of images.

Following our brief meditation, Roger told his story. He saw many different cars. He was the driver and I was the passenger in a sports car. There was a head-on collision. We both survived and moved on to a large black car. Roger felt nauseous and sick. He was attached to an intravenous line. Then we moved to another car and I was taking Roger to a professional conference. Roger listened and went along with the action, even as I became angry with a man at the conference. We were then in a golf cart, filming the movie, *Cast Away* (2000), about a man who survives a long period of isolation on a desert island. Roger drove to the edge of a cliff and crashed into the ocean. He awoke in a swimming pool in a resort and someone spoke: "Your car is waiting. Are you ready?" Finally, he and I were in a spaceship, fighting a battle with other spaceships. We were okay, intact, safe, even though we were fighting. Roger felt a shift in his body. He was letting go.

When he asked me to speak, I told Roger of a scene in a large black convertible. I was a passenger and Roger was driving. He took us to a cemetery and parked near his father's grave. He walked over to the tombstone and lifted it off the ground. It was light and became a scroll on which are inscribed the Ten Commandments. He took it in the car and drove back to the house. He excitedly told me of his discovery. Once inside, he took out a camera and filmed the scroll. It would become the centerpiece for a film he was making about the spiritual rebirth of the city.

After the experience, I asked him, "What was the ride like for you?" He replied: "I felt that your meditation led me to my goal—to sit back and enjoy the ride. It was like the feeling I had when my father finally turned on the music and the heater in the car 25 years ago. It was warm and despite the humiliation and the craziness, I was being taken home."

"But you were driving me," I said, "in both of our meditations."

"I was in control," he replied. "I knew where I had to go and what I needed to do. I just needed you to be there with me."

When the planes driven by terrorists crashed into the city, Roger reexperienced a time in his life, 25 years before, of humiliation and terror. To cope with these feelings, he shut down. Like Rip Van Winkle, he went to sleep. The sandman, that part of him that shut down the machinery of feeling, was in control. The events of September 11 were also an opportunity for Roger to revisit that time and to replay not only the public humiliation of his father's mental illness, but also the ride back home in the comfort of his father's car, the best vehicle he had to shepherd his son to safety. As Roger and I played out our car ride together, we discovered a new connection between guide and novice, between man and man. It is possible to go through many journeys, even those involving collisions, sickness, crashes, and battles, and still arrive intact, having enjoyed the journey. Roger noted that, in my story, the tombstone is transformed into commandments that complete the film, a story of resurrection.

"Maybe the towers were too high," said Roger. "Maybe my internal jihad was too fierce. Who knows? I think now is a time to rebuild."

Twenty-five years ago, a terrorist stalked Roger. It was his father. Feeling like a helpless child, Roger succumbed. He tried to fight back but ultimately felt humiliated and defeated in the role of son. The counterrole of mentally ill terrorist father was too overpowering. In search of a guide, Roger found a sandman to put him to sleep so he did not have to confront the terror again. When the terrorists hit New York on September 11, Roger was retraumatized, but ready to replay the defining event of his last 25 years.

In telling the story and taking a symbolic, playful car ride with a new guide, the therapist, Roger was able to review and rethink the episode. In the end, with a new guiding relationship, Roger was able to transform the meaning of *jihad* from uncontrolled terrorism to a journey toward meaning. With the new guide offering a vision of transformation, Roger, the son, discovered a way to father himself.

CONCLUSIONS

Play is generally a means of stepping back from the requirements and routines of everyday life and imaginatively creating an alternative reality and entering into it for no particular conscious reason, just for the fun of it. When the play is applied to a therapeutic process, as it is in drama therapy, a conscious purpose arises—to offer a commentary on, or corrective of, everyday life, thereby gaining a greater sense of control.

As we have seen, adults can play like children; and often this kind of play is therapeutic, especially in dealing with trauma. However, many adults in crisis are not ready to play, or, to be more precise, they are not able to play like children. In most instances, adults in need of therapy need to play like adults. This most often means, verbally and cognitively, sparring with language, telling stories, playing out alternative scenarios in thought, even meditating. But sometimes, when they are ready, after their stories have been told and witnessed, adults in drama therapy might be willing to take another step. By regressing and playing the roles of buildings and planes and fire hoses, even of children going for rides in their fathers' cars, they may, like those in the previous examples, experience a sense of control and balance. After the play, it can be equally rewarding to resume the adult consciousness and to reflect on the play and recognize its capacity to contain contradiction.

Play is a great balancer, a stage for heroes and villains, terrorists and firefighters, fathers and son, roles and counterroles. Because it isn't real, it can offer endless possibilities. Because it offers endless possibilities, it is essentially truthful, a rarefied reality.

REFERENCES

Assagioli, R. (1965). *Psychosynthesis: A manual of principles and techniques*. New York: Viking Press.

Bettelheim, B. (1976). *The uses of enchantment*. New York: Knopf.

Brockett, O. (1999). *History of the theatre* (8th ed.). Boston: Allyn & Bacon.

Brook, P. (1978). *The empty space*. New York: Macmillan.

Cast Away. (2000). Burbank, CA: Twentieth Century Fox and Dreamworks.

Cole, D. (1975). *The theatrical event*. Middletown, CT: Wesleyan University Press.

Emunah, R. (1994). *Acting for real: Drama therapy process, technique, and performance*. New York: Brunner/Mazel.

Emunah, R. (2000). The integrative five phase model of drama therapy. In P. Lewis & D. R. Johnson (Eds.), *Current approaches in drama therapy* (pp. 70–86. Springfield, IL: Charles C Thomas.

Evreinov, N. (1927). *The theatre of life*. New York: Harrap.

Goffman, E. (1959). *The presentation of self in everyday life*. Garden City, NY: Doubleday.

Hillman, J. (1983). *Healing fiction*. Barrytown, NY: Station Hill.

James, M., & Johnson, D. R. (1997). Drama therapy in the treatment of combat-related post-traumatic stress disorder. *Arts in Psychotherapy, 5*, 383–395.

Johnson, D. R. (1988). The diagnostic role-playing test. *Arts in Psychotherapy, 15*, 23–36.

Johnson, D. R. (2000). Developmental transformations: Toward the body as presence. In P. Lewis & D. R. Johnson (Eds.), *Current approaches in drama therapy* (pp. 87–110). Springfield, IL: Charles C Thomas.

Jung, C. G. (1971). *Psychological types*. Princeton, NJ: Princeton University Press.

Kelly, G. A. (1955). *The psychology of personal constructs* (Vol. 1). New York: Norton.

Kirby, E. T. (1975). *Ur-drama: The origins of theatre*. New York: New York University Press.

Knill, P., Barba, H., & Fuchs, M. (1995). *Minstrels of the soul*. Toronto, Ontario, Canada: Palmerston.

Landy, R. (1983). The use of distancing in drama therapy. *Arts in Psychotherapy, 10*, 175–185.

Landy, R. (1984). Conceptual and methodological issues of research in drama therapy. *Arts in Psychotherapy, 11*, 89–100.

Landy, R. (1993). *Persona and performance: The meaning of role in drama, therapy and everyday life*. New York: Guilford Press.

Landy, R. (1994). *Drama therapy: Concepts, theories and Practices* (2nd ed.). Springfield, IL: Charles C Thomas.

Landy, R. (1996a). Drama therapy and distancing: Reflections on theory and clinical application. *Arts in Psychotherapy 23*, 367–373.

Landy, R. (1996b). *Essays in drama therapy: The double life.* London: Jessica Kingsley.

Landy, R. (2000). Role theory and the role method of drama therapy. In P. Lewis & D. R. Johnson (Eds.), *Current approaches in drama therapy* (pp. 50–69). Springfield, IL: Charles C Thomas.

Landy, R. (2001). Role profiles: An assessment instrument. In R. Landy (Ed.), *New essays in drama therapy: Unfinished business.* Springfield, IL: Charles C Thomas.

Lewis, P., & Johnson, D. R. (Eds.). (2000). *Current approaches in drama therapy.* Springfield, IL: Charles C Thomas.

McNiff, S. (1992). *Art as medicine: Creating a therapy of the imagination.* Boston: Shambhala.

McNiff, S. (1998). *Art-based research.* London: Jessica Kingsley.

McReynolds, P., & DeVoge, S. (1977). Use of improvisational techniques in assessment. In P. Mc Reynolds (Ed.), *Advances in psychological assessment* (Vol. 4, pp. 222–277). San Francisco: Jossey-Bass.

Moreno, J. L. (1946). *Psychodrama.* Beacon, NY: Beacon House.

Murray, H. (1938). *Explorations in personality.* New York: Oxford University Press.

Perls, F. (1972). *Gestalt therapy verbatim.* New York: Bantam.

Petzold, H. (1973). *Gestalttherapie und psychodrama [Gestalt therapy and psychodrama].* Nicol: Kassel, Germany.

Rosenberg, Y. (1999). *Role theory and self concept.* Master's thesis, Lesley College, Tel-Aviv, Israel.

Seitz, P. (2000). *Drama therapy storytelling assessment: A comparison of mentally ill and normal neurotic stories.* Master's thesis, New York University.

Tangorra, J. (1997). *Many masks of pedophilia: Drama therapeutic assessment of the pedophile* Master's thesis, New York University.

Chapter 3 ————————————————————————

PSYCHODRAMA

Adam Blatner

Psychodrama is a method in which people explore their problems by enacting them in a role-playing fashion rather than by just talking. Developed around the mid-1930s by J. L. Moreno, MD (1889–1974), psychodrama is a complex of methods and concepts that can be applied in a wide variety of contexts (Blatner, 1995b, 1999, 2001). Moreno was the pioneer of the idea that enhancing the client's creativity was one of the major goals of therapy and that creativity can be most powerfully catalyzed by evoking the client's spontaneity. He found that improvisationally dramatizing the actual scenes in the client's life allowed for the equivalent of play therapy with adults. People could replay situations and discover better ways of reacting.

Acting-out, when done consciously, is quite different from acting-out as an unconscious defensive reaction. Indeed, it might be better to be termed *acting-in* because, in the course of spontaneously interacting physically with those who play a significant other in life, clients often discover deeper feelings, bring to the surface preconscious attitudes or beliefs, and get past their own tendencies to intellectualize or use other verbal defensive maneuvers (Blatner, 1996).

Many of psychodrama's ideas have been integrated into other methods. Satir's approach to family therapy was influenced by psychodrama's more directive and action-oriented style, and family sculpture was an adaptation of a psychodramatic method called *action sociometry* (Compernolle, 1981). Fritz Perls integrated the psychodramatic "empty chair" technique as an integral part of his approach to Gestalt therapy. Drama therapy and the other creative arts therapies have also integrated principles of fostering spontaneity and using action techniques. It is not necessary to learn everything about psychodrama to adapt its ideas and techniques. Learning something about this rich approach can fertilize and be integrated with many other approaches (Corey, 2000). Thus, as you read the following description, consider how you might be able to use these elements.

Rationale

As mentioned, psychodrama may be thought of as a group of methods that can facilitate the processes of therapy as conceptualized by a wide variety of other schools of thought, such as psychodynamic, reality therapy, and transactional analysis. The classical verbal techniques are thus enhanced by the dynamism of physical action and direct encounter. (Moreno was one of the first to use the term, "encounter," as well as the focus on the power of interacting in the "here and now.")

Psychodrama theory suggests that promoting a client's creativity is an important element in overall treatment. This and other theoretical advantages are described more in *Foundations of Psychodrama* (2000a), the book I wrote that discusses at length the intellectual basis for using action methods. When psychodramatic methods are used along with other approaches to therapy, the integration of the dynamics of action, imagination, and improvisation can make the treatment process even more effective.

One of Moreno's unique contributions to psychology was the insight that creativity can best be promoted through the activation of the person's spontaneity, the ability to respond afresh to a challenge, instead of responding simply according to old habits of thought or behavior. Spontaneity, in turn, is fostered through improvising in a predicament, exploring it, not just sitting back and thinking or talking *about* it. Active physical involvement adds to the warming-up to spontaneity because the active involvement opens a corresponding flow of intuitions, images, feelings, and insights that are otherwise distanced and blocked by more passive verbal modes of interchange.

Moreno experimented with spontaneity and found that a number of factors either facilitated or inhibited it. Being around people with whom one felt a good sense of rapport helped, and this is one of the elements in group therapy theory called *group cohesion.* Another element is a gradual process of everybody disclosing a bit more about themselves. But perhaps the most powerful element is the introduction of *playfulness,* not in the sense of silly frivolity or irrelevance, but rather in the sense of flexibility and tentativeness. To *play* a role means that it can be taken back and worked with—it doesn't have to "prove" anything about the role player's actual or final feelings or character. This makes the therapy session into a kind of "fail-safe" laboratory in which people can explore self-expression of feelings that are not generally acceptable in conventional society, much less in the sensitive context of many families.

Finally, there are a number of issues that are not easily addressed simply by talking about them—issues of inner conflict, unfinished business with people who are no longer alive, and other elements of *psychological truth.* Moreno used this term, *psychological truth,* to express his respect for the way that the most relevant complexes of attitudes and expectations often relate not so much to what actually occurs in life, but more to what never occurs, but still was anticipated, feared, hoped for, or wondered about.

Drama, then, became an even more powerful method than mere group discussion for exploring psychological issues with that combination of spontaneity and playfulness—not scripted drama in which someone else writes the story and the actors memorize and rehearse the parts, but improvised drama based on the real and imagined scenes of people's own lives. This method didn't just tell the story; it allowed the participants to pause and reconsider the underlying issues. In addition, from the insights that arose from this exploration, it allowed them to finally re-tell the story in a more life-affirming way, to make new decisions.

The method was psychodrama. To this basic structure, Moreno devised a number of devices, such as the double, role reversal, and replay, that allowed people to deepen their exploration of personal or group issues and look at situations from surprisingly new perspectives. There were also many other purposes and benefits (Moreno, J. L., 1947). Psychodrama seems a bit unnatural to those who have become accustomed to the purely verbal, "grown-up" way of behaving. However, at another level, it is very natural, partaking not only of the make-believe play of childhood, but also of the way that humans have used ritual and drama in healing for millennia.

History

Jacob Levy Moreno was born in 1889 in Bucharest, Romania, of Sephardic Jewish parentage. His family moved to Vienna when he was about six years old. As an older teenager and young man, he became inspired with the idea that creativity was a spiritual imperative. Indeed, for a while, he experimented with a kind of social-activist "religion of encounter" that he and some friends made up. He then finished his studies at the University of Vienna and began medical school (Marineau, 1989).

Vienna was one of the cultural centers of the world at the time, and the spirit of innovation was pervasive among the intelligentsia. When Europe was caught in the paroxysm of World War I, he was assigned as a consultant to a refugee camp. There he became impressed with the arbitrary way administrators assigned people to various dormitories, and how, instead, it might be better if the refugees would be allowed to choose their own subcommunities. (This was the beginning impulse for his later social psychological method called *sociometry.*) In addition, he saw the challenge of promoting spontaneity as a theme in beginning to change our social institutions.

Moreno also enjoyed the theater as an avocational interest but was impatient with what he felt to be fixed and decadent elements based on the separation between the playwright and the actor. After graduating from medical school, while working as a family physician in a suburb of Vienna, he organized an improvisational theater troupe—very possibly the first one. He called it *Das Stegreiftheater* (the *Theater of Spontaneity*) and gradually began to realize that the impromptu process tended to help people broaden and balance their personal role repertoires, and that it was healing.

Life was difficult in postwar Europe, so in 1925 Moreno immigrated to the United States and gradually became reestablished. In the early 1930s, he was consulting at Sing Sing prison in New York regarding group work. He gave a presentation on this topic to the American Psychiatric Association, where he proposed (and coined the term) *group psychotherapy.* In subsequent years, Moreno would be almost as interested in promoting group therapy in general as he was in developing psychodrama and sociometry—and he saw them all as integrated. During the same decade, he was also one of the pioneers in the role theory field (Biddle & Thomas, 1966, pp. 6-8).

In the 1930s, Moreno opened a sanitarium in Beacon, about 60 miles upstate from New York City, and began to implement his methods. He wrote, taught, and was prolific in his activities. In the late 1940s, he married Zerka Toeman, who gradually became the major exponent of psychodrama in the 1970s through the time of this writing (Blatner, 2000a).

For a variety of reasons—not the least of which was the mid-century hegemony of psychoanalysis—psychodrama, as a radical alternative, never became widely recognized. (A whole chapter on these reasons may be found in my *Foundations of Psychodrama* (Blatner, 2000a). Nevertheless, its influence has spread in more subtle ways.

APPLICATION

While some of the psychodramatic methods may be adapted and integrated with other therapeutic approaches, full enactment, *classical psychodrama,* is as complex as doing surgery. Like surgery, psychodrama must be learned by doing, with supervision by more experienced trainers. The textbook serves the function of intellectual orientation, but you shouldn't think of yourselves as being able to direct more complex enactments without the kind of training described in the

Directory and Certification Standards booklet published by the American Board of Examiners in *Psychodrama, Sociometry, and Group Psychotherapy* (2002; address in references).

Moreover, just as a surgeon must also be a competent physician, so a director of psychodrama must ground that practice in a broader knowledge of diagnosis and theory, a wider range of treatment methods in addition to psychodrama, and so on.

Although psychodramatic methods, in modified form, have many applications in nonclinical settings, such as education, professional and business training, conflict resolution in the community, religious workshops, programs for personal development, and the like, the emphasis in this book is on its use as a method of psychotherapy, which was also psychodrama's original purpose.

Basic Elements

A patient is helped to become the main actor, the *protagonist*, in an enactment of some aspect of his or her life. The process is facilitated by a *director* who is trained in the method, usually a fully trained psychotherapist. The enactment is aided by supporting players, called *auxiliary egos* by Moreno (and, more recently, often called just *auxiliaries*). These auxiliaries sometimes are played by trained assistants or co-therapists, but more often, other group members take on these helping roles. The players generally do the enactment in a special section of the room, to mark out the special and different, "as-if" status of the drama.

Generally, first is a warming-up process, which includes a number of elements: Promoting a sense of safety, symmetrical self-disclosure, and playfulness may be enhanced by a series of structured experiences (warm-ups).

There is a "knack" to leading action-oriented groups. Directors need to plan the warm-ups and the explanations so they are targeted to the size, makeup, and purpose of the group. The method itself is very flexible and can be adapted to almost any context, because it is not necessary to use the full "classical approach" to get many of the benefits of its varied components.

Because doing full, problem-oriented, therapeutic psychodramas can generate powerful emotions, the director should be *fully* trained in the use of the method. However, trained therapists in other approaches can still use some psychodramatic methods in the service of their own work.

Role playing is the most commonly recognized derivative of psychodrama. It tends to be more focused on how a problem should be dealt with, and there is less emphasis on deeply exploring the feelings of the clients or promoting a catharsis.

The second step, after warming up, is to set the stage. The person whose problem is to be explored—perhaps a problem common to many of the group members— is interviewed by the director, and begins to move from an abstract description of the issues involved to a fairly specific example. The main principle at this point is: If we can't stage it, see it, hear the words, then we don't really know what's going on. This is to counter tendencies of people to use abstract terms and "psychobabble" as an unconscious defense against really engaging the situation.

In setting the stage, there may be more or less time spent defining the imagined setting; the room dimensions; and the location of the door, windows, sofa, or sink. The next step clarifies the cast of characters. As the scene opens, who is in the room?

The Soliloquy

Sometimes a scene begins with the protagonist approaching a situation—going home after a year at college, getting ready for a job interview, or getting up to go to school on a day that something traumatic happened. This carries forward the warm-up, so that the protagonist can begin to remember what kinds of preliminary thoughts set up the ensuing scene. The soliloquy has the protagonist driving in a car, getting dressed, or walking around, perhaps with the director as a seemingly invisible inner countervoice to evoke more questions—a type of "double." (We'll describe the use of the double technique later.) Even though these thoughts may have been kept inside, not spoken aloud, they are spoken for the purposes of the psychodrama.

Saying words aloud—expression—is a powerful way to feel the reality of thoughts. The subconscious mind tends to numb, cloud, discount, and otherwise evade the clear assertion of many thoughts and feelings. The various defense mechanisms can operate continuously, subtly, and in concert, and be mixed with a variety of other avoidance maneuvers—ways of talking that create distance and a "dis-owning" of experience. Psychodramatic methods serve to counter this tendency by making experience more vivid; and saying things aloud, knowing that others are hearing these statements, helps to promote a sharper degree of awareness.

Involving the Auxiliary

The next scene usually involves another character, and sometimes the protagonist chooses one of the group to play that role. "Who here could be your dad?" the director asks. "Mark," says the protagonist. "Mark, come up and now you're dad." (Mark does so.) Variations are possible. The director could choose the auxiliary. Someone in the group might be warmed up and want to play the father and would indicate interest by raising his hand. In addition, the person chosen might not want to enter the drama. The director should emphasize the voluntary nature of the process—that it's okay for people to say no at any time during the action.

But how should the auxiliary behave? The director says to the protagonist (whom we call Joe for purposes of explanation), "Joe, role reverse, become Dad, and show us how he acts at the beginning of this scene." Even after the scene begins, there may be several actions and role reversals in which the protagonist becomes the other person and shows how the other person reacts. This helps the auxiliary warm up to the role. At a certain point, the auxiliary gets the sense of who dad is and begins to respond from the viewpoint of being Joe's dad.

Working in the Here and Now

One of the more common evasive maneuvers is that of narration—telling a story. Finding the story-like theme in our lives helps provide structure and meaning. However, the narration tends to be in words and in the past, or, if talking about an anticipated event, in the subjunctive tense: "I would. . . ." "I might. . . ." To add the vividness that brings a greater degree of ownership to the experience, psychodrama enacts rather than just talks about, and that enactment is refocused to be experienced "as if it's happening here and now." So when the protagonist starts to turn to the director and explain what happened (narrating in the past), the director needs to help redirect this behavior: "Show us, don't tell us. It's happening now."

A variation is to direct people to phrase their comments as direct statements *to* the other person, not to the director or audience. When Joe turns his head, shaking it, and says to the group, "He doesn't care about my feelings," the director says, pointing with his finger at "dad," "Tell *him* that!" Joe turns to his dad, played by Mark, and says, "Dad, you don't care about my feelings!"

The Double

This technique introduces the dramatic device, the voice-over, seen in many movies or television shows, in which the audience is allowed to hear the unspoken thoughts of the protagonist. Lacking the electronic technology, another auxiliary is used to play the double, the role of Joe's feelings, the things he might think but might not ordinarily say. This is a most productive role.

The art of doubling involves working to bring forth material that might be at the preconscious level, which refers to those things that register consciously in the mind but feel awkward or in other ways tend to be pushed away, inhibited, or denied. Saying such things helps open the general flow of ideas and insights that percolate up from the unconscious.

Again, the director should be attentive to the protagonist's feeling that what the double says is "ego syntonic"; that is, it feels accurate in expressing inner thoughts. Sometimes the double misses it and says things that don't feel right, and the director needs to reassure the protagonist that it's okay to disagree, to correct the double. The double, in turn, is instructed to attend to the protagonist's cues and not become so fixated on his or her own ideas that he or she "lays a trip" on the protagonist. Doubles who can't align with the protagonist should be kindly dismissed and another double chosen.

This is a very rich role, and psychodramatists in training spend a good deal of time practicing auxiliary roles, which involves an activity of role-taking—really imagining what it's like to be in the other person's predicament. Indeed, this activity is the essence of empathy.

Cutting the Action

The director should feel free to call "Cut!" to stop the scene. During the ensuing break, the director might interview or coach the protagonist or one of the auxiliaries. The spirit is that of the movie director who calls a cut in filming to make certain adjustments. It is assumed that the edited film will cover these interruptions. However, in movies about making movies, and in psychodrama, the audience is let in on the actual process of how the enactment is modified, and indeed, these modifications are the essence of the method.

Although one might read in newspapers about how some poignant situation is a "psychodrama," that is really a misuse of the term. Complex, emotionally loaded dramas, to serve as psychodramas, must include the additional element of opportunities for the main player to pause and reflect: Is this the way I want to play this role? Is this even the role I want to play? Can this role be renegotiated? Such questions allow old reaction patterns to be interrupted and a fresh view introduced. This is a great deal of what Moreno meant by the value of spontaneity—dealing with an old situation in a new way or a new situation in a more effective way.

The Mirror Technique

The mirror technique involves cutting the scene, pulling the protagonist out to the sidelines, allowing another auxiliary to play the protagonist's role, and observing. It is the dramatic equivalent of introducing videotape playback. The protagonist can see how he or she was acting, including nonverbal communications. After this, the protagonist may be allowed to replay the scene.

Replay and Role Training

The essence of rehearsal in drama, music, dance, and other activities is the opportunity to refine a behavior. Talking about and thinking can't replace the power of actual practice, involving the feeling of saying something directly, facing the possible anger or sadness of the other, wrestling with the situation, and refining one's chosen role behavior. Often a drama might at a certain point require a series of several replays, not just one, to practice a new or emerging role.

A related technique combines replay and the mirror with a twist: How would other people in the group handle a given predicament? Several people might get up and take the protagonist's role, showing how they might react. For example, if the challenge were that of resisting peer pressures to smoke or engage in unsafe sex, others could model and thereby practice their own self-assertive behaviors. In turn, the protagonist is free to pick up ideas—but not obligated to choose any particular idea—in reformulating the tactics or style in the next scene in which he or she again faces the awkward stimulus. This may be the most widespread use of the role-playing technique.

Sociodrama

Sociodrama is the application of psychodramatic methods for exploring in greater depths issues involving a single or narrow set of roles. In reality, people play a number of different roles, many of which conflict, and each of which have their own unique elements. Thus, Joe may have a wife who behaves in a specific way and a father who used to treat him in a very specific way. If Joe was wrestling with a conflict with his employer, it may in part involve pressures he's feeling with his wife and be distorted by old learning patterns from the relationship with his dad. That's psychodrama.

An example of sociodrama, in contrast, is an exploration in a group that is looking at how people work with their supervisors at their place of employment. It would investigate the issues shared by most people in relation to supervisors. Sociodrama addresses the challenges of a given role, but not the particulars of how that role plays out in an individual's life in interaction with that person's other roles (Sternberg & Garcia, 2000).

Admittedly, sociodramatic enactments can easily lead into a psychodrama; and in turn, psychodramatic enactments often have scenes that are really more sociodramatic—they deal with the whole way the culture defines a certain role. In therapeutic groups, this shift may be fine, but in educational or management groups, directors should be alert to this trend and strenuously resist the tendency to turn a given exploration of a role—a sociodrama—into a personal problem—a psychodrama.

Surplus Reality

One of the most powerful aspects of psychodrama is the capacity to enact not only what happened, but also, as Moreno said, "What never happened, what *could* never happen!" This, he said, is the *psychological truth,* and that may be more important than mere historical fact. Drama allows fantasies to be enacted, delusions, hallucinations, a meeting with the ghost of a person's ancestor, or an encounter with a child who was never born.

Because one of the more important goals of psychodrama is to help clients develop insight, introducing perspectives that hadn't been fully considered sometimes helps. "What if . . ." can open people up to desires or yearnings that they'd shut down many years earlier. What if you could repeat that humiliating birthday party when you were a kid, only do it so that it came out wonderfully? What if you could have a heart-to-heart talk with the parent who never listened, using the "reformed auxiliary ego" technique in which the parent not only listens, but really understands?

By this point, we hope that you are beginning to sense the many ways different clients might be able to benefit from playing out a wide range of scenes. Psychodrama is enormously rich, and this chapter can offer only a kind of appetizer to apprise you of its range and potential. You may be motivated to read more about it, take some workshops, and learn to use this valuable group of tools.

Role Reversal

Role reversal is simply the activity of changing parts. In setting up a scene, reversing roles can help show an auxiliary how the protagonist thinks the other person should act. It's a way to warm up the auxiliary, as mentioned earlier.

The more complex use of role reversal occurs later on, after the encounter has been proceeding for a while. At a certain point, it becomes appropriate for the protagonist to consider the viewpoint of the other person. Before that, he or she should have the opportunity to ventilate a bit, get in touch with his or her own feelings, and own the right to his or her own viewpoint. But then, there comes a time to relinquish egocentricity, to expand the mind to seek to really understand what it's like to be the other person.

Some forms of psychotherapy don't fully demand such widened awareness. However, psychodrama is, in part, based on a social psychology and has a streak of ethics, too. One need not end up agreeing with the other person, but true insight requires an appreciation of alternative perspectives, some empathy into the other.

When Joe in his psychodrama is invited by the director to role reverse, to become his supervisor, Ms. Smith, he finds himself saddled with a different set of role pressures. Supervisors have to balance their desires to help their subordinates with the constraints they are given by their superiors , company policy, and the needs of the subordinate's other co-workers.

In this role reversing, the director (in this case, a woman) may cut the action and then set up a mini-scene in which she interviews Joe, now in the role of his supervisor, Ms. Smith. What's it like to be in this job? What are its advantages, disadvantages? What kind of worker is Joe? What is your own bias regarding his request?

Admittedly, Joe (in the role of his supervisor, Ms. Smith) doesn't always know the answers to these questions, but he can guess; and, in fact, we all have our fantasies about others' motivations and experience. This just makes those fantasies more explicit. In addition, once they're brought into a state of heightened awareness, they're subjected to a correspondingly more complex capacity of the mind for rational analysis. So, while this one-way role reversal is not as good as having both of the actual people involved in a conflict there and able to give corrective feedback, it's still better than merely reacting according to old habits of attitudes and behavior.

Skill Training

A significant component in therapy should be the development of skills—not just information, but activities that deserve to be practiced and need to be learned experientially. Assertion training began to become a more recognized method in the later 1960s, and role playing is far more effective than just reading about it or hearing lectures. It's also powerful to not only learn to assert oneself initially, but also to respond in measured but forceful ways when the other person doesn't give in easily, keeps the argument going, or makes the argument escalate. Teaching parents to manage defiance in children also requires some of this behavioral practice (which psychodrama introduced and then was incorporated into behavior therapy).

Imagination Training

Psychodrama and its corollary idea of "surplus reality" encourage people to imagine. A number of other relatively recent imagery therapies do the same, but psychodrama, which preceded them, allows the imagery to be acted out, which adds the vividness of physical experience.

Drama requires a relatively concrete process of scene-setting. The idea is that we all, to some extent, are the audience; and if we can't "see it, hear it," we don't know what the client is talking about. As mentioned before, the requirement that the images be made specific helps to circumvent the defenses of rationalization and oververbalization, talking about and around but avoiding the real point.

For example, in doing grief work, staging a shared memory that is stated specifically draws into the mind images that had been suppressed, and with these, often, a load of emotions. A dying grandfather hearing a grandchild say, "I love you," may be nicer than hearing "I hate you," but it's so easy not to remember *why* the child found the old man lovable. More meaningful would be something such as, "I remember the time when we walked on the beach in Miami and you found a starfish and gave it to me—and I still have it on my mantelpiece." We can picture that scene a little bit. It would be even more powerful to stage that walk, feel the breeze, notice if the two were barefoot or had shoes—the emotions so often lie in the smaller details.

Role Theory

Moreno was one of the founders of role theory, a uniquely American contribution to sociology. *Role theory* is primarily a language or general way to approach thinking about psychology. One of its many advantages is that it can address dynamics at and between several levels of human functioning: somatic, intrapsychic, interpersonal, small group, larger group, and cultural. The role concept has now become commonplace, expanding from its origins in the theater (where it first described the "rolled-up" parchment script of the actors) to describing a function within a more complex system, sometimes having nothing to do with people at all. Therefore, its language is familiar.

The major advantages of role theory derive from its subtle association with its origin, the drama, because it implies that we are all playing roles. By extension, we can all choose to play those parts differently; we can learn to play them better; we can let go of a role, shift roles, balance roles, expand our role repertoire; and engage in other operations that shift these units of behavior, viewpoint, attitude, and social expectations around like pieces on a chessboard.

Drama is one of the arts, and we have come to think of artists as creative; therefore, people who play roles should bring some creativity to the task. In other words, role playing harkens back to the theoretical place of creativity in life. In addition, people like the idea of thinking of themselves as creative; it draws people forward in therapy or education or business; and it invites people to rethink their beliefs and consider new alternatives.

Role theory acknowledges the influence of the past, but tends to put more emphasis on the present predicament and immediately anticipated future. In the process of therapy, then, a careful evaluation of the real complexities of the role conflicts inherent in the client's actual life situation may give more relevant insights about the nature of the problem than the time spent on elucidating the details of early childhood.

The combination of recognition of the individual's existential predicament and its "user-friendly language" makes role theory a natural foundation for psychodrama. In addition, it is compatible with many, if not most, psychoanalytic theoretical constructs (as well as theoretical concepts in other approaches), which can then be discussed in a more understandable fashion.

Sociometry

Even before developing psychodrama, Moreno saw the therapeutic potential of groups—especially the helpfulness of administrators in hospitals, prisons, or schools that allowed people who prefer to affiliate with each other to do so in the arrangements of groups, dormitories, or projects. To assess people's interpersonal preferences—the spontaneous reaction that accounts for rapport—Moreno simply asked group members whom they'd prefer to be paired up with if engaged in some specific activity. He then tabulated the results and made plans accordingly.

For more mature group members, Moreno later found that sharing the information and helping the group deal with it could be a powerful way to explore very meaningful psychodynamic and interpersonal issues.

Sociometric methods may be used without using psychodrama, and psychodrama may be used without formally using sociometry, but the two approaches are in fact synergistic. Group workers of all types, including teachers and group play therapists, should pay attention to these issues of interpersonal preference—those flows of attraction and repulsion that go on in any group setting. (Moreno called this connectedness *tele.*)

Facilitating the Phases of Psychotherapy

Psychodramatic methods can catalyze a number of functions in therapy (Blatner, 1985). The process of psychotherapy has a kind of logical progress that, while not rigid, nevertheless offers some rational structure for the practitioner:

1. Entrance and support.
2. Initial contract and history-taking.
3. Focusing on a problem, going deeper, reviewing attitudes.
4. Formulation and recontracting.
5. Dealing with frictions in the helping relationship.
6. Re-Integration.

1. *Entrance* and *support.* The beginnings of therapy may be facilitated by using the principles of *warming up,* shifting the sense many patients have that their presentation needs to be neatly packaged. Warming up offers room to approach the problem gradually. If the client feels intimidated, the technique of *role reversal* with the therapist or others may reduce the fantasies of being judged and can also counter tendencies toward entitlement or unrealistic and magical expectations. In being supportive during this vulnerable phase, a modified form of *doubling* (which I call *active empathy*) lets the client know that the therapist is

willing to look at the situation from the client's viewpoint and be willing to be corrected if any impressions are mistaken.

2. *Initial contract* and *history-taking.* This function may be aided by the use of the portrayal of small *vignettes,* mini-enactments used to make the descriptions clear. Initial complaints are often vague or overly abstract. I say, "I don't know what you mean until I can actually visualize the scene." This quasi-dramatic approach helps to move toward specificity, reveals the nonverbal elements that shape the meaning of the interaction presented, and helps the client feel that the therapist understands the predicament. History-taking is also aided by the use of the *social network diagram* (originally called by Moreno "the social atom"). Essentially, this involves drawing a schematic picture with a symbol of the self in the middle and noting symbols for the relevant people in the client's social network, along with indications of how near or far the client perceives them to be, letting spatial distance suggest emotional distance. Lines may be drawn to indicate how the client feels toward each of those people and how the client thinks those others feel toward him or her. It's a most useful way of building the treatment alliance and getting information that feels relevant to the client.

3. *Focusing on a problem, going deeper,* and *reviewing attitudes.* This takes the therapy toward the "mid-game." Note that well into the process, an ongoing diagnostic process is going on. "Sometimes simply describing a behavior episode is not sufficient to reactivate all parts of the pattern. *Role playing* an episode may help the client become more fully aware of and understand all aspects of the experience" (Ford & Urban, 1998, p. 651). As part of this exploration of the underlying meanings of the behaviors and attitudes that are brought to the surface, the techniques of *doubling, role reversal, concretization, mirroring,* and *exaggeration* are often used. Using *surplus reality,* dreams or fantasies may be enacted, and *catharsis* sometimes accompanies this process.

As insights are gained, protagonists are helped to consider alternatives by being invited to *replay a scene differently,* and *role training* may be helpful for integrating new attitudes.

4. *Formulation and re-contracting.* It's often helpful to demystify the therapeutic process and discuss the overall understanding of the problem. Talking in terms of the roles being played and how they might be defined differently offers a relatively neutral language for this grounding of the treatment alliance (Blatner, 1993).

5. *Dealing with frictions in the helping relationship.* Frictions inevitably arise, and working what have also been called (misleadingly, I think) *resistances* and *transferences* can result in many insights. Techniques such as the *mirror* and *role reversal* are often helpful here. One common source of resistance, for example, is the projection that the therapist is being judgmental. By imagining what it's like to be a therapist and being interviewed in that role, clients may begin to

become more aware of negative expectations and to neutralize their force. Another source is the feeling that the therapist isn't "doing it right," and, again, if this can be identified, it may be explored by a modified role reversal and then a *replay* of the previous interaction, except the client has the opportunity to show what a "good" therapist would think and do.

6. *Re-integration.*   The re-integration function may be facilitated by enacting a *corrective scene,* using the *reformed auxiliary* technique for the protagonist to relive a traumatic situation so that it "happens" (in *surplus reality*) in a more positive fashion. Another way to promote integration is to have the client replay the scene in a more empowered fashion, to feel himself or herself become more self-assertive. *Role training* may be needed here, with actual *coaching,* perhaps some *modeling* by other group members, and encouraging and supporting more effective responses. Thus, the psychodrama serves as a laboratory for experimenting with alternative behaviors, a fail-safe place where clients can rehearse a wider range of reactions. (Some of these elements are illustrated in the following case review.)

Problems are often complex, involving a number of interrelated issues. After dealing with one facet of life, another situation is often raised. Therefore, therapy may well involve a repeat of the sequence, or several repeats. These may occur some months or years apart, with time away from therapy to consolidate skills. Issues of termination, follow-up, and other aspects of therapy must also be considered. Given the complexity of the process, there are many opportunities for the effective application of psychodramatic methods.

Areas of Application

Psychodramatic methods may be modified and applied in working with children in therapy (Bannister, 1997; Bannister & Huntington, 2002; Hoey, 1997), with patients with post-traumatic disorders (Kellermann & Hudgins, 2000; Hudgins, 2002), in family therapy (Blatner, 1994; Farmer, 1996), and other areas.

Bereavement

The process of grief work can be facilitated by a modified psychodramatic technique, if judiciously applied at certain phases in the grief process. Because a common experience compounding healthy grieving is the sense of being "unfinished," of not having said what had to be said, this process is allowed to be explored in fantasy: The "empty chair" technique is used to imagine the lost other and to ask questions and make statements. Through role reversal, the client can play out what he or she imagines the lost other might reply. The technique draws on the idea that deep down, people "have the answers" to many of their more emotionally meaningful questions (Blatner, 2000b).

Education

Role playing and sociodrama are derivatives of psychodrama, and they may be used at all levels of education. In the earlier grades, as creative drama, these modified approaches promote imaginativeness and mental flexibility—qualities that are needed in a changing world, and qualities that tend to be neglected in an educational system that becomes too oriented to knowing correct answers and taking tests.

A major application for these approaches is in the task of promoting social and emotional skills learning, "emotional intelligence," a movement in education that is gaining momentum (Blatner, 1995a). In addition, role playing is a powerful approach for enhancing a deeper comprehension of history, literature, and even some aspects of math and science (Blatner & Blatner, 1997, Chapter 14).

Role playing is also an important method for the experiential learning of interpersonal skills for all kinds of people who deal with human services, from sales to nursing to teaching medical students various themes; for example, talking to patients about dying, taking a more astute medical history, or dealing with difficult behaviors. This kind of teaching is also used in professional continuing education for all kinds of clinicians.

In these activities, the classical psychodramatic method is modified so that the protagonists no longer enact actual scenes from their own lives that are too self-disclosing, but rather, these situations are chosen by the group and the main players are representatives of clinicians in role. (This is in keeping with the previously mentioned differences between sociodrama and psychodrama.) A variety of social issues can be explored, and social and emotional learning skills may also be cultivated through a mixture of sociodrama and role playing.

Deepening Spiritual Understanding

An interesting variation of this approach is the sociodramatic exploration of stories from the Bible, or from other sacred scriptures or inspirational literature (Pitzele, 1998). The point again is to shift from mere instruction to a more experiential approach to appreciating the moral and spiritual difficulties involved in many of these cultural myths. Sociodramas can also be used in Sunday schools and with other religious groups (especially for teenagers and young adults) to address cultural and other ethical issues that have become socially relevant.

Recreation

Aside from its use as a problem-solving process, psychodramatic methods can also be modified and applied for the purposes of pure play. Some people take classes in improvisational theater. Others have engaged in "play for adults," reengaging in the simplicity of clowning, working with simple arts materials, and so on. We developed a creative drama variation, "The Art of Play," that allows participants to enact scenes based on characters in their imaginations (Blatner & Blatner, 1997). These approaches not only serve as an activity for socializing, but also enhance the capacity for mental flexibility, imaginativeness, spontaneity, and many other qualities.

Drama Therapy

Drama therapy evolved in the mid-twentieth century from helping inmates perform scripted plays and skits in hospitals and prisons, creative drama in education, and other sources, and in the 1970s became informed by psychodrama (Emunah, 1997). Its practitioners are more identified with their backgrounds in theater, while psychodramatists are primarily psychotherapists who then learn a specific dramatic approach. Still, there is increasing overlap in technique and valuable contributions from both fields. (This subject is addressed in more depth by Dr. Landy in Chapter 2 in this volume.)

A TYPICAL SESSION

(This session is somewhat of a composite and names and situations have been drawn from several sources, disguised, and fictionalized enough to not be associated with any actual person. Protecting confidentiality is one of the group process norms that is always addressed not only at the outset, but also every few sessions during the group.)

The structure of the action portion of a psychodrama follows the structure of a kind of spiral. It goes inward from the present to the past, and from the outward to the more inward parts of the mind, clarifying a trauma, an injunction, loosening the points of fixation a bit. The action then spirals outward again toward how a new decision might be made and practiced in the present and immediate future (Goldman & Morrison, 1984).

The Warming Up

Improvisational enactment requires a mixture of a feeling of motivation and a moderate degree of group cohesion. People sometimes come to a group knowing what it is they want to work on. Perhaps it was addressed in part by someone else in a previous session, and, in that case, these folks are already somewhat warmed up. At other times, the group is still "cold"—the issues aren't clear, nor are the procedures or even the sense that the people know each other.

The traditional analytic approach often allowed the silence itself to be a prod to anxiety, but I think that approach tends to accrue misleading sources of motivation. It's better to allow people to get in touch with their concerns about their own issues; and to do this, it sometimes takes a while just talking about why they're there, what their problems are, and introducing a bit of what the group approach will be.

Sometimes structured experiences or "warm-ups" are used, such as, for a beginning group, having the director suggest that everyone stand in a circle and say his or her name, accompanied by some gesture or action. This sets the norm for physical activity and nonverbal expressiveness. There are hundreds of different warm-ups; for example, using imagination or having small dramatic encounters with an empty chair, nonverbal interaction, or talking about a focused topic, such as the story of one's name and how the group members feel about their names.

Yalom (1975) notes—and I agree—that structured experiences should not be used too automatically, lest they obscure the natural group interaction that is inclined to happen. However, if things get slow or frozen, an appropriate technique can often function as an "ice breaker."

The example we give is a group that's already somewhat warmed up and has a fairly good level of group cohesion. In the course of a group therapy session in which it was understood that action methods would be used, one of the group of about eight clients, Alice (not her real name), a shy woman in her late 20s, was complaining about becoming inhibited in taking care of her needs. This is a common problem and other group members nodded in empathy. The therapist as director asked if she'd like to discover some of the roots of her inhibition and to perhaps find some ways to counter that, and she eagerly assented.

> **D** (for Director): "Okay, let's have the scene in which you didn't get your needs taken care of. Where did it take place?"
>
> **P** (for protagonist): "On the phone."
>
> **D:** "We can show phone conversations. Over here is you (invites the group member to get out of her chair and enter the stage area of the room, and she does so). Are you sitting, standing . . . and which room is it?"
>
> **P:** "It was my kitchen, and I was on a cell phone."
>
> **D:** "Okay, and the other person, where was he or she when you called?"
>
> **P:** "It was a she, a girlfriend, and I wanted to ask her to house sit for me while I went to another city to visit friends."
>
> **D:** (Registering this explanation, but not reacting to it now) "Guess where in her house she would have been." *(Anchor the action in imagery, in concrete settings, so that verbal generalities and explanations don't obscure the vividness of the memory or the capacity of the group to empathize.)*
>
> **P:** "In her bedroom, I think."
>
> **D:** "Okay, pick someone to be your friend."
>
> **P:** (looks around the room, chooses) "Betty."

D: "Betty, will you come up and be the auxiliary for Alice?" (Reaches out invitingly, and Betty gets up and enters the scene.)

"Okay, Alice, what's your friend's name?"

P: "Cecelia."

D: "Okay, Betty will be Cecelia in this scene, but first you be Cecelia and show how she answers the phone—warm up the auxiliary."

(I often weave in a bit of explanation to demystify the process, help them learn the procedure, and generate a bit of functioning of the observing inner self who remains grounded in the broader context of a therapy session and allied to a supportive therapist and group. Each time, it becomes a little less awkward and a little smoother.)

P (as Auxiliary, Cecelia): "Hello?" (Said in a friendly tone.)

(However trivial these small maneuvers may seem, they allow for the "lubrication," the warming up, of not only the protagonist, but also the auxiliaries and the group to the flow of the scene, as if to see it unfold. Another reason for having the protagonist show how the auxiliary should play the role, the nonverbal style especially, is so that the auxiliary does not inject too much of her own projections into it. The protagonist is the one who should be the co-director, so to speak, showing how the people react.)

D: "Okay, Betty, you be Cecelia now, and pick up the phone. Alice, do you call her? (She nods.) Okay, go back to your room over there, pick up your cell phone. 'Action'" *(This is the shorthand word for "go ahead and begin to interact as if it were happening in the here and now.)*

P: "Hello, Betty?"

D: "You mean Cecelia."

P: "Oh, yes, sorry. Hello, Cecelia?" (She begins to warm up to the scene.)

A1 (First Auxiliary, Betty): "Hello? Alice?" *(Now here the auxiliary took a chance—she injected a bit of her own spontaneity in guessing that Cecelia recognized the voice of her friend. It might not have been that way, but Alice responded naturally, so the director let it pass. A certain amount of auxiliary spontaneity often furthers the action. If the protagonist seems taken aback, the director might cut the action and check it out: "Was that the way it was?" If the protagonist says no, the director says, "Change parts and show us how the other person behaved.")* (Continuing the action:)

P: "Yes, it's me. Hi, how are you . . . (They do some small talk.) . . . I was wondering if you could . . . What are you doing next week?" (Here Alice becomes flustered and vague.)

D: "Freeze the scene." (Addresses Alice.) "Out of the scene, to us, make an aside."

P: "That's it. I can't ask her. It feels like it's too much to ask."

D: "Okay, let's hold this scene and come back to it later. There's another scene unfolding at this moment in your own mind: This is the inner drama, the voice-over, or maybe voices plural, different parts of you that may be in conflict. Let's set up another scene. Betty, you can sit down for now.

"Over here, Alice, will be you; (Setting up three chairs in a semi-circle and indicating the middle chair:) and here, to your right, the part of you that wants to ask for what you need. *(Restating the initial problem.)* And here (pointing to the left-hand chair) is a voice, or maybe two or three, who stop you from doing that. Let's hear what they say." *(Before assigning auxiliary roles, a bit of "auto-drama" is used, with the protagonist playing all the roles. Also, the scene in which several parts of the protagonist are presented is called the "multiple ego" technique.)*

P: (Goes to the right-hand chair.) "Well, this is okay, why don't you just ask her?"

D: "Shift roles."

P: (Goes to left chair.) "Wait, she might think this is too . . . (Hesitates trying to find the right word.) (Someone from the group/audience speaks up, caught up in the action: "Presumptuous!") . . . presumptuous." (Smiles embarrassedly.)

D: (Points to right chair, to see how much she'll dispute this.)

P: (Moves to more assertive side; but then can't answer.)

D: "Do you agree with her?"

P: "I don't know."

D: "So how are you going to find out if your friendship is strong enough to handle a request for a favor? Well, one way is to interview the other person. This is a kind of role reversal, a role taking. Let's have you in another scene: Become Cecelia, and I want to interview you as her."

P: (Takes role of Cecelia.)

D: "Cecelia?"

P: "Yes?"

D: "How long have you known Alice?"

P (as Cecelia): "Six years."

About three or four minutes is taken in a process of interviewing the protagonist in role of the other, reviewing the events of the relationship. The director aims the questions at why Cecelia would like Alice. What emerges is that while both parties have given and taken, Alice gives a good deal; and some of the details of how Alice has given of herself, her time, and her concern to Cecelia are brought out. *(The point here is to begin to break out of habits of egocentricity, which are not always self-inflating. Sometimes they're self-deflating. To see yourself as others might see you requires an active exercise of the imagination, made more vivid by enactment.*) The interview begins to wind up.

D: "So, Cecelia, you really care about this woman, Alice."
P (as Cecelia): "Yes, she's been a good friend.
D: "She *is* a good friend."
P: "She *is* a good friend."
D: "Okay, let's go back to the inner discussion, Alice, the three parts of you. From this chair on the left, you thought maybe you were being 'presumptuous' and then from this chair on the right, you couldn't answer. Want to try to answer now?"
P (as assertive self): "Yes. (Enters role, talking to other empty chair.) What do you mean 'presumptuous'? Alice has given a lot to Cecelia. She's done a lot. It's give and take, you know."
D: "Change parts."
P (as doubting self): "Yes, but people forget, and maybe, well . . ." (Trails off.)

Exploring Inner Attitudes

D: "Are there other voices in there?"
P: "Yes, but not so rational."
D: "Let's hear them; stand up and stand behind this left-hand chair."
P: (Enters even more doubting-self-role.) "Don't listen to her. You're just no good. You're just worthless! People aren't going to like you when they know you!" (Begins to cry a little, then looks up bewildered.)
D: "Wow. Are those voices in there, too?"
P: (Nods yes.)
D: "Well, that's not uncommon. (Turns to group.) Do some of you hear some of those words deep inside? (Several murmur 'yes.'). Okay, let's find out more of what all that's about. Alice, about how old were you when you heard those kinds of words?"
P: "About five."
D: "Let's see what happened."

Again they go through a process of setting up a scene, this time with a harried mother and a little girl wanting attention. Another auxiliary from the group plays the mother, and the protagonist takes that role initially to show how the mother behaved. The mother becomes impatient and blurts out the kinds of words used by the negative inner voice. The protagonist then takes her own role, protesting weakly, and crying a little.

The mother is then interviewed, with Alice, the protagonist taking the mother's role. Her life is reconstructed and her own stresses brought out, so that her impatience is clarified. In this case, it's a mixture of personal dissatisfaction, the mother's own feelings of worthlessness, and her wishing her child would be less timid temperamentally, more assertive. It's the old "I'll put you down in the hope that you'll rebel with some gumption" technique; and while it works in a few cases, more often than not, it simply reinforces the lack of gumption.

D: "So, those voices are in there, but they felt kind of real, didn't they, as if you had to believe them?"

P: "Yes, but I won't."

D: "Would you like to argue with yourself again, and this time, win the argument?" (Alice agrees and we re-stage the multiple ego technique, varying it: We have three auxiliaries sit in the chairs—Dorothy, Ed, and Fay—to play the confident voice; the middle self; and the doubting, self-effacing voice, respectively. Alice, the protagonist, is instructed to stand behind those three voices and coach them, egg them on, and at other times, to leave the scene and look on as the three voices argue with one another. This is known as the "mirror" technique, because it's as if she were seeing her inner dynamics in action, as if in a mirror. Then she re-enters the scene alone, back to the autodrama, playing the roles herself.)

P (as A2., playing first chair): "I'm going to affirm myself in this!"

D: "Change parts."

P (as A4., third chair): "You better watch out, you're worthless, no one cares."

Then, without the director's suggestion, she spontaneously gets up and moves to the middle chair, having caught on to the idea of enacting inner dialogue, and speaks as the choosing self. Turning to the doubting chair . . .)

P: "I'm not going to listen to you any more. You've run my life for too long."

Behavioral Practice

D: "Okay, let's have you really feel your own empowerment, not just in your voice, but in your body. (Here the action begins. Beginning to move out of the center of the psychodramatic 'spiral' toward behavioral practice.) Pick three people to portray your inner barrier, and we'll have you push through it to ask for what you need."

P: "Fay, George, and Harry." (They get up to become auxiliaries and play the role of an inner wall of inhibition.)

D: (To them.) "Your job is to hold on to each other, tightly enough so that Alice is going to have to work to get through you. Also, as she tries, you repeat all those negative words from her past."
(To the protagonist:) "Alice, no hitting, but shoving that doesn't really hurt is okay, wiggling, somehow to get through these three. And you can yell, shout positive affirmations, or whatever, to help you. Go."

P: (Struggles.) "I'm getting through you!"

The auxiliaries playing the "wall": "You can't, you're worthless! You're too weak!"

(As she struggles, a couple of group members can't keep quiet and erupt in rooting her on: "Go for it Alice!" Finally, she breaks through.)

D: "Well, how did it feel?"

P: (Eyes shining.) "Good . . . but, no, I didn't really try hard enough."

D: "Replay! Do it again, only (to the auxiliaries playing the wall) hold on to each other tighter. Action." (They sort of wrestle, but this time the protagonist can't break through.)

Group Member: "May I make a suggestion?" (Sometimes group members, although in the audience role, become involved enough to spontaneously volunteer something.)

D: "What?"

Group member: "I do T'ai Chi. She's trying to go over the top, using the top part of her body. (To Alice:) Put your center of gravity low, go through with your energy low."

D: "Would you like to try again with that suggestion?"

P: "Yes."

D: "Okay, replay." (The protagonist again approaches the "wall" and tries to wiggle through between their legs, and after a tussle, succeeds.)

(This is an example of behavioral training. Although somewhat symbolic in the struggling against an imaginary wall, it does have the elements of practicing, coaching, and re-trying a new behavior.)

D: "How do you feel now?"

P: "Good."

D: "Okay, let's play the original scene." *(Thus, coming full circle out of the psychodramatic spiral.)* They re-set up the first scene, with the group member Betty again as auxiliary playing Alice's friend Cecelia on the phone.)

P: "Hi, Cecelia, blah blah blah (to the director and group); we do the hi how are you small talk for about a minute. Okay (shifts back into role, talking on the phone), so, I called to ask if you'd visit my apartment and keep things together for me for a week while I visit my family out West. Or even stay there if you want?"

Betty: "Sure, no problem. Well, though, I should ask, what will be involved? I mean, do you have any major illnesses with your pets or anything?"

P: "Nothing like that. Just watering the plants and feeding the bird and taking in the mail and stuff like that."

Betty: "Okay."

P: "Say, I really appreciate this."

Betty: "Well, Alice, after the nice things you've done for me, I'm glad to be able to give you something back."

(At this point, the "energy" was declining, and it was time to cut the scene, rather than draw it out in excruciating detail. The director needs to sense this moment and think, as a dramatist would, that the figurative blackout as a scene closes often finishes a key moment or exchange.)

D: "Okay. Cut (the scene). (To the protagonist:) Are you feeling finished?"

P: "Yes."

D: "Then (turning to the group), let's have some sharing."

The Sharing

The director reorganizes a circle, with the protagonist and an empty chair next to her sitting still partly in the stage space.

D: "Alice has shared some of her life with you, and you've helped her explore it. At the end of a psychodrama, instead of analyzing her, what we do is share. That is, we share back what *in our own lives* has been touched or brought up from watching this enactment. Anyone?"

Usually, someone is warmed up by the drama and is ready to come up, sit in the chair, and talk to the protagonist. People may share both from their role in the drama or from their own role. Generally, when someone who was an auxiliary wants to share, after that sharing of what it was like in role, the director says, "Okay, thank you. Now de-role: Turn around, and say something like, "I am not your (mother, inner negative voice, whatever), I am (announce your own name). This affirms that you're distancing yourself from that part. Then share from your actual self as a group member."

Sometimes the sharing is relatively brief, and sometimes it goes on for quite a while. The disclosure of one person often invites others to disclose at that same level. Indeed, it is not uncommon for one drama to act as the warm-up for someone else who says, "I want to play out a situation with my spouse (or employer, or daughter, or some other relationship)."

CURRENT STATUS

Psychodrama as a field has continued to evolve and spread in influence and application. Despite the fact that most textbooks in psychiatry tend to cite only the original source material of Moreno's own writings from the 1940s and 1950s, many excellent books in this field have been published by others since Moreno's death. An updated list is kept on the author's Web site: www.blatner.com/adam/, and there are also extensive references on the Web site of the American Society of Group Psychotherapy and Psychodrama (ASGPP, 2002; wwww.asgpp.org). Most of the available books mentioned in the references and others may be ordered from an affiliated book service, Mental Health Resources (e-mail: mhr@ulster.net). Some of the relatively recent books that are significant—other than those mentioned elsewhere in this chapter—include those by Verhofstadt-Deneve (1999); Karp, Holmes, and Bradshaw-Tauvon (1998); Leveton (2001); and Z. Moreno, Blomkvist, and Rützel (2000).

In addition, an independent American Board of Examiners in Psychodrama, Sociometry, and Group Psychotherapy certifies those achieving full training and passing an examination. (Because many people do what they call *psychodrama,* this offers a way to find out who has actually completed the kind of training recognized by their professional colleagues.) At present, the training required for full certification includes the possession of a master's degree in one of the helping professions and over 780 hours of didactic/experiential work and specified supervision—to ensure a level of maturity and competence. The examination requires an understanding of ethical issues, knowledge of theory and practice, and an observation of the candidate's actual directing skills.

There are at present about 180 certified trainers and 200 certified practitioners in the United States. In other countries, increasing professional interest has resulted in the formation of national and multinational organizations, publication of books and journals, and the staging of international conferences. An estimated 10,000 practitioners have more than 200 hours of training in the world today, and half of those have more than 700 hours of training. Substantial organizations of psychodramatists have been formed in at least 25 countries, and there are interested professionals in many others. A number of these countries now have their own psychodrama journals (Blatner, 1997).

Moreno's journals went through several name changes and, beginning in 1980, the psychodrama journal was titled the *Journal of Group Psychotherapy, Psychodrama & Sociometry.* In 1997, reflecting an expansion of its scope, the name was changed again to the *International Journal of Action Methods.*

The national psychodrama association, the ASGPP (mentioned previously), continues to hold annual national conferences. The American Group Psychotherapy Association, once a bastion of psychoanalysis, has in the past few decades opened somewhat to other methods, including Gestalt therapy and psychodrama. Around 1973, Moreno helped found the *International Association for Group Psychotherapy* (IAGP); and in that professional association, in addition to group analysis, psychodrama also has a significant presence.

SUMMARY

Psychodrama offers many applications, both in clinical settings and beyond them, in education, community building, and other contexts. It should be considered a complex of techniques and concepts that complement rather than compete with other psychotherapeutic schools of thought. In this sense, psychodrama can vastly intensify and expand the power of those other methods. It should not be expected to work in the absence of good judgment, clinical experience, and discretion.

Psychodramatic methods are capable of significant modification, with some of the techniques being applied very simply, such as in role training those with developmental disabilities or in enhancing the repertoire of play therapists or rehabilitation counselors (Tomasulo, 1998).

The underlying and associated theoretical constructs also offer a valuable addition to other theories of psychology, helping to produce an approach that is more holistic and multidimensional. Role theory, for example, generates bridging approaches that connect psychosomatics, individual psychodynamics, family and small group processes, social psychology and sociology, and even considerations of culture and evolution.

Moreno started his *magnum opus,* a 1934 book on sociometry titled *Who Shall Survive,* with this provocative line: "A truly therapeutic procedure should have as its objective nothing less than the whole of mankind." His vision of the applications of sociometry, psychodrama, sociodrama, role playing, group therapy, and applied role theory—all as an integrated praxis—was that these were tools that could help in a remarkably wide range of not only psychotherapeutic, but also sociocultural, endeavors.

REFERENCES

American Board of Examiners in Psychodrama, Sociometry and Group Psychotherapy. (2002). *Directory of Trainers and Certified Practitioners.* Available from P. O. Box 15572, Washington, DC, 20003–0572.

American Society for Group Psychotherapy and Psychodrama. (2002). Membership Brochure. Available from 301 North Harrison Street, Suite 508, Princeton, NJ 08540, e-mail: asgpp@asgpp.org, Web site: www.asgpp.org.

Bannister, A. (1997). *The healing drama: Psychodrama and dramatherapy with abused children.* New York: New York University Press.

Bannister, A., & Huntington, A. (2002). *Communicating with Children & Adolescents: Action for Change.* London: Jessica Kingsley.

Biddle, B. J., & Thomas, E. J. (1966). *Role theory: Concepts and research.* New York: Wiley.

Blatner, A. (1985). The eclectic context of psychodrama. In *Foundations of Psychodrama.* San Marcos, TX: Author.

Blatner, A. (1993). The art of case presentation. *Resident and Staff Physician, 39*(2), 97–103.

Blatner, A. (1994). Psychodrama. In C. E. Schaefer (Ed.) *Family play therapy.* Northvale, NJ: Jason Aronson.

Blatner, A. (1995a). Drama in education as mental hygiene: A child psychiatrist's perspective. *Youth Theatre Journal, 9,* 92–96.

Blatner, A. (1995b). Psychodrama. In R. J. Corsini & D. Wedding. *Current Psychotherapies* (5th ed.). Itasca, IL: Peacock.

Blatner, A. (1996). *Acting-In: Practical applications of psychodramatic methods* (3rd ed.). New York: Springer.

Blatner, A. (1997). Psychodrama: The state of the art. *Arts in Psychotherapy, 24*(1), 23–30.

Blatner, A. (1999). Psychodrama. In D. Wiener (Ed.), *Beyond talk therapy: Using movement and expressive techniques in clinical practice* (pp. 125-143). Washington, DC: American Psychological Association.

Blatner, A. (2000a). *Foundations of psychodrama: History, theory, and practice* (4th ed.) New York: Springer.

Blatner, A. (2000b). Psychodramatic methods for facilitating bereavement. In P. F. Kellermann & M. K. Hudgins (Eds.), *Trauma and psychodrama: Acting out your pain* (pp. 41–50). Philadelphia: Jessica Kingsley.

Blatner, A. (2001). Psychodrama. In R. J. Corsini (Ed.), *Handbook of innovative therapies* (pp. 535–545). New York: Wiley.

Blatner, A., & Blatner, A. (1997). *The art of play: Helping adults reclaim spontaneity and imagination.* New York: Brunner/Routledge.

Compernolle, T. (1981). J. L. Moreno: An unrecognized pioneer of family therapy. *Family Process, 20,* 331–335.

Corey, G. (2000). *Theory and practice of group counseling* (5th ed.). Pacific Grove, CA: Brooks/Cole.

Emunah, R. (1997). Drama therapy and psychodrama: An integrated model. *International Journal of Action Methods, 50*(3), 108–134.

Farmer, C. (1996). *Psychodrama and systemic therapy.* London: Karnac Books.

Ford, D. H., & Urban, H. B. (1998). *Contemporary models of psychotherapy: A comparative analysis.* New York: Wiley.

Goldman, E. E., & Morrison, D. S. (1984). *Psychodrama: Experience and process.* Phoenix, AZ: Eldemar Corp.

Hoey, B. (1997). *Who calls the tune? A psychodramatic approach to child therapy.* London: Routledge.

Hudgins, M. K. (2002). *Experiential treatment for PTSD: The therapeutic spiral model.* New York: Springer.

International Journal of Action Methods. (1997). Available from Heldref Publications, 1318 18th Street, Washington, DC, 20006.

Karp, M., Holmes, P., & Bradshaw-Tauvon, K. (Eds.). (1998). *Handbook of psychodrama.* New York: Routledge.

Kellermann, P. F., & Hudgins, M. K. (Eds.). (2000). *Psychodrama and trauma: Acting out your inner pain.* London: Jessica Kingsley.

Leveton, E. (2001). *A clinician's guide to psychodrama* (3rd ed.). New York: Springer.

Marineau, R. F. (1989). *Jacob Levi Moreno, 1889–1974.* New York: Routledge.

Moreno, J. L. (1947). *Psychodrama* (Vol. 1). New York: Beacon House.

Moreno, Z. T., Blomkvist, L. D., & Rützel, T. (2000). *Psychodrama, surplus reality, and the art of healing.* London: Routledge.

Pitzele, P. (1998). *Scripture windows.* Los Angeles: Alef Design Group.

Sternberg, P., & Garcia, A. (2000). *Sociodrama: Who's in your shoes?* (2nd ed.). Westport, CT: Greenwood.

Tomasulo, D. J. (1998). *Action methods in group psychotherapy: Practical aspects.* New York: Accelerated Development.

Verhofstadt-Denève, L. (1999). *Theory and practice of action and drama techniques: Developmental psychotherapy from an existential-dialectical viewpoint.* London: Jessica Kingsley.

Yalom, I. D. (1975). *The theory and practice of group psychotherapy* (2nd ed.). New York: Basic Books.

Chapter 4

IMPROVISATIONAL PLAY IN COUPLES THERAPY

Daniel J. Wiener and David Cantor

This chapter presents an annotated case featuring Rehearsals for Growth (RfG), an application to relationship therapy of improvisational theater techniques. The writing is the result of a close collaboration between Dan, the founder of RfG, and David, the therapist of the case, who is a Certified RfG Therapist trained by Dan and was actively supervised on this case by Dan. The case narrative is written from David's point of view and is interspersed with Dan's italicized commentary.

IMPROVISATION, PLAY, AND RFG

Improvisation (improv) is the invention, in the moment, of behavior that satisfies an unexpected need or constitutes a novel, yet appropriate, response. RfG uses theatrical improv in the forms of either *exercises,* in which persons respond as themselves to a novel task, instruction, or situation; or *games,* in which persons respond to a given situation as characters other than themselves. In RfG, games and exercises are conducted both in a separate physical space from the ordinary therapy seating (like the theatrical stage) and in an imaginary realm set off from the real world, what Johnson (1992) terms the *playspace.* When improvising with others, persons (now termed *players*) co-create and perform invented "realities"

Daniel J. Wiener, Professor, Marriage and Family Therapy Program, Department of Counseling and Family Therapy, Central Connecticut State University, New Britain, CT. e-mail: wienerd@ccsu.edu. David Cantor, Staff therapist, Rimmon Pond Counseling Center, Seymour, CT. e-mail: DCantor@aol.com.

that exist only by mutual agreement of the players and audience; these realities exist only in the playspace and have the same validity as do the rules of a conventional game. Also, like games, these co-created realities are understood by all involved as having meanings limited to the stage or world of the game, in contrast to having "real life" consequences. For this reason, exploratory behavior can be attempted during improv play without the same degree of risk as behaviors undertaken in a nonplay context.

Good improvising has a lot in common with good relationship functioning: Both require cooperation, attending closely to others, and mutual validation. RfG uses improv games and exercises to assess relationship functioning, regularly finding a correspondence between difficulties in improvising together and problems in relating. These same RfG games and exercises are also useful as interventions to teach couples, families, and group members how better to connect and cooperate (Wiener, 1994).

RfG games and exercises shift the social context of reality to a more playful and fantastic mode, thus lessening fear of "real life" consequences of change and empowering exploratory behavior. When clients free their imaginations, they expand their use of self to include playing at being someone else and get unstuck more readily from habitual limitations in both personal and interpersonal behavior. Relationships can be shifted by improvising scenarios that expand emotional range, altering the social positioning of the players, and promoting cooperation by the sharing of control. As do other action (experiential) techniques, RfG opens alternative pathways to learning that do not rely exclusively on verbal processing. Although each RfG game and exercise has a definite structure and specific instructions, the therapist can always improvise, modifying or creating rules and conditions to suit the needs and opportunities of the moment during therapy.

Couples Therapy with Donny and Tracy

The following case narrative describes 10 couples sessions with Donny and Tracy, a couple married 10 years with two children, seven and four, who came into my (David's) office looking to renew a relationship that had gone "dead." They described themselves as having traditional Christian values, including gender roles. He works outside the home as a software consultant, and she works as a homemaker. Jointly, they had recently attempted a multilevel marketing business, but described it as a failure and a personal disappointment in that the values implied by the company's sales techniques did not comport with their own. They described themselves as fairly good as business partners, excellent as parental partners, but bad at being marriage partners. Four months earlier, they had attempted, unsuccessfully, five sessions of talk-only, communications skills-focused couples therapy.

Tracy's stated goals of the therapy were for receiving greater trust and respect from Donny, which included: understanding of her feelings; respect for her decision to attend to the needs of her ailing mother; and not to have her household decisions second-guessed, particularly those involving discretionary spending ("Don't treat me as a child!" she exclaimed, looking angrily at him). She also wanted greater intimacy from Donny, which she defined as more frequent displays of physical affection. For his part, Donny was less articulate about his goals in therapy. Careful questioning elicited the information that he wanted Tracy to respect his decisions because they were reasonable, logical, and best for the family. He wanted her to defer to his role as financial caretaker, especially because he regarded her choices as emotionally based and thereby potentially harmful to their family. Donny was clear that he came to therapy seeing no way to resolve their differences except for Tracy to capitulate. Both expressed fear that their marriage would collapse if they couldn't reach agreement, Tracy referring twice to the "deadness" in their current relationship.

When asked about this "deadness" of their relationship, she indicated that he did not want to be intimate with her; that every time she tried to connect with him, he disagreed or pointed out some minor inaccuracy in what she said, shutting down their whole interaction. He asserted that he was not shutting off intimacy, but rather simply stating "the objective truth" and that he needed to correct her whenever she either misunderstood or misrepresented what he had said. He further asserted that he was being rational and logical while she was being "too emotional," allowing her feelings to cloud what was actually being said and what the "right" decision to be made was, whether it was the right decision for her, for them, or for their family. Seeing the danger of getting drawn into a lengthy argument over hearing and accepting what the other one meant, I offered them a general reframing of their mutual goals in therapy— "to feel accepted by the other and to experience genuine closeness"—and asked if this was what they would regard as a satisfactory outcome. After some clarifying discussion, they both agreed it was.

As I observed their interaction, I became keenly aware that no matter what the issue, subject, discussion, or general interaction, on almost all occasions, *offers,* particularly when coming from the wife, were being *blocked* by the husband. *"The Blocking/Accepting distinction is fundamental to all of improvisation . . . An offer is any communication that signifies, indicates, or assures some aspect of social, historical, psychological or physical reality"* (Wiener, 1994, p. 59). *Blocking, which can be total or partial, is the invalidation of an offer, while accepting validates that offer. Blocking is regularly encountered in couples therapy, being at once a symptom and cause of interpersonal conflict. RfG both requires and teaches people to shift from blocking to accepting each other's offers.* Specifically, Tracy was offering Donny opportunities for closeness or ways to overcome obstacles to closeness, which he blocked by ignoring them and instead criticizing her "emotionality." In turn, he was blocked by her refusal to recognize how much her financial choices threatened him. With the idea of interesting them in cooperative, playful interaction, I shared this observation with Donny and Tracy, being careful not to alienate Donny by emphasizing his blocking over hers. I pointed out how bad feelings result from being blocked in general. Seeing that they understood and agreed with this point, which amounted to their accepting *my* offer, I further reframed their problem as a mutual desire to be fully accepted by each other, rather than blocked.

INDUCING PLAY

Play brackets experience so that it is socially permissible to explore alternatives to conventional behavior without the consequences that ordinarily ensue from such "real life" conduct. In couples therapy, partners who are often highly reactive to each other's behaviors are able to become more relaxed and tolerant of the same or similar behaviors from the other when performed in a play context.

To derive the benefits of RfG techniques in their therapy, Donny and Tracy had to participate, which in turn depended on my inducing them to try these techniques. Tracy, who had initiated the therapy and was the pursuer of change, seemed primed to try anything that would get Donny to be more understanding and sympathetic. For Donny to participate in RfG, however, I determined I would have to appeal to his sense of reason and logic. I first pointed out that blocking, though producing the impasse they came to therapy to overcome, served at least one useful purpose: to protect people from being forced to change by another. Yet, for them to experience the acceptance of each other's offers and the good feeling that flows from such acceptance, they would need to move beyond their blocks and accept my offer to try accepting. Observing their continued nervousness (and fearing that if an offer I made was blocked, it would mirror their stuck dynamic and reinforce their hopelessness), I decided that I needed to reduce their anxiety further before I invited them to try RfG exercises. I began by describing two specific RfG offer-and-acceptance exercises, MIRRORS (Wiener, 1994, p. 69, described on p. 72) and BODY OFFERS (Wiener, 1994, p. 68, described on p. 73). *All RfG exercises and games, and indeed all improv enactments, are based on the acceptance of offers. These two exercises train clients to attend to each other's nonverbal offers and can be enacted successfully only by one player accepting the offers of the other.* At this point, I modeled speaking to them in GIBBERISH (p. 82), playfully telling them beforehand that I would be conveying the wonders of offer-acceptance games to

heal relationships, but in gibberish (nonsense speech with accompanying emotional tone and gestures signifying meaningful communication). *David is helping
reduce their anxiety by modeling enactment rather than urging them to try activities outside their experience. By "going first," he reduces the social distance
between therapist and clients and models the courage to do something "undigni-
fied." He also models the humorous, playful attitude that helps most clients move
into and benefit from RfG techniques and is also reducing his own anxiety by
warming himself up to play.* Afterward, I noted to the couple that it was hard to
feel blocked by the other if you're responding to each other in gibberish. To the
contrary, you find yourself wanting to respond to the other's gibberish offers by
responding in kind.

Next, I modeled STATUS CUES (Wiener, 1994, pp. 114–115). *"Status," as
used in RfG, refers to behavior signifying relative importance. In a dyad, high-
status behaviors signal that the player is more important than the other, while
low-status behaviors signal less importance. Status cues are culture-specific behaviors that reliably signal high-, equal-, or low-status.* I did this out of an awareness that Tracy and Donny were demonstrating status inequality in their
interaction with each other, with Donny assuming a high-status "I know I'm
right" attitude and Tracy, a low-status "I'm just a frightened child" one. I began
taking on character by standing up, assuming different postures, and soliloquiz-
ing on the shifts in status accompanying my altered physical positions. *Here
David alternates between performing in role as the characters he takes on and as
himself commenting and explaining what he is doing in role.* In addition, I allowed myself to briefly play characters that I felt emerging by adding a line or
two of dialogue to the physical gestures. Again, I explained to Donny and Tracy
what I was about to demonstrate to them before I actually did it, as well as describing to them what was happening to me immediately before I did it. In this
way, I hoped my demonstration would show them how these RfG techniques facilitate taking on positions different from the habitual ones they were in now. I
also intended that, through their participation, they could gain further experiences of having their offers accepted, as well as accepting those of the other—a
win-win situation. Taking advantage of the humorous and more relaxed mood
that had been established, and noticing their engagement, I took the opportunity
to ask them if they would be interested in a little exercise for them to try before
they went home; both assented. What I offered them was a blocking exercise to
try together. I emphasized that, although a blocking exercise, it would be done
together, with each other's cooperation and collaboration. Thus, by simply
agreeing to attempt it, they would already be accepting each other's offers.
*Here, David is using a strategy of getting the couple to agree to cooperate in play-
ing a game by the same rules (process alignment), which is an effective way of
overcoming a blocking impasse, even when the rule is to block (nonalignment of*

content). At this point in the therapy, Donny was unaware that he was blocking Tracy in real life. I proceeded to explain and demonstrate NON-VERBAL BLOCKING (Wiener, 1994, p. 61) of each other's offers, turning my body away, avoiding eye contact, and seeming to attend to something else when they addressed me. Donny expressed his concern that, because they would just be playing it here, this exercise would not be authentic and therefore of no relevance to their real lives. I addressed his concern by emphasizing that play is, at its core, accepting the offers of those we're playing with, and that was exactly what I wished for them and what they had asked for. As for relevance of how this would relate or help them in their real lives, I asked him to humor me by putting it to a test. I assured him that I could handle being wrong and the worst-case scenario was that it would prove a waste of one minute of his time. He smiled and agreed to try it.

I had them sit in two chairs in the middle of the room facing each other, instructing them to take turns nonverbally (physically) blocking any made-up verbal statement by the other. They proceeded to block each other's offers quite skillfully. As one block, Donny even got up, walked away from his chair and out of the room. I had them take turns stating and blocking for three rounds apiece, encouraging them to enjoy the process of finding ever-new ways to block. When finished, I asked them how they experienced these exercises. Tracy reported a lot of discomfort; it felt to her much like what happened frequently in real life. Donny reported, almost gleefully, that it had been fun. I surmised this was because he had permission to do in the enactment what he was being criticized for doing in the relationship. *At this point, David is less concerned with validating each partner's blocking of the other than of inducing participation with RfG enactments.* When asked what it was like to cooperate, to have agreed to do this experience together, they both indicated that, because they didn't do anything together anymore, it was different from what they were used to. Before the session ended, I reassured Tracy that in the next session we would build on the game just enacted so that she would experience having an offer accepted. I then asked Donny if that sounded okay to him. He said, "Yes, I want to accept her offers; it's just that if I accept her offers, I'll have to give up on my own." I ended the session by reassuring them both that, through these RfG techniques, they would find a way to accept the other's offer without fear that they would have to forgo their own offers being accepted. *David offers frequent reassurances of the effectiveness of the work by reminding them that the techniques are intended to bring them a sense of satisfaction through completion, of achieving an experience that they want, and which they have had in the past.*

I began the second session by revisiting my observations on their stuck dynamic where they didn't feel listened to or understood. At the time, although Donny had mentioned it in the first session, I was not consciously aware of the rational/emotional split between them; he wanted her to think more (to use more logic and reason), and she wanted him to feel more. He believed that her emotional expressiveness interfered with her own logic and reason and feared that his validation of her feelings would leave no room for her to acknowledge his logic. For her part, Tracy feared that accepting his logic would leave no room for his accepting of her feelings. Thus, they were stuck in a demoralizing impasse that neither of them expected could be overcome. When I did become consciously aware of this split and their hopelessness about it, I wanted to use it not simply for insight as an end in itself (for what good is being aware of an impasse when there is a concurrent belief that it is unalterable?). Rather, I wanted to use it as a beginning, as a tool to intensify their motivation to try new techniques as one way out of their impasse. With the belief that sharing this insight would lead them to more and more committed participation, I shared my observations with them, repeating that RfG techniques offer an experience of accepting differences that, instead of threatening their belief systems, would actually bring them closer together.

Picking up on Tracy's reminder that we had finished the last session without giving each a chance to have an offer accepted by the other, I asked them if they wanted to experience that in this session; they agreed. Before beginning, I reminded them that what we were embarking on was achieving their main goals of therapy, namely to feel accepted by the other and to experience genuine closeness. For emotional resonance and as a way to shift the emotional affect for the series of exercises that was next to come (YES, BUT-YES, AND; Wiener, 1994, pp. 64–65), I borrowed the phrase from the first session, which Tracy had used and Donny had liked, that they were both looking for "a soft place to land."

Reminding them of the nonverbal blocking they had already done in the previous session, I now instructed one of them to make any statement, after which the other was to block verbally by changing the subject or responding with a non sequitur. I demonstrated by asking Donny to say something to me ("I like gin and tonic") and responded with a verbal block ("It isn't raining as hard as yesterday"). As in the first session, they found themselves quite skilled at this blocking, although not comfortable with the feeling of being blocked. Reassuring them that we would soon get around to accepting offers, I next instructed them to block physically while accepting verbally. For each of these instructions, I demonstrated first by having Donny or Tracy say something to me (make the verbal offer), after which I modeled my version of how I might follow the instruction. They readily participated and commented afterward that it felt like a block despite the verbal acceptance. I now instructed them to invert the last process by instructing them to accept verbally, but block emotionally through the tone of their voices. This led to a humorous exercise, where I asked them to block verbally but accept both emotionally and physically. Although Donny was more adept and playful during this last process, Tracy reported enjoying watching Donny's inventiveness and was not critical of herself for being comparatively less creative. I then instructed one of them to make a verbal offer and the other to respond with a verbal block beginning with "Yes, but . . ." I had them continue on one subject "Yes, butting" each other on each turn until they were really feeling sick and tired of it. This last instruction was given with the intent of reminding them that this enactment was collaborative and that they were playfully assisting each other to succeed in "feeling sick and tired." *By offering the couple numerous blocking exercises first, David primes them for the full acceptance of offers that they had been waiting for, here and in their life outside the therapy room.* When they reported that they were sick and tired of being sick and tired, I offered them (at last!) the possibility to say "Yes, and . . ." in response to the other's statement. They did so readily and with a moderate degree of enthusiasm, commenting that it felt good to hear the acceptance and noting that replacing the word *but* with *and* made a big difference. Both reported that it was a relief not to be rejected by the other no matter how preposterous their own statement was.

Building on this sentiment, I offered them the heightened satisfaction of full acceptance by offering a version of IT'S TUESDAY (Wiener, 1994, pp. 133–134). *In this game, a brief scene is started by one player making a trivial statement. The other player "overaccepts" by creating a monologue beginning with an emotionally neutral "Yes, and" response, and, on successive lines increases the emotional intensity step by step to an ecstatic crescendo to complete the scene.* They played this exercise fully, reporting enjoying it immensely because they felt so completely accepted. They also reported the relief of not having to hold back their acceptance of the other. They said that with nothing to lose, they would always rather accept, even enthusiastically, than block. Regarding the feeling of having nothing to lose, Donny remarked that it was exactly the opposite situation in real life where they felt angry and were at a distance from each other. In a flat tone, he stated that accepting each other's offers in the real world would be fake and could lead to some bad decisions and consequences. Tracy got upset with this comment, indicating that he never considered her point of view valid and always dismissed her feelings about anything as being "too emotional." *At this juncture, the couple regresses in the processing of a positive experience, activating old wounds, fears, and resentments. David chooses simply to comment on his observations and again reassures them that they can co-create a different reality from what they have had in the past.* Addressing Donny's concern about fakeness, I asked him if continuing to do these exercises outside the therapy office would likely result in their interaction being more fake, less fake, or the same. He said, "the same or less fake."

I asked each of them the same question regarding closeness and each responded, "(resulting in) the same or greater closeness." I asked these questions both to show Donny that I was being responsive to his concerns (and thus not blocking his offer of concern) and to reorient him to objectively (logically) evaluate the usefulness of the RfG techniques. Having gained his partial validation of their usefulness, I ended the session with the reassurance that, with their permission, I would continue to offer other RfG techniques as tools for achieving their therapeutic goal of authentic closeness.

The third session began with their complaint that they could not agree on anything and that they couldn't agree to disagree because they had impending big life choices, especially around the spending and budgeting of money; agreeing with the other meant giving up too much. I offered my observations on their interaction, pointing out numerous examples of one partner's offers that were being blocked by the other. I reminded them that they could disagree without emotionally blocking or invalidating each other and mentioned some other RfG games, exercises, and enactments where they could experience acceptance even as they were blocking the content of each other's offers. In this way, they could maintain their differing positions, yet feel close to each other or, at least, be cooperative in their disagreement. They showed signs of real interest in this, at which point I offered them another version of agreeing to disagree in game form with an exercise called NO, YOU DIDN'T (Wiener, 1994, p. 74). In this game, one partner invents a story while the other one interjects "No, you didn't" or "No, it wasn't" at frequent intervals. The Storyteller then accepts this block, incorporating the changed information into the story and advancing the story line in a new way, which soon again gets blocked, and so on. Both tried the Storyteller and Contradictor roles and reported enjoying this exercise while feeling closer to each other as a result of it, because they could disagree without being angry with each other. They related that, because they disagreed on so many things in real life, it was a relief to learn that disagreement itself wasn't necessarily a relationship-breaker. The session ended with my reassurance that I would continue to offer experiences that I thought could create what they wanted—authenticity and closeness.

In the fourth session, I invited them to explore memories of a time when they had felt authenticity and closeness, which led me to introduce HOW WE MET (Wiener, 1994, p. 103), an RfG game in which they could co-tell the story of how they first met. First, I had them co-tell an improvised story as characters, followed by the co-telling of their real story. In co-telling the imagined story, they both showed much humor, with Donny adding affectionate quips regarding Tracy's attractiveness and Tracy inventing story elements in which she appreciated his humor, solidity, and stability. I had them immediately follow this game with their co-telling of the real story of how they met, which followed a line similar to the imagined one. I chose to have them tell the stories in this order, imagined followed by actual, because I knew that they had had a positive courting experience, but had noticed earlier that they didn't wish to acknowledge it or perhaps had given up on the possibility of ever again retrieving "that loving feeling." I surmised that an imagined story of how they first met would take the pressure off; with my encouragement or directing to remain positive, they would realize their ability not only to think positively about their relationship, but also to experience the real affection they had for each other underneath all the familiar resentments. This experience had the potential to pave the way for a positive reactivation of their earlier romance, bypassing the blocks that these resentments had created. On hearing their positive comments about the enactment and sensing their emergent gentler feelings toward each other, I asked if they wanted to try an exercise in which they could feel their closeness on another level. When they indicated yes, I offered them a holding exercise I adapted from Imago Therapy (Hendrix, 1992) in which Tracy would hold Donny's head in her lap. I offered this as a way to experience the emotional closeness they had when they first met and offer them an experience of reclaiming it after all the intervening years. When Donny hesitated, asking to know the purpose of the exercise, I gave him exactly these reasons of reclaiming lost qualities and experiences, whereupon he agreed to participate. Donny reported during and after the exercise that he did not like to be on the receiving end of the holding because "Her hands felt like they don't care for me," which made him angry. The discussion that followed revealed how both of them felt uncared for by the other, resulting in both being afraid to ask or give to the other for fear of being rejected. I pointed out how this, too, was a version of blocking each other's offers. I told them I understood that the blocking came from fear and resentment, but could be overcome gradually by simply experiencing an acceptance of each other's offers through previously experienced RfG techniques. I chose this moment to characterize the process of change as an experience that need not be labeled as good or bad, but rather as something different from the miserable stuckness they reaped as a result of their blocking. I noted that the holding exercise, although not enjoyed, offered valuable information about wounds that needed to be healed—namely, their mutual fear of becoming vulnerable so that they could receive nurturance and love. I reassured them that, no matter what their experience had been (for instance, no one having been there for them when they did reach out for support, touch, and love), they could ask for and get nurturance and love now, while taking the time to notice and work on their fears about receiving them. I stated that the body holds not only great fear, but also great longing to be free of the fear. *Exercises involving touch or holding offer ways both to experience and transcend the fear of attaining authentic closeness*

(Fallon, in press). Seeing their receptivity, I took the opportunity to recontract with them around their willingness to try RfG techniques in the therapy. They agreed to continue to be open to my offers for them to participate. The rest of this session and the following two sessions (the fifth and sixth) were talk sessions in which they constructively acknowledged to each other when, how, and why they thought things had gone sour between them.

During our seventh meeting, I reframed the holding exercise attempted in the fourth session as an exercise in receiving, rather than giving, touch. I emphasized the receiving aspect because I guessed that Donny could experience his underused feelings through receiving touch and that Tracy wanted her love to be received (accepted) and not blocked, just as much as she wanted him to give to her when she needed love and understanding. I remembered how Donny was critical of the way she had held him in the previous exercise, and I wanted to take the pressure and focus off her and return focus of each to self. I also didn't want the exercise to backfire with recriminations of how the other wasn't sufficiently loving, revisiting their whole stuck, hostile dynamic of blocking each other, instead of supporting and understanding each other's fears. Noting the difficulty Donny had experienced, I offered them the MIRRORS exercise (Wiener, 1994, p. 69) that I had described during the first session as a safer way to practice receiving or accepting a physical offer. *In MIRRORS, the players are positioned to face each other and assigned the initial roles of Leader and Follower. The Leader begins slow, continuous physical movement from the waist up, which the Follower imitates. Both maintain eye contact in silence throughout. The therapist occasionally calls out "Switch!" signaling the exchange of Leader and Follower roles, while the movement continues. Toward the end of the exercise, the therapist calls out "Mutual!" as a signal for mirrored movement to continue without either designated as Leader or Follower.* MIRRORS is safer than exercises involving touching because the Follower has only to copy the movements of the leader and there is no physical contact involved to bring up fears of rejection or fears that the other does not want to give. Yet, the sustained eye contact in silence for two or three minutes heightens intimate connection. They agreed and participated readily in the MIRRORS exercise, with Donny playfully making occasional sudden, hard-to-imitate movements when in the Leader role. Tracy could have taken this as a competitive action, but she smiled appreciatively. During the enactment after I had called "Mutual," both slowed down their movements and attended to each other with greater intensity. Later they reported that, although their ability to move simultaneously was only intermittent, they felt very close to each other. *In my extensive experience using* MIRRORS *with couples, any attainment of mutuality between partners is prognostic of improvement from the therapy* (Wiener, 1998).

Following the verbal processing of their experiences with MIRRORS, I took them through another game I had described in the first session, BODY OF-FERS. *In BODY OFFERS, the first player places his or her body in a position as a statue; then the second player attends to this physical offer by responding with his or her own body offer in any position affected by the first player's. The first player says "Thank you" to acknowledge acceptance of the offer, and they switch roles for another round.* The discussion that followed centered on how satisfying it was to have offers accepted, yet each again expressed the earlier-stated concern of how to translate this experience into their real lives. I was surprised by their return to skepticism and decided to postpone attempting the holding exercise. Accordingly, I responded by proposing they do an enactment, a scene in which they were to play characters with a similar stuck relationship, but were to find a way out of the stuckness by acceptance of offers leading to their characters' experiencing closeness. I explained to them, particularly to Donny, that if they role-played their "real selves," I feared that their actual fears, resentments, and frustrations with each other would interfere with expe-riencing the authentic closeness they really wanted. Noting their statement in the first session that they were good business partners but bad marriage part-ners, I offered them a scene as business partners with an absolutely equal sta-tus relationship in which they could take on fictional character names. I wanted to endow Tracy with more status in role so that she could empower her character to deal assertively with Donny rather than continuing to rely on me to confront him. *David's choices here not only offer the clients an experience beyond their familiar dynamic but also work to disengage him from the role as Tracy's spokesman.* They liked this idea and named themselves Fred and Mary, partners in an import-export business, playing out a scene in which Mary made offers to come to her family parties while Fred refused her invitations by giv-ing a lame excuse every time. During process breaks in the scene after each block, I instructed them to continue the scene with Mary getting angry with Fred both for not accepting her invitations and for his lame excuses. This would empower her to express anger from an adult's, rather than a child's, sta-tus position. This break was quickly followed by another in which I instructed Fred first to accept her offer of greater friendship with an expression of how much he liked her and wanted to meet her family, and then to accept Mary's in-vitations, offering with Fred's "real" reason for blocking Mary's offers to at-tend her frequent parties. His character's "real" reason was left for him to improvise, provided it had nothing to do with her, disparaging or otherwise. Because Fred liked Mary and wanted to be with her and her family, I suggested this reason had something to do with himself (Fred) that was too embarrassing for him initially to admit to her. *Similar to the earlier instruction David gives Mary to be angry with Fred, this instruction offers Donny an opportunity to go*

beyond previous habitual behavior in self-disclosure and acknowledge his block-
ing of her offers. RfG often uses scenes to rehearse behaviors in displaced roles
and fictional circumstances that are too risky or disagreeable to attempt as one-
self. David here is providing a great deal of direction/structure to their impro-
vised scene, as he has specific goals in mind. Under other circumstances, an
RfG therapist might choose to stand aside once the scenario is proposed for a
scene, allowing clients to discover and explore without the use of process breaks.

Following enactment of these scenes as Mary and Fred, both felt an immense sense of relief: Tracy, on having her character's offer accepted; Donny,
on his character's being able to overcome fear and accept her offer. I told
them that they could stay as these characters if they so chose, or use them as
needed to enact scenes in character between sessions.

The following (eighth) session began with a spontaneous report of how
much they were enjoying playing Fred and Mary, calling to each other from
separate rooms and making up all sorts of embarrassing reasons (blocks) why
they couldn't do household chores and errands and agree to other requests (offers) by the other. I asked them if they wanted to take the next step toward their
intimacy and closeness goal by doing the holding exercise again. This time I
noted that they seemed more receptive to each other and were experiencing a
greater willingness to receive each other's touch. Additionally, Donny reported no anger or fears of rejection as he had experienced the first time. They
then reported a perking up of their recently nonexistent sex life when they
could be Fred and Mary. I surmised that status had something to do with their
sexual intimacy. When asked about the effect, if any, of their status equality as
Fred and Mary, Tracy indicated that playing equal status reduced her anger at
being treated like a little girl, relaxing and allowing her to be more playful
with Donny/Fred. He reported that he liked her taking on a higher status than
in real life, that he respected someone who thought highly of herself, and that
it was fun when she was not afraid to play as an equal with him.

I now had them try a nonverbal status exercise, first with Donny standing
over Tracy (who was seated), assuming a high-status posture. To further exaggerate the status inequality, I instructed him to adopt an "I know better than
you" attitude, while Tracy was instructed to take on a "little girl" posture and
attitude. After allowing them a few moments to experience the effects of this,
I next instructed them to explore shifting their attitudes, gestures, and relative
physical positions, noticing how these changes internally and relationally affected their experience of status shifts. After some experimenting, Donny reported not feeling comfortable with his own high-status behavior and feelings
of disrespect toward her in a low-status position. For her part, Tracy felt
intimidated like a little girl, just as in real life, when playing low-status. This

brought into awareness her prior angry feelings at his financial mistrust of her. I next had them reverse positions, with Tracy, now standing over a seated Donny, assuming the attitude, "I know better than you," while Donny was instructed to think to himself, "I'm a little boy." Tracy had difficulty in fully taking the high-status position and reported being afraid of hurting Donny's feelings. By contrast, Donny enjoyed playing the humbled little boy to the hilt. In the discussion following these unequal status enactments, they both reported contrasts with the Fred and Mary enactments, where their characters had held equal status and where they had been freely able to voice their needs and wants in character. I commented that when they view status as something they can play at, rather than either as a personality trait or a fixed condition of their relationship, they can each choose status independent of the status choice the other is making, freeing themselves from feeling controlled by the other. *David is making a key point here, as couples often ascribe unfair and coercive power tactics to their partners' status maneuvers. When status is viewed as elective expressive behavior on the part of both partners, the responsibility shifts away from being controlled by the other to making one's own choices.*

During the ninth session, the couple reported the positive effects of playing Fred and Mary at home as waning and that they seemed to be returning to their old stuck dynamic, with unequal status cues and the ensuing resentments. I offered a new round of NO, YOU DIDN'T (p. 70) as a way to experience being blocked without feeling put down. This "have your cake and eat it, too" experience, as described by Tracy, was well received by both. For the first time, Donny reported his awareness of using blocking words without any accompanying blocking energy. Wanting them to leave the session with a positive experience of accepting offers and making supporting each other more important than being right, I followed with instructing them to revisit the YES, BUT-YES, AND exercise (p. 68), this time building to a crescendo of enthusiastic acceptance in the "yes, and" part of the exercise. Building further on this positive feeling, I also had them revisit BODY OFFERS (p. 73) with the expectation that they would have a more positive experience this time than when they had done it before. They did so, this time adding to the physical offers a line of dialogue apiece and ending one body offer with a scene in which they spontaneously began a game of "leap frog." Looking back on this event, I realize that this also offered them the opportunity to learn about healing relationship wounds inflicted in the past—that just because a previous experience went badly didn't mean that subsequent ones have to go badly also.

In the tenth session, we revisited head-holding and BODY OFFERS to experience receiving and accepting physical offers, because Donny had a previously-noted difficulty with receiving touch in his family of origin. For her part,

Tracy wanted him to both give and receive touch as a sign of his love. Unlike the previous head-holding, Donny now reported receiving at a deeper level, without scrutiny of how she was giving but with self-focus on the sensation and the emotional "taking in" of her giving. To deepen the experience further, I offered the instruction of touching by holding hands while discussing a disagreement. As they did so, I asked them to report how open they felt in the moment to receiving from the other. Predictably, they both reported a decrease in their receptivity during the disagreement. I then asked each to touch his or her own heart while I said, "Bring compassion into your heart, knowing how scary it is to take in the other's energy, position, point of view, and feelings." They now reported more receptivity, but still experienced some holding back. Next, I asked both to say where, in their own bodies, each was experiencing fear or holding back; then, using the hands not on their hearts, to touch that fear spot on the other's body. The energy palpably shifted; they sighed, maintained eye contact, and leaned in toward each other. Tracy was both smiling and quietly tearing; Donny said he was very relaxed and experiencing an opening out toward her. As they evidently wanted to stay in this place, I allowed a few minutes to pass without saying anything. When they moved spontaneously into a hug, I asked them to express whatever they wanted to say about what they were experiencing. Tracy said, "This is what it was like at the beginning of our relationship!" Donny said, "This is different from the beginning. Then I was kidding around a lot. This is something I never got growing up." "Would you like more of this?" I asked. He said, "Sure, I'd love it!" I commented that this is what results when you make supporting and attending to each other, and accepting offers from the other, more important than being right, regardless of whether your reasons for being right are rationally or emotionally based.

EPILOGUE

As the work has continued, Donny and Tracy have oscillated between accepting from/opening to each other and their former resentment-driven blocking/judging dynamic. Donny has become less defensive, often listening quietly without interrupting. Tracy is expressing her opinions and feelings more assertively and directly (actually, less emotionally driven). She seems significantly less collapsed and powerless. Their communication patterns have shifted considerably; there is seldom overt blocking, and they have greater receptivity to the other's point of view, lessened fear of expressing point of view, and little fear that disagreement will result in the collapse of their relationship. When beginning a session, I notice how their energy has changed since the beginning of treatment—they now feel like a team, rather than each holding himself or herself apart or against the other.

Increasingly, they come into sessions spontaneously asking for help with getting back to the "good stuff," even suggesting previous or new exercises to get themselves unstuck. My role has become more responsive to their initiatives, so that therapy has become truly collaborative. In the last session as of this writing, they reported that they had just begun a new joint business venture in which their collaboration in setting up the business felt much more to their mutual liking.

However, all is not resolved. Tracy declared that she still doesn't feel fully trusted as an equal partner financially. Donny has conceded that he still is emotionally reactive toward her overspending the household budget, and this reactivity has carried over to their new venture. This case has been fairly successful—even though the work is not complete, a strong foundation has been laid in trust, mutual fun, and personal growth for them to address both unresolved and new challenges in their relationship.

REFERENCES

Fallon, M. (in press). Using psychodramatic techniques and client-on-client touch in couples therapy. In D. J. Wiener & L. K. Oxford (Eds.), *Action methods in conjoint psychotherapy*. Washington, DC: APA Books.

Hendrix, H. (1992). *Keeping the love you find: A guide for singles*. New York: Pocket Books.

Johnson, D. R. (1992). The dramatherapist in-role. In S. Jennings (Ed.), *Dramatherapy: Theory and practice* (Vol. 2). London: Tavistock/Routledge.

Wiener, D. J. (1994). *Rehearsals for growth: Theater improvisation for psychotherapists*. New York: Norton.

Wiener, D. J. (1998). Mirroring movement for increasing family cooperation. In T. S. Nelson & T. Trepper (Eds.), *101 more interventions in family therapy* (Vol. 2, pp. 5–8). *New York: Haworth Press.*

DEVELOPMENTAL TRANSFORMATIONS IN GROUP THERAPY WITH THE ELDERLY

David Read Johnson, Ann Smith, and Miller James

This chapter describes the basic principles and methods of a play therapy modality, called *Developmental Transformations,* with elderly populations. We attempt to communicate the potential significance of play with the elderly and illustrate these methods by several case examples.

PLAY AND THE ELDERLY

The elderly is such an interesting term for a condition that clings to ambiguity and contradiction. Perhaps it refers to a certain age in years, such as 70 or 60 or (God forbid) 50? Perhaps a state of infirmity or illness or weakness is implied: To be elderly means to be sick and old. Or, perhaps it is merely a state of mind involving feeling that you have lived long and seen much, whether that is accompanied by fatigue or exhilaration. Being elderly is a mixture of being wise and old, sick and immune-contradictions that can give rise to either irony or annoyance.

The term *play* similarly slips through our grasp: Play can mean a game or hobby or interest that is taken very seriously. Play can mean being "playful," which means not taking things very seriously. Some play/creative therapists use play to access serious issues, while others attempt to achieve a state of playfulness as an end in itself. These attitudes roughly correspond to adopting a tragic versus a comic view of life.

In our American culture, adults are subject to social constraints regarding their display of seriousness and playfulness: To be too serious is often seen as a sign of anxiety, difficulty, or rigidity; while being too playful leads to not being believed, trusted, or authorized. Paradoxically, the elderly are less subject to these constraints because of the perception that they are no longer upholding the economic or social structure of society. Thus arises the common stereotype of the rigid, old person "set in his ways," the curmudgeon who insists on repeating the same things each day, expounds worn-out opinions and stories, and views the world concretely, in all senses of the word. Death and stillness surround this stereotype: sitting in his chair, lying in her bed, waiting. Against this stereotype is contrasted another—that of the youthful, playful, whatever-may-care elderly, who tell off-color jokes, encourage young people to take risks, travel to far-off places, and embrace spontaneity and surprise, usually to the delight of others. It is not unusual for these elderly to be featured at the end of the nightly news shows; the message is that a person can be victorious over death—he or she can spit in the face of destiny. Between these mostly imaginary stereotypes lies the quiet playfulness of many older people, who find a mixture of spontaneity and custom in their activities of gardening, fishing, carpentry, or knitting, activities lying somewhere in between work and play, craft and improvisation. Thus, we reluctantly return to the notion—though we can cite no research—that the elderly may be no different from younger adults or even children in the range of their playfulness.

The position we take in this chapter is not that the elderly are in need of play, or that play can be used as a method of processing serious concerns, but rather that each person may have areas that are not allowed entrance into a *playspace;* that is, are not permitted the natural transformations of perspective, meaning, and development. Our task through a play therapy approach is to gently dislodge their grip on this sustaining framework, giving permission for the elderly to more fully enter the natural flow of time and being in which each of us is suspended.

DEVELOPMENTAL TRANSFORMATIONS

Developmental Transformations is a method of drama therapy that uses free play as a central concept (Johnson, 1982, 1991, 2000; Johnson, Forrester, Dintino, James, & Schnee, 1996). As such, Developmental Transformations can also be seen as a play therapy method. The method was developed out of creative arts therapy work with a number of clinical populations, including the elderly (Johnson, 1985, 1986; Sandel & Johnson, 1987; Smith, 2000), schizophrenics (Johnson, 1984; Schnee, 1996), and veterans with combat-related posttraumatic stress disorder (Dintino & Johnson, 1996; James & Johnson, 1997). It is also currently applied in individual therapy with normal-neurotic adults (Johnson, 2000). The approach has been deeply influenced by dance therapy (Johnson, 1993), experimental theatre (Grotowski, 1968; Spolin, 1963), educational drama (McCaslin, 1990; Way, 1967), and play therapy with children (Axline, 1989; Schaefer & O'Connor, 1982).

Over the course of development of this approach, numerous theoretical perspectives have been incorporated to understand the processes involved. These have included the psychological perspectives of cognitive development (Piaget, 1951; Werner & Kaplan, 1963), psychoanalysis, particularly free association (Freud, 1920/1966; Kris, 1982), object relations theory (Jacobson, 1964; Klein, 1932), client-centered therapy (Gendlin, 1978; Rogers, 1951), authentic movement (Whitehouse, 1979), and dance therapy (Sandel, Chaiklin, & Lohn, 1993); philosophical perspectives of existentialism (Sartre, 1943) and deconstruction (Derrida, 1978); and the spiritual perspective of Buddhism. These widely divergent sources have been used to understand aspects of the therapeutic method, concepts of the self-structure, and images of being.

The work with elderly populations has been conducted largely in nursing homes and senior centers, and was influenced by many previous contributors to the use of the arts with the elderly (Caplow-Lindner, Harpaz, & Samberg, 1979; Weisberg & Wilder, 1985; Weiss, 1984). Developmental Transformations was initially conducted in small groups, but has since been applied to individuals, large groups, and milieu/community interventions (Sandel & Johnson, 1987). A training institute has been established to provide in-depth training in the method to clinicians with the appropriate background, though many of the basic clinical principles can be easily applied by any play-oriented therapist.

THEORETICAL RATIONALE

The central concepts of Developmental Transformations include (a) the playspace, (b) embodiment, (c) encounter, and (d) transformation.

The Playspace

The *playspace* is the mutual agreement among the participants that what is occurring is in play. The playspace is the container of the entire therapeutic action in Developmental Transformations. Verbal discussion or processing occurs in the playspace, not at the end of the session outside the state of play. The kind of play that takes place in the playspace is free improvisation, in which clients are asked to play out dramatic movements, sounds, images, and scenes based on thoughts and feelings they are having in the moment. Thus, as these thoughts and feelings change, the scenes, characters, and actions change. Similar to meditative practice, the client is asked to allow thoughts and feelings to arise, to engage with them, and then to let them go as others arise. In Developmental Transformations, this process takes place in an embodied, interactional, and dramatic form, rather than sitting in silent meditation.

Inevitably, thoughts and feelings arise that do not seem playable to the client. The therapist's job is to help the client maintain the state of play through these moments, often by temporarily shifting to other images. Over time, the goal is for the client to be able to play with the unplayable. The play process serves the deconstructive process, largely through repetition. As difficult issues repeatedly arise, are then avoided, and are then addressed again, the client and therapist find ways of playing with different aspects of the issue until, with time, the issue becomes like a cliché and loosens its grip on the client, who eventually lets what is to come next arise.

The playspace is defined by three fundamental and necessary conditions. First, there must be a *restraint against harm*. When playing with someone who pushes a little too hard or gets a little too angry, we say, "Hey, that was too hard, remember it's only pretend!" and thus articulate a boundary condition. Play ends when harm occurs; play deteriorates rapidly when harm is possible. Thus, in our work, when clients fear harm, when the action is getting "too real," their energetic presence diminishes and their playspace shrinks. These are signals to the therapist. When the playspace is strong, more intense issues can be represented, including aggression, hate, sexuality, love, and intimacy. Representing love or horror is not equivalent to living love or horror.

Second, the playspace is a *mutual agreement:* A person cannot be in a playspace alone. When we play together, we look to see confirmation from the other that he or she understands that we are pretending. In this way, knowing that the other is in play with us *is* the playspace. If the father wearing a mask sees that his young child seems intimidated or afraid, he moves the mask more to the side, revealing more of his face, until he sees the recognition by the child that it is Daddy under the mask. Once this mutuality has been reestablished, the play can continue.

Third, the playspace is intrinsically a *discrepant communication,* meaning that reality and fantasy (and thus the boundary between them) are revealed simultaneously. In the previous example, the father shows both the mask and his real face; in theatre, the proscenium stage frames the imaginal world of the play. Other activities such as magic, lying, or disguise attempt to reduce the discrepant elements so that a person is made to believe that what he or she sees is real. Play, on the other hand, is a lie that insists on revealing itself as a lie. To be in the playspace is to know the boundary between fantasy and reality.

Together, these three characteristics—restraint from harm, mutuality, and discrepancy—provide a basis for the proposition that the playspace, as defined here, has a moral or ethical dimension (Johnson, 2000).

The next three central concepts of Developmental Transformations are derived directly from the notion of the playspace, expressed in the arenas of the body, interpersonal relationships, and the process of development.

Embodiment

Developmental Transformations places value on the body as the source of thought and affect. Following Piaget and other developmentalists, this method uses body activation to evoke sensorimotor, then imagistic, and, finally, lexical representations of thoughts and feelings, and it attempts to maintain an energetic, physicalized environment in which the therapeutic process unfolds. Using embodiment as a foundation for interventions provides a concretization that many clients benefit from; it tends to minimize intellectualization and avoid well-rehearsed schemas that are often verbalized; and the stimulation of kinesthetic sensations often evokes unique imagery and memory that may not otherwise be accessed.

Encounter

Developmental Transformations also places value on the exploration of the interpersonal encounter among group members and with the therapist. The content of the play may initially involve generic problems in interpersonal relationships, then more specific matches and/or mismatches among individuals' social roles, and eventually move to the deeper existential anxieties of being in the presence of another, of being seen and grasped by another consciousness. Because of this emphasis, the therapist joins the client(s) in the playspace, allowing them to use him or her as their *playobject*. Real objects or props are not used in this method because they serve as displacements from potential interpersonal encounters (Johnson et al., 1996). Here, it is the therapist who becomes the client's projective playobject, or toy.

Transformation

The principle of transformation is embraced because the stream of consciousness, the flow of images and feelings, is always changing. Thus, as images and roles arise and are played with in the therapy session, the method allows for and encourages the letting go of these scenes and ideas so that the next ones pressing for expression can be acknowledged. In this sense, the aim of the work is not to crystallize core issues or explore specific problems, but rather to achieve a certain success in tolerating and being with a person's own and the other's embodied presence. Thus, the method attends to those moments when the play becomes stuck or impeded, called *impasses,* and attempts to help the participants discover or rediscover their freedom within these intimate bonds.

Summary

For elderly clients, these principles are directly relevant to their major concerns. Embodiment immediately confronts the elderly client's attitude toward his or her own body, including fears of illness, limitation, disability, and ultimately death. Asking a client to move his or her arm may bring up worry about pain or memories of times when movement was a joy. Movement also has meaning in terms of life, for the dead do not move; to move even just a little is to defy death.

Encounter raises issues of presence, of being gazed at and grasped by another. Fears of being ignored, "treated like furniture in the hall," objectified by medical personnel, being hidden from sight, being a burden to their families, being a "has-been," wishing to disappear—all are potential reactions of elderly clients to being encountered. Pride and humiliation are the coin of this realm, and they can cripple interpersonal relations.

Transformation is change, development, and growth—all threatened by age and disability. Why not narrow your field to what is safe and known; why not play the same song now, until the end; what is the point of being spontaneous, now? Each moment in a session when a transformation occurs, clients are asked to let go of a previous image or scene and embrace a new one, not yet fully known. The desire to hang on, to maintain, to hold tight, is tested numerous times in each hour. Each passing image must be mourned, when many have had enough of mourning.

Therefore, working toward embodied encounters in the playspace could be seen as the opposite of dying, that immobilized, unseen, unchanging still point that we imagine is waiting for us.

IMPLEMENTATION: CLINICAL PRINCIPLES

Establishing the Playspace

The therapist's main task is to help the client enter and remain in the playspace. Important in this process is the healing charisma of the therapist, who, by showing spontaneity, creativity, and humor, encourages the client to engage in the imaginal realm. Rather than encouraging participation in play from the sideline, the therapist represents himself or herself more as having come from the imaginal realm, and reaches out to the client, encouraging him or her to follow, as Alice follows the Rabbit down the hole. The therapist must find some symbolic means to indicate to the client that he or she is partly "elsewhere." This can be a colorful item of clothing, a manner of speaking, or posture. Because the playspace is established as an understanding between participants, it is important that the therapist draw clients into a play mode and get their acknowledgment that they are there. Over time, this activity on the part of the therapist helps create what we call a *therapeutic persona,* consisting of both real and imaginal components (Johnson, Agresti, Nies, & Jacob, 1990).

Throughout the therapeutic process, the therapist begins where clients are capable of playing and moves into territory that they have had some difficulty playing with. These areas are inevitably more personal concerns about their current situation; relationships with loved ones or authorities; fears of illness, disability, or death; or painful memories. In this sense, it is not accurate to say that the playspace is a pretend space, for what will eventually be played with are very real things.

EXAMPLE

In one nursing home, the drama therapist had to go room to room to gather the clients, all of whom were in wheelchairs. This was a laborious process, made more burdensome by numerous obstacles that the clients, staff, and families placed in his way. The more serious he became about this problem, the larger the problem grew. One day, simply out of a feeling of surrender, as he was meandering down the hallway, he shouted out, a bit too loudly, "Drama therapy group!" in a somewhat singsong manner. To his surprise, one of his group members, supposedly deaf, shouted back from her room, "Drama therapy group!" As the weeks went on, the therapist incorporated this "gathering song" and soon not only clients but also staff members responded to him, and "Drama therapy group" could be heard in call-and-response form, all along the corridor. Now resistance diminished, and nursing staff volunteered to wheel clients to the room, all the while basking in the belief that the drama therapist was obviously a silly person. Ironically, the breakthrough occurred exactly when the therapist was no longer afraid of being seen as a silly person, and his status in the institution rose instead.

Engaging Clients in Bodily Movement

It is critical in this approach for there to be bodily movement. Because, for many elderly clients, so much of their lives has become absent, establishing their presence becomes an essential intervention. The awareness of presence is facilitated by moving your body, and by witnessing others move their bodies. Bodily movement also allows the therapist to track more accurately the flow of energy in the clients, for after each intervention or introduction of a new element, the rise or fall in the group's energy is the determining factor in the therapist's next action.

Group sessions, therefore, nearly always are begun in wordless movements in unison and allowed to develop from these movements. The therapist attends to the qualities and variations in movement qualities of each member, picking up silently on them in his or her own movement. The therapist models being embodied throughout the session. As images and, eventually, verbalization emerge from these movements, movement is maintained. For example, the therapist may be in the role of an incompetent medical doctor when a client reports a real memory of a past medical complication. During the verbalization, the therapist maintains his gestural/postural behavior indicative of his imaginal role to sustain the possibility of engaging the client in the ongoing scene. The real memory is not transformable, because it occurred; however, the situation of the memory can be incorporated into the scene with the therapist/doctor, allowing the thoughts and feelings associated with it to enter the playspace.

> **Client:** (Reporting a real story.) "And then the doctor took out the needle and dropped it on the floor, and I saw that the nurse looked at him as if he was a klutz and had done this many times before."
>
> **Therapist:** (As doctor, using a funny voice he had been using for the character.) "That's terrible, John. Now in my case, I have never dropped equipment. Let me show you."
>
> **Client:** "I guess so, but you have no idea how I felt; I wanted to knock his block off!"
>
> **Therapist:** (Pretending to pick up some equipment and then dramatically dropping it onto the floor.) "Oops, these electrodes go somewhere (turning to another client); can you hold these electrodes? Which one is the red one?"
>
> **Client:** "You're just like him, an idiot!"
>
> **Therapist:** "Now, John, steady now, this won't hurt much, if I can just find the red one."
>
> **Client:** (Pretends to bop the doctor over the head with a club. The doctor falls to the floor.)
>
> **Therapist:** "Nurse! What happened? Where's the red one? Who's the patient?"
>
> **Emily:** (As Nurse) "You are, you idiot! Come on everyone, let's hook him up!" (Several members put pretend electrodes on him.)
>
> **John:** (Delighted) "Ah, and I found the red one!" (Putting it on him.)

The therapist successfully brings a personal memory into the playspace, allowing the client to more fully embody the feelings inherent in the memory.

Despite the value of the actual, reported memory, the goal in this method is to sustain the transformative potential of each person's underlying flow of affect and imagery.

Being Available as a Playobject

The reverse transference, which has been noted by clinicians working with the elderly (MacLennan, Saul, & Weiner, 1988; Meerloo, 1955), occurs when older clients project not only parental but child images onto their therapists, who are often much younger than they are. However, we have found that the reverse transference is merely one aspect of a more general condition: that elderly clients tend to express interest in their therapists. (All clients have interest in their therapists, but perhaps elderly clients feel less constrained to express it.) This natural arrangement is incorporated by the Developmental Transformations therapist in taking on the role of the client's playobject (Johnson, 1992).

By allowing and encouraging clients to express and expand on their thoughts and feelings about the "therapist" as a persona in the playspace, often a great deal of energy is mobilized that is highly revealing of the clients' issues, concerns, and strengths. This process also allows the therapist to be directly engaged in the dynamics of a relationship with the clients, which provides him or her a great deal of therapeutic power. Once a particular therapeutic persona has been sufficiently developed and invested in by clients, the therapist's task is to heighten their encounter with it by presenting the character to them with greater intimacy.

For example, in one session, the clients had often expressed interest in why the therapist had not had any children, and thought that he should have some soon. The therapist attempts to move this real concern into the playspace.

Therapist: "Well, perhaps you're right, I should have a child."
Client A: "Good! Tell your wife to get on it right away."
Therapist: "Don't you think I'd be a great father?"
Client B: "Excellent."
Therapist: "In fact, I plan to raise the child myself, because my wife works."
Client C: "Men don't know how to raise young children."
Therapist: "Yes, but I am a modern man (laughter). I can do it. Let me show you! Someone give me an infant."
Client C: "I wouldn't give you mine."
Therapist: "No, really, here is one. (Pretends to hold a baby, which he does in a particularly awkward manner.) Now let's see, I know, I'll change its diaper!"
Client B: "This is going to be a disaster!"
Therapist: (Showing difficulty, nearly drops the baby.) "Oops. That was close."

Client A: "You remind me of my husband. I didn't let him in the same room with our daughter until she was two."

(Other clients begin to comment on their past child-rearing memories, as the therapist continues to work with the child. Eventually, he passes the pretend baby around the circle, as each one demonstrates a child-care activity such as feeding, diapering, or disciplining. Past (real) and present (imaginal) are woven together. The therapist's tolerance of the clients' interest in his real life has been turned into a deepening of the playspace and a revelation of the clients' real lives. The therapist's self-disclosure has remained minimal and of a generic meaning.)

In general, the therapist's countertransference and/or real characteristics can be used as stimuli for the clients' play. What guides the decision of the therapist is whether the image facilitates the flow of energy in the play. Thus, as long as the therapist attends to the clients' response to the emergence of a particular image or situation, the source of it (client or therapist) is less relevant.

Establishing Nonlinear Norms

Developmental Transformations seeks to establish a nonlinear process, in which the roles, stories, and images that are currently being expressed and played with are open to be replaced by those that are emerging, even if such replacement appears to disrupt a meaningful, sequential story. It is therefore essential that the therapist be attentive not only to what is being played with *(the existent),* but also what is about to rise up from within group members *(the emergent).* The emergent images are often first seen as discrepant variations in current roles or stories. These discrepancies become the material that the therapist uses to shape the next intervention. Thus, typical dramatic structures such as plot, consistency of character, storyline, ending, moral, and climax-denouement, are intentionally disrupted through such methods as repetition, transformation of the scene, introduction of divergent elements, and shifting attention to discrepant elements in a scene. As the therapist brings attention to the emergent images, he or she helps the group let go of the existent scene to fully embrace what is coming. This method thus differs from others that use convergent interventions to reduce discrepancies in the service of maintaining the organization of the play.

EXAMPLE

In the following group of elderly clients, a family scene was being enacted.

Therapist: (As son) "Dad, I am old enough now to take the car out by myself."

George: (As father, sternly.) "You may be old enough, but you are not responsible."

Therapist: "Oh, Mom, please let me!"

Emily: (To father, smiling.) "Now, dear, aren't you being a little harsh?"

George: "Harsh? Am I being harsh?"

Therapist: "Harsh?" (A feeling of some levity springs forth among the group; the repetition of the word *harsh* and the incongruent giddy feeling are indications of an emergent image; the therapist attends to these.)

Emily: (Looking at therapist, but speaking about George.) "He's always been a little *harsh* with me." (At this point, two members of the group giggle; Emily is positively seductive.)

Therapist: (Softly) "Why, Mother, it's always been so easy to be *harsh* with you."

Emily: "Son, you are so *fresh!*"

George: "Yes, *fresh!*"

Therapist: "I am fresh, you are harsh. (Pause.) Let's all say that together."

All: (With a rise in the energy.) "I am freshhh, you, are harshhh." (This is repeated three times. Several members begin to continue the Sshhh sound. Several put up their fingers to their mouths as if indicating: "Be quiet." The therapist opens his mouth to speak and the entire group "ssshhhs" him, with great delight. Other members then follow suit, opening their mouths to speak only to be ssshhhed. The action appears to make complete sense to the entire group, though it is not possible to put that meaning into words here.)

By attending to the discrepant elements arising within organized scenes, the therapist allows the unfolding of a new, as yet unnamed, entity. The resulting process, however, is far from unorganized—it has been organized at a different level.

IMPLEMENTATION: GROUP THERAPY PROCEDURES

Groups do not often leap into free play, so the therapist uses a developmental perspective to help members gradually achieve higher levels of play. The therapist accomplishes this task through interventions in five dimensions of play behavior: ambiguity, complexity, media of expression, interpersonal demand, and affect expression (see Johnson, 1982). These are based on developmental principles described by Piaget (1951) and Werner and Kaplan (1963), among others. *Ambiguity* is the degree to which the therapist does not determine the spatial configuration, tasks, or roles in the group at a given moment. *Complexity* is the degree to which these space, task, and role structures include multiple elements (such as numerous, different roles). *Media of expression* refers to the level of representation of the action along the developmental continuum of movement, sound, image, role, or word. *Interpersonal demand* is the level of interaction required among members, as well as whether the roles are expressed in inanimate, animal, or human form. *Affect expression* is the degree to which the action and imagery is personal (i.e., about self vs. a fictional character), and intense (i.e., superficial vs. aggressive, sexual, or intimate).

In general, the group session begins at the earliest developmental level, which means therapist-directed sound and movement, in unison, with little interaction, and impersonal, nonintense imagery. The therapist gradually makes interventions that increase the developmental level of one or more of these dimensions toward greater ambiguity, complexity, interpersonal demand, and intense, personal imagery. The therapist uses the group's responses to these interventions (in terms of fluctuations in the energy or flow of the play) as a signal of whether to continue or to linger at a particular level. It is important to understand that the therapist's attention is largely on these developmental dimensions, not on the content of the client's imagery or scenes, nor on an agenda of planned exercises or structures. This is because the Developmental Transformations therapist is managing the state of play, not the content of the play.

For many clinical populations, typical stages of the (usually one-hour) group session include greeting, unison movement and sound, defining, personification, structured role playing, unstructured role playing, and closing. A more detailed description of these stages is included in Johnson (1986). Group work usually begins by inviting the group members into the playspace (greeting), and then engaging in unison movement while sitting in a circle (unison movement). Over a period of time, transient images begin to arise (defining), followed by more organized roles/characters (personification), which then may be focused on for a period of time (structured role playing), only to dissolve again into more free-flowing improvisation (unstructured role playing). The departure from the playspace occurs during the closing ritual. We have found that as groups become more familiar with the method, and as the therapist becomes more seasoned, these stages become less distinct.

In longer term therapy, participants have the opportunity to develop a much deeper sense of trust in the process and in the ability of the playspace to contain and express their core anxieties and insights. The overt content of the play thus deepens, moving from the level of social role to personal history to here-and-now experience among the participants. This method is best designed to evoke and process basic existential issues, in contrast to addressing current life problems. For the elderly in particular, this type of work speaks to the questions of "What's the point?" or "Why bother caring anymore?" as opposed to symptom reduction.

CASE ILLUSTRATIONS

A Small Group Session

The following transcript is based on a Developmental Transformations session that occurred in a long-term nursing home in New York City. Client identities have been disguised, and some events have been changed to make aspects of the method more explicit. Reflections on the session-in-progress are noted in brackets. Although several of the ten clients had participated in other drama therapy groups, this particular group was only a few weeks old, and several of the clients had never participated in drama therapy. Most of the clients were dealing with intense physical problems, such as complications from stroke, heart failure, and diabetes, among other medical conditions. Many of the group members also had some form of dementia, although not of sufficient severity to prevent their participation in the group's activities. Following is a description of each of the clients:

> Alan, 90, dementia, heart disease, poor circulation; large, physically imposing, in wheelchair, bilingual English/Spanish, can be verbally/physically abusive to staff, not enthusiastic about groups.
>
> Andrea, 95, alcoholic, dementia, ambulatory, former taxicab driver, talkative, sociable.
>
> Bill, 82, stroke, expressive aphasia, wheelchair, religious, occasional angry outbursts but sociable.
>
> Debbie, 79, depression, mild dementia, walks short distances with a walker, sociable and cooperative.
>
> Jackie, 88, stroke, schizophrenia, memory deficit, teacher, active group participant.
>
> Jocelyn, 69, paranoid schizophrenia, mistrustful of others, but participates in activities.
>
> Manny, 80, heart attack, ambulatory, Hispanic, abusive to wife, inappropriate sexual behavior, plays guitar.
>
> Mark, 68, stroke, heart disease, uses walker, poor background, active, sociable.
>
> Myron, 80, dysphoric, wheelchair, poor eyesight, estranged from mentally ill wife.
>
> Sandra, 80, ambulatory, grew up in Caribbean, active in groups, superficially pleasant.

The group took place in a common dining area on one of the nursing home units. The group was kept as private as possible by closing the doors to the dining room and discouraging staff from entering during the session.

[GREETING PHASE:] The therapist (AS) arranges the group in seats or wheelchairs in a circle, and then gives a brief explanation of the name and purpose of the group, indicating that "everywhere there are signals or invitations for you to hang it up, to be still, to die, for your life to be over. But in this group, we are going to work to remind ourselves that we have so much life left, to breathe life into our bodies and play together. Okay? So let's begin by doing some breathing." The therapist then leads the group into taking deep breaths and slowly letting out sounds on the exhalation.

[UNISON SOUND AND MOVEMENT PHASE:] Soon, simple hand motions (e.g., lifting, twisting) are added that everyone performs in unison. Mark makes a hand gesture with the words "Can't do it." Everyone follows him, repeating the movement and phrase. Each person then introduces a variation, for example, saying "Can't do it" matter-of-factly, opening the hands away from each other, or doing it by waving the hands in a snobby, elite way.

Therapist: "Do it toward your neighbor." (They do.)
Therapist: "Do it to the people across from you." (There is a burst of energy and laughter.)

[Reflections: *There is a feeling now of being above it all; we can't do it because we don't need to do it; we have others to do it for us.*]

Alan: Wags his finger, "Heh, heh, heh." (Everyone follows.)
Jackie: "Sounds like a donkey."
Myron: "Ha, ha, ha." (Everyone follows. The sound changes to that of witches cackling. The group turns into witches.)

[*Note the rapid transformation of images. It is important not to grab onto an image such as "Can't do it," because it rapidly shifts to something else. At this phase in the group, the importance is to simply build some momentum and continually note the level of energetic flow of the play. DEFINING PHASE:*]

Therapist: "Here we are again as witches. This happened last week, too."
Jackie: "We need a house to haunt."
Therapist: "How can we haunt the house?" (One by one, they think of different ways to haunt the house. Ghosts, spider webs. They act these out together.)

[*From haughty to haunting, the feeling here is both an empowered one and an emergent sense of loss, as in being mere ghosts of our former selves.*]

Mark: "Dracula!"
Therapist: (Moves into the center of the circle and acts out Dracula for them, baring her teeth and approaching each one in turn.)

Jackie: "First, they say I have long teeth. Then they say I have no teeth."
Therapist: (Now as a toothless Dracula.) "Argghh!" (Laughter, delight.)

[The feeling is now powerlessness, an impotent ghoul, a sexual being that no longer can touch or be touched, only the desire to control remains.]

Myron: "No, now she's a bat!"
Therapist: "A bat? Now I'm a bat?"
Andrea: "Yes, a blind bat."

[Now blind as a bat . . . the references now fully evoke bodily deterioration, disability, dependency. Yet, there is a feeling of need, of wishing to be helped, of looking for redemption somehow, or seeking love.]

Therapist: (Reaches out to individual clients, sometimes touching them lightly. Some reach back, some hold her hand, some shy away pretending to be disgusted or afraid. The clients are energized and laughing. Someone starts clapping. Others join in, and the clapping turns into a rhythm.)
Jackie: "Sounds like an old horse."
Mark: "A bunch of horses."
Therapist: (Taking the role of an old horse as she walks around the center of the circle. PERSONIFICATION PHASE:) "Oy, my back hurts."
Mark: "You don't have a saddle."
Bill: "No—no——no teeth!" (Laughter.)
Alan: "You have nothing in the world. I am like you!"
Sandra: "You have a limp."
Therapist: (Faithfully renders all of these images.)

[Despite the levity, the room seems filled up with loss. The character has lost everything: body, senses, family, friends. The therapist silently remembers a recent personal loss.)

Myron: (Singing) "The old gray mare ain't what she used to be." (Everyone joins in. Much laughter.)
Therapist: "No, I'm not what I used to be. (To Myron) Are you what you used to be?"
Myron: "No, I am not. Definitely not."
Therapist: (Asks each person in the circle. One at a time they answer "No.")
Manny: "No, Miss, I am not what I used to be."

[The therapist uses Transformation to the Here-and-Now, *which means that while staying in role as the horse, she addresses the clients as clients, though some ambiguity remains as to whether they are answering "for real" or as a*

character in this ongoing drama. That ambiguity is sought at this moment, for it provides the freedom to speak the truth, or lie. Perhaps it is this that allows Manny, a proud and guarded man, to admit to a weakness.]

Therapist: "You're not? Yes, I can see. Neither am I."
Myron: "You're just like the rest of us."
Therapist: "I'm in good company."
Alan: "You're in the right place."
Debbie: "You're home."
Jocelyn: (Laughs nervously and loudly. The energy in the room drops.)

(The therapist senses a feeling of anxiety, of wanting to go no farther down this path, of images of homes that perhaps were not the best, of family members who brought pain—not solace, of brokenness.)

Therapist: (Again in role as the old gray mare) "Can you help me? I need something, but I don't know what exactly."
Debbie: "A feedbag."
Jackie: "An apple."
Therapist: "I lost my teeth in this apple. You can probably find yours in there, too!" (Laughter.)
Bill: "Here, you can have my teeth." (He pretends to pull out his false teeth and offers them to the therapist. People roar with laughter. There is a pause.)

[There is now a buoyant feeling in the room, a lift gained by the welcome retreat from the emergent shadow encountered moments before. However, the therapist assumes that what is to emerge comes on its own, and it is not her job to force it into the playspace. This assumption is supported by a feeling of anticipation held by the group. There is more to say. As the silence continues, the therapist merely looks around the circle at the group members. STRUCTURED ROLE-PLAYING PHASE: Myron speaks first.]

Myron: "The biggest for me was losing my eyesight. I so much loved to watch things: sunrises, flowers, people. I try to see them in my mind's eye now, but it isn't the same."
Debbie: "I lost my parents when I was young, maybe 30. That was a long time ago. I could have used their advice so many times. But, what is there to do?"
Therapist: "What other losses have people had?"

(Several other members mention their losses, with a mixture of poignancy and puck.)

Bill: "Do you have any idea what it is like to be in this wheelchair all day? I think about the times I could walk and run, I was a sports nut, you know, skiing, hiking. This is tough."

Andrea: "But you have your mind. It is worse to lose your mind." [The therapist has an initially negative reaction to this comment, as if Andrea is invalidating Bill's and others' losses out of a fear of suffering and death. However, the group members react positively to her comment, as if reminded of a pleasant summer day.]

Andrea "We still have things that make life good." (People nod in agreement.)

Therapist: "Okay, let's put all those good things we still have into our Magic Box." [The MAGIC BOX is a pretend box that is kept in the ceiling and brought down by everyone raising their arms and pulling it down with a hum. The lid is then opened.]

Therapist: "What do we have?" (Members put in "my sense of humor," "love from my son," "being together here," "no bowel problems.")

[The therapist, though beset with various judgmental thoughts and therapeutic agendas, tries to put these aside and continue to faithfully render the flow of the group's play, based on the evidence of their energetic involvement, which remains high.]

Therapist: "Now, let's close the lid and return the Magic Box to the ceiling."

(The group does so with a giant, "Whoosh!" and then several members spontaneously applaud. There is clearly a good feeling in the group. CLOSING RITUAL:)

Therapist: "So it seems we were able to accomplish our goal for today, which was to breathe some life into ourselves. I was touched to hear about the burdens you have been facing, for they are certainly big ones."

Myron: "Not as bad as the old gray mare's!" (Laughter.)

Therapist: "No, definitely not that bad. So let's end the group for today. As usual, we will close our eyes, take a slow breath in, and then out. Okay, open your eyes, take the hand of your neighbor, and look around the room at each person. (They all do so in silence.) See you next week!"

Discussion

This is an example of an early Developmental Transformations session in a nursing home context. The group had met for only three weeks before this session and demonstrated a high degree of cohesion and cooperation. The therapist structured the opening and closing, and offered herself as the central playobject during the main action of the session. Her attention centered on sustaining a state of engaged play rather than the content of the issues arising from the group, though she had numerous personal reactions to these. Importantly, when the group moved forward into more effectively laden issues, it often made a quick retreat into safer topics. The therapist did not interfere with this ebb-and-flow of the group's play, trusting that each foray into darker territory left a note of familiarity that allowed the group to imagine returning at a later time. The group was not at a point that it could move into unstructured role playing, which is not unusual for groups at this stage of development. This session did appear to achieve a level of communication, sharing, and affective release around some significant issues for these elderly clients.

A Large Group Session

Developmental Transformations can also be applied to large group meetings, in which clients are usually arranged around tables in the dining room, facing the front. An excellent format is to use a public address system with one or two microphones, connected by long extension cords so that the emcees can walk into the audience. In this format, the two therapists attempt to take different angles on a particular issue and recruit audience members to articulate one side or the other in a point-counterpoint type of interaction. The purpose is to maintain a dynamic, slightly off-balance atmosphere that calls out for participation from the group "to put things right."

The central principles of Developmental Transformations are adhered to: The large group is invited into a playspace by the therapists, who take on an enhanced "therapeutic persona" (Johnson et al., 1990). The therapists emphasize interpersonal encounters both with the clients and each other, and allow the focus to be directed to them as the central playobjects (or characters) in the unfolding action. Through their movement in space and by varying their proximity with the clients, the therapists are cognizant of the need for embodiment. Transformation is achieved by the therapists' picking up not on the overt content but on the divergent affect or imagery that is evoked by the various encounters. In this way, the issue being discussed changes over the course of the session and the therapists do not attempt to stick to one topic.

In this example, the therapists (Dr. Johnson and Dr. Jacob) were staff members of the nursing home and led a weekly community meeting. Each had a microphone with an extension cord and moved through the room to clients who signaled them they wished to speak. Over the past several weeks, Dr. Johnson's therapeutic persona could be characterized as a somewhat pitiful remnant of the patriarchy, which had meaning in the context of the arrival of a new administrator who was female. Dr. Johnson began:

Dr. Johnson: "What's on people's minds today?"

Eloise: "Not much."

William: "Aren't you supposed to lead the discussion?"

Dr. Johnson: "I'm supposed to lead the discussion?"

Dr. Jacob: "Yes, aren't you supposed to lead the discussion? You're the leader, aren't you?" [The leaders do not have any preset ideas about the issues to be explored, and plan to pick up on whatever is offered them.]

Dr. Johnson: "Yes, of course I am the leader. Don't I look like a leader?"

Margaret: "Yes, you are big and strong!" (Laughter.)

Dr. Johnson: "Thank you, Margaret."

Dr. Jacob: (To a member showing disdain) "What's your view?"

Frank: "You call that leadership?" (Laughter.)

Dr. Jacob: "But he appears to be big and strong?"

Frank: "Yes, but is there anything up here (pointing to the head)?"

(Laughter.)

Dr. Johnson: "Ellen, they don't believe in my leadership! (Moves close to her and smiles.) But you do, don't you?"

Ellen: "Oh, yes." (Very submissive.)

Dr. Johnson: (To Dr. Jacob) "Now here's a very intelligent woman! Ellen, don't you think strength is a critical part of being a leader? Think of our generals, our presidents! Who do you want? A wimp? Someone who has *feelings?*"

Ellen: "Oh, no!"

Dr. Johnson: "You want a REAL MAN, don't you, Ellen?"

Ellen: "Yes, a real man!"

Dr. Jacob: "What's your view, Bill?"

William: "I think people like that have gotten us into real trouble."

Dr. Jacob: "What do you mean?"

William: "Like despots and dictators."

Dr. Johnson: "You think I'm great, don't you, Andy?"

Andy: "Not really."

Dr. Johnson: "Andy! (Steps closer, looming over him.) You think I'm great, DON'T YOU?"

Andy: "If you say so." (Laughter.)

Dr. Johnson: "That's what I want to hear!"

Dr. Jacob: "Ever come across anyone like this before?"

Greta: "Yeah, my husband. (Laughter.) He was very bossy and thought I should do what he commanded. He was a stern man." [There is a great deal of energy in the room at this point, which the leaders use to guide them.]

Dr. Jacob: "A lot of men act like this, don't they?"

Greta: "You'd better believe it."

Dr. Jacob: "So how did you handle it?"

Greta: "I pretended to do what he said."

Dr. Johnson: (To Bob) "So Bob, man to man, don't you think men deserve to be the head of the family?" [Here the leaders shift the focus from Dr. Johnson to family relationships, following the group's response to Greta's contribution.]

Bob: "Absolutely."

Dr. Johnson: "That's how it was in your family, right, Bob?"

Bob: "Well, actually, my wife was the boss." (Laughter.)

Dr. Johnson: "Bob, you let her take over!"

Bob: "I never had a chance."

Dr. Jacob: (To Emily) "How about in your family?"

Emily: "I had him wrapped around my little finger."

Dr. Jacob: "Really. He let you do that?"

Emily: "Women are stronger than men in general. That's why men die off earlier."

Dr. Johnson: (stomps around) "This is terrible. This is going in the wrong direction. Where are the men anyway? Look here, the patients are mostly women; the staff are mostly women! Andrew, look at this place, most of the staff are women, right?"

Andrew: "Right."

Dr. Johnson: "And you are the PATIENT, right? And here, the PATIENT is the one in charge, right?"

Andrew: (Does not answer.) [There is a definite drop in the flow of energy in the room, indicating to the therapists that there is some anxiety about addressing the nursing/patient power relationship.]

Dr. Johnson: "Andrew!"

Andrew: "Not really."

Dr. Johnson: "Andrew, this is awful. You are a man, you have had a long career as a manager, you have been a successful husband and father and grandfather, and you are telling me that AS A MAN you are not in charge here! You can tell us. What can they possibly do to you?" (Dr. Johnson and Andrew look at each other.)

Andrew: (Playfully) "Women can do a lot."

Dr. Johnson: "Hmm, come to think of it, I imagine you're right."

Andrew: "Frankly, I'm not sure if I ever was in charge."

Dr. Johnson: (Becoming very upset) "Oh no, this is terrible!"

Dr. Jacob: "Now don't become so upset, Dr. Johnson!"

Dr. Johnson: "I am upset! This is frightening, this is horrible, this is impossible."

Dr. Jacob: (In a directive way) "Now CALM DOWN."

Dr. Johnson: "Yes, Dr. Jacob." (Laughter.) [The leaders have now moved away from the previous issue back to Dr. Johnson, in response to the decreasing playability in the room.]

Dr. Jacob: "You see, you have to be strong with them. Right?"

Emily: "Right. That's how I did it with my husband. Though you have to be careful."

Dr. Jacob: "What do you mean, Emily?"

Emily: "Sometimes they get violent."

Dr. Jacob: "Then what do you do?"

Emily: (Tearfully) "You cry. You leave home for the night. You wait for him to come back and apologize." (Long silence in the room, though the flow appeared to be high again.)

Dr. Johnson: (To Eloise) "Is an apology ever enough?"

Eloise: "No, never enough. But what else can you do?"

Dr. Johnson: "I don't know. That would be a hard one to figure out."

Eloise: "It's a problem."

Dr. Jacob: "Is it a problem?"

Emily: "It's a problem." Silence. [This was a remarkable moment, because nearly all in the room were on the edges of their seats, and the silence was filled with many layers of this issue: past family abuse, present nursing/ patient conflict, and the pitiful Dr. Johnson, all woven together.]

Dr. Johnson: "So Dr. Jacob, I apologize for getting so upset earlier. I don't think it really matters if I am the leader or not. I had a good time hearing from everyone here about this issue."

Dr. Jacob: "I agree. But you are going to have to work on your feelings, I think."

Dr. Johnson: "Perhaps you're right about that. But how?"

Dr. Jacob: "After the group, I want to see you in my office."

Dr. Johnson: "Yes, Ma'am." (Laughter.) [The leaders, cognizant of the time as well as the intensity of feeling, again drew the attention back onto their therapeutic personas.]

Dr. Jacob: "So, thank you, everyone, for coming today. I think we made some progress in discussing the topic of leadership, though we certainly did not come to any conclusions! See you next week."

Discussion

In this example, the guise of the therapists' playful personas allowed this large group of nursing home residents to name and speak about several important issues related to power dynamics, both in the nursing home itself and in their past relationships. The discussion served to normalize these problems, providing permission for these issues to be addressed directly during real interactions in the institution. Indeed, because nursing staff were in attendance at this meeting, sensitivity to these issues increased, and client-staff violent incidents remained extremely rare.

This approach does not require agendas or even particular knowledge on the part of the therapists, other than comfort in improvisation and being the object of large group projections. The talk show format used here provides a normative structure that most participants are familiar with; therefore, it serves as an organizing influence in the session.

Influencing an Entire Milieu

In one Veterans Administration nursing home, the collective influence of the creative arts therapy groups, holiday ceremonies, and theatrical plays that had been performed began to be felt in all areas of the milieu. Introducing norms of playfulness and creativity into an institutional environment may have, in the long run, far more positive effect on the health of its clients than a series of disconnected treatment components, however competently run (Sandel & Johnson, 1987). Originally, the nursing home did not celebrate any major holidays, because staff were often on vacation on those days. This included National Nursing Home Week, which was ignored largely because the staff identified themselves as the Veterans Administration, not a nursing home. The first attempt to acknowledge this week was met with resistance and concern, because it brought to awareness that the unit was a nursing home. The first several years, the week was acknowledged by a special ceremony held in the dining room, in which the hospital director and other staff spoke about the importance of the nursing home, some awards were given, and a blessing spoken. The next year, the staff felt they wanted to celebrate the week by putting on a health fair, in which the whole hospital was invited to come and see what the nursing home was like. This was the first time the nursing home opened itself to scrutiny from others, requiring staff and patients to don "presentational" personas that had otherwise been discarded in the previously self-contained unit.

The following two years, the staff and clients organized a talent show, again inviting the rest of the hospital to attend. The first talent show was a somewhat standard display of the staff's and clients' limited talents, including some singing, dancing, and reading of poetry. The second one, however, demonstrated a much higher degree of playfulness and spontaneity, with participants presenting more idiosyncratic aspects of themselves. For example, a male and female patient sang a love song to each other, hamming it up tremendously. In a magic act, the psychologist—assisted by two patient amputees—sawed the head nurse in half, only it went "wrong" and (fake) blood spilled out onto the floor, to the howls of staff and clients, who understood the actors were making fun of their very real competition with each other. The head nurse, the typical stoic and rock-hard manager, the kind of person everyone would love to saw in half, became instantly loved.

With the success of this project, the following year the staff and patients went well beyond previous efforts and transformed the unit into a truly remarkable playspace. For months, the patients, staff, and a new medical director planned the event, which had been suggested by one of the patients. The event was the re-creation of a 1920s speakeasy, in which the dining room was transformed into a gambling casino and saloon, with staff as the employees. As people arrived in the unit from the elevators, however, they entered a "funeral parlor," in which a real casket was displayed with a staff member lying in it (welcoming the public), a physically imposing male staff member playing an organ, and a very sexily dressed staff woman "in mourning." Word was passed around before the event that to get into the speakeasy (which was hidden behind the funeral parlor screen), you had to say "Harry and Mo asked for me." The entire hospital became interested in this event (the casket being set up in the nursing home turned more than a few heads), so much so that the hospital police asked if they could stage a fake raid on the speakeasy, which was arranged, to the delight of everyone. The new medical director of the nursing home was arrested and hauled off by the police.

This event, by being so deeply involved in a mutual playspace for the whole unit, brought out a liveliness and meaningfulness in nearly every client and staff member. Instead of being ashamed of their status as a nursing home, they were the pride of the entire hospital. The event simultaneously re-created a historical event of importance to the clients, played with the notion of death in a dramatic way, and overturned the shame of the unit by making others in the hospital hope to gain entrance into the home, where the action was.

The following year, the unit staged a wedding, in which the unit social worker married his female intern (well, actually, their characters got married). The unit medical director, a female, who was really pregnant at the time, played his mistress; and other clients and staff played the whole gamut of both families, one of which was a lower-class Mafia family, and the other an upper-class and uptight New England family. Again, the hospital was invited for the black tie affair. To standing room only, the hospital chaplain conducted the ceremony, and the dance afterwards included ballroom dancing (with rotating globe above), and a dance exhibition by the same psychologist and head nurse who tripped over each other, ending up in a heap on the floor. The issues addressed included sexuality, staff-client intimacies, and ethnic and social class dynamics. The wedding brought back memories that were processed in the various therapy groups. Only because the staff were not afraid to be seen this way could these issues be addressed in play, with no known incidents of confusion or misunderstanding among the clients.

Discussion

Though certainly not the standard group therapy intervention, the healing effects of such milieu interventions cannot be underestimated. In this example, the principles of Developmental Transformations were followed: The playspace was established and maintained, staff offered themselves as the clients' playobjects, embodied action was emphasized whenever possible, and attention was paid to emergent images in the community rather than proscriptive agendas based on what staff had learned was therapeutic for their clients. Rather, the staff was able to trust that what emerged from participants' playfulness would be meaningful and relevant to them. This proved to be true, and allowed one Veterans Administration nursing home to be deeply transformed.

CONCLUSION

Developmental Transformations is a play therapy approach that can be applied in a variety of contexts in work with elderly clients. The application of improvisational play that emphasizes embodied encounter gives rise to many important issues for elderly clients. Following developmental principles in which the flow of play is maintained by constantly altering the level of structure, complexity, and interpersonal demand, the therapist can successfully implement this approach even with severely disabled clients. Perhaps most uniquely, this approach uses the therapist's own participation as an object of playful encounter, made even more possible by the reverse transference often existent in these groups.

These principles also support the application of Developmental Transformations in larger group meetings and in the milieu, and offer a course of action for transforming agencies and communities into more healthy playspaces, characterized by restraint from harm, mutuality, and the disclosure of boundaries between reality and fantasy.

The limitations of this approach include the need for a high degree of spontaneity and improvisational skill in the therapist, and a willingness to actively participate in the developing playspace. Second, this approach may be difficult to integrate in other formats because of its emphasis on process and lack of discrete structures that could be applied. Third, this method is designed to address more existential issues, rather than specific symptoms or life problems, and so may not be applicable in situations where a focus on a particular issue is appropriate. Nevertheless, Developmental Transformations can be used in short- or long-term therapies; in individual, group, and large group formats; and with severely disturbed or high functioning populations. In addition, the central principles of playspace, embodiment, encounter, and transformation may be useful to the creative play therapist in enhancing his or her therapeutic style.

REFERENCES

Axline, V. (1989). *Play therapy.* Boston: Houghton Mifflin.

Caplow-Lindner, E., Harpaz, L., & Samberg, S. (1979). *Therapeutic dance movement: Expressive activities for older adults.* New York: Human Sciences Press.

Derrida, J. (1978). *Writing and difference.* Chicago: University of Chicago Press.

Dintino, C., & Johnson, D. (1996). Playing with the perpetrator: Gender dynamics in developmental drama therapy. In S. Jennings (Ed.), *Drama therapy: Theory and practice* (Vol. 3, pp. 205–220). London: Routledge.

Freud, S. (1966). *Introductory lectures on psychoanalysis.* New York: Norton. (Original work published 1920)

Gendlin, E. (1978). *Focusing.* New York: Bantam.

Grotowski, J. (1968). *Towards a poor theatre.* New York: Simon & Schuster.

Jacobson, E. (1964). *The self and object world.* New York: International Universities Press.

James, M., & Johnson, D. R. (1997). Drama therapy in the treatment of combat-related PTSD. *Arts in Psychotherapy, 23,* 383–396.

Johnson, D. R. (1982). Developmental approaches in drama therapy. *Arts in Psychotherapy, 9,* 183–190.

Johnson, D. R. (1984). The representation of the internal world in catatonic schizophrenia. *Psychiatry, 47,* 299-314.

Johnson, D. R. (1985). Expressive group psychotherapy with the elderly. *International Journal of Group Psychotherapy, 35,* 109–127.

Johnson, D. R. (1986). The developmental method in drama therapy: Group treatment with the elderly. *Arts in Psychotherapy, 13,* 17–34.

Johnson, D. R. (1991). The theory and technique of transformations in drama therapy. *Arts in Psychotherapy, 18,* 285–300.

Johnson, D. R. (1992). The drama therapist in role. In S. Jennings (Ed.), *Drama therapy: Theory and practice* (Vol. 2, pp. 112–136). London: Routledge.

Johnson, D. R. (1993). Marian Chace's influence on drama therapy. In S. Sandel, S. Chaiklin, & A. Lohn (Eds.), *Foundations of dance/movement therapy* (pp. 176–192). Columbia, MD: American Dance Therapy Association.

Johnson, D. R. (2000). Developmental transformations: Towards the body as presence. In P. Lewis & D. Johnson (Eds.), *Current approaches to drama therapy* (pp. 87–110). Springfield, IL: Charles C Thomas.

Johnson, D. R., Agresti, A., Nies, K., & Jacob, M. (1990). Building a therapeutic community in a nursing home through specialized groups. *Clinical Gerontologist, 9,* 203–217.

Johnson, D. R., Forrester, A., Dintino, C., James, M., & Schnee, G. (1996). Towards a poor drama therapy. *Arts in Psychotherapy, 23,* 293–306.

Klein, M. (1932). *The psychoanalysis of children.* London: Hogarth.

Kris, A. (1982). *Free association: Method and process.* New Haven, CT: Yale University Press.

MacLennan, B., Saul, S., & Weiner, M. (1988). *Group psychotherapies for the elderly.* Madison, CT: International Universities Press.

McCaslin, N. (1990). *Creative dramatics in the classroom and beyond.* New York: Longman.

Meerloo, J. (1955). Transference and resistance in geriatric psychotherapy. *Psychoanalytic Review, 42,* 72–82.

Piaget, J. (1951). *Play, dreams, and imitation.* New York: Norton.

Rogers, C. (1951). *Client-centered therapy.* Boston: Houghton-Mifflin.

Sandel, S., Chaiklin, S., & Lohn, A. (Eds.). (1993). *Foundations of dance/movement therapy.* Columbia, MD: American Dance Therapy Association.

Sandel, S., & Johnson, D. (1987). *Waiting at the gate: Creativity and hope in the nursing home.* New York: Haworth.

Sartre, J. P. (1943). *Being and nothingness.* London: Methuen.

Schaefer, C. E., & O'Connor, K. (Eds.). (1982). *Handbook of play therapy.* New York: Wiley.

Schnee, G. (1996). Drama therapy with the homeless mentally ill: Treating interpersonal disengagement. *Arts in Psychotherapy, 23,* 53–60.

Smith, A. (2000). Exploring death anxiety with older adults through developmental transformations. *Arts in Psychotherapy, 27,* 321–332.

Spolin, V. (1963). *Improvisation for the theatre.* Chicago: Northwestern University Press.

Way, B. (1967). *Development through drama.* London: Longman.

Weisberg, N., & Wilder, R. (1985). *Creative arts with older adults.* New York: Human Sciences Press.

Weiss, J. (1984). *Expressive therapy with elders and the disabled.* New York: Haworth Press.

Werner, H., & Kaplan, S. (1963). *Symbol formation.* New York: Wiley.

Whitehouse, M. (1979). C. G. Jung and dance therapy. In P. Lewis (Ed.), *Eight theoretical approaches in dance/movement therapies* (pp. 51–70). Dubuque: Kendall/Hunt.

PART II

THERAPEUTIC HUMOR

Chapter 6

INTEGRATING HUMOR INTO PSYCHOTHERAPY

Steven M. Sultanoff

Humor in psychotherapy is a curious concept—integrating humor, generally a light, playful, and even distracting experience, with psychotherapy, which for many is a highly focused, "serious" process. Yet, from Freud to the present, clinicians have been intrigued by humor as a potential tool in the therapeutic process.

The experience of a humorous event not only feels good, but also can help provide perspective on life's challenges. Humor can serve as a vehicle through which to communicate and confront with a minimal amount of stress placed on the relationship.

Humor has the distinctive ability to enhance interpersonal relationships. In addition, its capacity to reduce interpersonal tension and reestablish stretched relationships has resulted in its being labeled a *social lubricant*.

While humor has many therapeutic benefits (including its ability to change emotional distress and cognitive distortions as well as enhance the therapeutic alliance), its use as part of the psychotherapeutic process is not well understood. In this chapter, you will learn about the therapeutic nature of humor and how humor can be integrated into the therapy process.

Correspondence concerning this article should be addressed to Steven M. Sultanoff, PhD, Humor-Matters™, 3972 Barranca Parkway, #J-221, Irvine, CA 92606. Electronic mail may be sent to ssultanoff@humormatters.com.

HISTORICAL PERSPECTIVE

While humor has probably been a core element of humanity since human beings first walked the earth, one of the earliest references to the healing potential of humor comes from the Bible in Proverbs 17:22 (KJV): "A merry heart doeth good—like medicine—but a broken spirit drieth the bones." Seventeenth century physician Thomas Sydenham agreed when he said: "The arrival of a good clown exercises a more beneficial influence upon the health of a town than the arrival of twenty asses laden with drugs."

Freud (1928) expressed interest in humor, but his emphasis was primarily on humor as a coping mechanism used by the client rather than as a potential treatment strategy for the analyst. While Freud may have sparked some initial interest in humor in the therapy process, it is the modern theorists and practitioners (like Albert Ellis) who have been most outspoken and supportive of the concept of humor as a specific intervention tool for the therapist.

The concept of a humorous intervention by the therapist has appeared as a component in most modern models of psychotherapy. In his book on theories, Corey (2001) states: "One procedure to counteract painful affect is humor. A therapist can demonstrate the ironic aspects of a situation. If clients can even briefly experience some lightheartedness, it can serve as an antidote to their sadness" (p. 317).

One element that appears to be missing in the literature on the therapeutic value of humor is a model or rationale connecting humorous interventions to potential outcome in psychotherapy. One of the goals of this chapter is to present both a rationale for the integration of humor into psychotherapy and a model of intervention that demonstrates how humor serves to meet the same clinical goals as most modern theories of psychotherapy.

DEFINING MOMENTS OF HUMOR

The Universal Traits of Humor

Why is it that some people experience humor in a particular situation, while others do not? When two people experience the same event and react differently, that difference is based on each individual's unique perception. If that unique perception in the individual includes stimulation by one of the universal traits of humor, the individual experiences the event as humorous.

While it is clear that sense of humor varies widely among individuals and groups, it is the presence of one or more of the universal characteristics of humor that make events more likely to be perceived as funny by the observer.

Among the universal characteristics that may produce a humorous response are the experiences of:

- Incongruity.
- Absurdity, ludicrousness, or ridiculousness.
- An unexpected future.
- A pleasant surprise.
- Being startled.
- "Getting it."
- Emotional chaos remembered in tranquility.

A *sense of humor* can be defined as the ability to perceive one or more of the universal characteristics. Therefore, a person's sense of humor involves the capacity to appreciate those universal characteristics. A discussion of each follows.

Incongruity

When a stimulus is perceived as *incongruous,* it is likely to be experienced as humorous. A cartoon depicting a man reading a sign that says, "Sensitivity training . . . this way, stupid!" illustrates the incongruity of *sensitivity training* and calling a person *stupid.* An individual who perceives this incongruity will likely experience such a cartoon as humorous. Oxymorons (pairs of words that go together but mean the opposite of each other) are often experienced as funny based on their incongruity. Examples of oxymorons include *jumbo* shrimp, *act* naturally, *working* vacation, *definite* maybe, *same* difference, and *genuine* imitation. It appears that the cognitive process of attempting to make sense of incongruity triggers a humorous response in us.

Absurdity, Ridiculousness, and Ludicrousness

A stimulus that results in some absurd, ridiculous, or ludicrous perception may be experienced as humorous. A clinician using exaggeration to describe a client's personal situation or perception is demonstrating the use of absurdity to trigger a humorous response. Simple exaggeration can be particularly effective with clients, because the clinician takes the client's circumstance or situation and "stretches" it to absurdity, thus helping the client gain perspective.

For example, consider a client who was excessively worried about doing something to "mess up" her two-year-old child's life. Her parental belief was, "Almost anything I do could ruin my child's life, and that would make me an awful person." As part of the therapy, she was working to change her exaggerated belief to a more realistic belief—that she was not likely to ruin her child's life by her normal everyday interactions with her child.

During one therapy session, she mentioned that she and her husband had purchased a new house, but the color was an "awful" yellow. Given the clinician's understanding of the client's propensity to worry excessively about how her actions might affect her child, the clinician responded, "There you go again. Are you trying to ruin your two-year-old's life? How could you make him live in an awful yellow house?"

The absurdity (experienced through exaggeration) of suggesting that living in an "awful" yellow house would cause emotional harm to her son triggered her humorous response. The perspective offered by this humorous intervention also helped her connect to many other events in her life where she feared she could cause harm.

The Unexpected Future

A stimulus may also be perceived as humorous when an *expected* future is replaced with an *unexpected* one. The more unexpected the event, the more likely it will be perceived as humorous. Often the punch line of a joke presents an unexpected future or result. Slapstick comedy is a common source of unexpected future, as are cartoons.

Envision a cartoon in which a man is sinking in quicksand. He calls to his faithful dog and says, "Lassie, go get help!" The next cell of the cartoon depicts Lassie lying on the therapist's couch . . . "getting help." In this cartoon, it is the unexpected result of Lassie's seeking a different type of help that may be perceived as humorous.

Pleasant Surprise

Another quality of a stimulus that may make it humorous is the presentation of a pleasant surprise. When we are mildly surprised or tricked, the experience may result in our feeling delighted. Children love to be tricked. We can see this in their reaction to experiencing magic, for example.

Businesses often use the pleasant surprise to promote their services. Examples include the sign on a plumbing repair truck that reads, "A flush beats a full house" or the sign on a muffler shop that says, "No appointment necessary. We will hear you coming."

The pleasant surprise is sometimes used as a simple form of communication. Examples include the door on the psychiatric ward that reads, "Please do not disturb further," or the sign on a parking space at a garden nursery that says, "Reserved for plant manager." The pleasant surprise can also be used to playfully poke fun at the human condition as illustrated by the sign on the maternity room door which reads, "Push, push, push."

Pleasant surprises can also include visual absurdities such as an ornamental propeller spinning on the back of a sports utility vehicle. Whether in the form of a "play on words" (as illustrated by the slogans), or in the form of an out-of-context visual (like the propeller), the pleasant surprise can trigger a mirthful response.

The experience of the pleasant surprise frequently does not result in laughter. It can, however, stimulate a sense of being delightfully amused, or trigger an appreciation for the clever nature in which it is presented.

Being Startled

Being startled may also create a humorous response, if the stimulus is quickly perceived to be nonthreatening. Imagine a boat gliding across a smooth lake. Suddenly the boat bounces over the wake of another boat. The resulting splash causes one of the passengers to get sprinkled with a few drops of icy water. After a moment of mild shock (surprise), she starts laughing. In the course of events, she was startled, quickly evaluated the situation as nonthreatening, achieved a sense of relief, and then laughed.

Had the splash resulted in her getting drenched, she might have been concerned about being wet and chilled or about damage to her possessions, in which case, the event would have been perceived as somewhat threatening or annoying and therefore, not humorous. It is only when the threat is quickly evaluated as harmless that a humorous reaction may result.

The television show "Candid Camera" is a classic example of the element of surprise and experiencing a startle that is quickly perceived as harmless. It was after the star of the Candid Camera prank heard those famous words, "Smile— you're on Candid Camera" that the situation was quickly perceived as harmless and, along with a sense of relief, came the delight and amusement of the victim.

Getting It

For some individuals, it is not the incongruity, the surprise, or being startled that is funny, but it is simply the "getting it." Sometimes it is the cognitive appreciation, or the joy of solving the twist in the situation that is experienced as humorous. We sometimes hear people exclaim, "I get it!" as an indicator of this discovery.

Because different individuals "get it" at different paces, this type of response to humor "rolls" across an audience similar to the flow of the wave cheer at a sporting event. The following story illustrates both "getting it" and the importance of understanding context of the situation and relating to that context:

Renee Descartes, the famous philosopher, was on a flight from Paris to New York. The flight attendant approached Mr. Descartes and asked, "Can I get you a drink?" to which Descartes replied, "I think not." And then, he disappeared!

While, as the reader, you may have made an immediate connection, alternately, you may be pausing to let the story "sink in." On the other hand, you may not get it at all and are studying the situation and perhaps even rereading the story—trying to make some sense of it. If you "get it," you may find it funny, and if so, the pleasure you derived from this story was in the "getting it." The "I get it" type of humor often does not trigger laughter; however, it does frequently stimulate cognitive and/or emotional responses in the individual.

To get the humor in this story, you must be able to place Descartes in the context of being the philosopher who is known for creating the statement, "I think—therefore, I am." If you associate Descartes with this statement, the concept of his comment, "I think not," and his disappearing make sense.

To further illustrate the nature of "getting it," consider a client who lives in a two-level apartment where the entire second floor is cluttered with over 100 storage boxes, filled mostly with "junk." During her therapy session, she expresses her dissatisfaction with these boxes but adds that the first floor of her apartment is organized and uncluttered, to which the therapist responds, "But upstairs is another *story*." If the word *story* is emphasized and its double meaning understood by the client, she may perceive the comment as funny or amusing.

Emotional Chaos Remembered in Tranquility

While a stimulus that presents incongruity, surprise, or startle may be perceived as humorous, James Thurber proposed: "Humor is emotional chaos remembered in tranquility." We have all heard the expression "It wasn't funny at the time!" (*The Oxford Dictionary of Modern Quotations,* 1991, p. 217.) Clients who develop the capacity to look at past trauma and, in the present, perceive humor that was not apparent at the time will relieve much of their emotional distress. Humor may be experienced when the chaos of the past is viewed at a peaceful moment in the future. Clients who do not readily see the humor in hindsight may benefit by exploring ways of revisiting a past event with humor. Most of us have stories about experiencing traumatic events, which may not have been funny at the time. Clients can be taught to reevaluate the trauma of the past by seeking an absurdity, incongruity, or amusing nature associated with the traumatic event. Survivor groups (e.g., cancer survivors) are filled with humor about the process of recovery. While humor does not reduce the seriousness of an illness or traumatic event, it certainly lightens the load of coping with the trauma and aids in the healing process by offering perspective and assisting the client on the path toward recovery.

The Experience of Humor

While we often assume that a person's sense of humor is based on his or her expression of laughter, "*sense* of humor" or individual experience of humor is far more complex. An individual's reaction to a humorous stimulus may be observed through the physiological response of laughter, but a humorous reaction can also include the individual's emotional and/or cognitive changes as a result of the stimulus. The emotional and/or cognitive effects are, for the most part, not outwardly expressed and, therefore, not apparent to the observer. The *experience* of humor, therefore, is a complex interaction involving an individual's physiological response (laughter), emotional response (mirth), and/or cognitive response (wit) to a humorous stimulus (Sultanoff, 1994).

To effectively apply humor to the process of psychotherapy, it is crucial for the clinician to understand the nature of humor as *experienced* by the client. The *sensation* of humor for clients begins with a stimulus, such as a play on words, exaggeration, cartoon, joke, story, pratfall, or event. Clients must then perceive the stimulus, process its meaning in their individual context and, if the stimulus meets that individual's "humor criteria," it will trigger a physiological, emotional, and/or cognitive response. It is ultimately the potential of humorous interventions to stimulate the client's *experience* of laughter, mirth, and/or wit that makes them most effective.

Summary

While a person's sense of humor is highly idiosyncratic and individualized, it is based on the person's awareness and perception of a stimulus that is presented in the context of one or more of the universal traits. The universal qualities of the stimulus-receiver interaction increase the probability of a specific event's being perceived as humorous. These include the presentation and perception of incongruity, absurdity, surprise, expected replaced with unexpected, a nonthreatening startle, getting it, and, finally, chaos remembered in tranquility.

Once a stimulus is perceived as humorous, it triggers a reaction in the individual. This reaction may be physiological (laughter), cognitive (wit), or emotional (mirth), or a combination of these experiences. Therefore, the total sensation of a humorous event is a complex interaction of a stimulus, an individual's perception, and the resulting reaction.

THEORETICAL MODEL FOR THE USE OF HUMOR IN PSYCHOTHERAPY

Psychotherapy is a process in which therapists, based on their specific theoretical framework, create intervention strategies that are designed to promote change in clients' emotions, behaviors, cognitions, and/or physiology. Each of these four aspects of the human system interacts with the others so that a change in one aspect (e.g., emotion) is likely to create change in another (e.g., behavior). Humorous interventions have therapeutic power because they have the capacity to stimulate changes in all four areas. There are numerous ways a therapist can integrate humor into psychotherapy. Humorous interventions can serve as (a) a treatment strategy for use in helping clients change their emotions, behaviors, cognitions and/or physiology, (b) a diagnostic tool, and (c) a medium with which to create emotional warmth, therefore building and strengthening the therapeutic alliance.

With researchers in psychoneuroimmunology continuing to investigate the interrelationships between and among emotions, cognitions, and health; and with the proposal that psychologists begin to pursue a science of positive psychology (Seligman & Csikszentmihalyi, 2000), therapeutic humor is poised to become a key factor in the future of mental health applications.

Research on the relationship between emotions and health has focused primarily on the impact of distressing emotions, while generally neglecting the impact of uplifting emotions (Salovey, Rothman, Detweiler, & Steward, 2000). The importance of positive subjective experience in the maintenance of health and well-being is becoming a focus for psychological investigations (Salovey et al., 2000).

According to Seligman and Csikszentmihalyi (2000), "The field of positive psychology at the subjective level is about valued subjective experiences: well-being, contentment, and satisfaction (in the past); hope and optimism (for the future); and flow and happiness (in the present)." They suggest that, while negative emotional experiences are more urgent and therefore tend to be the focus of health intervention, positive human traits may in the future be found to serve as both a buffer against, and a prevention for, psychological and physical distress. Humor and its impact on health, well-being, and the psychotherapeutic process appear to be natural additions to the intervention strategies of therapists.

The fundamental goals of psychotherapy are to help clients *feel* better and/or *act* differently. These goals can be achieved by creating interventions that influence any one of the four basic human processes: moods, behaviors, thoughts, and physical reactions (Greenberger & Padesky, 1995). These core aspects comprise an interactive system of human experience whereby changes in one influence each of the others. As illustrated in Figure 6.1, these four processes interact inside an individual and are affected by external input (stressors/stimuli) generated from the environment (Greenberger & Padesky, 1995; Padesky & Mooney, 1990).

Each of the theoretical approaches to psychotherapy focuses on one or more of these aspects as its central target of change. Gestalt, person-centered, and humanistic approaches primarily address emotions as the target of change. Behavioral psychotherapy focuses primarily on changing behavior. Cognitive and rational-emotive therapies focus primarily on restructuring cognitions as the target of intervention, and the purpose of psychopharmacology is to create biochemical changes in the human physiological system.

As illustrated by Padesky and Mooney (1990) and supported by research as reviewed by Salovey et al. (2000), the four elements of the human system are highly interactive. Changes in any of these central aspects of human experience stimulate changes in any or all of the other aspects. While the specific effects and specific

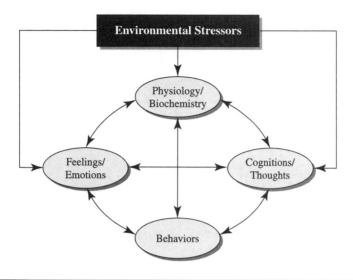

**Figure 6.1   Interactive model of human experience. From "Clinical Tip: Present-
ing the Cognitive Therapy Model to Clients," by C. A. Padesky and
K. A. Mooney, 1990, *International Cognitive Therapy Newsletter, 6,*
pp. 13–14. Copyright 1990 by Padesky and Mooney. Reprinted with
permission.**

mechanisms may not always be apparent, it is clear that the targets of psychotherapeutic intervention (moods, behaviors, cognitions, and physiology) are
indeed influenced by the environment and are interactive with one another.

The therapeutic nature of humor in psychotherapy evolves from its capacity to
stimulate change in all four of these central aspects of human experience (Sultanoff, 1992). Therapists, therefore, who learn to effectively integrate humorous
interventions into their therapeutic framework, increase their ability to help
clients relieve emotional distress and generate new, healthier behavior (Gelkopf
& Kreitler, 1996).

Fry (1992) describes the "humor process" as consisting of a stimulus, an emotional response, and a resulting behavior. The model presented in Figure 6.2 ex-
pands Fry's description to include cognitive and physiological/biochemical
reactions to humorous stimuli. As illustrated, the experience of a humorous stimulus affects one or more of the four aspects of the human experience. As a humorous stimulus activates any one aspect, it is likely to influence the other aspects.
According to Gelkopf and Kreitler (1996):

It is evident that the emotional and cognitive aspects of humor are closely interwoven and interact with each other. Thus, optimism, for example, may be considered as a direct effect of the cognitive aspect of humor or as a mediated effect of

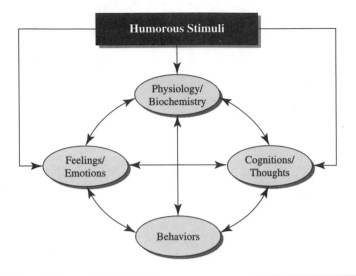

Figure 6.2   Interactive model of human experience as influenced by humorous stimuli.

the change of mood characterizing humor. Similarly, the decrease in hostility may reflect a direct emotional change or a mediated cognitive effect due to the increase in positive attitudes toward people or of a light-hearted, easy going view of the world. (p. 247)

Humor Influences Emotions

The impact of distressing emotions on physical health has been extensively investigated (Salovey et al., 2000). Chronic anxiety, depression, and anger are correlated with heart disease; anxiety is associated with gastrointestinal disorders; and depression influences the function of the immune system.

The experience of humor changes distressing emotional states. Humor relieves depression (Gelkopf & Kreitler, 1996; Porterfield, 1987) and reduces the impact of stressful events (Bizi, Keinan, & Beit-Hallahmi, 1988; Martin & Dobbin, 1988; Martin & Lefcourt, 1983). The experience of humor may also serve as a vehicle for discharging and relieving pent-up emotional conflict (Rosenheim & Golan, 1986). Moran (1995) found that a humorous stimulus reduced subjects' ratings of their anxiety, although they found no reduction in their ratings of depression. Mark Twain said, "Humor is the great thing, the saving thing after all. The minute it crops up, all our hardnesses yield, all our irritations and resentments slip away, and a sunny spirit takes their place."

It has been suggested that a humorous experience and distressing emotions (depression, anxiety, anger) cannot simultaneously occupy the same psychological space (Sultanoff, 1997). In those moments of experiencing humor, emotional distress dissolves. While feelings of distress may return, the experience of humor—at a minimum—provides momentary relief.

Humor Influences Behavior

The experience of humor affects how a person behaves. It has been reported that patients who experience humor from their family physicians file fewer lawsuits against their doctors (Levinson, Roter, Mullooly, Dull, & Frankel, 1997). It has also been noted that soldiers who activate their senses of humor when experiencing a stressful event perform better in these situations (Bizi et al., 1988).

As individuals experience humor, they feel emotionally uplifted and "connect" well with others (Richman, 1996). There appears to be a positive correlation of sense of humor with exhibition, gregariousness, assertiveness, and creativity (Thorson, Powell, Sarmany-Schuller, & Hampes, 1997). Individuals experiencing distress tend to withdraw and disengage from relationships and opportunities, while individuals experiencing humor become more energized, attentive, and pursue connections with others, thus changing their behavior.

Humor Influences Cognitions

While it is common for an individual to attribute fluctuations in mood to external stimuli, it is the client's interpretation of life's events that is the major determinant of emotional reactions (Beck, 1976; Ellis & Harper, 1979). It is the *meaning* that the client assigns to an event that is the primary influence on that client's emotional reactions. According to Shakespeare's *Hamlet,* "There is nothing either good or bad, but thinking makes it so."

The relationship between belief systems and both physical and emotional health is becoming increasingly clear. Optimism, personal control, and sense of meaning are associated with mental health (Seligman, 1998), while positive beliefs are related to physical well-being (Taylor, Kemeny, Reed, Bower, & Gruenewald, 2000).

The experience of humor offers a client alternative ways to perceive daily events. Humor provides perspective (Gelkopf & Kreitler, 1996; Richman, 1996; Rosenheim & Golan, 1986) and increases problem-solving abilities (Rosenheim & Golan, 1986; Thorson et al., 1997).

By enabling a client to gain perspective, humor invites the client to examine and change distorted thinking patterns. Corrections of unhealthy, distorted beliefs translate directly into emotional and behavioral changes (Beck, 1976; Ellis & Harper, 1979). Rollo May stated, "Humor is the healthy way of feeling a 'distance' between one's self and the problem; a way of standing off and looking at one's problem with perspective."

It has been suggested that humor can also help clients gain a healthy psychological distance from meaningful, traumatic events (Sultanoff, 1995). Use of humor can reduce the emotional impact on those facing disasters, by providing the opportunity for those in crisis to view their situations from an alternative (and perhaps incongruent) perspective. After disastrous hurricanes in the United States, many homes were reduced to rubble. It was not uncommon to see homemade, humorous signs posted at such sites with phrases saying, "Gone With the Wind," "House for Sale—Half Off," or "House for Sale—Some Assembly Required!" These survivors chose to reduce their distress by creating perspective in their lives by being playful with incongruity and by doing the unexpected.

Perspective helps create distance (whether emotional, geographic, or temporal) from traumatic events (Sultanoff, 1995). Ashley Brilliant has said, "Distance doesn't make you any smaller, but it does make you part of a bigger picture." Humor helps create distance from traumatic events by providing perspective that may change the way clients view the events.

In addition to providing perspective, humor can change thinking patterns by presenting incongruities. It is the cognitive resolution of incongruities that helps shift rigid thinking patterns. A cartoon depicting a client reading a sign which says, "Sensitivity Training: This Way, Stupid!" illustrates incongruity. The juxtaposition of *sensitivity training* and *stupid* causes the mind to attempt to resolve the incongruity. There is no logical resolution as the concept of "sensitivity training" and calling someone "stupid" cannot logically coexist and, therefore, the resulting reaction is often the experience of humor.

Norman Cousins (1979) labeled this experience of mental incongruity as "train wrecks of the mind." Clients dedicated to a rigid personal belief system can become "derailed" when presented with an incongruity. Incongruities help "snap" a client's thinking and unblock "stuck" cognitive processes. The presentation of incongruity and the resulting resolution of the incongruity (through the experience of humor) can challenge and "unstick" distorted and rigid thinking patterns associated with a variety of emotional distresses. The resolution of incongruities also helps stimulate problem-solving skills by encouraging divergent thinking and activating previously inaccessible ideas and alternatives (Gelkopf & Kreitler, 1996).

Humor Influences Biochemistry

A number of studies have reported that the experience of laughing—as a result of receiving a humorous stimulus—leads to positive biochemical changes. When individuals laugh, they have decreased levels of stress hormones (Berk et al., 1989) and increased levels of antibodies (Berk et al., 1989; Dillon, Minchoff, & Baker, 1985–1986; Martin & Dobbin, 1988). During laughter, many body systems (such as cardiovascular, muscular, and skeletal) are activated or "exercised" (Fry, 1992). As a result of this physical activation, biochemical changes occur—many of which have not yet been studied.

In summary, humorous stimuli are capable of creating positive changes in emotional, behavioral, cognitive, and physiological states. It is this potential that makes humorous interventions a powerful tool for use in the psychotherapeutic process.

THE FUNCTION OF HUMOROUS INTERVENTIONS IN PSYCHOTHERAPY

Humor as a Diagnostic Tool

Not only does the experience of humor serve to change emotions, behaviors, cognitions, and biochemistry, but also humorous interventions can be used to *diagnose* a client's current cognitive state—as well as progress—in treatment. A client's capacity to experience a stimulus as humorous requires that the client be aware of the context in which the stimulus is presented and perceive the twist (incongruity, absurdity, surprise, etc.) that places the stimulus out of context. If a client is unable to *perceive* the twist, it is possible that the client's cognitive process is rigid and, therefore, the client is less able to generate perspective in relation to personal environmental stressors. A humorous intervention can serve as a diagnostic tool to assess the rigidity of the client's thinking pattern. Such diagnosis can assist the therapist to assess the strength of irrational belief systems and faulty underlying assumptions.

Using humorous interventions to identify changes in a client's underlying distorted thought patterns (such as irrational beliefs or faulty assumptions) can help evaluate the success of cognitive restructuring. For example, during her first therapy session, a client explained that "bad things happened" to her because she was "stupid." On subsequent visits, she was treated with a traditional cognitive therapy approach, helping her to restructure that belief system. On her tenth visit, she reported that another "bad thing had happened," but she could not explain why it had occurred. Her therapist insisted that she knew why, but she insisted that she did not. Finally, her therapist looked directly at her and exclaimed, "It happened because you are stupid!" After a brief moment of shock (startle, the unexpected), she burst out laughing.

Her ability to perceive the ludicrousness of a bad event being associated with her "being stupid" triggered her laughter. Diagnostically, she perceived that her belief that bad things happened because she was stupid was indeed ludicrous, indicating her progress in treatment from the first session (when she would not have made the connection and would have agreed with the statement) to the tenth session (where it seemed ridiculous to her).

Had the client failed to see the absurdity of the statement (and perceived that the event in fact did happen because she was stupid), this would indicate (diagnostically) that she had not yet integrated the new belief that bad things can happen, regardless of her intellectual abilities. Whether her reaction was to perceive the ludicrousness of the statement or to agree with the absurd belief, observing her reaction to the humorous stimulus from the therapist served as a diagnostic tool to help assess her progress. Diagnostically, her therapist purposely used this interplay to assess her progress in her ability to restructure her faulty assumption.

Humor as Treatment

While humor can be used to build the relationship, energize the client/therapist interaction, and assess the client's thought process and progress in treatment, it can also be used as a direct intervention strategy. Because the major goals of therapy include helping clients change distressing emotions and/or ineffective behaviors, and therapists are trained to create interventions that influence feelings, behaviors, cognitions, and/or physiology, the use of humorous stimuli that influence one or more of these areas has the potential to help clients create positive changes for themselves. Psychotherapists can integrate humorous interventions into their treatment modalities so that their humorous responses to clients become part of their "therapeutic repertoire."

Because humor directly changes a person's emotional state, it can be used as a treatment modality to relieve distressing emotions. Clients can be taught to use humor to relieve anxiety, depression, and anger. Through the purposeful use of humor, clients can learn that they can both *relieve their emotional distress* and be empowered to *manage their emotional reactions.*

For example, a client who was "dedicated" to maintaining her depression insisted that she wanted to feel less depressed. As part of her treatment, her therapist integrated humorous interventions. After each of the first few humorous interventions (presented over several sessions), she responded to her therapist, "I hate it when you do that (say something humorous)." She became increasingly annoyed with her therapist's use of humor until finally the therapist inquired, "What is it about my use of humor that bothers you?" Instantly she emphatically replied, "When you make me laugh, I don't feel depressed!"

In a moment of insight, the client perceived the incongruity that, even though she wanted to feel better, she was upset when her depression was taken away or dissolved. The humorous interventions (treatment) helped to lighten her depression while, unconsciously, she continued to be dedicated to maintaining her emotional distress.

A depressed client who experiences and is receptive to humor in therapy can learn *experientially* that, for at least that moment in time, the intensity of the depression fades. Clients can be taught to consciously seek humorous experiences outside the therapy sessions as ways of managing their emotional distress. A cognitive psychotherapist can use humor to explore and/or test a client's faulty assumptions by exaggerating the client's perception leading to a ludicrous conclusion. For example, if a therapist knows a client experiences test anxiety, the therapist can exaggerate the client's *failure* on a test to result in the client's having to drop out of school, becoming unemployed, and then being destitute. The absurdity of this illogical progress of events—starting with failure on a test and leading to being destitute—can result in a reframing for the client. When clients realize that they have illogically distorted their situation, they are better able to regain a healthier, more realistic perspective.

Humorous interventions can also help manage anxiety. Hans Selye, the renowned stress researcher, said, "Nothing erases unpleasant thoughts more effectively than concentrating on pleasant ones." In therapy, clients can be asked to describe personal situations when they laughed so hard that they fell down or became tearful (a physiological reaction). Clients can then be asked to describe how this humorous reaction impacted their emotional state during the original event and now as a memory. Generally, clients who experience these humorous memories in session report a reduced level of emotional distress (such as anxiety). The therapist can then help clients integrate humorous memories (or similar images) into daily experiences when they are anticipating or experiencing anxiety. In this way, clients can enhance their ability to manage their anxiety by developing humor skills, which can reduce anxiety.

During six months of cognitive restructuring with a social phobic client, I was attempting to increase his belief in his ability to manage his anxiety (and therefore manage his panic attacks). In previous sessions, we had addressed many of his core beliefs such as, "I have to be seen as perfect by others or it means I have no value" (a common belief among clients with anxiety and panic disorders) and, "If I panic, I will be out of control and that would be awful." While his panic attacks had significantly diminished, he continued to experience occasional attacks and remained avoidant of social interactions.

At the beginning of a session and as an introduction to the humorous intervention, I asked the client to rate his anxiety level on a scale of 1 to 10. That rating provided a baseline of his anxiety.

I then asked him to raise his anxiety two levels on that 1-to-10 scale. (Most clients are able to raise their emotional distress on such a scale. Teaching clients to raise and subsequently lower their distress teaches them that they have some ability to manage their emotions.) After he raised his anxiety two levels, we discussed how he accomplished that task so he would understand his role in increasing his distress. (When asked, "How did you raise your anxiety?", most clients reply with something like, "I just thought about an anxiety-provoking situation." I ask, "What specifically went through your mind?" This question generally leads to an assortment of cognitive distortions, most of which—in the case of anxiety—have to do with performance.)

As a humorous intervention, I asked him to share with me two situations when he had laughed so hard that he fell down. (I often ask for a situation where the client laughed so hard he or she wet his or her pants, but for a social phobic, this image has obvious drawbacks.) After he described each situation, I again asked him to rate his anxiety. He indicated that it had dropped below his baseline. I then asked him what that meant to him, and after a period of discussion, he realized that creating a humorous image, in fact, reduced his anxiety.

The impact for this client included changes in all four target areas for psychological therapeutic interventions:

- He *changed his thinking* by incorporating the accurate belief that, "I can lower my anxiety by visualizing a humorous event." (Note that the belief alone that he can manage anxiety reduces the anxiety.) As with other types of imagery, visualizing a humorous past event serves as a distraction to the client. Because increased anxiety is based on a particular thought pattern, and, if the client is prevented (through imagery, for example) from engaging that pattern, the anxiety diminishes or disappears. Any neutral or pleasant image can serve this purpose; thus, this advantage is not strictly associated with the experience of humor. With panic disorder, beliefs by the client that he or she can manage the panic attack will, in fact, reduce or eliminate panic. In this case, the client's observation, in session, that the imagery reduced anxiety and the strengthening of the belief that he could manage the panic can result in a new belief system that reduces or even eliminates panic.
- He *changed his emotional state* (anxiety) directly by integrating the sensation of humor. (Distressing emotion and humor cannot occupy the same psychological space.) When a client experiences humor, the emotional distress dissolves. Because the imagery of the humorous event creates a similar (although probably not as intense) emotional reaction as was experienced during the original event, the emotional sensation of humor serves to counteract the emotional sensation of anxiety. The emotional uplifting of the humorous memory replaces the emotional distress.
- He *changed his physiological sensations* by reimaging the humorous event. Research suggests that stress hormones are reduced after heartfelt laughter. While it is impossible to observe the physiological changes that are created by humorous visualization during session, some physiological reactions to

imagery can be measured by biofeedback techniques. While the research on physiological changes from a humorous experience has focused on the changes resulting from *laughter,* it is probable that the visualization of a *humorous* experience (without laughter) also stimulates biochemical changes that serve to reduce the physiological correlates of anxiety.

- He *changed his behavior* and, by incorporating the use of imagery and changing his beliefs about his ability to manage his emotional distress, he demonstrated his increased willingness to approach social events.

During future sessions, we practiced imaging social events leading to increased anxiety, followed by imaging humorous events to decrease anxiety level. In practice, the client, when beginning to feel anxiety about social interaction, would revisualize one of his humorous events to lower the level of anxiety to what he considered manageable. After the integration of this process into his life, his panic attacks completely stopped.

Humor and the Therapeutic Alliance

Research has consistently indicated that the primary factor for client change in psychotherapy is the nature of the therapeutic alliance. (Carkhuff & Berenson, 1967; Corcy, 2001; Rogers, Gendlin, Kiesler, & Truax, 1967; Strupp, 1960; Truax & Carkhuff, 1967). Psychotherapy as a relationship is unique, and the methods by which therapists build intimacy in the therapeutic alliance are generally different from the methods by which they build intimacy in other types of relationships.

Most interpersonal relationships develop intimacy through the process of mutual self-disclosure and mutual solicitation of information. Basically, to build relationships, we disclose, and we ask questions.

Most psychotherapeutic theoretical orientations have a bias against therapist self-disclosure as part of the therapeutic process. In addition, the extensive use of questions by the therapist (except for diagnostic purposes and primarily at intake) is discouraged.

How then do therapists develop intimacy in the therapeutic relationship? All traditional therapeutic models identify empathy—the capacity to understand the client combined with the ability to communicate that understanding to the client—as essential for the development of the therapeutic alliance. In therapy, clinicians use the skill of *empathic responding* (defined as the ability to consistently and accurately reflect the client's emotional state and the meaning of that state to the client) as the core intervention to develop and strengthen the therapeutic alliance.

It is through the experience of being understood by the therapist that the client connects with and learns to trust the therapist. Empathy feels good to the client and demonstrates understanding of the client by the therapist.

Humorous interventions help build the therapeutic relationship (Gelkopf & Kreitler, 1996; Richman, 1996) and have great potential to deepen the therapeutic alliance, because they can result in positive accepting, empathy, cohesion, and belonging (Richman, 1996). Therapists who are able to create humorous interventions from a genuinely warm and caring perspective can increase their connection with their clients. Just as empathy demonstrates a level of caring and understanding and builds the therapeutic relationship, the use of humor can enhance the bond between therapist and client. To use humor spontaneously in session, the therapist must "know" the client at deeper levels. The client's experience of feeling "known" (through the therapist's use of humor) strengthens the therapeutic alliance.

While the use of humor may enhance the therapeutic relationship, Kubie (1971) cautions that humor may also be potentially destructive to the therapeutic relationship. Kubie states, "The author believes that the use of humor by the psychiatrist is potentially destructive to the psychotherapeutic relationship. Humor has its place in life. Let us keep it there" (p. 866).

While Kubie is accurate in his observation that "humor is potentially destructive," he fails in his ability to accept that the clinician is sufficiently skilled to either carefully select appropriate humor or be capable of perceiving when the humorous intervention has a negative effect on the client. Kubie assumes that the clinician is not capable of addressing the impact of a humorous intervention on the client.

Many interventions in therapy have the potential to be destructive. Interpretations or confrontations *could* be detrimental to the therapeutic alliance, yet it is unlikely that Kubie would suggest that clinicians abandon these types of responses.

Kubie's statement is more accurately interpreted as a suggestion to therapists who use humor to question their motivation, as well as to evaluate how a particular intervention might be useful for the client. Humorous interventions can be harmful, but, in the hands of a skilled clinician, can serve as an extremely positive experience for the client.

Because the client places trust in the therapist and is, therefore, more vulnerable to emotional harm, the risk of using humor in psychotherapy is greater than the risk of using humor in other relationships. The purposeful intention of using humor in psychotherapy must clearly be for the benefit of the client and not for the therapist's personal gratification or pleasure. By using humor, the therapist may risk alienating the client. The therapist may be perceived as not taking the client's issues seriously and/or may be perceived as less competent and, therefore, less capable of helping. Effective use of humor as a therapeutic tool requires that the therapist analyze and maximize the potential for clients to integrate humorous interventions.

In addition to strengthening the therapeutic alliance, humor has the added benefit of infusing energy into the therapy session. As the therapist (or the client) uses humor, the energy between clinician and client is heightened. The heightened energy creates greater receptivity to the work of therapy and increases presence of both the therapist and client. Heightened energy tends to keep both therapist and client involved in the therapeutic process.

Communicating with Humor

Humor is frequently used as a vehicle for communication. A restaurant that posts a sign reading, "Children left unattended will be towed at the owner's expense," is one example of humor as a vehicle to communicate a message. While the notion of children being towed is absurd, the presentation of the absurdity (being towed) in the context of reality (please manage your children's behavior) helps parents hear and act on the request.

Humor can enhance communication as a nonthreatening way of delivering a message from the therapist to the client. Cartoons that poke fun at situations similar to those of the client may provide the client with a visual message, when a more direct statement from the therapist might not be communicated as well. A cartoon depicting two mothers talking while a rebellious teenage son appears in the background, with one mother saying to the other, "Do you think it is too late to sue my obstetrician?" is an example of a cartoon that might communicate a therapist's empathy for a mother struggling with a teenage son.

PREPARING TO USE HUMOROUS INTERVENTIONS

Because of the risk that a humorous intervention might be experienced by the client as nontherapeutic or even harmful, it is essential for the therapist to evaluate the client's potential to receive a stimulus as humorous. The potential for any intervention to be successful is based on numerous factors, including the strength of the therapeutic alliance, the relative closeness of the proposed intervention to the client's present emotional and cognitive states, and the strength of a client's defense mechanisms that may be engaged to protect the client when emotionally threatened by a particular intervention.

To use humorous interventions effectively in psychotherapy, it is helpful for the therapist to:

1. *Plan appropriate humor* for use in therapy.
2. Be willing to *risk using humor* as a therapeutic tool.
3. *Assess the client's personal style* of humor and receptivity to humorous interventions.
4. *Select humor that is genuine and congruent* with the clinician as a person.

5. Be capable of *self-monitoring motivation* for using humor.
6. Be prepared to *respond to the client's reaction* to the humorous intervention.

Planning to Use Humor

While the process of psychotherapy (to the untrained observer) may appear to be one of spontaneous reactions by the therapist, it is in reality a process in which the therapist chooses a response carefully, based on training and experience. In this way, psychotherapy is a process that is *planned,* because each clinical response is selected from a repertoire of potential therapeutic responses, based on the clinician's understanding of the specific needs of the client.

A clinical response is *spontaneous,* based on the particular moment in therapy and on the client's presentation at that moment. Therapy is, therefore, a process of *planned spontaneity*—the therapist spontaneously responding in the moment, based on planning reflected by the therapist's training and expertise.

The process of planned spontaneity also applies to the therapeutic use of humor. The therapist prepares by practicing humor outside therapy and by gathering specific "humor tools" such as cartoons, anecdotes, jokes, puns, signs, and props, which illustrate a variety of life's events that might be faced by clients. The practice outside therapy, along with the preplanned humor tools, prepares the clinician to use humor spontaneously with clients in chosen moments when the therapist believes it is most likely to be therapeutically beneficial.

Risking the Humorous Intervention

As with any advanced therapeutic intervention, using humor adds an element of risk to the clinical process. The therapist's training and careful preparation of planned humor does not guarantee that the client will experience an intervention positively. To use humor effectively, the therapist must be willing to risk that the intervention may not result in the intended positive effect. Therapists who are unwilling to take risks in their interactions with clients tend to become static and unable to help clients move forward. As T.S. Eliot said, "Only those who will risk going too far can possibly find out how far one can go."

Assessing a Client's Sense of Humor and Receptivity to Humor

Before presenting a humorous intervention, it is helpful for the therapist to assess the client's personal level of sense of humor and receptivity to humor to match a specific intervention to that client. Assessing the role humor plays in a client's life, as well as the kind of humor to which the client is receptive, can provide a guideline as to when and under what circumstances the client may be most open to a humorous intervention.

Assessing the client's readiness to receive a humorous intervention is not an easy task, but several guidelines can assist in choosing an appropriate time. Clients can be asked directly what they find humorous. As clients share the experiences they find humorous, they will exhibit changes in their levels of animation and energy, which can reveal styles of humor with which they are most connected. By uncovering the types of humor clients enjoy, therapists can attempt to adapt humorous interventions to match clients' styles.

For example, a client who tells jokes may relate better to the therapist who shares jokes and anecdotes (auditory), while a client who enjoys the more visual stimulus of cartoons may be more receptive to viewing copies of comic strips such as "Peanuts," "Cathy," or "For Better or Worse." When clients identify with the predicaments faced by the characters in comic strips, they are more likely to connect with the humorous messages in those cartoons.

Being Genuine with the Use of Humor

Rogers et al. (1967) emphasize the importance of genuineness in all aspects of the therapeutic relationship. Willard Scott has said, "We should be proud of who we are. Then we can laugh at ourselves. Being natural—being yourself—goes right at the heart of humor."

To use humor effectively, a therapist must offer it genuinely and comfortably. Humorous interventions must be congruent with the therapist's own clinical personality style as a human being. Humor that is not genuine is likely to be perceived by the client as manipulative, phony, and insincere. Honest humor, evolving out of the therapist's caring for the client, is more likely to be trusted and, therefore, positively experienced.

Self-Monitoring of Therapist's Motivation to Use Humor

As is true throughout therapy, it is important for therapists to self-monitor their use of humor to be sure that they evaluate their motivation for using this type of intervention. *Therapeutic* humor emanates from a clinician's empathy and desire to be helpful to clients, while *toxic* humor evolves from a therapist's own personal needs (such as expressing frustration, impatience, or disappointment). It is imperative that therapists continue to monitor *why* they are using humor in therapy. Self-monitoring is intended to ensure that the use of humorous interventions is in the service of the needs of the client and not those of the therapist. It is helpful for therapists to ask themselves, "How will this humorous intervention be helpful to my client at this moment in therapy?"

THE CLIENT'S EXPERIENCE OF THERAPEUTIC HUMOR

Gelkopf and Kreitler (1996) discuss the potential impact of humor on a client's emotional, cognitive, and physiological states. Therapeutic humor, as experienced by the client, stimulates one (or more) of three reactions—wit, mirth, and laughter (Sultanoff, 1994). The client experiencing *wit* cognitively "appreciates, understands, or gets" the humor; the client experiencing mirth "feels" an internal sense of joy or pleasure; and the client experiencing *laughter* may become aware of physiological and behavioral changes in reaction to a humorous stimulus. When a client laughs, physical bodily functions are activated, resulting in an increase in respiration and blood flow, as well as an activation of the muscular system (Fry, 1992).

A client receiving a humorous intervention may experience any or all of these three processes. Because each of these processes has therapeutic value, and because each one stimulates the others, a humorous intervention that stimulates all three has the greatest therapeutic impact.

When wit, mirth, or laughter is experienced, the four aspects of human experiences (emotions, behaviors, cognitions, and biochemistry—which are the focus of psychotherapeutic interventions) may be individually or collectively engaged, maximizing the potential benefit of the humorous intervention for the client. While a humorous intervention by the therapist is designed to change emotions, behaviors, cognitions, or biochemistry, it is the client's internal experience of wit, mirth, and/or laughter that has the potential to be ultimately therapeutic.

Addressing the Client's Reaction to the Humorous Intervention

What if a humorous intervention does not work? What if the client does not perceive the clinical interventions as humorous or reacts negatively to the therapist's use of humor?

In the process of psychotherapy, it is not only the specific interventions by the therapist that are healing, but also the therapist's capacity to address the client's *reaction* to the intervention that are crucial for client growth. While many humorous interventions may be effective by themselves, others may require that the therapist follow up, especially when the client has a negative reaction to the intervention.

To be effective, many humorous interventions require that the therapist address the impact of the humorous intervention on the client. As with any clinical intervention—interpretation, confrontation, exploring transference, and so on—a fundamental aspect of the therapeutic process is to address the impact of the intervention on the client. This is equally true for humorous interventions. Whether clients perceive and respond to the stimulus as humorous or respond in some other fashion, it is the responsibility of the therapist to explore the client's reaction with the client.

INTERVENTIONS

Humorous interventions in psychotherapy are intended to be therapeutic. According to the Association for Applied and Therapeutic Humor (AATH), therapeutic humor is:

> Any intervention that promotes health and wellness by stimulating a playful discovery, expression, or appreciation of the absurdity or incongruity of life's situations. This intervention may enhance health or be used as a complementary treatment of illness to facilitate healing or coping, whether physical, emotional, cognitive, social or spiritual. (n.d.)
>
> Clinicians may employ a variety of humorous "intervention strategies." The two general categories of humorous intervention strategies are client-oriented *personalized* interventions and client-oriented *generic* interventions.

Client-Oriented Personalized Interventions

Client oriented personalized interventions are based on the unique clinical history between client and therapist. This type of humor, when shared with someone outside the relationship, may not be perceived as amusing. This is the typical humor of the "in joke."

In a client-oriented personalized intervention, the therapist creates a humorous stimulus that is tailored to the client in the context of the therapy. For example, one client who was a self-proclaimed packrat complained about the excess of boxes cluttering her apartment. In previous sessions, she had gone to great lengths to convince the therapist of the extreme nature of her situation. She brought pictures to session that showed stacks of boxes and described climbing over boxes to access her closets. Her efforts implied that not another box could fit in her overcrowded apartment!

In session while explaining that her parents were moving, she indicated that she was going to their home to retrieve many boxes filled with her possessions. She stated to her therapist, "Just what I need . . . more boxes! What am I going to do with all those boxes?" to which the therapist answered, "I'm not sure; how high are your ceilings?" The client immediately burst out laughing.

The effectiveness of the intervention was based both in the shared context (of the stacked boxes) and on the perception of absurdity (of piling the boxes even higher). Her therapist's humorous empathy stimulated her understanding of the intensity of her "boxed-in" situation. The mutually shared perception of the client and the therapist, based on the absurdity of adding more boxes, created a context in which the therapist could create and insert this specific humorous intervention. This particular intervention was tailored to this client for this situation and would not be appropriate in any other therapist-client interaction. The humorous intervention, therefore, was client-oriented and, while presented spontaneously by the therapist, was personalized to their shared clinical history.

While most client-oriented humorous interventions evolve from the bond that develops between client and therapist, on occasion (and for the purpose of generating a connection) an intervention can be initiated without first establishing the relationship. This type of intervention is more risky, as the client and therapist do not yet share an interpersonal trust base, which would generally serve as a foundation to keep the relationship connected even in the face of negative client reactions. When a therapist uses humor before establishment of the trust base, there is greater risk to the relationship, because the client may adversely react to the intervention.

While the use of humor in an early session is generally not recommended until the relationship develops, there are some occasions when such an intervention may be effective. A new client entering treatment indicated on the intake form that, over the past year, she had sought therapy three times with three different therapists—and each time she terminated after the second visit. During the intake, her therapist explored this pattern. The client explained that in each case, when she began to feel close to the therapist and reveal her hidden emotions and deeper issues, she abandoned the therapeutic process. Her therapist asked her what she wanted in therapy, to which she replied she wanted to avoid "emotional distress" and feel "comfortable and safe." To that, the therapist responded, "It seems like you want an uninvolved and somewhat distant therapist—one who will help you remain unemotional so that you can feel comfortable and safe." She looked at the therapist with a momentary quizzical look and then laughed.

This client's experience of humor was based on her capacity to perceive the incongruity between the process of therapy (to establish a close relationship between therapist and client and to explore distressing emotional issues) and her goal of maintaining emotional comfort and safety. She perceived the ludicrousness of how her own behavior of abandoning the therapeutic process had prevented her from receiving the help she desired. Her capacity to perceive that what she wanted was ludicrous triggered her humorous response.

When this client arrived for her second session, the therapist began the session by stating, "As this will be our last session, I wonder if there is anything in particular you would like to avoid talking about?" Again, the client looked quizzical for a moment and then laughed. In this statement, the clinician had presented two points of incongruity. First, the therapist addressed her history of dropping out after two sessions by presenting the second appointment as termination. Second, the therapist again validated her fear about getting "into" her issues, by establishing the incongruity of seeking treatment while preventing it from becoming effective.

This client remained in therapy for about a year and terminated only because she moved out of the area. Her ability to connect with this therapist and remain in therapy may have partially been a result of the initial use of humor to establish the relationship (which she had not been able to do on the prior three attempts with other therapists).

This example further illustrates a client-oriented personalized intervention. The therapist's intervention was designed for this particular client and would not be relevant to any other. When humorous interventions are tailored to the specific client, they illustrate a deeper level of empathy and understanding that the therapist is able to achieve with the client. The client who is able to receive this empathy is more likely to feel understood, and the trust base between client and therapist strengthens.

Another example of client-oriented personalized humor involved an adult client who chose to avoid contact with her father. She was struggling with her belief that, "I *should* see my father," which conflicted with her desire, "I do not *want* to see him." After about ten sessions in which she mastered cognitive restructuring of many of her distorted beliefs, a statement such as "I *should* see my father" became "Do I *want* to see my father?" This successful integration was apparent when she announced she was having a college graduation party, the family was coming, and she was trying to decide if she *should* invite her father. Very calmly and seriously, her therapist said directly to her, "You *absolutely should* invite your father to your graduation." She looked at her therapist, smiled with eyes twinkling, and laughed triumphantly, "Of course, I *should,* but I do not *want* to, and I am perfectly okay if I choose not to invite him."

This spontaneous use of exaggeration ("You absolutely *should*") was designed exclusively for her and her particular situation. While the use of exaggeration is a common method for creating a humorous intervention, the specific *content* of this exaggeration was relevant only to this client and to the history and context of the therapeutic relationship.

Note that this client's ability to laugh at the therapist's "should-ing" was a diagnostic indication that she was incorporating the cognitive shift from "shoulds," "musts," "oughts," and "have to's" to "wants," "desires," "preferences," and so on. That shift was evident in her ability to perceive the absurdity of her former belief, "I *should* see my father and if I do not, I am a bad person," which through therapy had been replaced by the new belief, "I can choose to see my father if I want to, and I am a good person whether I see him or not."

Humorous interventions can help the client resolve both current and past emotional distress. One client who was particularly sensitive to criticism had recently had a baby. While getting her hair cut, she took the baby with her to the salon. Just as her hair was finished and she was ready to leave, it began to rain. As she was leaving the salon, her hairstylist said, "It's raining outside. Be sure to cover the baby." Although the hair stylist's comment was meant to be caring and not critical in any way, the client immediately felt embarrassed and attacked. She mumbled, "Okay" and hurriedly left the salon.

In session after the client recounted this story, her therapist asked her to brainstorm responses that she could have made to the stylist. Among the possible were aggressive responses such as, "It's none of your business" and passive responses such as, "Okay" or "Yes, I know." Among the response possibilities the client created were several nonaggressive humorous responses such as, "Don't worry about the baby, he could use a shower," or "Don't worry about the baby. We had him Scotchgarded at the factory." These last two responses are examples of applying the concept, "When the world gives you lemons, make lemonade."

Through the creation of the humorous responses, the client experienced emotional relief from the distressing memory and practiced using humor to directly address future distressing moments. With continued practice, this client could integrate the humorous process and be able to address similar situations with humor rather than react with emotional distress.

Client-Oriented, Generic Humor

Client-oriented, generic humor is generated when the clinician creates an intervention by selecting from a previously assembled (by the therapist) collection of humorous stimuli. These interventions can vary greatly but often are presented as cartoons, jokes, stories, props, and so on, which are designed to illustrate a variety of common client issues. Included among the many issues that can be illustrated through humor are depression, anxiety, interpersonal relationships, male issues, female issues, parenting issues, obsessive-compulsive behavior, codependency, and dependency.

A therapist can maintain a collection of cartoons to share with a client at an appropriate moment in therapy. One such cartoon that might help provide *perspective* to clients concerned about whether people like them shows the cartoon character "Ziggy" lying on a psychiatrist's couch. The psychiatrist says, "It is not that the whole world is against you; there are billions of people who don't care one way or the other." Because this cartoon illustrates a commonly experienced issue, it may be appropriately shared with many different clients who share this same concern.

The presentation of the cartoon intervention was client-oriented because it was selected to address the client's issue. It was also generic in that the same cartoon could be used with many clients who exhibit the same issue.

In addition to being generic, this humorous intervention was planned, because the therapist previously secured the cartoon and anticipated its potential usefulness in therapy. By its very nature, client-oriented, generic humor is planned because it requires that the clinician collect humorous stimuli that have the potential to become part of the therapeutic process. The therapeutic benefit of this particular cartoon lies in its ability to change cognitive process by helping the client to gain perspective.

There are countless cartoons available that illustrate a humorous perspective on emotional distress, interpersonal relationships, male and female differences, family issues, and so on. A therapist can develop a repertoire of applicable cartoons to keep available in the therapy office for those times when a client's presentation matches the message that the therapist wants to send using a particular cartoon.

In addition to cartoons, generic humor may be presented through jokes or stories that illustrate a variety of client experiences. Clients who are graduate students often learn that graduate school takes far longer to complete than they initially expected. A "light bulb" joke that pokes fun at the situation of graduate school might stimulate some insight and relief for this client. One good example might be: "How many graduate students does it take to change a light bulb?" Answer: "Just one, but it takes six years."

Another classic light bulb joke that may help clients who are "stuck" and/or resistant is: "How many therapists does it take to change a light bulb?" Answer: "Just one, but the light bulb really has to *want* to change." This same light bulb joke might provide perspective to psychology interns who are frustrated trying to get their clients to "change."

The most effective humorous intervention is tailored to the needs of the specific client (client-oriented). These interventions represent humor that is either specifically designed for the client (personalized) or humor that pokes fun at issues common to many clients (generic).

Prop-osition

While *verbal* humor is probably more frequently used by therapists, *visual* humor (in the form of props) may also add a unique intervention strategy. A prop may serve as a humorous stimulus, thus providing the therapist with another medium through which to stimulate the client's experience of humor. Therapists are generally more unfamiliar with, and, therefore, more uncomfortable with, this form of humor. Props can assist the therapist to visually and even kinesthetically alter the "serious" flow of therapy. As with verbal humor, props can be used to present any of the universal traits of humor.

I keep many props in my office. One of the simplest to keep and use, and most often requested, is the "magic wand." At least once a month, one of my clients wishfully asks for a "quick fix" to his or her problems, often directly requesting a magic wand remedy. Once I hear this request, I get up, cross the room, pull my wand from its hiding place, and with a wave and flick of the wrist, "magically" relieve their distress.

The sudden surprise and whimsy of a magic wand "cure" generally trigger a humorous reaction, followed by a discussion of the client's wanting a quick fix, and then acceptance that it may not be the solution to the problem. This sudden playful interaction generally builds the therapist's relationship with the client, while at the same time, helping the client gain some perspective on the challenges being addressed.

I also keep a red clown nose in my pocket. In fact, I carry it everywhere I go. I use it at fast food drive-up windows, on airplanes (to quiet a screaming child), at airport ticket counters (to give the agent a laugh), and so on. In therapy, I rarely don my red nose, but on occasion there is an appropriate therapeutic moment.

One such opportunity occurred when one client, having recently seen the movie "Patch Adams," asked if I knew anything about the health benefits of humor. Because my therapeutic use of humor is interwoven into my more traditional clinical interventions, my clients are unaware of my unusual specialty in therapeutic humor. While the client was talking, I inconspicuously reached into my pocket to grab my red nose. Then with my nose tucked in the palm of my hand, I faked a sneeze, covered my face, and when I removed my hands, my red nose appeared, surprising my client. Both the client and I chuckled and then a discussion of humor, depression, and emotions ensued.

With another client, who was severely depressed and had occasional psychotic symptoms, I used my red nose as a humorous prop to pull her out of what appeared to be the onset of a psychotic episode. The client became extremely depressed during session, and I was concerned she would lose touch with reality (which had occurred during some previous sessions).

I put on my red nose and, when she saw me, she laughed, brightened up, and much of her immediate depression dissipated. The nose helped her to reconnect to me and to reality (if sitting with a therapist with a clown nose is reality).

Juggling balls can be an extremely useful prop in therapy to serve as a kinesthetic experience representing numerous life circumstances. Occasionally, when a client is experiencing multiple stressors and unrealistically expecting to masterfully be able to handle them all, I grab a juggling ball. Using masking tape, I mark it with one stressor; for example, work. Then I give it to the client to juggle. Most clients can accomplish the task of juggling one ball. Then I add a second ball illustrating another stressor; for example, relationship. Now the client has two balls to juggle. This is somewhat more difficult but generally achievable. Then I add a third ball representing another stressor—financial struggles.

At this point, most clients feel as though they cannot juggle three balls. Each stressor increasingly taxes the system until all the balls fall down. The surprise of integrating juggling into the more serious therapy session generally adds an element of humor for the client. The use of increasing the number of balls to be juggled serves as a parallel—helping clients understand how, as life's stressors increase, a person's ability to manage the stressors becomes limited. The activity is experienced as a challenge, a representation of stressors of life, and as fun.

The analogy of the experience of juggling and handling too many real life stressors such as relationships, work, children, health, and so on that tax the individual's emotional system is further developed as we discuss how the client can become more "practiced" (juggling the balls or managing the stressors) so that the tasks or challenges become more manageable. The parallel between the real stressors accumulating and the increasing number of juggling balls becomes readily apparent; and the clients have fun, play, and laugh during the experience. Like many other experiential activities, the juggling balls are remembered (both visually and kinesthetically) and, therefore, understanding *how* stressors overload all of us is also remembered.

Another example of integrating a prop into treatment involves the use of "mental floss." Mental floss consists of a thin plastic tube that is worn around the back of the head like a headband (though hidden in the wearer's hair), with the ends of the tube beginning and ending behind each ear. A string (or floss) is threaded through the tube and hangs out about eight inches at the ends of the headband just behind each ear.

To use the floss, the wearer holds the end of each string (on either side of the head) and pulls the string back and forth through the tube. From a distance, it appears as if the string is passing through or flossing the brain (hence mental floss).

I once worked with a couple; the husband—who was generally playful—was reported by his wife to be grumpy in the mornings. During our couple's session, I asked him to describe his morning routine of preparing himself for the day. After listening to him, I reached to my desk and put on my mental floss. As I demonstrated its use, I said to the husband, "I want you to keep this in the bathroom and, when you get up in the morning, I want you to look in the mirror and 'floss'."

Both he and his wife laughed. For the next few sessions, I asked him if he had been flossing, and he reported that he had. I then asked his wife if there had been any change in his grumpiness, and she reported that, since he began "flossing," his morning moods had lifted dramatically.

Humor as Homework

When offering humor as homework, as in all homework types of interventions, the activity is best when tailored to the specific individual. The most simple humor homework assignment is to have the client consciously increase his or her opportunities to experience humor. To encourage this process, it is important for the therapist to identify the types of stimuli that trigger a particular client's sense of humor.

As an initial approach, I ask clients directly, "What do you find funny?" I am looking for categories (such as cartoons, comedians, jokes) and then more specifics (such as Peanuts, Robin Williams, light bulb jokes). I also investigate their favorite communication vehicles (video, audio, text, Internet, multimedia, etc.).

If I am going to suggest a homework activity, I want to maximize its potential for success by matching the task to my client's "sense" of humor in style and content. To suggest a joke book or other humorous reading to a client who does not like to read limits the possibility of success, compared to asking a client who listens to audiotapes while commuting to listen to a tape of his or her favorite comedian.

CLIENT-INITIATED HUMOR

The use of humor is not restricted to the therapist. It is common for clients to share humor in the therapeutic relationship. Client-initiated humor can serve many purposes, including reducing emotional distress (as illustrated by nervous laughter). Vaillant (1977, 2000) suggests that the use of humor by an individual is an "adaptive and mature" defense mechanism, which helps the client directly examine emotionally painful events and memories. Clients may also use humor to gain perspective or to achieve some sense of superiority or mastery. In addition, clients may engage humor to connect or join (developing a closeness) with the therapist, by sharing a joke or story.

No matter what form the client's use of humor takes, it can serve as a diagnostic indicator of his or her progress in treatment. Clients who are using humor to cope with distress may be attempting to reduce the stress without addressing the underlying issues. Nervous laughter is one such process. Diagnostically nervous laughter may indicate the importance for the therapist to explore the issues stimulating the laughter. The therapist wants to help the client gain awareness into the process of using nervous laughter to cope with emotional distress.

The specific use of humor by a client can indicate increased perspective illustrated by changes in beliefs about self and, therefore, be a diagnostic indicator of the success of cognitive restructuring. For example, I was treating a bright, attractive, narcissistic young man who held an MBA from Harvard University. His narcissistic personality made it difficult for him to develop intimate relationships even though, on the surface, he was friendly, conversational, and attractive.

In general, narcissistic personality clients do not enjoy humor offered by therapists (and others) because the center of focus is diverted away from themselves. Narcissistic personality clients also keenly dislike humor of which they themselves are the target. Being the target of humor may trigger a "narcissistic injury."

The client in this example was in treatment for his narcissistic personality when, after about six months of therapy, he told me the story of the Midwestern farmer who was walking across Harvard Square in search of the cafeteria. The farmer approached a very stately looking gentleman, who happened to be a Harvard English professor. The farmer asked, "Excuse me, sir. Can you tell me where the cafeteria is at?" The professor looked at him somewhat disdainfully and replied, "At Harvard, we do not end sentences with prepositions!" Undaunted, the farmer paused a moment and said, "Then excuse me, sir. Can you tell me where the cafeteria is at . . . ass hole!"

By telling that story, this narcissistic, Harvard MBA (who identified himself with the professor) was clearly laughing at his own narcissism and sharing his ability to laugh at himself with his therapist. Diagnostically, his ability to openly make fun of himself indicates the breaking up some of his narcissistic thinking.

As clients begin to laugh at themselves through use of therapeutic humor, their inner core of self-esteem is enhanced. Laughing at yourself indicates, "I am okay and can reveal my insecurities."

HUMOROUS INTERVENTIONS AND THE CLIENT

Context, Culture, and the Perception of Humor

For clients to perceive the humor in any stimulus, such as jokes or anecdotes, they must have the context of the humor in their personal experience. This context provides a background through which the client filters the stimulus and, if the stimulus has one or more of the universal traits of humor, it will be experienced as humorous.

Jokes, anecdotes, and humorous events shared in a group such as friends, family, or (more broadly) ethnic groups, may be experienced as funny by insiders but not by outsiders. The insiders share a history of interaction and, therefore, have developed a common context through which the stimulus is perceived. Outsiders do not usually share the same interactive history and, therefore, do not perceive the same context in the same way.

Cultural differences and even differences within culture subgroups create different contexts from which to perceive humor. Because a therapist cannot possibly know all the many contexts in a culture or in an individual, it is important to evaluate each individual client as to his or her personal receptivity to maximize the potential of any humorous intervention.

Individual and cultural belief systems influence whether a stimulus is perceived as humorous. One such belief in some cultures is, "One should not enjoy humor or laugh at a funeral." While this is true in some cultures, the Irish wake is a good example of a serious event that is experienced with a great deal of levity.

Cultural differences are usually determined by the rules of a person's culture when compared with another. These rules become part of the individual's context or perception of the world and, therefore, greatly influence the individual's experience of humor.

While the universal traits that trigger a humorous response remain consistent across cultures, the context or belief system that filters the events varies. The result is a dramatic difference in the experience of humor across cultures. A challenge to the therapist is to understand both the client's cultural *and* individual frames of reference, which creates the context of his or her view of the world, so that humorous interventions can be designed to match that client's sense of humor.

Matching Sensory Modalities

We all sense humor through three primary modalities (auditory, visual, kinesthetic), but each of us is likely to be dominant in one. The most successful interventions target the most dominant sense without ignoring the potential of the others. The therapist who is able to present humorous interventions involving multiple modalities and who is sensitive to the primary receptive modality of the client will be able to create interventions that are most suited for the client.

To stimulate the *visual* client, *showing* a cartoon or recommending a video has greater impact than *describing* the cartoon or *verbally telling* a joke or story. While the *auditory* client may connect to the verbal presentation, the kinesthetically oriented client may be more energized or "tickled" by attempting to juggle balls or feeling the "touch" of a magic wand, which, in addition to stimulating visual sense, creates a sensual experience for the client. A skilled clinician attempts to integrate *all* sense modalities into the clinical process, while emphasizing the modality best suited for the client.

Gender Differences

While a sense of humor ultimately is highly individualized, it appears that, in addition to the influence of cultural context, men and women have somewhat different styles of "sense" of humor. Men appear to be more stimulated by slapstick and physical humor, as well as humor about sex and bodily functions. Male humor tends to include more superiority (put down) and aggression.

Women tend to gravitate toward humor about interactions, relationships, people, successes, and support. Women tend toward humor that is empathic and sensitive to the plight of others. Women are more likely to make fun of *situations,* while men are more likely to make fun of *people.*

Gender differences shift as the psychological well-being and motivation for humor are considered. Emotionally stable men display less put-down or aggressive humor, while emotionally stable women tend toward a playful humorous style.

While culture and gender clearly play a role in determining an individual's personal sense of humor, it is ultimately individuals who cultivate and create their own unique processes for evaluating an event as humorous. Virginia Satir stated, "The event does not determine *how* to respond to the event. That is purely a personal matter. The *way* in which we respond will direct and influence the event more than the event itself."

While a client's humorous response is determined primarily by the unique perception of the individual, a therapist must also be sensitive to the culture and gender differences that may influence whether a particular stimulus is perceived as humorous.

EXPANDING THE THERAPIST'S SENSE OF HUMOR

The renowned "philosopher" Br'er Rabbit observed, "Everybody's got a laughing place. Trouble is . . . most folks won't take the time to look for it."

Integrating humorous intervention into clinical practice follows a process similar to the integration of any therapeutic skill. Just as the *skill* of empathy is based on the capacity of a therapist to *feel* empathic toward another human being, the use of humor is predicated on the clinician's ability to *feel* and perceive humor.

Assuming that the therapist has the capacity to *feel* empathic, the clinician has the basis from which to *learn* empathic intervention. The same process applies to humorous interventions. Therapists who have a core capacity to experience humor can be *trained* to increase their sense of humor and to integrate humor into therapy.

Effective integration of clinical skills is based on a combination of academic (cognitive) learning and experiential (applied) learning. To integrate empathic skills, clinicians repeatedly practice these skills outside the therapy hour. In addition, therapists-in-training receive supervision of their clinical work.

To learn to integrate humor into therapy requires that the clinician be skilled in basic therapeutic interventions and have a developed sense of the therapy process. With such a foundation, the clinician can develop specific skills by practicing humor skills outside the therapy hour.

To learn and practice humor skills, clinicians can gather humorous material (jokes, cartoons, stories, etc.) and practice sharing them with friends, family, and other social contacts. The more clinicians practice humor in nonclinical settings, the more humor becomes integrated into their clinical work.

In addition to the practice of using cartoons, jokes, word play, and so on, clinicians who can expand their comic vision by perceiving the humor in the world around them will expand their sense of humor, making them more capable of creating humorous interventions in session.

Clinicians who in nonclinical settings figuratively view the world through "Groucho glasses" develop a greater sense of the humor in their surroundings. For example, while flying on Virgin Atlantic Airlines and sitting near the galley, I noticed the flight attendants filling a canvas bag with cans and plastic. When they were finished, they lifted the bag revealing the bag's label—"Virgin Recycling." I may have been the only passenger onboard who perceived the humor in that particular label! This illustrates the concept of developing your *comic vision.*

As another example, consider the sign on Interstate 5 just north of San Diego, California, that reads: "Cruise Ships: Use Airport Exit." As I drove down the freeway and saw this sign, I wondered just how many cruise ships use the airport exit! It was my "misperception" of the intended meaning of this sign that triggered my "funny bone."

Therapists who want to expand their comic vision can do so by increasing their humor activities and perceptions. Therapists can learn and practice jokes and stories, collect cartoons, perceive humor around them, use props for play, and practice increasing their humor quotient. It is the humorous practice in nonclinical settings that prepares the clinician to more effectively interpret humor into clinical practice. As Dr. Seuss said, "There to here . . . Here to there . . . Funny things are everywhere."

CONCLUSION

The integration application of humor to psychotherapy can be particularly powerful because it has the potential to activate changes in all four of the core aspects of human experience (emotional, behavioral, cognitive, and physiological) that are targeted by the major theoretical approaches. Humorous interventions can be used as treatment (by helping to positively change emotions, behaviors, cognitions, and physiology), for diagnosis, and for building the therapeutic relationship.

Central to the effective use of humor by the therapist is tailoring interventions to the specific client. This takes both practice and planning. It is also crucial for the therapist to assess the client's potential receptivity to humorous interventions and to respond to the client's reactions to those interventions. The most effective use of humor occurs when, as with empathy, therapists are able to integrate humor into their own core being so that humor becomes an integral part of their interactions with clients.

HUMOR RESOURCE LIST

Humor Organizations

Association for Applied and Therapeutic Humor
1951 West Camelback Road, Suite 445
Phoenix, AZ 85015
602-995-1454   602-995-1449 (fax)
http://www.aath.orgoffice@aath.org

International Society for Humor Studies
Don Nilsen
Executive Secretary, ISHS
English Department
Arizona State University
Tempe, AZ 85287-0302
602-965-7592   602-965-3451 (fax)
www.uni-duesseldorf.de/WWW/MathNat/Ruch/humor.html
don.nilsen@asu.edu

HumorMatters™
3972 Barranca Parkway, # J-221
Irvine, CA 92606
949-654-4500 (phone/fax)
http://www.humormatters.com
ssultanoff@humormatters.com

The Humor Project
110 Spring Street
Saratoga Springs, NY 12866
518-587-8770
http://www.humorproject.com

REFERENCES

Association for Applied and Therapeutic Humor. (n.d.). Retrieved from http://www.aath.org.

Augarde, T. (Ed.). (1991). *The Oxford Dictionary of Modern Quotations* (p. 217). New York: Oxford University Press.

Beck, A. T. (1976). *Cognitive therapy of emotional disorders.* New York: New American Library.

Berk, L. S., Tan, S. A., Fry, W. F., Napier, B. J., Lee, J. W., Hubbard, R. W., et al. (1989). Neuroendocrine and stress hormone changes during mirthful laughter. *American Journal of the Medical Sciences, 298*(6), 390–396.

Bizi, S., Keinan, G., & Beit-Hallahmi, B. (1988). Humor and coping with stress: A test under real-life conditions. *Personality and Individual Differences, 9*(6), 951–956.

Carkhuff, R., & Berenson, B. (1967). *Beyond counseling and therapy.* New York: Holt, Rinehart and Winston.

Corey, G. (2001). *Theory and practice of counseling and psychotherapy.* Pacific Grove, CA: Brooks/Cole.

Cousins, N. (1979). *Anatomy of an illness as perceived by the patient.* New York: Norton.

Dillon, K. M., Minchoff, B., & Baker, K. H. (1985–1986). Positive emotional states and enhancement of the immune system. *International Journal of Psychiatry, 15*(1), 13–18.

Ellis, A., & Harper, R. (1979). *A new guide to rational living.* North Hollywood, CA: Wilshire Book.

Freud, S. (1928). Humour. *International Journal of Psycho-Analysis, 9,* 1–6.

Fry, W. F. (1992). The physiologic effects of humor, mirth, and laughter. *Journal of the American Medical Association, 267*(13), 1857–1858.

Gelkopf, M., & Kreitler, S. (1996). Is humor only fun, an alternative cure or magic? The cognitive therapeutic potential of humor. *Journal of Cognitive Psychotherapy: An International Quarterly, 10*(4), 235–254.

Greenberger, D., & Padesky, C. A. (1995). *Mind over mood.* New York: Guilford Press.

Kubie, L. (1971). The destructive potential of humor in psychotherapy. *American Journal of Psychiatry, 127,* 861–866.

Levinson, W., Roter, D., Mullooly, J., Dull, V., & Frankel, R. (1997). Physician-patient communication: The relationship with malpractice claims among primary care physicians and surgeons. *Journal of the American Medical Association, 277*(7), 553–559.

Martin, R. A., & Dobbin, J. P. (1988). Sense of humor, hassles, and immunoglobulin A: Evidence for a stress-moderating effect of humor. *International Journal of Psychiatry in Medicine, 18*(2), 93–105.

Martin, R. A., & Lefcourt, H. M. (1983). Sense of humor as a moderator of the relation between stressors and moods. *Journal of Personality and Social Psychology, 54,* 520–525.

Moran, C. (1995). Short-term mood change, perceived funniness, and the effect of humor stimuli. *Behavioral Medicine, 20,* 32–38.

Padesky, C. A., & Mooney, K. A. (1990). Clinical tip: Presenting the cognitive therapy model to clients. *International Cognitive Therapy Newsletter, 6,* 13–14.

Porterfield, A. L. (1987). Does sense of humor moderate the impact of life stress on psychological and physiological well-being? *Journal of Research in Personality, 21,* 306–317.

Richman, J. (1996). Points of correspondence between humor and psychotherapy. *Psychotherapy, 33*(4), 560–566.

Rogers, C., Gendlin, E., Kiesler, D., & Truax, C. (1967). *The therapeutic relationship and its impact.* Madison: University of Wisconsin Press.

Rosenheim, E., & Golan, G. (1986). Patients' reactions to humorous interventions in psychotherapy. *American Journal of Psychotherapy, 40*(1), 110–124.

Salovey, P., Rothman, A., Detweiler, J. B., & Steward, W. T. (2000). Emotional states and physical health. *American Psychologist, 55*(1), 110–121.

Seligman, M. (1998). *Learned optimism: How to change your mind and your life* (2nd ed.). New York: Pocket Books.

Seligman, M., & Csikszentmihalyi, M. (2000). Positive psychology: An introduction. *American Psychologist, 55*(1), 5–14.

Strupp, H. (1960). Nature of the psychotherapist's contribution to treatment process. *Archives of General Psychiatry, 3,* 219–231.

Sultanoff, S. (1992, July/August). The impact of humor in the counseling relationship. *Laugh It Up, Publication of the American Association for Therapeutic Humor* (Vol. 1). Retrieved January 10, 2002, from www.humormatters.com/articles/explore.htm.

Sultanoff, S. (1994, July/August). Exploring the land of mirth and funny: A voyage through the interrelationship of wit, mirth, and laughter. *Laugh It Up, Publication of the American Association for Therapeutic Humor* (Vol. 3). Retrieved January 10, 2002, from www.humormatters.com/articles/explore.htm.

Sultanoff, S. (1995). Using humor in crisis situations. *Therapeutic humor, 9*(3), 1–2. Retrieved January 10, 2002, www.humormatters.com/articles/crisis.htm.

Sultanoff, S. (1997). Survival of the *witty-est;* Creating resilience through humor. *Therapeutic Humor, 11*(5), 1–2. Retrieved January 10, 2002, from www.humormatters.com /articles/resilience.htm.

Taylor, S. E., Kemeny, M. E., Reed, G. M., Bower, J. E., & Gruenewald, T. L. (2000). Psychological resources, positive illusions, and health. *American Psychologist, 55*(1), 99–109.

Thorson, J. A., Powell, F. C., Sarmany-Schuller, I., & Hampes, W. P. (1997). Psychological health and sense of humor. *Journal of Clinical Psychology, 53*(6), 605–619.

Truax, C., & Carkhuff, R. (1967). *Toward effective counseling and psychotherapy.* Chicago: Aldine.

Vaillant, G. E. (1977). *Adaptation to life.* Boston: Littlem Brown.

Vaillant, G. E. (2000). Adaptive mental mechanisms: Their role in a positive psychology. *American Psychologist, 55*(1), 89–98.

Chapter 7 ————————————————————————————————

HUMOR AS A MODERATOR OF LIFE STRESS IN ADULTS

Herbert M. Lefcourt

HISTORICAL BACKGROUND

While a sense of humor is commonly regarded as an asset today, this has not always been the case. Philosophers such as Plato (in *Philebus*), Aristotle (in *Poetics*), Hobbes (in *Leviathan*) and Rousseau (in *Lettre a M. d'Alembert*) have characterized humor as an expression of hostility and a means of aggression. For these philosophers, the derision and denigration that can be involved in laughter at others' expense, most often directed at ugliness and deformities in others, made humor seem undesirable and cruel. Laughter was said to reflect the more unattractive aggressive qualities of humans that resulted in the victimization of others. Aristotle suggested that "comedy aims at representing man as worse, tragedy as better than in actual life" and "the ludicrous is merely a subdivision of the ugly" (Piddington, 1963). It is instructive to recall that until the end of the nineteenth century, for example, it was routine for the fashionable "upper classes" to tour mental institutions, enjoying a good laugh at the expense of pitifully disheveled inmates who were often shackled to their cages. The films *Elephant Man* and *The Wild Child* (based on J. Itard's famous case study, *The Wild Boy of Aveyron*) provide good reminders of how people visited fairgrounds to gawk and laugh at deformed and diseased persons. Even today, "freak shows" are not unknown among itinerant circus companies.

Lengthy debates about whether humor can be regarded as a blessing or a curse have been proffered in the writings of Robertson Davies and Umberto Eco. In the third book of Robertson Davies' (1975) classic *Deptford Trilogy,* titled *World of Wonders,* for example, there is a prolonged discussion among the protagonists about whether humor and joking aren't the province of the devil rather than a gift from God. They argue that joking about the past is a way to diminish its importance, and of "veiling its horror." This "veiling of horror" is said to simply prepare people to accept yet further horrors, and is held responsible for human failure to learn how to avoid the circumstances that produce misery. Humor, in these terms, is essentially evil because it prevents people from learning what they need to know if they are to survive without further duress. As one of Davies' characters notes, "Only the Devil could devise such a subtle agency and persuade mankind to value it" (p. 92). Interestingly, this "veiling of horror," which is viewed so negatively by the protagonists in Davies' novel, comprises what psychological humor theorists mean when they speak of humor positively as an emotion-focused coping strategy, a means by which emotional responses may be mitigated.

A disputation about humor is highly salient in Umberto Eco's novel, *The Name of the Rose* (1980), in which humor plays a more central role in the story than it does in Davies' work. Two monks, who become the major antagonists in this wonderfully engaging mystery, enter into an intense dialogue about the nature of humor in a dramatic scene shortly before one or both of them are likely to be killed by the other. The malevolent monk, who was responsible for a series of mysterious deaths among his follow monks, reveals his hatred and dread of humor in arguing that it is blasphemous because it has the potential to destroy faith and the "order of the universe." His contention is that if humor were allowed to undo the fear of God, humans would inevitably come to revere the profane, "the dark powers of corporal matter." Humor is seen as a nullifier of obedience and a tool for insurrection. The second monk, who is the mentor of the assumed writer of this memoir-like novel, counters this position, arguing, much as modern day humor advocates might, that puritanism is the very hell that threatens to make life an agony in the here and now. He asserts that the use of fear and terror (and murder of would-be insubordinates in this case), while supporting order, reflects the devil's "arrogance of the spirit, faith without smile, truth that is never seized by doubt" (p. 477).

While philosophers have argued about the value of humor, physicians seem to have held humor, or at least laughter, in positive regard for some time. In a delightful article titled "A Laugh a Day: Can Mirth Keep Disease at Bay?" Jeffrey Goldstein (1982) cited contributions of physicians and philosophers from the thirteenth through the nineteenth centuries, presenting a series of priceless testimonials for and against the value of humor for health. Among them is one by Gottlieb Hufeland, a nineteenth-century professor, who is quoted as saying:

> Laughter is one of the most important helps to digestion with which we are acquainted; the custom in vogue among our ancestors, of exciting it by jesters and buffoons, was founded on true medical principles. Cheerful and joyous companions

are invaluable at meals. Obtain such, if possible, for the nourishment received amid mirth and jollity is productive of light and healthy blood. (p. 22)

In the thirteenth century, a surgeon named Henri de Mondeville suggested that laughter could be used to facilitate the recovery from surgery: "The surgeon must forbid anger, hatred, and sadness in the patient, and remind him that the body grows fat from joy and thin from sadness" (Goldstein, 1982, p. 22).

In the sixteenth century, Joubert (1579) claimed that laughter produces an excessive blood flow that helps to create healthy-looking complexions and vitality in facial features. Laughter was, therefore, said to be aligned with recuperative forces that contribute to a patient's wellness.

Another testimonial from a sixteenth-century physician was offered by Richard Mulcaster, who believed that laughter could be thought of as a physical exercise promoting health. "He wrote that laughter could help those who have cold hands and cold chests and are troubled by melancholia, since it moveth much aire in the breast, and sendeth the warmer spirites outward" (Goldstein, 1982, p. 22).

In the early years of the twentieth century, James Walsh, a medical professor at Fordham University, wrote the book *Laughter and Health* (Walsh, 1928). In that volume, he states:

The best formula for the health of the individual is contained in the mathematical expression: health varies as the amount of laughter. . . . This favorable effect on the mind influences various functions of the body and makes them healthier than would otherwise be the case. (p. 143)

It would seem, then, that where many philosophers and theologians, and those concerned with morality and religion from earlier centuries, excoriated humor and laughter as reflecting malicious delight at the failings and misfortunes of others, physicians were more observant of the health benefits of laughter and humor. This latter orientation has received strong support in recent decades in the writings of Norman Cousins. In *Anatomy of an Illness,* Cousins (1979) described the important therapeutic role of humor as he struggled with a life-threatening disease. In Cousins' case, the use of humor may have helped to change the course of his disease, a point he came to emphasize in two subsequent books concerned with healing processes during encounters with different diseases (Cousins, 1983, 1989).

Among the earliest psychological contributions depicting the positive effects of humor was that of William McDougall (1903, 1922). McDougall suggested that laughter could reduce the impact of social forces that otherwise might undermine rational behavior. Laughter was described as a device for avoiding an excess of sympathy for a suffering compatriot, therefore saving us from depression, grief, and other potentially destructive emotions. This position parallels recent writings about humor as a means of alleviating distress (emotional arousal). Mc-Dougall (1922) wrote:

> The possession of this peculiar disposition (laughter) shields us from the depressing influence which the many minor mishaps and shortcomings of our fellows would exert upon us if we did not possess it, and which they do exert upon those unfortunate persons in whom the disposition seem to be abnormally weak or altogether lacking. It not only prevents our minds from dwelling upon these depressing objects, but it actually converts these objects into stimulants that promote our well-being, both bodily and mentally, instead of depressing us through sympathetic pain or distress. And now we see how the acquirement of laughter was worth while to the human species; laughter is primarily and fundamentally the antidote of sympathetic pain. (p. 299)

Similarly, Freud, in his book *Jokes and their Relationship to the Unconscious* (1905), described laughter as a release of defensive tension that had been aroused by circumstances preliminary to the laugh. Tension was said to be elicited by anything that could provoke feelings or thoughts associated with anger and sexuality in situations where their expression would be inappropriate. When ego defenses that inhibit such emotional expression proved to be unnecessary, as when a joker provides a punch line to his story and thereby relieves the listener of possible emotional responses, the energy exerted in inhibiting emotional responses was said to be released in laughter. In Freud's writings, similar to McDougall's, he hinted at the beneficial effects of humor in reducing the impact of emotional duress.

Freud also wrote a brief paper titled "Humor" (Freud, 1928), wherein he presented a view of humor that differentiated it from "wit" and the "comic." Humor was said to represent the internalization of parental forgiveness that enables an individual to gain perspective and relief from the emotions attendant on disappointments and failures. Humor involved the reinterpretation of failures as being of lesser importance or seriousness than had initially been believed, thereby transforming such failures into "mere child's play." In this way, humor becomes a means of coming to terms with disappointments and averting episodic anxiety and depression. It is this form of humor, described by Freud and hinted at by McDougall, that characterizes much of contemporary research on humor as an alleviator of emotional distress.

Current Perspectives on the Role of Humor in Human Affairs

Norman Dixon (1980) has proposed that humor may have evolved as an alternative to feelings of anger, which become less adaptive when humans begin living in less nomadic and more populous groups. As Jared Diamond (1997) has noted, anger and violence become less acceptable means for resolving conflicts if people have to live in proximity in stable societies. As long as people are nomadic, following herds of animals or continually seeking new places with more clement weather and edible plants, violence can be a hit-and-run affair. Nomadic perpetrators of violence do not often remain in proximity to camps or neighborhoods where friends and relatives of a murdered family member might come seeking vengeance as would be the case in stable food-producing societies. As Dixon argued, the expression of anger and aggression become maladaptive in settings where populations are stable. Here, humor may have evolved as an alternative response to the annoyances and irritations that could otherwise escalate into violence and murder. The contemporary epidemic of "road rage" is an example of anger-driven aggressive responses to interference by strangers that may have characterized nomadic societies. Crowded urban settings provide similar opportunities for violence as did nomadic societies. Urban metropolises are places where the intersection of paths between strangers rarely recurs, and violent offenders can hope to retreat from their misdeeds without being recognized. For survival purposes and feelings of security in the urban milieu, road rage seems to be the very sort of emotional expression that must be subdued, if not by humor, at least by law.

If humor helps to avert the likelihood of violence between people, it also can enhance interactions within social groups. As Bonanno and Keltner (1997) found, bereaved persons who smile and laugh as they speak about their deceased spouses are judged to be more attractive and appealing to their interviewers than are those who remain solemn. If people can laugh about what had been a difficult or even dreadful experience, they become more approachable. Laughter, smiling, and humor signify that the mourner is ready to make a return to more normal social interactions, which, in turn, makes it easier for others to approach them. To this end, Keltner and Bonanno (1997) assert that laughter gives evidence that the bereaved person is becoming more involved in current ongoing social experiences and is in the process of retreating from a life of reminiscence and relationship with deceased persons. These developments enhance the likelihood that people will become reinvolved in their social groupings, which, as a consequence, may protect them from the effects of ongoing stresses.

Could these contentions about the positive roles that humor and laughter play in facilitating social interaction be the very same phenomena that early philosophers held up to such ridicule? Obviously, humor comes in many forms, and laughter can be derisive on some occasions and supportive on others, though some theorists insist that humor is always derisive, with laughter signifying victory over others (e.g., Gruner, 1997).

In his longitudinal study of Harvard men titled *Adaptation to Life,* Vaillant (1977) described humor as a "mature defense mechanism" and differentiated between "self-deprecating" humor and wit, the latter being perceived as a hostile form of humor from which pleasure is obtained in the denigration of others. The former was described as adaptive because laughing at ourselves while undergoing stress can serve to lessen the emotional impact of those stressful events. Wit or hostile humor, on the other hand, was thought to be an aggressive means for controlling others and, therefore, less likely to afford relief when a person is on the receiving end of stressful experiences. There is no acceptance of the inevitable, no relief from taking yourself too seriously in humor that is characterized by competition and aggression. Only in self-directed humor whereby people laugh at their own disappointments and failings was relief to be expected. Vaillant described humor that could reduce the seriousness with which failure is regarded as being among the most mature of ego defenses.

In recent research, Janes and Olson (2000) offer support for the differentiation between self-deprecating and hostile humor. Disparaging humor was found to be intimidating to those who observed it even if they were not its target. In the presence of hostile joking, people exhibited more conformity and became more fearful and sensitive to rejection than did those who observed self-deprecating humor. Self-deprecating, as compared to disparaging, humor evidently does not have the dampening effects on the well-being of observers. The latter may result in social isolation of the comic even if the expression of dislike for his ridiculing humor is not made obvious by "fearful" observers. On the other hand, self-deprecating comics may continue to enjoy the pleasure of social engagement because their humor does not arouse the fear of rejection among observers.

Currently, self-directed, as opposed to disparagement or hostile humor, is regarded as an asset. If Dixon's (1980) assertion that humor evolved as an alternative to the experience and expression of anger is correct, it obviously would be the nonhostile form of humor that would prove most adaptive and arousal-reducing, the sort that Freud presciently labeled *humor* in that brief but seminal paper describing humor as an emotion-focused coping strategy.

Individual Differences in Humor

The assessment of humor has always been problematic because of social desirability. Few persons readily admit to having an inadequate sense of humor. Gordon Allport (1961) found that 94% of people questioned reported that their sense of humor was average or above average. In early measures of humor, however, the issue of self-promotion was skirted by simply assessing preferences for one kind of humor or another (sexual, aggressive, nonsense, etc.). Typical of the approach was Tollefson and Cattell's (1963) *IPAT Humor Test of Personality* wherein respondents judged the funniness of 100 different jokes. The resulting scores reflected their appreciation of each of five humor factors, which, assumedly, reflected certain underlying personality characteristics. O'Connell (1960) and Eysenck (1942, 1943) developed similar measures in which the appreciation of jokes and cartoons comprised the subject matter. In a review of these early measures, however, Babad (1974) concluded that such preferences for types of jokes or cartoons were not related to important criteria such as peer ratings of the respondents' senses of humor. Consequently, when my colleagues and I began our research into humor, we decided to use different approaches to investigate humor as a personality characteristic.

In our early studies, we adopted the aforementioned Freudian view of humor— that people with a good, as compared to a poor, sense of humor could take themselves and their experiences less seriously. To pursue our investigations, we constructed two scalar measures of humor, the *Situational Humor Response Questionnaire* (SHRQ; Martin & Lefcourt, 1984) and the *Coping Humor Scale* (CHS; Martin & Lefcourt, 1983). Both were then deployed in studies examining the stress-moderating effects of humor.

In the SHRQ, respondents are asked to describe how often and to what degree they are apt to respond with mirth in situations that could be as irritating as they might be amusing. Reactions could range from not being amused at all to laughing aloud. In hindsight, this measure seems to be assessing a readiness to experience humor in lieu of annoyance or anger; accordingly, the SHRQ can be thought of as an index of emotion-focused coping whereby unsettling emotions are circumvented or short-circuited by laughter. In the CHS, however, respondents are queried as to their deliberate use of humor to alter difficult circumstances. This differs from the SHRQ in that the focus is on actively changing the stressful nature of a situation rather than undoing its negative emotional effects. Thus, the SHRQ is more intrapersonal and the CHS is more interpersonal in focus. These two instruments overlap each other and yet are dissimilar as evidenced by typical correlations of approximately .25 (rarely exceeding .50). Both scales manifest acceptable internal consistencies and temporal stabilities, encouraging their widespread use. Martin (1996) has documented the reliability and validity data for the SHRQ and CHS based on a decade of research. Martin (1998) has more recently reviewed findings obtained with most of the scalar measures that have been used in humor research.

In a series of validity studies, the CHS and SHRQ, along with subscales from the *Sense of Humor Questionnaire* (SHQ; Svebak, 1974), have been found to be associated in the predicted directions with a number of criteria, including the following:

- Laughter during an interview.
- Peer ratings of humor.

- Positive moods.
- Self esteem.
- Mirth expressed during failure experiences.
- Witty remarks and funniness while creating impromptu comedy routines.
- Humorous content of narratives produced while watching stressful films.
- Funny comments produced spontaneously during tests of creativity.

The results have been supportive. One consistent finding, however, needs to be highlighted. The SHRQ seems to be more predictive of male humor, whereas the CHS is more predictive of female behavior. These sex-specific findings have also emerged in subsequent research and have led to discussions about the different meanings and manifestations of humor for males and females (for discussions, see Lefcourt, 2001; Lefcourt & Thomas, 1998).

Research Findings Linking Humor and Stress

The results from our first studies evaluating the power of humor as a stress moderator lent support for the hypothesized "emotion-focused coping" role that had been advanced previously by Freud, McDougall, and Cousins. Significant moderating effects were found for our and Svebak's (1974) scalar measures of sense of humor and for tasks we created that required the active production of humor. Specifically, with higher scores on each of the various humor measures, we found less mood disturbances as people dealt with potentially stressful life circumstances. Higher scores on the various measures of humor were associated with lower scores on self-ratings of depression and irritability regardless of the frequency and intensity of the life stressors.

Several investigators have attempted to replicate and expand on our findings. The two initial follow-up investigations offered conflicting evidence for the stress-moderating role of humor. In the first study, which yielded disconfirming results, Porterfield (1987) used both the CHS and SHRQ to predict emotional responses to life stressors. Elevated humor was associated with lower scores on a measure of depression, but no interactions were found between humor and stress in the prediction of depression. Thus, humor seemed to be a simple correlate and not a potential moderator of moods displayed in stressful circumstances. Differences in sample characteristics between Porterfield's and our investigation may account for some of the divergence in our findings. Although Porterfield had secured a large sample ($N = 220$) of undergraduates, the initial depression scores exhibited by his sample were substantially higher than normative (more than one standard deviation higher than the normative means for the measure). A common problem in depression research is that among persons with elevated scores, it is often difficult to produce any beneficial effects. This may have contributed to Porterfield's failing to find moderator effects for humor.

In the following year, Nezu, Nezu, and Blissett (1988) reported a study with strong confirmatory findings. In this investigation, both the CHS and SHRQ were evaluated for their moderator effects on the relationships between life stress, depression, and anxiety. Two parallel data sets were collected. One was cross-sectional in which stress and dysphoria were measured at the same time, and the other was prospective with dysphoria measured subsequent to the stressful experiences. Nezu et al. found significant main effects and interactions between stress and humor in the prediction of depression, at both times of testing. In the prospective analysis, where earlier measures of depression and anxiety were entered as covariates in predicting the later measures of same, the analyses were even stronger than at the first cross-sectional prediction of depression. In both the cross-sectional and prospective data sets, however, depression scores increased with stress primarily among subjects with low scores on either the CHS or SHRQ measures of humor. Those persons who scored high on humor varied little with changing levels of stress and were always less depressed than their low-scoring counterparts. On the other hand, the results obtained when anxiety was the dependent variable were unrelated to humor.

In summarizing these early findings, we could conclude that in certain circumstances, humor has been found to alter the emotional consequences of stressful events. In others, however, humor has been found to be a negative correlate of dysphoria regardless of the levels of stress that subjects had undergone. The latter findings suggest that humor could be regarded as similar to traits such as well-being, optimism, or cheerfulness.

In the ensuing years, a number of studies have been reported with further varied results. I have summarized and discussed these elsewhere (see Lefcourt, 2001; Lefcourt & Thomas, 1998). In brief, humor has most often been found to be associated with lesser indications of dysphoric affect. The role of humor as a stress moderator, however, has not been clearly resolved. Nevertheless, a number of investigations attesting to the beneficial roles that humor may play in concert with other psychological characteristics known to reduce the impact of stress encourage us to maintain our original hypotheses about humor as a stress moderator.

For example, Carver et al. (1993) reported on the ways a sample of women coped with the threats involved with undergoing surgery at an early stage in the development of breast cancer. While these investigators' primary interest was in the effects of optimism as a moderator of the relationship between illness-as-a-stressor and emotional responses, they also explored the effects of other coping mechanisms, including the women's use of humor during this period. In each of five assessments at presurgery, postsurgery, and then at 3-, 6-, and 12-month follow-ups, the use of humor—being able to joke and laugh about breast cancer itself—was found to be positively correlated with optimism. In turn, optimism and the use of humor were found to be negatively associated with distress at all five periods. Because distress involved in coming to terms with life-threatening illnesses such as cancer may leave a person more vulnerable to the ravages of that illness through immunosuppression (Kiecolt-Glaser et al., 1987), optimism and humor can be positive assets in the struggle against serious illness. Given the nature of the very real stressful circumstances explored in this study, the positive effects for optimism and humor are compelling and, once again, suggestive of their stress-moderating roles.

In another approach to the study of stress moderation, my students and I have studied the affective responses of people who have been led to contemplate their own mortality. The assumption underlying this research was that many of the questions comprising life event measures of stress contain intimations about the deaths of loved ones and of the respondents themselves. In one study (Lefcourt et al., 1995), students were led to think about their own deaths through the completion of a series of tasks: completing a death certificate in which students had to guess at the cause and time of their future deaths, composing a eulogy that they would like to have delivered at their funerals, and constructing a will disposing of the worldly goods that they anticipated having at the time of their deaths. Scores indicative of mood disturbance had been assessed before and following these "death exercises." As predicted, most persons exhibited an increase in mood disturbance, reporting more depression, tension, anger, and confusion following completion of the death exercises. The only exceptions to this trend were among those persons who had scored high on a measure assessing "perspective-taking humor." These persons showed little or no change in their moods following completion of the death exercises. The perspective-taking humor measure consisted of an index reflecting appreciation and comprehension of a set of Gary Larson's *Far Side* cartoons (Larson, 1988), which had been specially selected for their "perspective-taking" character. Each of the cartoons required "distancing" to be appreciated and understood. That is, respondents had to be capable of perceiving the nonsense in everyday human activity to comprehend and enjoy the humor inherent in these cartoons. Perspective-taking humor, the ability to assume a humorously distant position from everyday life, seems to have provided some protection from the dysphoria that commonly results from the contemplation of our mortality.

In a second study concerned with humor and mortality (Lefcourt & Shepherd, 1995), humor was used to predict the willingness to become an organ donor. We reasoned that the very act of signing an organ donation form required, if only for a moment, recognition of the possibility of sudden and accidental death. The recognition of that possibility, however brief, would be aversive enough that most people would never get around to signing an organ donation form. To confirm that belief, we first found that organ-donation signing was related to behaviors indicating acceptance, as opposed to dread of death. For example, willingness to visit a mortally ill friend and readiness to discuss death with one's parents and relatives were positively associated with the signing of organ donation forms. This led us to assert that persons who had signed their organ donation forms were generally less phobic about death-related thoughts and behaviors. In turn, when organ-donation signing was examined for its relationship to humor, it was found to be positively associated with both the SHRQ and our cartoon measure of perspective-taking humor. These data were interpreted as indicating that humor reveals a tendency to not regard ourselves too seriously. Not being overly serious about ourselves allows us to acknowledge feelings and thoughts about mortality without succumbing to morbid affects.

In a previously mentioned set of studies, humor, observed during interviews conducted six months after the loss of a spouse, was used to predict how well persons would eventually come to terms with the loss of their loved ones (Bonanno & Keltner, 1997; Keltner & Bonanno, 1997). These investigators found that adjustment favored survivors who could laugh while they were speaking about their former partners. Those who could laugh during interviews reported that they felt less anger and were enjoying their lives more than they had immediately following their spouses' deaths. Like humor, laughter could be said to reflect a distancing from the grief attendant on death, allowing the person to recover and enjoy current life more fully.

In these studies, humor and laughter seem to provide a degree of protection from morbid affects, enabling people to cope with thoughts and feelings about death. Because the very process of thinking about death can arouse anxiety and dread (Becker, 1973; Solomon, Greenberg, & Pyszczynski, 1990), humor may be thought of as a positive asset that allows us to continue our daily lives despite surrounding perils that always serve to remind us of the ephemerality of our lives. The traumatic events of September 11, 2001, had that very effect. People throughout the world were led to think about their fragility and the suddenness with which their lives could be snuffed out. The attendant depression was palpable and even experienced in rural Western Australia where I was ensconced at that time. Though the events were so horrendous to consider, it wasn't very long before black humor arose that allowed for or simply indicated the restoration of positive affect in the face of such horror. [Note the November 12, 2001, issue and the cover of the December 10, 2001, issue of the *New Yorker* magazine in which jokes about security (a restaurant is chosen not for the quality of its cuisine but because of the presence of armed muscular guards) and the sounds of previously unknown names (e.g., "I just love saying Jallalabad") appeared. The cover of the December 10 issue exhibited a map of the greater New York area with neighborhoods renamed with -stan as a suffix (e.g., Yentastan) became a best-selling poster.] As a point of interest, however, direct references to the destruction of the Twin Towers in New York were nowhere to be found in these cartoons. Most dealt indirectly with the crisis, focusing on terror from incongruous positions of comfort and security. It may be some time before such reminders of death and destruction may be handled with humor.

Investigations concerned with the effects of stress often direct their attention to coping styles that facilitate or obstruct optimal functioning under threatening conditions. Coping methods that involve avoidance or denial of impending stressful experiences are said to leave persons more vulnerable to those stressors than coping styles that involve awareness and active dealing with stressors (Janis, 1958; Lazarus, 1966). In a series of studies, humor has been found to be associated with more active and confrontative coping styles and negatively related to avoidance and denial.

In the previously mentioned Carver et al. (1993) investigation, use of humor and optimism were found to be positively correlated, and both were associated with lesser distress in response to breast cancer. In addition, optimism and humor were associated with positive reframing and were negatively related to denial and behavioral disengagement. Other investigators have found similar patterns of coping styles associated with humor.

Rim (1988) found humor to be associated with positive reframing but negatively related to suppression, the tendencies to seek succorance and to blame others, and substitution, the latter being examples of avoidance coping responses made to stressful events.

Humor has also been found to be associated with "approach" coping styles by Kuiper, Martin, and Olinger (1993) in their study of students' responses to academic examinations. These authors found the CHS to be positively associated with the degree to which students appraised exams as challenging rather than threatening. As well, the CHS was found to be positively related to distancing and confrontive coping, subscales from the *Ways of Coping Scale* (Lazarus & Folkman, 1984). These latter findings suggest that persons who use humor as a coping mechanism are apt to engage in problem-focused coping with minimal emotional responses during their encounters with stress. In support of this contention, these authors also found that the CHS was negatively correlated with trait measures of perceived stress (S. Cohen, Kamarck, & Mermelstein, 1983) and dysfunctional attitudes (Cane, Olinger, Gotlib, & Kuiper, 1986), the latter of which assesses dysfunctional self-evaluative standards that are associated with vulnerability to dysphoria.

Studies that have examined the relationship between humor and coping styles lend support to earlier research investigations suggesting that humor can play a role as a moderator of stressful experiences. Coping styles that are associated with humor seem to be the kind that augur active confrontation with the sources of stressful experiences, helping to reduce distress, if not immediately, after sufficient time has elapsed to allow for a change in perspective.

Humor and Stress-Related Physiological Processes

Humor has been found to be associated with physiological responses associated with stress. For example, Berk et al. (1989) examined the effects of humor on neuroendocrine hormones that are involved in classical stress responses. Experimental subjects watched a 60-minute humorous videotape during which blood samples were taken every 10 minutes. Control group subjects were provided with an equivalent "quiet time" during which they were exposed to neutral stimuli. Blood samples were later assayed for corticotropin (ACTH), cortisol, beta-endorphin, dopac, epinephrine, norepinephrine, growth hormone, and prolactin, all of which usually change during stressful experiences. Of these eight neuroendocrine hormones, five were found to have notably decreased among experimental subjects while remaining stable among control subjects. Berk et al. concluded that mirthful laughter modifies or attenuates some of the neuroendocrine and hormone levels that are associated with stress.

Newman and Stone (1996) found that the act of creating a humorous monologue to accompany a stressful film (the industrial accident film used in lab studies of stress; Lazarus, 1966) had a marked effect on heart rate, skin conductance, and skin temperature. In contrast to subjects who were asked to create a serious monologue to accompany the film, those creating a humorous monologue evinced lower heart rates and skin conductance levels and higher skin temperatures than their "serious" counterparts. Therefore, active humor creation seemed to have had an anxiety-reducing effect during the presentation of this stressful film. That the film had been stressful was evident because heart rate and skin conductance had both increased as the film progressed while skin temperature declined, all three returning gradually to baselines several minutes after the film ended.

Finally, we (Lefcourt, Davidson, Prkachin, & Mills, 1997) have found evidence with regard to humor as a stress moderator that may shed some light on the occasional variability of results and conclusions notable in this literature. Subjects in our study engaged in five stressful tasks; during each, blood pressure was monitored at regular intervals. In general, systolic blood pressures increased above resting levels, reaching a peak toward the end of each stressful task, and then receded toward resting levels after a further five minutes had lapsed. When humor scores were examined opposite blood pressure, similar patterns were found during the performance of each task. Women who scored high on the CHS measure of humor invariably exhibited lower mean blood pressure levels than women who scored low on the CHS and men, regardless of their humor scores.

However, men who scored high on the CHS exhibited higher mean systolic blood pressures than men who scored low on that measure, and this was maintained throughout the testing sessions, even during rest periods. Although the results were not as consistent as they were with the CHS, men who scored high on the SHRQ often manifested lower systolic blood pressures than men who had scored low on that scale. Among women, the results with the SHRQ were less evident. The SHRQ, then, seemed more related to lower blood pressures among males, whereas the CHS was more predictive of lower female blood pressures and higher male blood pressures.

These contrasting findings suggest that some of the variations in previous results in the study of humor as a stress moderator may be attributable to the mistaken aggregation of data from males and females. Discussion of these findings is available elsewhere (Lefcourt, 2001; Lefcourt & Thomas, 1998). Evidence deriving from the early stress-moderator studies—from research concerning the resistance to dysphoria while thinking about mortality, from investigations linking humor with active, approach-coping styles, and from studies connecting humor with stress-related physiological processes—shows us that humor is a positive asset, a "wired-in" response that serves to enhance our well-being, protecting us against the ravages brought on by stress.

INTERVENTIONS FOR IMPROVING SENSE OF HUMOR

Although there is evidence attesting to the role that humor can play in moderating the impact of stressful experiences and there is much anecdotal lore (and some suggestive scientific research) about the beneficial effects of humor for health and well-being, there is a surprising dearth of literature concerning how people can improve their sense of humor. Several programs have been designed to encourage the development of humor (Goodman, 1983; McGhee, 1994; Salameh, 1987; Ziv, 1988). With the exception of McGhee's efforts, however, there has been little attempt to subject these programs to any form of rigorous evaluation or empirical testing. Even McGhee's attempted assessment consisted of only a follow-up questionnaire measuring self-reported change in humor. Given the social desirability issues in the assessment of humor, it would seem highly problematic to obtain validity data in this fashion. Negative self-ratings of changes in a person's sense of humor would, in effect, reflect a denial of obtaining benefits from McGhee's program, something that might be difficult to do for a person who places a premium on being liked.

Some attention has been given to the use of humor in various psychotherapeutic enterprises (Fry & Salameh, 1987, 1993), but these efforts have consisted largely of descriptive accounts of humor use by therapists rather than a focus on the improvement of humor among clients. Recently, Nevo, Aharonson, and Klingman (1998) described a more systematically designed program to increase the use of humor among a sample of Israeli schoolteachers. In failing to find definitive results, this study revealed more about how difficult it was to conduct suitable outcome research than it was about the substance of the results. Good naturedly, these researchers admitted to several flaws in their investigations. Nevertheless, they did present a useful model for programs designed to improve sense of humor. Their program was based on Ziv's (1981) distinctions between the appreciation, production, and disposition toward humor. Nevo et al. expanded the dispositional element to include motivational, emotional, social, and behavioral components of humor that became targets for instruction in their program. In essence, they sought to alter their subjects' desire to improve their humor and enhance the cognitive skills associated with humor, such as rapid shifting of cognitions, tolerance of childishness, playfulness, and the like. Ultimately, they sought to alter their subjects' abilities to produce and appreciate humor, but failed to demonstrate such changes. Aside from basic sampling problems, the measures of outcomes—ratings by peers or completion of cartoons or creativity tasks—were difficult and unlikely to change within the 20-hour period during which the programs were completed. Nevertheless, the authors' description of their plans of operation could provide a good starting point for anyone wishing to conduct such research.

If you did little else, the encouragement of flexible thinking, of learning to generate multiple responses to singular stimuli, and lessening the fear of rejection for attempts at being comical or provoking laughter could be good starting points for investigators wishing to enhance the humorous capacities of their subjects. To this end, I would like to propose a set of procedures that I believe might be helpful in facilitating changes in a person's access to humor. These procedures reflect a distillation of methods useful in the modification of other behaviors that we might try applying to the task of enhancing a person's sense of humor. What I am suggesting is really a micromanagement of individuals' responses that are regarded to be components of humor production and humor appreciation. My contention is that previous failures at enhancing humor capacity have most likely resulted from researchers making premature leaps to distant goals following training procedures that have not been carefully designed to alter components of humor.

Each of the tasks undertaken by Nevo et al. (1998) could no doubt play a role in helping people to increase their propensity to be funny. However, as an initial consideration, it is important that each element or task to be presented be done in such a way that success for the client is highly probable. Because most people have a fairly stable evaluation of their own sense of humor, those who would be seeking to improve their sense of humor would probably be a select group of people who believe that they are inadequate in that realm. And, because they have experienced their own relative humorlessness with consistency over time, they regard it as a trait and, therefore, would probably not hold out too much hope of change. Consequently, each step toward "making humor" must be simple or, at least, not too large a leap.

If the target is the production of humor (becoming funny), a first task to be mastered might be to simply involve the provision of alternative responses to simple stimuli. This could be accomplished in word association tasks in which the person could be asked to generate a whole series of different responses to the same word. This would result, at the least, in an increase in verbal output and, optimally, in learning to produce a wide range of responses to particular stimulus words. Given the likely success at this procedure, you might then shift to the description of inkblots similar to the ways in which the *Rorschach Inkblot Test* is administered. A person might be asked to provide different responses to each of several inkblots. Again, this should lead to an increase in output, a necessary condition for bisociative processes that are, in turn, prerequisite to the creation of humor.

Following successes in making multiple responses to words and inkblots, this process might be extended to pictures of people in action as in the Thematic Apperception Test (TAT). Here, the humorist-in-training might be asked first to tell a story in which he or she describes what is happening in the picture. Subsequently, the client could be asked to create a different story about that picture. This could be done several times, a procedure that would have become familiar in the word association and inkblot tests. When the individual seems to have become capable of multiple responses as he or she looks at any one picture, word, or inkblot, the next chore introduced might focus on the speed of the responses. For example, the target could be shifted to seeing how many responses the client can offer in a given length of time. As speed of offering multiple responses increases, the person is readied for the next target, the rapid offering of widely divergent responses to a single stimulus.

Jokes that involve the widely different ways in which particular persons are apt to view certain human conditions can be offered as examples. For instance, jokes involving observations by Catholic priests, Muslim clerics, and Jewish rabbis are common and often draw on sudden shifts in perspective. Jokes about farmers' daughters, ethnic and racial groups, and the like often derive their humorous quality from the widely divergent ways in which members of these different groups view a range of phenomena, from religion to sex to money. The goal to be emphasized in this task is to offer responses that are as different from one another as it is possible to be. The mentor would have to be encouraging and avoid making the person seem foolish in a process where silliness would be more readily seen than humor. Fearing failure at being funny and looking foolish while trying to make others laugh are great enough obstacles to be overcome that the therapist must resist making any judgmental comments as the individual struggles to offer divergent responses during his or her training. Comedians often speak of their fears of "flat audiences" before whom their jokes fail. If professionals, who should be inured to such dread given their lengthy experience with different kinds of audiences, find such experiences nightmarish, the novice or amateur is all the more likely to suffer embarrassment and humiliation given negative responses for their efforts.

If and when the person becomes fluent at creating multiple responses to the specific stimuli presented, has developed speed in the process, and has become capable of producing widely divergent responses, the next step could be a transfer of training to social stimuli. This would involve creating multiple, divergent responses to social stimuli in quasi-realistic situations, as in films or television broadcasts. Offering alternative responses to potentially funny social situations could then become a well-practiced skill to be learned before turning toward the task of doing the same in arousing situations that are not ostensibly funny. The stressful films that have been used in research concerning stress and, more recently, humor, could be employed. As described in earlier research, the films used by Lazarus to induce stress in laboratory situations could be used as training films. While humor researchers have used these films as assessment devices for measuring individual differences in the uses of humor, the same films could be used as training devices or performance outcome measures that might reflect the learning of humor production. This could be the occasion for a transfer of learning from how to make funny commentary to potentially humorous events to more stressful, less potentially funny circumstances. Films concerned with accidents or painful experiences could be presented with instructions encouraging the production of humorous monologues. Models of such humor creation could be employed. Similar procedures could then be adopted in role-playing situations as well where stressful experiences are presented in scripts. Years ago, I used role-playing procedures in which subjects had to tell a friend about failures and difficulties that were embarrassing to discuss (Lefcourt, Antrobus, & Hogg, 1974). Some subjects did respond with humor, though it proved to be relatively rare because it was too difficult for most of our subjects to accomplish. Perhaps given the kind of training we are discussing, humor production might have been more common.

As a brief addendum, the responsiveness of the trainer or peers to the trainee's efforts could also be varied, proceeding from total acceptance to qualified responsiveness. That is, the trainee might learn to take greater risks in trying to produce humor if he or she could become more tolerant of failure in the process. Becoming desensitized to listeners' responses could become a target of training with the goal of overcoming fear of rejection. Learning quips to relieve the anguish of nonresponses or jeers could provide just enough security that trainees might become better able to risk failure in front of others as they attempt to be funny.

Thus far, we have focused on steps leading toward the production of humor in stressful situations. Perhaps as important is our responsiveness to humorous possibilities that occur around us. The appreciation of humor entails recognizing shifts in meaning, the changes in perspective that inhere in given circumstances. As opposed to the divergent cognitions that were discussed with regard to producing humor, convergent thinking may be as important when we consider the enhancement of humor appreciation. If people can recognize accidental or purposeful overlaps in thinking about stressful situations, the consequent finding or recognition of humor in those situations may be as useful as the creation of the same for alleviating the effects of stress.

Again, if the trainee is to begin the process of recognizing potentially funny elements in stressful events, he or she must become capable of convergent thinking, being able to perceive commonalities among ostensibly different stimuli. As a start, I could imagine training people to become good at solving tasks such as the Mednicks' *Remote Associates Test* (Mednick, Mednick, & Mednick, 1964) in which subjects are asked to come up with an object that is relevant to three different stimuli that seemingly have little in common. For example, "ball" would be the correct response if subjects were asked what "snow, dance, and basket" have in common. Learning to quickly recognize remote commonalities with simple verbal stimuli may enhance the likelihood of recognizing other convergences in realistic stressful events. Being able to respond positively to the convergent thinking evident in cartoons or humorous stories about events such as the September 11 attack on the United States might help to alleviate some of the anguish that is still being experienced at this time. If we doubt that such events can ever be rendered less depressing by humor, it is always instructive to recall that humor and laughter occurred even in Nazi concentration camps (E. A. Cohen, 1953).

We may best encourage the production and appreciation of humor if we begin by analyzing these tasks into their component elements. Once these components are recognized, the trainee can be introduced to the steps toward mastery of those elements as small and gradually learned skills. Such teaching would ideally be tailored to the individuals in question if the gradual behavior changes are to be assured. To my knowledge, no such programs have been tested, although the Nevo et al. program, in their analysis of what makes for humor and their attempt to implement a training program where mastery of those components of humor is attempted, was closest to what I am proposing. Unfortunately, the performance criteria seemed too far removed from the training that had been proffered. Gradual increments in the skills involved in the production and appreciation of humor may prove to be a more useful direction for humor education to take.

SUMMARY

Although scholars have long expressed an interest in the meaning and uses of humor, we still do not have a substantial body of reliable empirical information about the functions of humor. Nevertheless, enough convergent evidence exists to suggest that humor is a valuable psychological asset that can play a role in reducing the negative effects of stressful experiences. Given its potential benefits for dealing with difficult circumstances, I have proposed a number of procedures for enhancing peoples' abilities to produce and appreciate humor. While even less empirical data exists regarding methods for increasing humor potentials, the procedures suggested in this chapter derive from knowledge about the components of humor that may help to serve as a promising introduction to humor enhancement research.

REFERENCES

Allport, G. (1961). *Pattern and growth in personality.* New York: Holt, Rinehart and Winston.

Babad, E. Y. (1974). A multi-method approach to the assessment of humor. *Journal of Personality, 42,* 618–631.

Becker, E. (1973). *The denial of death.* New York: Free Press.

Berk, L. S., Tan, S. A., Fry, W. F., Napier, B. J., Lee, J. W., Hubbard, R. W., et al. (1989). Neuroendocrine and stress hormone changes during mirthful laughter. *American Journal of the Medical Sciences, 298*(6), 390–396.

Bonanno, G. A., & Keltner, D. (1997). Facial expressions of emotion and the course of conjugal bereavement. *Journal of Abnormal Psychology, 106*(1), 126–137.

Cane, D. B., Olinger, L. J., Gotlib, I. H., & Kuiper, N. A. (1986). Factor structure of the Dysfunctional Attitude Scale in a student population. *Journal of Clinical Psychology, 42,* 307–309.

Carver, C. S., Pozo, C., Harris, S. D., Noriega, V., Scheier, M. F., Robinson, D. S., et al. (1993). How coping mediates the effect of optimism on distress: A study of women with early stage breast cancer. *Journal of Personality and Social Psychology, 63*(2), 375–390.

Cohen, E. A. (1953). *Human behavior in the concentration camp.* New York: Grosset & Dunlap.

Cohen, S., Kamarck, T., & Mermelstein, R. (1983). A global measure of perceived stress. *Journal of Health and Social Behavior, 24,* 385–396.

Cousins, N. (1979). *Anatomy of an illness.* New York: Norton.

Cousins, N. (1983). *The healing heart.* New York: Norton.

Cousins, N. (1989). *Head first: The biology of hope.* New York: Dutton.

Davies, R. (1975). *World of wonders.* Toronto, Ontario, Canada: Macmillan.

Diamond, J. (1997). *Guns, germs, and steel: The fates of human societies.* New York: Norton.

Dixon, N. F. (1980). Humor: A cognitive alternative to stress. In I. G. Sarason & C. D. Spielberger (Eds.), *Stress and anxiety* (Vol. 7, pp. 281–289). Washington, DC: Hemisphere.

Eco, U. (1980). *The name of the rose.* New York: Harcourt, Brace, Jovanovich.

Eysenck, H. J. (1942). The appreciation of humor: An experimental and theoretical study. *British Journal of Psychology, 32,* 295–309.

Eysenck, H. J. (1943). An experimental analysis of five tests of "appreciation of humor." *Educational and Psychological Measurement, 3,* 191–214.

Freud, S. (1905). *Jokes and their relation to the unconscious.* Leipzig, Germany: Deuticke.

Freud, S. (1928). Humor. *International Journal of Psychoanalysis, 9,* 1–6.

Fry, W. F., & Salameh, W. A. (1987). *Handbook of humor and psychotherapy: Advances in the clinical use of humor.* Sarasota, FL: Professional Resource Exchange.

Fry, W. F., & Salameh, W. A. (1993). *Advances in humor and psychotherapy.* Sarasota, FL: Professional Resource Exchange.

Goldstein, J. (1982). A laugh a day. *Sciences, 22,* 21–25.

Goodman, J. (1983). How to get more smileage out of your life: Making sense of humor, then serving it. In P. E. McGhee & J. H. Goldstein (Eds.), *Handbook of humor research* (Vol. 2, pp. 1–21). New York: Springer-Verlag.

Gruner, C. R. (1997). *The game of humor: A comprehensive theory of why we laugh.* New Brunswick, NJ: Transaction.

Janes, L. M., & Olson, J. M. (2000). Jeer pressure: The behavioral effects of observing ridicule of others. *Personality and Social Psychology Bulletin, 26*(4), 474–485.

Janis, I. L. (1958). *Psychological stress.* New York: Wiley.

Joubert, L. (1579). *Treatise on laughter.* Paris: Chez Nicolas Chesneav.

Keltner, D., & Bonanno, G. A. (1997). A study of laughter and dissociation: Distinct correlates of laughter and smiling during bereavement. *Journal of Personality and Social Psychology, 73*(4), 687–702.

Kiecolt-Glaser, J. K., Fisher, L., Ogrocki, P., Stout, J. C., Speicher, C. E., & Glaser, R. (1987). Marital quality, marital disruption, and immune function. *Psychosomatic Medicine, 49,* 13–34.

Kuiper, N. A., Martin, R. A., & Olinger, L. J. (1993). Coping, humor, stress, and cognitive appraisals. *Canadian Journal of Behavioural Science, 25*(1), 81–96.

Larson, G. (1988). *The far side gallery 3.* Kansas City, MO: Andrews & McMeel.

Lazarus, R. S. (1966). *Psychological stress and the coping process.* New York: McGraw-Hill.

Lazarus, R. S., & Folkman, S. (1984). *Stress, appraisal, and coping.* New York: Springer.

Lefcourt, H. M. (2001). *Humor: The psychology of buoyancy.* New York: Kluwer Academic/Plenum Press.

Lefcourt, H. M., Antrobus, P., & Hogg, E. (1974). Humor response and humor production as a function of locus of control, field dependence and type of reinforcements. *Journal of Personality, 42,* 632–651.

Lefcourt, H. M., Davidson, K., Prkachin, K. M., & Mills, D. E. (1997). Humor as a stress moderator in the prediction of blood pressure obtained during five stressful tasks. *Journal of Research in Personality, 31,* 523–542.

Lefcourt, H. M., Davidson, K., Shepherd, R. S., Phillips, M., Prkachin, K. M., & Mills, D. E. (1995). Perspective-taking humor: Accounting for stress moderation. *Journal of Social and Clinical Psychology, 14,* 373–391.

Lefcourt, H. M., & Shepherd, R. (1995). Organ donation, authoritarianism and perspective-taking humor. *Journal of Research in Personality, 29,* 121–138.

Lefcourt, H. M., & Thomas, S. (1998). Humor and stress revisited. In W. Ruch (Ed.), *The Sense of Humor* (pp. 179–202). New York: Mouton de Gruyter.

Martin, R. A. (1996). The Situational Humor Response Questionnaire (SHRQ) and the Coping Humor Scale (CHS): A decade of research findings. *Humor: International Journal of Humor Research, 9*(3), 251–272.

Martin, R. A. (1998). Approaches to the sense of humor: A historical review. In W. Ruch (Ed.), *The Sense of Humor* (pp. 15–62). New York: Mouton de Gruyter.

Martin, R. A., & Lefcourt, H. M. (1983). Sense of humor as a moderator of the relation between stressors and mood. *Journal of Personality and Social Psychology, 45,* 1313–1324.

Martin, R. A., & Lefcourt, H. M. (1984). The Situational Humor Response Questionnaire: A quantitative measure of the sense of humor. *Journal of Personality and Social Psychology, 47,* 145–155.

McDougall, W. (1903). The nature of laughter. *Nature, 67,* 318–319.

McDougall, W. (1922). A new theory of laughter. *Psyche, 2,* 292–303.

McGhee, P. E. (1994). *How to develop your sense of humor.* Dubuque, IA: Kendal & Hunt.

Mednick, M. T., Mednick, S. A., & Mednick, E. V. (1964). Incubation of creative performance and specific associative priming. *Journal of Abnormal and Social Psychology, 69,* 84–88.

Nevo, O., Aharonson, H., & Klingman, A. (1998). The development and evaluation of a systematic program for improving sense of humor. In W. Ruch (Ed.), *The Sense of Humor* (pp. 385–404). New York: Mouton de Gruyter.

Newman, M. G., & Stone, A. A. (1996). Does humor moderate the effects of experimentally-induced stress? *Annals of Behavioral Medicine, 18,* 101–109.

Nezu, A. M., Nezu, C. M., & Blissett, S. E. (1988). Sense of humor as a moderator of the relation between stressful events and psychological distress: A prospective analysis. *Journal of Personality and Social Psychology, 54*(3), 520–525.

O'Connell, W. E. (1960). The adaptive functions of wit and humor. *Journal of Abnormal and Social Psychology, 61,* 263–270.

Piddington, R. (1963). *The psychology of laughter: A study in social adaptation.* New York: Gamut Press.

Porterfield, A. L. (1987). Does sense of humor moderate the impact of life stress on psychological and physical well-being? *Journal of Research in Personality, 21,* 306–317.

Rim, Y. (1988). Sense of humor and coping styles. *Personality and Individual Differences, 9*(3), 559–564.

Salameh, W. A. (1987). Humor in integrative short-term psychotherapy. In W. F. Fry & W. A. Salameh (Eds.), *Handbook of humor and psychotherapy: Advances in the clinical use of humor* (pp. 195–240). Sarasota, FL: Professional Resource Exchange.

Solomon, S., Greenberg, J., & Pyszczynski, T. (1990). A terror management theory of self-esteem and its role in social behavior. In M. P. Zanna (Ed.), *Advances in experimental social psychology* (Vol. 24, pp. 93–159). New York: Academic Press.

Svebak, S. (1974). Revised questionnaire on the sense of humor. *Scandinavian Journal of Psychology, 15,* 328–331.

Tollefson, D. L., & Cattell, R. B. (1963). *Handbook for the IPAT Humor Test of Personality.* Champaign, IL: Institute for Personality and Ability Testing.

Vaillant, G. E. (1977). *Adaptation to life.* Toronto, Ontario, Canada: Little, Brown.

Walsh, J. J. (1928). *Laughter and health.* New York: Appleton.

Ziv, A. (1981). *Psychology of humor.* Tel Aviv, Israel: Yachdav.

Ziv, A. (1988). Teaching and learning with humor: Experiment and replication. *Journal of Experimental Education, 57,* 5–15.

———————————————————————

Chapter 8

THERAPEUTIC HUMOR WITH THE DEPRESSED AND SUICIDAL ELDERLY

Joseph Richman

This chapter focuses on the life enrichment and life-saving functions of humor, primarily with the depressed and suicidal elderly. The therapeutic influence of humor, however, is universal, not limited to the elderly or patients in psychotherapy.

For example, I recently gave a talk on humor and lifestyles (Richman, 2001) to patients at a medical rehabilitation center. At the end, an elderly man in a wheelchair who could barely speak above a whisper said, "Without humor, you're dead." He was very disabled but not depressed. As with this man, humor can enrich and even save life for everyone.

HUMOR AND ITS APPLICATIONS

Therapeutic humor rests on three foundations: knowledge of the principles of therapy, the principles of social influences, and, of course, the principles of humor.

The field of humor is a study in itself, with extremely wide applications. It is found in all human activities: literature, art, folklore, teaching, and all forms of healing. Theories of humor and laughter have abounded in the philosophical literature for some 2,500 years, from Plato and Aristotle to the writings of sociologists, psychologists, and physicians of the present. Umberto Eco's medieval mystery novel, *The Name of the Rose* (1994), is based on the legendary lost book that Aristotle allegedly wrote on humor. In the novel, the work was buried in the shelves of a monastery library. The authorities feared that the influence of humor would be so great as to undermine their society. (I gave away the ending, but the book is still worth reading.)

The positive effects of humor have been recognized since Biblical times: "A merry heart hath a cheerful countenance, and doeth good, like a medicine" (Proverbs 15:13 and 17:22 KJV). Humor is associated with good health and longevity; as Joel Goodman, director of the Humor Institute of Saratoga, New York, said, "He who laughs, lasts." In ancient Greece according to Cornford (1914/1961), the main function of comedy was to make the crops grow. You might say that comedy was used as a form of social therapy. There may be a link between this ancient function of comedy and the present day finding of its healing influence.

This chapter describes the principles and theoretical background of humor in general and illustrates the clinical processes and procedures of humor in therapy, with an emphasis on the disturbed and suicidal elderly. Humor, when properly applied, enriches therapy, increases the mutual enjoyment of client and counselor (the terms are used interchangeably in this chapter, as are *patient* and *therapist*), draws people closer together, and even saves lives.

Humor and Dreams Compared

Freud (1905/1960) compared humor to dreams. Both operate at more than one level, the manifest and the latent, and both permit the expression of forbidden drives, thoughts, and attitudes. The manifest level in most jokes appears in the story line or train of thought, based on ordinary discursive logic (the secondary process). The latent level follows in the "punch line," based on a more plastic and poetic form of thought (the primary process). The first part represents the overt or conscious thoughts, while the second reveals the more covert, unconscious, and unknown aspects.

The major difference from dreams is that jokes perform a social function. People need to share jokes and stories with others. Because the techniques of jokes permit the expression of forbidden thoughts and feelings, humor becomes an acceptable way of stating truths that are otherwise unspoken.

Freud's theory echoed those of the English writers of the Eighteenth Century Enlightenment, who saw the function of comedy as the exposure of vice and hypocrisy (Milburn, 1966) and the definition of laughter and humor by the philosopher Croce (1922/1953) as "War against all forms of insincerity."

Humor and Therapy

Several theories, including Freud's, are valuable for understanding the theory and practice of therapeutic humor. Zwerling (1955) pointed out that we laugh at that which makes us most anxious. It follows that the laugh is always on and, it is hoped, with the joke teller or the one who laughs. Monro (1951) emphasized that humor can present new or alternative ways of looking at the world, a feature he called *universe changing.*

Many philosophers, writers, and psychologists have emphasized the hostility behind humor and laughter. Humor, however, is not that simple or easily explained. Hostile humor can be destructive, but the use of hostility that is benign, and not destructive, can have a therapeutic effect. In fact, the inhibition of humor for fear that it will be hostile can have a decidedly negative effect. (See, for example, Assessment Example 11, later in this chapter.)

The therapist's ability to deal with hostility is especially important in the treatment of suicidal and severely suicidal patients. There is often an element of magical thinking in the suicidal, where the expression of anger is considered dangerous and deadly, leading to damage and even the death of loved ones. The expression of hostility in a safe setting, such as in a therapist's office, where all survive and, in fact, become closer, is very therapeutic. Such hostility, in fact, permits the emergence of a loving relationship.

Other writers have emphasized the humanistic and kindly attributes of humor. J. B. Priestley (1976) declared that "Humour at its best has some root in affection" (p. 10). Supporting evidence for the positive physiological, psychological, and social effects of humor and laughter have been summarized by Fry (1986).

Humor is a social phenomenon that essentially requires the presence of others. One major factor is the sheer pleasure of communication. Susanne Langer (1948), in her concept of *symbolic realization,* said that the communication of a person's experiences to others in the form of symbols is a universal human need. Despair may result when this need is disconfirmed and people are not provided with an opportunity for symbolic realization.

All of these components, the physiologically healthy qualities, the psychological techniques that permit the expression of forbidden but important truths, the social sharing and cohesion, and the joys of communication are implicated in the therapeutic effects of humor and laughter.

Humor has another meaning, an attitude of "good humor," that transcends joking and laughter. It refers to a general approach toward life and people. The results of good humor are a sense of well-being, social cohesion, and the formation of positive relationships.

Kris (1952), in his concept of "Regression in the service of the ego," noted that humor is associated with ego strength and mental health. His view was supported in a research study by Grossman (1977). Grossman found that subjects who tested high in ego strength liked jokes in their problem areas, while those low in ego strength disliked jokes in their problem areas. Allport (1937, 1968) stated that a sense of humor is a component of maturity. It is likely that mature people with a sense of humor tend to be high in ego strength and are able to laugh at jokes that touch on their problems.

THE SENSE OF HUMOR

A *sense of humor* is a personality attribute that is broader than just being funny or able to appreciate jokes. People with a therapeutic sense of humor possess four or more of the following attributes:

1. They are competent and sensitive, knowing when and when not to use humor.
2. Their humor is part of a positive approach and a meaningful philosophy.
3. They can listen, appreciate the humor of others, and respond so as to facilitate the treatment process.
4. Socially, they are warm and constructive, appreciative and responsive. They can put people at ease and help maintain high group morale. Their social awareness includes knowledge of the negative attitudes of society toward the ill elderly and the use of humor to overcome ageism.
5. They have a seemingly paradoxical attitude; they can be detached yet involved, a trait that applies not just to humor. *Tuesdays with Morrie* (Albom, 1997) described how Professor Morris Schwartz of Brandeis University faced his terminal illness, including the experience of pain, by doing just that—being involved yet detached. As a result, his final months became a growth experience and an affirmation of life.
6. A similar attitude is present in therapeutic humor. Therapists with a sense of humor can take some distance and, at the same time, care about alleviating the problems faced by their patients and others.
7. Their humor can touch on universal truths and experiences and make reality more bearable when times are rough.
8. When you combine these features with acceptance, commitment, genuineness, accurate empathy, and experience, you are describing the attributes of a successful counselor or therapist who is qualified for therapeutic humor.

SOCIAL ATTITUDES

Attitudes toward the elderly as seen in humor have been examined in several studies, including Palmore (1971) and Richman (1977). Several more studies are described in Nahemow, McCluskey-Fawcett, and McGhee (1986). They all found that bias and nonacceptance of the elderly were significantly related to social attitudes.

For my attitude study, I collected a hundred examples of humor concerning the elderly from a variety of joke books and classified them according to their major themes. More than half of the jokes were negative: Becoming old was associated with physical, sexual, and mental decline, becoming less attractive, and above all, DEATH.

However, a sizable minority of jokes conveyed a positive attitude, including an appreciation of the wisdom that grows with age, an admiration of the mere act of becoming old (as one 100-year-old said, "Yeah, but look how long it took me"), and good-natured laughter at decline.

Is Aging as Unpleasant as Most Jokes Suggest?

Because we laugh at what makes us most anxious (Richman, 1995; Zwerling, 1955), a joke makes a statement about the joke teller. Jokes about the elderly are not created by the elderly, but by younger people, usually males. Their jokes reflect the joke writers' areas of anxiety, together with those who laugh. It might be as accurate to ask, "Is being young as anxiety-laden as the jokes created by the young suggest?"

If so, negative emotions have positive potentials. In terms of growth and adjustment, anxiety is not necessarily something to avoid. Humor can help us identify and overcome the anxiety. In other words, humor depends on what you do with it. It can be used to avoid looking at, or else confronting and overcoming anxiety. The key to anxiety avoidance versus anxiety reduction is the distinction between laughing with or laughing at. Laughing *at* avoids the message. Problem awareness and anxiety resolution are facilitated by laughing *with*.

Youth Good, Age Bad?

Ours is a youth-oriented society, but the bias against the elderly is thousands of years old, a heritage from ancient pagan attitudes.

There is a story in Greek mythology about twin sons, age 22, who were unusually good to their mother. For example, they once pulled her in a chariot from one town to another. The gods were so filled with admiration that they granted both sons the gift of an early death, so that they would never have to bear the ills of becoming old.

This adoration of youth and rejection of age is outmoded today, largely as a result of the biomedical advances and healthy lifestyles that have developed in our era. Nevertheless, the ageist bias has been "bought" by many older persons.

Joan Rivers, for example, was interviewed on public radio (March 25, 1999), where she said it was a terrible fate, having to deal with the handicaps of getting old. The interviewer, Leonard Lopate, noted that some cultures look with respect upon their elders. Ms. Rivers replied, "But we live in the United States, in this culture." Unwittingly, Ms. Rivers acknowledged that this "terrible fate" was socially based.

Fortunately, most people can respond positively to positive attitudes. I was voting early in a primaries election, and the lady registering me said, "You're 21," meaning I was the 21st person registered. "My age?" I asked. "You wish," she said. I thought about that and finally responded, "Actually, no." The two registrants, one Democrat and one Republican, both elderly, agreed.

HUMOR AND ASSESSMENT: THE PERSON BEHIND THE LABEL

The term *assessment* can be broadly defined as the application of educated and applied understanding, often with specially designed evaluation instruments. Assessment is a complex activity, not limited to those who are ill or pathological. The following examples give an idea of the wide-ranging and valuable uses of assessment.

ASSESSMENT EXAMPLE 1: THE INCREDIBLY SHRINKING LADY

Eileen A. was a 30-year-old, white, single, pregnant woman, who was admitted to the psychiatric ward of a general medical hospital with the diagnosis of schizophrenia. She had developed the belief that she was shrinking and had become very tiny. She became pregnant immediately after learning that her father was dying of lung cancer.

During the course of psychological testing, she told two jokes:

> There was this switchboard operator in an office, and she was taking calls. One of the people who called asked for a Mr. Fukauer. She called for him, but there was no answer. So she went to one of the girls in the office and said, "Excuse me, I'm new here. Do you have a Fukauer?" The girl said, "A Fukauer! We don't even have a ten-minute coffee break."

The patient appears as an innocent who asks another worker a business question, which is misinterpreted as a sexual one. She finds herself in sexual situations without an awareness that she is doing so; or conversely, that she unconsciously sexualizes the nonsexual situations she is in. The dynamic implication is that of hysteria. The patient then told a second joke.

> There was a little boy with a speech defect, so he went to his mother and said, "Mommy, why do I talk like this?" (very nasally). She said, "I don't know, ask your father." He went to his father and said, "Daddy, why do I talk like this?" His father said, "I don't know. Go out and play." He went outside and saw the milkman. He

went over to the milkman and asked him, "Mr. Milkman, why do I talk like this?" The milkman replied, "Beat it, kid; do you want to get me in trouble?" (in the same nasal tone).

This was also a joke typical of pseudo-stupidity. In fact, there had been a clinical suspicion of mental deficiency that the psychological tests ruled out. These stories illuminated the patient's real life situation, her reactions to the trauma of her father's terminal illness, and her becoming pregnant. Her bizarre symptom of shrinking became best understood, not as a symptom of schizophrenia, but as a stress reaction to a life crisis. She was expressing a longing for the time when she was very small and cared for and did not have to face the strains of adult life.

ASSESSMENT EXAMPLE 2: POSITIVE RECOMMENDATIONS (CONTRIBUTED BY DR. SAUL GROSSMAN)

A 40-year-old woman was applying for a disability pension. She had graduated from law school and passed her bar examination. However, she never practiced, because she developed a progressive neurological disease that prevented her from doing so. During psychological testing to determine her eligibility for disability, she told a joke:

> A man at a bar saw an attractive woman in the lounge and had the bartender take her a note he wrote, inviting her for a drink. The woman looked at the note and at him, and came over. "I want to explain," she said, "that I can't accept your invitation because I'm a lesbian." "A lesbian? What's that?" asked the man. She replied, "I'll give you an example. You see that beautiful young woman in the lounge? I feel like going over to her, tearing off her clothes, and making passionate love to her." The man began crying at the bar. "Why are you crying?" she asked. He said, "I'm a lesbian, too."

This joke illustrates Freud's theory (1905/1960) that jokes use the same complex techniques as those found in dreams. They consist of a displacement to a trifle ("crying at the bar"), a play on words or a pun (the "bar" as becoming a lawyer and a place to drink), and, in the punch line, a conversion into the opposite.

The overt theme was that of a man flirting with a woman and declaring he is a lesbian, which was why he was "crying at the bar." The covert themes include continued grief and depression at losing her opportunity to practice at the bar and an insistence that she is normal. In joke parlance, the man's statement that he is a lesbian because he is attracted to women means he is "normal." The implication is a need for the joke teller to appear or be normal. The further implications are that she needs treatment—not just a disability pension—for her depression and that her wish to be normal includes a wish to function. The recommendation follows for vocational counseling, to find areas where she can work and achieve satisfaction.

ASSESSMENT EXAMPLE 3: A CONCEALED PROBLEM, REVEALED IN THE PUNCH LINE

Assessment is a continuing process. It takes place during therapy, as well. Genevieve S., an 85-year-old woman, was referred to the geriatric clinic after insisting she had colon cancer. Benign polyps had been removed from her intestines, and she did not have cancer. She was assigned to me for psychotherapy. In the first session, she spontaneously ended the meeting with a story. The following joke also illustrates dream-like techniques in jokes:

> An elderly man was sitting on a park bench, crying. Another man sitting next to him asked, "Why are you crying?" The man explained: "My wife left me, and I married another woman, who is a complete angel. She can't do enough for me. She makes the most delicious meals. We go to shows and operas that are wonderful, something I never did before. And our sex life is marvelous, better than it ever was." "So why are you crying?" asked the other man. He replied, "I forgot where I live!"

Jokes, like dreams, can be overdetermined. There is usually more than one reason or explanation. That is one reason that assessment and treatment should be comprehensive. In Genevieve S.'s case, depression that quickly responded to medication and psychotherapy was present. However, the more pressing problem was symbolically expressed in the punch line, "I forgot where I live."

She was a widow who lived alone for many years, and she had taken care of herself and her home. However, she had recently fallen down the cellar stairs while going to check the boiler. She then realized that she could no longer live alone in the large house where she had lived for 55 years and raised her children. She could not face her most pressing problem, but fortunately, she communicated it in her joke.

ASSESSMENT EXAMPLE 4: YOU THINK YOU HAVE A SON; YOU THINK YOU HAVE A FATHER!

Two jokes were involved. The first was told by a middle-aged doctor of my acquaintance:

> A man went to see a rabbi for help. "Rabbi," he said, "have I got a son! All his life he would never listen to me. I never could do anything with him, and now that he's grown up and thinks he's a man, he wants to marry a gentile girl. I feel terrible, Rabbi."
>
> "You think you've got a son," said the Rabbi. "I'm a rabbi and yet my son married a gentile girl and converted to Catholicism. Then his wife died, and after that, he became a priest. So you think you've got a son!"
>
> "That's terrible, Rabbi," said the sympathetic listener. "But at least when I have troubles, I come to you and talk it over and feel better. But who can you talk to?"
>
> "I talk to God," replied the rabbi.
>
> "And what does God tell you?"
>
> "He tells me," 'You think you've got a son!' "

This joke humanizes the rabbi, a man of God, and even God himself. The major theme is the ubiquity of father-son conflicts.

Shortly after telling this joke, the doctor asked if I could test his son, who was in psychotherapy; and his psychiatrist requested that he be evaluated. I tested the son, who told the following joke:

> A priest makes it a habit to go to hospitals, giving people hope and faith. He goes to one patient in an oxygen tent. The patient has difficulty breathing. The priest keeps talking and the patient is turning blue and can't speak. The priest then asks him to write a note, and the patient does. And just as he finishes writing it, he dies. The priest runs around frantically, then recalls the note, which he read. It said, "Get your fucking foot off my oxygen hose!"

Together, the stories depicted a father-son relationship in trouble. Both seemed trapped by the son's efforts to achieve autonomy and independence despite the well-meaning efforts of his father to be helpful. The two jokes depicted different views of the same problem. The problems pointed to the tasks of treatment-to help the son deal with an adolescent identity crisis and, in the process, help both generations become able to separate and yet maintain their relationship.

ASSESSMENT EXAMPLE 5: THE PROGNOSIS FOR MARITAL ASSESSMENT

A 50-year-old man was referred for testing by a marital therapist. In the course of the examination, I asked for a joke, and he complied with the following, "in keeping with this visit":

A couple was seeing a marital therapist. The man said, pointing to his wife, "Whatchamacallit says I ignore her."

In this example, the client communicated an awareness that he plays a part in their marital problems. The prognosis was for a successful outcome of marital therapy, as was indeed the case.

ASSESSMENT EXAMPLE 6: THE PHYSICAL EXPRESSION OF A LIFESTYLE PROBLEM

Allan B. applied to the mental hygiene clinic with the presenting complaint of depression. He told the following, as his favorite joke:

A man went to a clothing story. The salesman convinced him to buy an ill-fitting suit by having him hold his shoulder down, his right leg up, and his body twisted. After leaving the store, a man approached him and asked, "Where do you buy your clothes?" "Why do you ask?" The man replied, "Anyone who could fit a cripple like you must be terrific."

The joke symbolically depicted him as trying to satisfy other people and not himself. His effort to maintain a lifestyle based on a false self resulted in depression and many problems in living. He was dissatisfied with his job, his marriage, and his social relationships, and he suffered from severe back pains! He needed therapy to move him toward a more authentic self. The recommended treatment for his aching back included help in making the proper choices in his varied lifestyles.

EXPANDING THE BOUNDARIES OF THERAPEUTIC ASSESSMENT

You need not be a medical or psychiatric patient to benefit from the insights and self-knowledge of humor. Humor can also contain valuable messages that should be addressed and listened to. Sometimes the message to the self is potentially lifesaving but not heeded.

ASSESSMENT EXAMPLE 7: A MESSAGE TO THE SELF

A policeman walked over to a drunk who was leaning against a building and said, "What are you doing here?" The drunk said, "Holding up the building." The policeman said, "Move on." The drunk moved on, and the building fell down.

This story was told by Bernard Kalinkowitz, then chairman of the department of clinical psychology at New York University. Shortly after telling the story, Dr. Kalinkowitz had a heart attack. The story could be seen as a metaphor, with the building, the policeman, and the drunk all symbolizing different parts of the self and the stress that the joke teller was undergoing. Would it have made a difference if Dr. Kalinkowitz had seen his joke as a message and a warning?

The context in which humor occurs must be taken into account. Dr. Kalinkowitz was in a hotel room with friends and colleagues during a convention, and we were sitting around telling jokes, enjoying the pleasure and the sharing of laughter.

I am not suggesting that those of us who heard Dr. Kalinkowitz should have interpreted his story. However, I am suggesting that his choice of the joke may have been based on a covert awareness of the stress he was under as the head of an outstanding department of clinical psychology, and a pioneer in organizing a university-based psychoanalytic institute. In such nonprofessional contexts, the one to heed the message is the joke teller.

ASSESSMENT EXAMPLE 8: YOU'VE GOT MARITAL PROBLEMS!

My wife and I visited some old friends who had been married 40 years. In the course of the evening, I was reminded of a joke:

> A couple were celebrating their 50th wedding anniversary. They were both in good health, except that the wife was a little deaf. She had also made all the arrangements for the party at their home and invited a great number of guests. It was a grand and glorious success. At the end of the evening, the couple was sitting on the terrace. The man took his wife's hand and said, "I'm proud of you." The woman looked at him and said, "I'm tired of you, too."

In this example, the ones to heed the message may be those listening to the joke. A week after our meeting, the husband phoned and said his wife had requested a divorce. I don't know why I told that story. It may be coincidental, but possibly I was in touch with something in their expressions or behavior.

ASSESSMENT EXAMPLE 9: THE SELF-ESTEEM OF A BRILLIANT TEACHER

Sometimes humor can express a lifestyle or attitude based on the sublimation or resolution of problems. The joke in this example was told by Albert Ellis in the course of a symposium on humor:

A man was walking down the street, and he passed by two women. One of them said, "Doesn't he have a wonderful build." The other replied, "Don't be silly; those are his keys."

(The interpretation that follows is based on my associations, which were very different from Dr. Ellis's, and must, therefore, be accepted with a grain of projection.) The story describes two women talking about a man. One woman expresses admiration, and in the punch line, the other woman is disparaging him for not being what he seems.

The overt theme expresses wishes to be noticed and admired. At a less conscious level as seen in the punch line, his self-esteem depends on what others are thinking of him. That could be particularly meaningful for Ellis, the originator of rational-emotive behavior therapy. A major goal of his treatment is to free the patient from an excessive dependence on approval or disapproval by others.

STORIES AT THE INTERFACE BETWEEN ASSESSMENT AND THERAPY

ASSESSMENT EXAMPLE 10: NEGATIVE THINKING CREATES NEGATIVE JOKES

A joke can often communicate a crisis in the marriage and whether it can be resolved. In a debate on humor and political correctness (*Humor,* 1997), one man told the following joke:

A guy comes home and tells his wife he has been completely wiped out in the stock market. He tells her that he will have to sell their house, summer home, cars, her furs, and her jewels. And what is even worse, she will have to get a job so they can pay their debts and eke out a meager existence. She screams in horror and dismay, opens a window of their condominium apartment, and jumps fifteen floors to her death. The man looks up and says, "Thank you, Paine Webber."

Negative thinking brings up negative jokes. The joke teller commented, "I loved this one when I was going through a divorce."

ASSESSMENT EXAMPLE 11: POLITICAL CORRECTNESS CAN BACKFIRE

Hostility in humor that is benign and not destructive is better than no humor at all. Directing humor toward someone affirms the person's existence.

In the same debate on humor and political correctness (*Humor,* 1997), Don Nilsen was reminded of the following situation:

> A Black student came to Arizona State University and was asked to room with two Whites. The two Whites would tease each other and joke constantly, often saying things that appeared on the surface to be hostile. However, they didn't tease, joke with, or say anything hostile to the Black.
>
> The Black told the housing office that she wanted to move to a different place. When asked why, she responded that her roommates didn't like her. When the two roommates were confronted, they responded that they liked her very much, but they were just trying to be politically correct. By being politically correct, they had made the Black student invisible.

INTRODUCTION TO THERAPY

The use of humor in psychotherapy is widespread. The literature contains a rich body of clinical examples from therapists of different schools and theoretical persuasions, ranging from psychoanalysis to behaviorism. These therapists document the positive effects of humor during treatment (see, for example, Buckman, 1994; Fry & Salameh, 1987; Strean, 1994). Some objective research on the results of humor in therapy has appeared, with reports of positive findings (Andrus Volunteers, 1983; Ljungdahl, 1989).

Humor has another and larger meaning, referring to a general approach toward life and people. It is part of positive thinking, usually called "good humor." The results of good humor are a sense of well-being, the formation of positive relationships, and an increase in social cohesion.

The goals of therapy with the elderly are to reduce stress, relieve symptoms, provide meaningful insights, increase appropriate social behavior, and help in determining the most appropriate goals. The best therapy relies heavily on the patient's assets. That is true, even when dealing with profoundly depressed and suicidal patients, as well as those who are mentally defective or neurologically damaged.

A Prescription to Treat Ageism

Good-natured laughter is a valuable antidote against ageism. An outstanding example was Ida Davidoff, a friend and colleague, who retired in her 80s as a family counselor and gave lectures on creative aging. She described the seven stages of human development as infancy, childhood, adolescence, youth, middle age, late middle age, and "you're looking good." Ida could also laugh at our looks-oriented society; for example, she commented about relations between the generations: "The only reason we can stand young people is that they look so good."

Ageism is especially prominent in elderly patients prone to depression and suicide. Dr. Davidoff demonstrated that elderly patients can be helped to laugh at ageist stereotypes.

Developmental Tasks and Ageism

The young and the old have different problems and life tasks, and their different problems in living are a major part of their conflicts and distress. However, generation differences can result in similar behavior:

> A little boy was sitting on the curb, crying. An old man passed by and asked, "Why are you crying, Sonny?" The boy said, "Because I can't do what the big boys do." So the old man sat down and cried, too.

Life is filled with problems, no matter your age, but not necessarily because of your age. Those elderly who cannot tolerate the problems of aging today were usually not able to tolerate the problems of yesterday. The figures in the previous drama are from different generations and have different developmental tasks, but both suffer from not accepting their ages. Erik Erikson (1950) described the developmental task of latency-age children to develop areas of competence outside the home, in school, with friends, and adults other than their parents. The developmental tasks of the older adult include generativity, that is, to be a teacher and guide for the young; and ego integrity, to see his or her life as a painting or work of art, and, near its completion, to see it was good.

REPRESENTATIVE EXAMPLES IN THERAPY

THERAPY EXAMPLE 1: CRISIS IDENTIFICATION

Humor can point to problems with extraordinary sharpness and effectiveness. In this example, a therapy group in a mental health clinic was being discontinued because the group leaders were leaving. During their last session, they discussed how distressed they felt and their need for further treatment. Dr. Gerald Bauman and I tested the entire group with interaction testing, in which all participants must agree on one answer. As the last item, the group members were asked for a joke. One of them told the following:

> The motors of an airplane had stopped working. The passengers became panicked, but the pilot reassured them that there were parachutes for everyone. He gave one man the parachute, showed him how to put it on, and told him, "Jump, count to 10, and then pull this string." The pilot then jumped. As the pilot was gliding down with his parachute open, he saw the passenger, who stuttered, plummeting to

earth, saying, "0-o-one, t-t-t-two, th-th-th-three. . . . " The members of the group laughed heartily, and voted unanimously to consider this their favorite joke.

The overt theme of the story was the effort of the pilot to help a passenger survive. The covert theme was the failure of that effort, with the result that the passenger was falling to his doom. This was evidently a valid metaphor of the crisis faced by the group members, with the dissolution of the group leading to feelings of panic. It was the responsibility of the clinic to help the members obtain the help they needed. The group joke criticized the irresponsibility of the clinic for eliminating the group without making any provisions for further help.

THERAPY EXAMPLE 2: HUMOR AS SELF-THERAPY

The next example involves a man whose most pressing problem was dealing with the loss of a spouse, which is a frequent precipitant of depression, suicidal feelings, and even a completed suicide. The widower, in his late 70s, started dating women. He confided to his son that he had trouble with his sexual functioning. He then told his son a joke:

> A man's wife died, and eventually he started going out with other women. He met a 20-year-old woman. They fell in love and decided to get married. His children feared that the resulting physical stress would be too much for him and insisted he see a doctor for a thorough checkup. The man returned from the medical examination in great spirits. He told his son, "The doctor said I'm in great shape, and I can have plenty of sex, and even told me how often." He then asked his son, "How many times a week is semiannual?"

After telling the joke, his son reported that his father felt relieved and continued to make a better adjustment. The technique, a conversion into the opposite, enabled the man to laugh at his trying to act like a more youthful Lothario.

THERAPY EXAMPLE 3: THE PATIENT'S SENSE OF HUMOR

Clinically depressed and suicidal patients have recovered from their disturbed state because of their sense of humor.

Henry S. was a 75-year-old man who described himself as depressed and suicidal since the age of 10. He said, rather proudly, that he had been through every form of treatment and medication, including numerous hospitalizations, as well as individual, group, and family therapy. Nothing helped. He also suffered from severe medical ailments, including a stomach operation and Parkinson's. His second wife left him after the onset of his Parkinson's symptoms. Nevertheless, Mr. S. demonstrated the saving grace of a sense of humor.

In psychotherapy, he was gloomy and preoccupied with fears of mental decline. In session after session, he was obsessed with the fear that he was losing his mind and becoming crazy. The session would end with his asking me if I thought he was crazy, and I would reassure him. During one meeting, I became tired of this ritual. When he asked if he was crazy, I said, "You're as crazy as I am." He looked at me for a few moments and finally said, "As bad as that!"

He continued to improve and was discharged to a residence near his family, with whom he had reconciled with the help of the family therapy that was part of his treatment.

THERAPY EXAMPLE 4: HUMOR AND A SUICIDAL MAN

Suicide is the outcome of continued depression and hopelessness without relief. Humor is not recommended at the height of a suicidal state. Other interventions are required first—including medication and dealing with the hopelessness and despair. In the next example, I dealt with a recurrence of hopelessness, in part, with humor.

The patient was a 60-year-old man with cancer that had spread to various parts of his body, and who saw suicide as the only solution. He had been an active man with many interests, but he had completely collapsed. The cancer had spread, and he felt there was no reason to do anything, because there was no time. He responded positively to suggestions that he write an "ethical will" for his children and others, setting forth his values and principles of the good life. He also resumed his social life and became significantly less suicidal.

He had a setback in his medical treatment and became hopeless again, evidently in response to his oncologist's attitude. During one session, he said that he was feeling "bad vibes" from his oncologist. He said the doctor "seems to be losing hope," and the patient was clearly doing the same. I told the patient about the paper by Harold Searles (1975), on the patient as therapist to his therapist, then suggested he ask the doctor directly, "Are you starting to lose hope?" and try to help the doctor. The patient reacted to my advice with disbelief. His wife, however, said she would see to it that the doctor receives such feedback. The patient seemed to feel better. I then was reminded of a story:

> A man came over to a doctor and said, "I don't know if you remember me. I was in the hospital a few years ago, feeling terribly sick. I felt it was the end. One morning, you came into my room with a bunch of other doctors behind you. You looked

at my chart; then you turned to the other doctors and said one word to them. Right then and there I knew I would be all right." "What did I say?" asked the doctor. "You said, pointing to me, 'This man is moribund!' That was the turning point, and I recovered."

I told the couple that the joke showed the value of hope, no matter what the doctor thought. The patient in the joke recovered, not because of the treatment, but because of the patient. The message to my patient was, "Don't lose hope."

THERAPY EXAMPLE 5: USING THE THERAPIST'S DEFICITS AS AN ASSET

Peter V. was a 78-year-old, chronically depressed, suicidal, and alcoholic holocaust survivor who became acutely suicidal when his wife became terminally ill and died. (Other details of this case are presented in Richman, 1995).

Peter phoned to cancel our initial appointment because he became ill with the flu, and said, "I felt so sick I thought I was going to die." "Don't die before you see me," I said. "That's funny," he said.

I rarely respond with humor in the first session, much less over the telephone with someone I have not met before. In this instance, I felt comfortable following my intuition.

In both individual and group therapy, Peter developed a very positive relationship, but continued to say he was hopeless, with the only solution being to jump from the window of his 17th floor apartment. During one individual session, he described his shock and dismay after World War II, when he discovered that he was the only member of his immediate family who had survived the holocaust. What followed were years of maladjustment, failure, and hopelessness.

I listened sympathetically and for the moment ignored some papers that had fallen from my desk. He picked them up while saying in despair, "How can I live like this!" I said, "You can stick around and help me when I am being a klutz." Peter laughed and left in a good mood.

There were many reasons for Mr. V.'s overall improvement, including the good doctor-patient relationship and the opportunity to ventilate, while I listened without interrupting. In addition, the unexpected and spontaneous appearance of humor, with its humorous affirmation of his worth, even when he was in such psychological pain, was also a meaningful experience.

At the next group therapy session, Peter demonstrated some humor. The members were describing what they do when they feel bad or upset. One woman said she goes for a walk with her brother; however, they usually end up in an argument. Peter said, "Why don't you argue with me? Then I'll get mad and feel better."

THERAPY EXAMPLE 6: CAN WE REALLY LAUGH AT DEATH?

Mr. O. was a 71-year-old man who came to the geriatric clinic with the symptom of uncontrolled and heartbreaking sobbing, with no known precipitant or feelings. He responded well to antidepressant medication, combined with supportive couple's therapy. After two months of treatment, however, his symptoms returned with full force. He denied any precipitant, until his wife reminded him of the recent death of a close friend, from heart disease. He then said, "I'm afraid I am going to die." "No one knows the day of his death," I replied, and was reminded of a joke:

> There was a 95-year-old man with a very bad heart who bought a lottery ticket and won $5 million. His family was afraid to tell him the news, for fear the shock would be too much for him. They asked their family physician to notify him gently. The doctor came to visit the old man and asked, "What would you do if you won $5 million?" "I would give half of it to you," said the old man. And the doctor dropped dead.

The patient and his wife laughed heartily at the joke. It was contagious, and I joined them. There was no reoccurrence of Mr. O.'s anxiety and depressive symptoms, in part, because we laughed together at death. The answer to the question, "Can we really laugh at death?" is "Yes, but not alone."

THERAPY EXAMPLE 7: GOOD HUMOR CONFRONTS THE DEATH WISH

Mrs. Sally V. was an elderly woman who had made a serious suicide attempt that would have been fatal except for a chance phone call from a friend. When Mrs. V. did not answer the phone, her friend called 911. Mrs. V. was hospitalized, revived, and made a good physical recovery. I saw her in the hospital with her son, daughter-in-law, and two grandchildren. The patient agreed to see me after discharge; she came for individual and family therapy for two years.

In our first session with the family, Mrs. V. reassured the family that she was no longer suicidal, but added that she wanted to die and expressed regret at being revived. Nevertheless, her behavior changed. She became a feisty and out-spoken old woman, in contrast to her demure, self-effacing behavior in the past.

She also may have become more honest. At the first session, she told the family that she was really 80, to their surprise. There may seem to be little difference between 79 and 80, but the decades often have a symbolic significance. Seventy-nine was only a number, but 80 meant that she was old. The significance of aging was the dominant theme in our two years of psychotherapy. She was particularly fearful of becoming feeble, helpless, and dependent on the care of others.

One session with her 50-year-old son, Donald, in attendance was a turning point. She asked that I help her commit suicide should she be unable to take care of herself and need help. "I want you to pull the plug," she said. I realized she was not talking only to me, and turning to Donald, asked, "How would you feel if your mother became feeble and helpless and you had to feed her? He said, "I agree with Mother. I would want you to pull the plug."

At that point, I became the Good Humor man. I accepted their views cheerfully, discussed how to prepare a living will and obtain a power of attorney, and the session went on to other topics. Toward the end, I commented to Donald, "You are still very young. (At my age, I could say that) You might find taking care of and feeding your mother is not so distasteful when you are a few years older." Donald completely agreed. He added, "After all, I never had that experience so I don't know what I would really do."

The session ended and the participants left. Mrs. V. lagged behind and said to me, "I have such a good feeling." It was clear that her request for assisted suicide was based on fears of being powerless, abandoned, and unloved. Her son's reconsideration that he might take care of her provided her with a rare reassurance that people cared. That made all the difference and led to a glowing sense of well-being.

THERAPY EXAMPLE 8: TURNING LAUGHING *AT* INTO LAUGHING *WITH*

Good humor is not humor in the sense of creating laughter or smiling. It refers to the qualities of someone with a positive attitude, who is interested and accepting of others, but does not necessarily indulge in humor as usually defined. Good humor contains many of the qualities of therapeutic humor, such as a sense of timing, positive thinking, and a meaningful philosophy that is part of his or her professional life (see Richman, 2001).

A middle-aged woman in an outpatient clinic was sitting in the waiting room after a therapy session. She refused to leave and was upsetting the office staff. At her therapist's request, I sat in when he took her back to his office.

The patient complained that she was not given enough medicine. "I had a patient with the opposite problem," I told her. "He refused medication because he was a former drug addict and was afraid the antidepressant medication would be habit-forming."

The woman then displayed much inappropriate laughter and false gaiety, which turned into bitter anger. She suddenly accused me of laughing at her. "A little," I admitted, "but I would much rather be laughing with you." Do you think I have a sense of humor?" she replied. "Yes," I said. She said, "If I didn't have a sense of humor, I would have killed myself a long time ago." She left in good spirits and no longer demanding more medication.

I am good-humored and comfortable with demanding and complaining patients, because I listen to them, knowing there is a meaningful message behind their complaints. However, that patience developed slowly, after several years of seeing difficult patients. The recommendation follows: If possible, do not avoid patients who give you a hard time. Try, instead, to understand the basis of your irritation and work it out. If the difficulties are based on the realistic qualities of the patient, increased perhaps by unresolved problems of the therapist, and if the therapist cannot work through these barriers, it is best to seek other and more compatible clients. If you can learn to tolerate and deal effectively with such patients, the resulting treatment can become a growth experience for both.

THERAPY EXAMPLE 9: AN ABSURD FAMILY SESSION WITH UNEXPECTED RESULTS

Carl Whitaker has called his form of treatment "Psychotherapy of the Absurd" (1975). The method is a unique combination of paradox, poetry, and farce. In Whitaker's hands, therapy becomes an occasion for creative growth in both the patients and the families who come to see him. The following example (from Keith & Whitaker, 1978) was not presented as humor. Nevertheless, what happened was worth reporting. It was so outrageous, incongruous, absurd, and uncanny as to defy categorization.

During family treatment with a 30-year-old, very psychotic, very disruptive male, the patient made any therapeutic work impossible by his behavior. One of the therapists, Dr. Whitaker, exploded, ordered the patient to shut up, sat him down in his chair, then took a glass of water and emptied it over his head. The patient became violent and was sent to the seclusion room. The therapist sentenced himself to the same seclusion room, and the rest of the meeting was conducted by the cotherapist.

It was revealed at the next session that the father had done something similar when the patient was 10 years old and being disruptive. He had poured a bowl of cereal over his son's head. At that time, however, the father had been ostracized from the family and from then on was forbidden to exercise any discipline or influence. The therapist's action put the father's parallel behavior 20 years ago in a new perspective. It was a good example of "universe changing" or "relabeling," unusual for many reasons, and the only nonverbal example I know. The patient lost his psychotic symptoms and was discharged from the hospital in a week.

Regarding the remarkable recapitulation of the father-son episode, it might be argued that the therapist was just lucky, and that, in some serendipitous manner, his out-of-control behavior simulated the family dynamics. However, Carl Whitaker has been recognized as one of the two greatest psychotherapists of our time. (The other is Milton Erickson.) As his colleague, Keith commented, "It is not unusual for the therapist (i.e., Dr. Whitaker) to be able to rocket into the family's irrational stratosphere in the way exemplified" (Keith & Whitaker, 1978, p. 76).

I can only hypothesize that Dr. Whitaker was not only in touch with the unconscious of the patient, but with the unconscious of the entire family (Richman, 1996). My further hypothesis is that this contact is based on an ability to recognize minimal behavioral cues and facial expressions.

Therapeutic Humor in Medicine

Humor can help transcend the fear of death and lead to personal growth and the enjoyment of life. The function of humor and comedy is to successfully confront those aspects of the human experience that arouse the most fear and dread.

THERAPY EXAMPLE 10: THE COUPLE AND THE BRAIN SURGEON

Humor is valuable in the doctor-patient relationship of all health professionals, including all physicians, especially oncologists and other surgeons who must deal with matters of life and death daily.

A Death of One's Own (1978) is Gerda Lerner's memoir of the struggles of her husband Carl, and of the entire family, to cope with the brain tumor that eventually ended his life. When Carl was scheduled for brain surgery, the doctor told them the following story:

A man went to a bar and asked for the usual. The bartender brought him a double martini. The doctor gulped it down and asked for another. Same routine. After the third round, the customer heaved a deep sigh. "Feeling better?" the bartender asked sympathetically. The man nodded. "Had a hard day? How's the brain surgery going, Doc?" "Not bad," the man said.

Mrs. Lerner was at first upset with the doctor for telling such a joke at such a time. But "Carl was laughing uproariously with real enjoyment," she reported, "and before I knew it, I was laughing, too . . . In the months to come, we would increasingly find sentimentality, pity, or a tragic stance unbearable and ludicrous. We had, without knowing, shaped our attitude that day" (Lerner, 1978, p. 28).

What made the difference was the interaction between doctor, patient, and patient's wife. The doctor was willing to risk telling a joke at a time when the patient might have been feeling downcast, and Carl was receptive, showing an ability to laugh at a life-threatening condition. He could because the joke humanized the medical profession and the doctor-patient relationship while acknowledging the possible inadequacies of the healing arts. As a result, Carl felt less alone. Rather than assuming the role of the dying man who has been separated from the living, Carl could see himself as still part of life and society.

THERAPY EXAMPLE 11: A PATIENT'S HUMOR REDUCES ANXIETY

Group therapy can be particularly helpful when other group members are of the same age and have the same problems. In such a setting, laughing at your age and decline leads to greater self-acceptance. The fear of Alzheimer's disease is a major source of fear in the elderly. Sharing humorous stories is a major form of reducing the anxiety. The following example is from a geriatric group in an outpatient clinic. A 75-year-old man told of becoming terribly upset about his lapses in memory.

He then recalled the story of a doctor who was giving a lecture on aging. "There are three signs that you are getting old," he said. "One is that your memory is bad. And, uh, uh, I can't remember the other two."

The primary function of this joke in the group therapy context was the expression and sharing of a meaningful and nearly universal problem of today's elderly—the fear of dementia. The entire group, who were elderly but cognitively intact, responded with recognition of their own fears.

THERAPY EXAMPLE 12: THE HEALING EFFECT OF A PUN

Mr. T. was a 78-year-old retired standup comedian, who suffered from a variety of severe illnesses, including heart disease and a chronic obstructive pulmonary disorder. He was a highly negative and pessimistic man, who resisted all forms of medical as well as psychiatric and psychological treatment. He was seen in a combination of individual and group therapy. In every treatment form, he expressed strong feelings of hopelessness.

In one group therapy session, he declared, "I know what's wrong with me, and there is no hope. I can only go downhill, and I know what the end is." The other group members tried to cheer him up, reassure him, and suggest alternative attitudes. With consummate skill, he "proved" they were wrong. Sara, one of the women in the group, said, "You should be more positive."

"I'm positive my condition is hopeless," he replied. The group was taken aback at his pun, and no one could respond. I finally turned to Sara and said, "You're a great straight man." The ghost of a smile passed Mr. T.'s lips.

Sara also had a history of depression. Shortly after the previous exchange, Sara was asked how she was feeling. "I just want to die, that's all," she said. Mr. T. became very upset and replied, "We all love you." He then tried to cheer her up by making funny one-liner remarks, such as, "Once upon a girl, there was a time."

Following the session, there was a dramatic and long-lasting improvement in Mr. T.'s medical, as well as psychiatric, condition. The groundwork may have been prepared gradually and cannot be attributed to any one event, but the improvement followed immediately after that humorous exchange. The positive change suggested a gratification of his need to be noticed. The response to his humor helped create a shift from obtaining attention through medical complaints, to the satisfaction from a social interaction with the group. Not to be disregarded was his harking back to his standup days, by taking the audience aback with his pun on "positive."

DISCUSSION

Despite the vast differences in style and theory among those who have used humor in their therapeutic practices, successful therapeutic interventions contain features in common. Therapeutic humor requires a therapist with a sense of humor, possessing such personal qualities as warmth, accurate empathy, and acceptance (Truax & Carkhuff, 1967). The therapist should also possess a solid background of experience in psychotherapy. The skills of the humor therapist include the ability to communicate on a primary process level, a sense of timing and the effective use of surprise and novelty, a sensitive awareness of the boundaries of what is socially appropriate and permissible, and an attitude of realistic optimism.

To repeat, therapeutic humor means much more than joking or saying funny things. Therapeutic humor is part of a positive view toward life and people—not just patients.

The use of humor illuminates the diagnosis, the treatment plan, and the specific problems in living. These are important for treatment and cure, but they do not tell the whole story. Jokes and humorous stories reveal the nature of the doctor-patient relationship, and show how much the doctor and the patient have in common.

Using Humor in Therapeutic Practice

The first rule in therapeutic practice is to listen without trying to be humorous in a forced or irrelevant manner. The second rule is that humor should be resorted to infrequently. Humor is like fine liquor. It should be taken judiciously and not often. Too much humor is worse than too little. Third, remember that the goal of the humor is therapeutic, not for the personal gratification of the therapist. Nevertheless, the therapist can enjoy and be part of the positive and accepting atmosphere in which humor thrives.

Therapeutic Humor and the Setting

A cheerful and positive setting is conducive to therapeutic humor. As Greenwald (1987) said, "Humor can help create a therapeutic atmosphere of freedom and openness." The setting is interactive, "a phenomenon preeminently interactive, immanent, impromptu" (Goodchilds, 1972, p. 176). The setting encourages this atmosphere of spontaneity and freedom. The permission to be humorous facilitates the free sharing of a person's deepest concerns, resulting in a decrease in inner anxiety and an increase in social cohesion.

Both humorous and nonhumorous interventions reflect the personality and training of the therapist. Analytic therapists interpret; experiential therapists interact; behaviorists reinforce, decondition, or guide imagery. Humanistic and client-centered therapists listen and respond empathically. Skilled and experienced therapists use any and all of these, with or without humor. There are significant commonalities between humorous and nonhumorous interventions (Richman, 1996c).

The following describes what typically happens in the family treatment of suicidal patients. It is a nonhumorous example from Richman (1986):

> During my family sessions with suicidal patients, angry outbursts and accusations abound and sometimes threaten to escalate out of control. I respond with approval and commend the family for being good patients by letting it all hang out. Although that is not funny, my response resembles the "conversion into the opposite," which is one of the techniques of humor. I praise what is often criticized or considered a problem, and follow through with a further exploration of the situation. For example, death wishes are ubiquitous in suicidal situations. I encourage their expression

and interpret them (validly) as an expression of exasperation, rather than a literal death wish. That is an example of relabeling, the therapeutic version of "universe changing."

The result is an increase in cohesion. Family members are often astonished to find that their open expressions of angry feelings were not destructive and that everyone remained intact. The outbursts cease and are replaced with astonishment.

Insensitive and Inappropriate Humor

Not all humor possesses a healing influence or advances a sense of cohesion and acceptance. Humor can serve as a hostile attack on an opponent. It can be used as a defense in the service of denial or avoidance. People, including patients, can become the objects of scorn and rejection. Such events are behind the criticism that the use of humor by neophytes or poorly trained therapists is potentially destructive and serves the narcissistic needs of the therapist rather than the treatment goals of the patient (Grossman, 1977; Kubic, 1971). Kubie was referring to negative and nontherapeutic humor. In contrast, therapeutic humor is oriented toward helping the patient, not the therapist, although both can laugh together. Therapeutic laughter is kindly, tolerant, and brings people together.

These are statements that apply to all our therapeutic endeavors. Why did Kubie single out humor? Some therapists are more concerned about themselves than their patients, period. While such an attitude can be concealed, it becomes particularly evident under the microscopic clarity of their humor.

SUMMARY

Therapeutic humor can reduce stress, improve functioning, and decrease anxiety and other symptoms. The sharing of positive humor, whether in therapy by the patient and therapist, or outside therapy between friends or family members, results in increased social cohesion and decreased alienation.

An atmosphere and a context that permit the freedom to be humorous are part of therapeutic humor. The freedom to be humorous can lead to the freedom to uncover hidden truths or to question authority, like the king's jester in medieval times.

A positive doctor-patient relationship and working alliance usually precedes the use of humor. The human nature of the relationship decreases alienation, helps the patients realize that their problems are universal, and brings them back to the family of mankind.

All of the components touched on in this chapter—the physiologically health-ful qualities of humor, its ability to permit the expression of otherwise forbidden but important truths, the social sharing and increase in cohesion, and the joy of communication—are implicated in the therapeutic effects of humor and laughter. No one who can laugh at himself or herself can commit suicide, because positive humor is a celebration of life and love. When these are present, laughter and psychotherapy form a fruitful partnership.

REFERENCES

Albom, M. (1997). *Tuesdays with Morrie.* New York: Doubleday.

Allport, G. W. (1937). *Personality: A psychological interpretation.* New York: Holt, Rinehart and Winston.

Allport, G. W. (1968). *The person in psychology.* Boston: Beacon Press.

Andrus Volunteers. (1983). *Humor: The tonic you can afford.* Los Angeles: University of Southern California, Andrus Gerontology Center.

Buckman, E. S. (Ed.). (1994). *The handbook of humor: Clinical applications in psychotherapy.* Malabar, FL: Krieger.

Cornford, F. M. (1961). *The origin of attic comedy.* New York: Anchor. (Original work published 1914)

Croce, B. (1929). Translated by Douglas Ainslie *Aesthetic.* London: Macmillan. (Original work published 1920)

Eco, U. (1994). *The name of the rose.* New York: Harcourt Brace.

Erikson, E. (1950). *Childhood and society.* New York: Norton.

Freud, S. (1960). Jokes and their relationship to the unconscious. *The standard edition of the complete psychological works of Sigmund Freud* (Vol. 8). London: Hogarth Press. (Original work published 1905)

Fry, W. F., Jr., (1986), Humor, physiology and the aging process. In L. Nahemow, K. A. McCluskey-Fawcett, & P. E. McGhee (Eds.), *Humor and aging* (pp. 81–96). Orlando, FL: Academic Press.

Fry, W. F., Jr., & Salameh, W. A. (Eds.). (1987). *Handbook of humor and psychotherapy: Advances in the clinical use of humor.* Sarasota, FL: Professional Resource Exchange.

Goodchilds, J. D. (1972). On being witty: Causes, correlates, and consequences. In J. Goldstein, H. Jeffrey, & P. McGhee (Eds.), *The psychology of humor* (pp. 173–193). New York: Academic Press.

Greenwald, H. (1987). The humor decision. In W. F. Fry & A. Salameh (Eds.), *Handbook of humor and psychotherapy: Advances in the clinical use of humor.* Sarasota, FL: Professional Resource Exchange.

Grossman, S. (1977). Humor and psychotherapy. In A. Chapman & H. Foote (Eds.), *It's a funny thing, humour* (pp. 149–152). New York: Pergamon Press.

Humor: International Journal of Humor Research. Debate on political correctness and humor, 1997, 10.

Keith, D. V., & Whitaker, C. A. (1978). Struggling with the impotence impasse: Absurdity and acting-in. *Journal of Marriage and Family Counseling, 4,* 67–77.

Kris, H. (1952). *Psychoanalytic explorations in art.* New York: International Universities Press.

Kubie, L. S. (1971). The destructive potential of humor in psychotherapy. *American Journal of Psychiatry, 127,* 861–866.

Langer, S. K. (1948). *Philosophy in a new key.* New York: New American Library.

Lerner, G. (1978). A death of one's own. New York: Simon and Schuster.

Ljungdahl, L. (1989). Laugh if this is a joke. *Journal of the American Medical Association, 261*(4), 558.

Milburn, D. (1966). *The age of wit, 1650–1750.* New York: Macmillan.

Monro, D. H. (1951). *Argument of laughter.* New York: Cambridge University Press.

Nahemow, L., McCluskey-Fawcett, K. A., & McGhee, P. E. (Eds.). (1986). *Humor and aging.* Orlando, FL: Academic Press.

Palmore, E. (1971). Attitudes toward aging as shown by humor. *Gerontologist, 11*(31), 181–186.

Priestley, J. B. (1976). *English humour.* New York: Stein and Day.

Rivers, J. (1999). Interview with Joan Rivers by Leonard Lopate on Public Radio, March 25, 1999.

Richman, J. (1977). The foolishness and wisdom of age: Attitudes toward the elderly as reflected in jokes. *Gerontologist, 17,* 210–219.

Richman, J. (1986). *Family therapy for suicidal people.* New York: Springer.

Richman, J. (1995). The lifesaving function of humor with the depressed and suicidal elderly. *Gerontologist, 35*(2), 271–273.

Richman, J. (1996). Points of correspondence between humor and psychotherapy. *Psychotherapy, 33*(4), 560–566.

Richman, J. (2001). Humor and creative life styles. *American Journal of Psychotherapy, 33*(4), 560–566.

Searles, H. F. (1975). The patient as therapist to his analyst. In *Countertransference and related subjects* (pp. 380–459). New York: International Universities Press.

Strean, H. S. (Ed.). (1994). *The use of humor in psychotherapy.* Northvale, NJ: Aronson.

Truax, C. G., & Carkhuff, R. R. (1967). *Toward effective counseling and psychotherapy: Training and practice.* Chicago: Aldine.

Whitaker, C. A. (1975). Psychotherapy of the absurd: With a special emphasis upon the psychotherapy of aggression. *Family Process, 14,* 1–16.

Zwerling, I. (1955). The favorite joke in diagnostic and therapeutic interviewing. *Psychoanalytic Quarterly, 24,* 104–115.

PART III

SANDPLAY/DOLL PLAY

Chapter 9 ———————————————————————————————

USING SANDPLAY IN THERAPY WITH ADULTS

Rie Rogers Mitchell and Harriet S. Friedman

Sandplay therapy gives adult clients the opportunity to portray, rather than verbalize, feelings and experiences that are often difficult to express in words. Therapists and clients alike have found that Sandplay scenes, created with sand, water, and miniatures in a shallow box, serve as a window into the unconscious that contributes a surprising, new vantage point from which to nurture and experience healing and transformation.

Play therapy with children, using toys and other objects, is a widespread and conventional form of treatment for children; using it with adults, however, who possess a conceptual language, is unconventional. Nevertheless, language only partially succeeds in conveying intensely felt emotions, affects, and tensions that even adult clients are often unable to express, control, or understand. Play offers an avenue to communicate these inner experiences and perhaps touch deeply buried wounds.

Using Sandplay with adults may offer them the opportunity to play creatively and express themselves spontaneously, without words, for the first time since they were children. Through the free experience of play, the cognitive-logical mind is put aside, and the innocent, unsophisticated, and unconscious elements of the psyche, heretofore repressed, are allowed to emerge. Once these elements are made available, healing energies can be released to help the individual perceive and deal with life issues. Through this experience, unrealized aspects of the personality can be discovered, made conscious, and integrated, leading to a sense of greater balance and wholeness and an enriched, more satisfying life.

In this chapter, we provide an overview of basic Sandplay principles intended for practitioners who wish to deepen and expand their work with adults by using a creative, playful approach that activates healing energies in the unconscious. To accomplish this goal, a historical and theoretical perspective of Sandplay therapy is followed by a description of how to use Sandplay with adults, including Sandplay equipment needed, role of therapist, introduction of the tray, the Sandplay process, and an understanding of Sandplay pictures. We also illustrate how the healing process unfolds and highlight understanding of Sandplay pictures through a case study of an adult woman.

ORIGINS OF SANDPLAY: HOW IT ALL BEGAN

The therapeutic technique of *Sandplay,* which involves placing miniatures in a shallow box filled with wet or dry sand to create a scene, was originated in 1929 *by children* working therapeutically with London physician Margaret Lowenfeld. She furnished her playroom with miscellaneous small toys and two zinc trays, one filled with sand and the other with water. In less than three months, her child clients had spontaneously combined these elements and created a new technique; children called this experience, "making their world." Lowenfeld used the *World Technique* to observe and objectively record children's emotional states of mind. Her worldwide presentations on this new approach were enthusiastically received because the technique offered a way to record children's communication through their natural language of play by sketching or photographing the scene (Lowenfeld, 1979).

Twenty-five years later, in 1954, Dora Kalff was completing her training at the C. G. Jung Institute. Because of her ongoing interest in helping children, she attended a lecture given by Margaret Lowenfeld in Zurich. Deeply impressed by Lowenfeld's World Technique and intrigued with pursuing it further, Kalff told her friend, C. G. Jung, about the new approach. Jung himself remembered attending a 1937 conference in France where he had formally responded to a presentation given by Lowenfeld. He encouraged Kalff's interest in pursuing this technique, recognizing the potential of using miniatures and sand to reflect images from the unconscious. Kalff then contacted Lowenfeld about the possibility of working with her in London. Lowenfeld agreed and Kalff studied with her for one year in 1956 (Mitchell & Friedman, 1994).

Upon returning to Zurich to continue her work with children, Kalff began the creative process of attempting to integrate her Jungian-based approach with what she had learned from her work with Lowenfeld. During this period of incubation, while her own ideas were crystallizing, she had little contact with Lowenfeld or with others in the Swiss psychological community, for she was the only Jungian analyst working with this technique in Switzerland (Mitchell & Friedman, 1994).

Because of her Jungian training, Kalff had the vision to recognize that the emerging symbols in the sand tray objectified the energy and movement of the unconscious and provided a natural therapeutic modality for clients not only to communicate their inner and outer worlds, but also to heal psychic wounds. Kalff (1980) noted that if the therapist could provide a positive therapeutic environment, that is, a "free and sheltered space" (p. 29), the vital connection between the externally oriented conscious ego and the internally oriented unconscious self could be established. After many years of observing how participating in Sandplay (her name for the technique) seemed to help children become more balanced and spontaneous, she began using this technique extensively with adults and found it to be equally beneficial.

In the late 1950s, after Kalff had consolidated her own Jungian-based theory, Lowenfeld and Kalff exchanged letters (now stored in the Lowenfeld Archives in Cambridge). In this correspondence, Kalff expressed her appreciation to Lowenfeld and agreed to give her credit for originating the technique. They also agreed that Kalff would use the term *Sandplay* to describe her work, so as not to confuse it with the World Technique.

In addition to Lowenfeld's World Technique and Kalff's Sandplay approach, the term *sand tray* is also used to refer to the use of miniatures in a shallow box filled with sand. *Sand tray* is a generic term and is not connected with any particular theoretical perspective. The term is used appropriately when the tray is being used for research or as an assessment instrument, and when it is used with more than one individual (e.g., families, couples, and groups), as well as in situations where no "observing other" is present, or when the therapist is an active participant in a directive or interactive capacity.

SANDPLAY THEORY: WHY SANDPLAY WORKS

A basic premise of Sandplay therapy, in the Jungian tradition, is that the psyche possesses a natural tendency to heal itself, given the proper conditions. Similar to how our physical wounds heal under beneficial conditions, the psyche also has an instinctual wisdom that emerges when left free to operate naturally in a protected environment.

Dora Kalff believed that the aim of Sandplay is to activate healing energies at the deepest level of the psyche by using miniatures and the sand tray to reflect the client's inner world. By this activity and through the experience of free and creative play, unconscious processes are made visible in this three-dimensional form, much like the dream experience. Thus, Sandplay provides a vehicle for the unconscious to let itself be seen and known.

According to Jungian theory, the self, the "seat" of wisdom, located in the unconscious, is the central ordering principle of the entire personality. In the conscious part of the psyche, the ego has the role of maintaining a sense of personal identity and mediating between the conscious and unconscious realms, yet it still needs to be directed by the self. When the self and ego operate together, a person feels more balanced and alive, and more empowered to manifest or actualize the full range of his or her potential. However, the impact of trauma, loss, abuse, or other damaging life experiences can create a state of disequilibrium between the ego and self.

Through the process of playfully creating and reflecting on the sand trays, individuals often retrieve lost memories, early childhood experiences, and unverbalized material. Therapists (Miller, 1979) have observed that through the Sandplay process, psychological, cognitive, and relationship changes can occur, and the client becomes calmer and more at peace. Positive energies and strengths are activated and "recorded" in the trays, as are conflicted, split off, and anxiety-provoking aspects of the psyche. The sand tray provides a stage on which unconscious material can be exposed and examined. In this externally expressed form, the unconscious can be more easily understood and integrated by the conscious ego, creating a bridge between the ego and the self. Sandplay harmonizes the vital relationship between the inner and outer worlds, self and ego. Dora Kalff (1971) found that "In most cases where the constellation of the Self was made impossible during childhood, it can be recovered. This can happen at any stage of life, whatever the individual's age may be" (p. 18).

Several attributes of the Sandplay experience facilitate and enhance the healing that occurs in the process of creating and integrating a tray: turning the focus inward, activating healing energies, giving expression to the unconscious, creative stimulation, presence of the other, integrative viewing, and review and reflection.

1. *Turning the Focus Inward.* Putting one's hands in the sand and shifting and moving it around is a kinesthetic experience that moves the focus away from the outer world—the conscious mind—and inward, to the body, and ultimately to one's internal realm.

2. *Activating Healing Energies.* As the individual scans the collection of miniatures, some items seem to be invested with a magnetic draw. The client's attention is drawn to them, and they are chosen because of the unconscious symbolic meaning that is projected onto these objects. Once this internal energy field has been established, activating the healing aspects of the unconscious becomes possible.

3. *Giving Expression to the Unconscious.* Sandplay materials offer an opportunity for unconscious psychic components, previously held in check, now striving to break through, to be unconsciously and symbolically revealed in the sand scenes.

4. *Creative Stimulation.* In participating in this expressive process, the client has the opportunity to sense the stirring and emergence of his or

her own creative and healing powers and become aware of something bigger and more inspiring than himself or herself. This experience is occasionally accompanied by an extraordinary moment, similar to a profound insight or deep spiritual awakening.

5. *Presence of the Other.* The unconscious moves freely to deeper levels as the Sandplay experience unfolds in the presence of another, the therapist, who mirrors and accepts (without judgment or analysis) what the psyche has presented.

6. *Integrative Viewing.* The viewing of the Sandplay creation promotes increased consciousness and integration of unconscious material by bringing it into tangible three-dimensional form. Interpretation is unnecessary and may hinder the unfolding process.

7. *Review and Reflection.* Sometime after the completion of a series of trays, healing is enhanced through client's and therapist's reflecting on the Sandplay process and analyzing the trays together. Moving understanding closer to conscious awareness continues the vital link between the self and the ego.

GETTING READY: MOVING THEORY INTO PRACTICE

Sandplay therapy requires the use of a shallow tray, sand, water, and small items/miniatures. These concrete materials engage tactile, visual, olfactory, and kinesthetic senses. The silence of the experience has an impact on the auditory sense as well.

The Sand Tray

The sand tray serves as the container for psychological transformation. It provides a secure space, where the client is free to concentrate his or her imagination on the immediate experience, within the protective bounds of the tray.

Most Sandplay therapists have two trays available, one with moist sand and the other with dry sand. The damp sand can be molded, while the dry sand is fluid and pleasant to the touch; both have their own unique, subtle scent.

The dimensions of the sand tray are central to the experience of the free and protected space. The sand tray has specified dimensions (19.5×28.5 inches with a depth of 3 inches), is placed at a height of approximately 30 inches, and is painted blue on the inside to give the impression of water or sky. The size allows the client to view the scene in one glance without shifting the head from side to side. Thus, the tray provides a theatre for total freedom of fantasy but has a built-in limitation;

that is, the size of the box. It provides a secure holding environment, often referred to by the Greek word *temenos* (i.e., a psychological container or sacred
space). Some therapists place the tray on the floor; however, there seems to be
consensus among Sandplay therapists (Patty Scanlon, personal communication,
June 22, 2000) that this can promote a forced regression and influence the direction of the therapeutic process (Signell, 1981).

The Sand

Sand represents instinct, nature, the maternal, and the feminine healing powers
of Mother Earth (Kalff, 1980). Normally, light, fine-grained, sterilized sand is
used. Each tray is normally half-filled with sand, usually about 10 to 15 pounds.

The Water

Water is central to the Sandplay process as it is not only symbolic of the unconscious, but also plays an integral part in the transformation process. Practically
speaking, water is used several ways in the tray:

- To cause a form to disappear and a new one to emerge.
- To dampen the sand to better mold and shape it.
- To alter or soften.
- To flood or immerse.
- To dissolve an existing scene.

To keep the sand properly moistened, most Sandplay therapists dampen the
sand in one of the trays with about a quart of water every third day or so. The
sand should be left only slightly damp, and it should be moldable to the touch.
Most therapists keep an additional amount of water on hand in a pitcher and/or
spray bottle for the client's use.

Besides pouring water directly into the tray, clients also select objects that
represent water, such as pieces of mirror, shiny lids, or flat dishes containing actual water. They also brush away the sand from the interior of the tray, exposing
the blue bottom, when they want to represent a lake, river, or ocean.

The Miniatures

The available figures should represent a cross-section of all animate and inanimate items encountered in the external world as well as the internal imaginative
world. These miniatures help trigger the inner experience and facilitate the expression of the feelings, emotions, or situations depicted in the sand tray.

The creation of a collection is a personal experience for each therapist, reflecting his or her own individuality, qualities, and knowledge. There are no recommended standards regarding either number or variety of miniatures; however, the variety and types of objects are important considerations in developing a collection that offers sufficient and well-rounded choices that stimulate the imagination. For example, the collection should contain objects that serve as earthy, aggressive, ferocious symbols, as well as those reflecting ordinary life and spirituality.

When new clients enter an office of a Sandplay therapist, they are often startled to encounter hundreds of miniatures and small objects arranged and categorized by type on open shelves. Major categories are:

- *People*—adults and children of many nationalities, races, and religions in various walks of life, as well as heroes and villains.
- *Fantasy figures*—folklore, monster, witch, fairy, demon, and common cartoon figures.
- *Animals*—wild and domestic, including fish and birds.
- *Vegetation*—trees, bushes, hedges, grass, and flowers.
- *Buildings and other constructions*—houses, churches, schools, hospitals, castles, and tepees, as well as fences, bridges, and gates.
- *Vehicles*—road, rail, sea, air, and outer space, as well as construction and helper transport.
- *Universal symbols*—sun, moon, stars, mirrors, shapes, and religious symbols.
- *Miscellaneous items*—street signs, furniture, implements, and weapons.
- *Multipurpose materials*—string, marbles, driftwood, mosaics, candles, shells, rocks, pods, feathers, and paper.

Amatruda and Simpson (1997) give special attention to including symbolic representations of basic elements, such as earth (e.g., caves, bulldozers, miniature shovels, miners), water (e.g., boats, divers, sea life, shells), fire (e.g., candles, stoves, firefighters), and air (e.g., windmills, pilots, birds in flight, feathers).

A wide range of items from which to choose is especially important when working with adults. The scale of miniatures should be about the same (approximately one to six inches in height for standing human figures); too large a variety of sizes may seem confusing to clients. Furthermore, large figures call too much attention to themselves, while small ones tend to get overlooked. However, a wonderful and appealing figure should not be excluded if it comes into the therapist's hands; a client may want to use a large miniature, for example, to make a strong statement, or use a small miniature to suggest a newly emerging state. Clients have a phenomenal ability to integrate whatever proportions are available. For example, if only a large miniature or a relatively unimportant figure is available, it is usually placed to one side, while important small miniatures are placed in the center of the tray.

Sometimes Sandplay therapists fall into the trap of trying to acquire the "perfect" collection. Although it is important to have representative miniatures from the categories previously listed, the quantity and quality of the collection are only two factors that facilitate healing. Given a "free and protected space," the psyche can be trusted to find its own way with a less than perfect collection.

Understanding the symbolic meaning of the selected miniatures and what is happening in the tray can be gleaned from books, lectures, workshops, and other personal and educational experiences that add richness to your symbolic literacy.

Displaying Miniatures

If miniatures and objects are displayed on shelves and arranged in "family" groupings, such as ordinary people clustered together, groups of wild animals, groups of domestic animals, and groups of religious figures, clients can easily scan the groups and identify which particular miniatures hold a magnetic draw for them.

It is important that the miniatures remain consistently located, not only on the shelves, but also in the client's mind. When clients leave the session, they often think about the miniatures and make imaginary sand trays in their minds. Finding the same objects on the same shelves provides a constant and dependable environment that helps build the belief that your internal process can also be present, constant, and dependable. However, good Sandplay work can also be done by therapists who do not have a permanent setup and move between locations, taking their equipment with them.

Even though there are difficulties involved with a mobile Sandplay setup, many therapists feel it is worth the time and trouble. Pet and building supply stores may carry plastic trays of approximately the correct sand tray size, which then can be painted blue on the inside. Although heavy to carry, sand is a critical part of the process and far more preferable to grains (e.g., corn or rice) or other lighter-weight granular materials. The task can be minimized by carrying only enough sand to cover the bottom of the tray completely. A basic collection of miniatures and objects can be transported in a fishing tackle box or lightweight bags with handles and displayed on whatever surfaces are available.

Preparation of Therapist

The most important aspect of using this technique is the preparation and personal development of the individual therapist. Estelle Weinrib (1983) speaks of the naïveté of some therapists who consider the addition of a sand tray to their practice:

It would be an unfortunate misunderstanding to believe all one needs is a tray with some sand, a collection of small objects, and a dictionary of symbols. Just companioning a patient while he makes pictures will not accomplish much, nor will interpreting pictures as though they were dreams. (p. 29)

Becoming an effective Sandplay therapist is an engaging and circuitous process that requires the ability to receive, facilitate, and understand the profound experiences and imagery that this medium can evoke. Comprehensive clinical training, involvement in your own personal therapy, and experience as a practicing therapist are all important. It is recommended that therapists interested in Sandplay training read and take courses in Sandplay, Jungian theory, and symbolism, and complete their own Sandplay series to enhance understanding of the therapeutic process as it unfolds in this particular medium; a Sandplay consultation group experience can be helpful. To the extent that therapists have experienced and found meaning in their own Sandplay journeys, they will be able to grasp the meaning and implications of their clients' sand trays.

THE SANDPLAY PROCESS: WHAT YOU'LL NEED TO KNOW

Although the Sandplay process may appear to be straightforward, and even simple, the complexities of the approach soon become apparent. Most important is the presence of a therapist who values the healing powers of the unconscious and is able to provide a safe space for the client. The enticing invitation, "Would you like to make a picture in the sand?" is most often followed by questions from the client and explanations from the therapist. With an affirmative response, the therapist asks the client to begin by touching the sand and then surveying and selecting miniatures. These small objects find their own unique places in the sand, eventually creating a finished scene. At the conclusion, the client may make comments about the scene; however, interpretations by the therapist are not given at this time. After the client leaves, the therapist photographs the scene; these pictures are stored, awaiting the completion of the client's Sandplay process (i.e., multiple scenes that seem to come to a resting place). Sometime later, the client and therapist may view the photographs and reflect on and decipher the content of the trays and the process itself.

Role of the Therapist

The role of the Sandplay therapist is to establish a free and protected space in which the client can relax and let his or her internal state be accessed and expressed. This free and protected experience is similar in feeling to what Winnicott

(1965) describes as "being alone in the presence of the mother." In the Sandplay session, the client can trust enough to allow connection with and express his or her inner world, eventually leading to contact with the inner self (i.e., the ground of a person's own being).

Similar to the "good enough" mother, who is present and accepting but not intrusive, most Sandplay therapists sit at the client's side and a little behind, hardly seen (except out of the corner of the eye), yet whose presence is essential. This procedure helps to establish trust and rapport beyond verbal interaction, including an unconscious connection between client and therapist. When this space can be provided, the client can truly relax and access his or her imagination, so that the internal world can be safely experienced.

Introducing Adult Clients to Sandplay

Over time and with experience, Sandplay therapists evolve their own personal style of introduction. However, most Sandplay therapists agree on three basic principles:

- The introduction should communicate a respect for the Sandplay process and its ability to access the healing powers of the unconscious. The therapist conveys this respect either verbally, through the initial explanation, or nonverbally by his or her ability to contain and hold this experience as it unfolds.
- Therapists using Sandplay attempt to convey an open and nonjudgmental attitude, implying that whatever emerges in the tray is appropriate and acceptable—that there is no right or wrong way of doing Sandplay.
- Sandplay therapists convey, either verbally or nonverbally, that specific suggestions for Sandplay themes do not come from the therapist. The therapist is nondirective; clients may create any type of picture in the sand.

Adults often need encouragement to begin Sandplay, for they experience uncomfortable feelings when thinking about playing in the sand and are often fearful of what will be unexpectedly revealed in their trays. Adults who are dedicated to focused, cognitive approaches in their own lives may be particularly reticent, and may even denigrate this type of nonverbal process.

Introducing the tray to adults involves listening to their concerns while observing their nonverbal communication. Encouraging the creative imagination to become a partner in the process often helps the adult client bridge his or her initial discomfort so that he or she more freely participates in the Sandplay. Conveying to the client that Sandplay is an opportunity to access otherwise inaccessible parts of himself or herself that communicate something that cannot be expressed in words can be intriguing and often helps overcome reluctance.

Many Sandplay therapists do not immediately suggest Sandplay to adult clients. Instead, they first use traditional talk therapy, establish a strong therapeutic relationship, and wait until the time is right. Typically, the right time arrives when a client feels stuck, needs a deeper or creative experience, needs to know or understand something in a different way, needs to access early wounding experiences, or is particularly interested in connecting to the unconscious. Then the Sandplay therapist might suggest that the adult client make a sand picture by simply saying that Sandplay provides an opportunity to move to a deeper level of understanding.

If the client agrees to try this new activity, the therapist invites him or her to touch and move the sand (to become grounded). At this point, the sand acts as a magnet; and before clients realize it, their hands are autonomously sifting the sand, making tunnels, shaping mountains, runways, and riverbeds. It is then suggested that the client leisurely look over the shelves of miniatures, and select those figures that capture his or her attention and seem to be asking to be placed in the sand tray.

Accompanying the Sandplayer

During the Sandplay, therapists most often take process notes and draw a rough sketch of the finished tray, with any changes noted. When taking notes, the therapist needs to remain attuned to the Sandplayer's verbal and nonverbal communications, as well as his or her own feelings during the session. Process notes typically include the following:

- The type of tray the client chooses (the wet or dry).
- The manner in which the sand is touched and/or sculpted.
- If water is added; how the miniatures are examined, selected, or not selected.
- The order in which the miniatures are selected and placed in the tray (particularly, first and last miniatures).
- The location of miniatures in the tray.
- Changes made.
- Client's comments.
- Therapist's impressions and feeling reactions.
- Dialogue that occurs.

During the making of a sand picture, little verbal exchange happens between client and therapist, other than the occasional comment about a miniature or a feeling generated by making the scene in the sand. The therapist may offer help in finding a particular miniature but normally acts as a silent witness, observing and recording the process, until a recognizable point occurs and the Sandplay process comes to a resting place. The client often announces that he or she has finished.

After a sand picture has been created, the therapist may inquire about the client's feelings in making the tray or personal responses to the tray itself. Sometimes the client is asked if the sand picture has a name; other times the therapist might observe the placement of a miniature (e.g., "Oh, I notice the cowboy is pointing at the tiger"). Either before the client leaves or immediately after, the therapist photographs the tray and disassembles it out of the client's view.

The therapist does not interpret the tray to the client, nor does he or she suggest that the picture be changed in any way. Sandplay therapists believe that the Sandplay picture is a "snapshot" of the psyche and/or unconscious. Just making the Sandplay picture itself is therapeutic; verbal interpretation at the time is unnecessary. Giving directions or asking what is going to happen next in the tray directs the process, takes the experience out of the moment, emphasizes the performance aspect, and puts the therapist in the driver's seat—rather than letting the psyche freely move in its own individual direction.

It is essential that the Sandplay process and the therapist are allied with and supportive of the healing energies of the Self, rather than the ego desires of the therapist or client. When the therapist moves into the cognitive realm too quickly by verbally analyzing the tray or giving directions to the client to move miniatures or create or amplify a particular scene, these are ego-driven activities that interfere with the client's internal process. These kinds of directions occur in response to the therapist's anxiety that a miniature (representing an aspect of the client's psyche) is in jeopardy, discomfort with shadow material, or fear of the unknown. When the therapist does not trust the process and instead imposes his or her need to bypass difficult issues in favor of a momentarily cheerful resolution, the client's natural internal process is at risk of being compromised.

To facilitate the deepest transformation, the therapist must be willing to witness the perilous aspect of the client's journey, the "dark night of the soul," and assist emerging healing energies as well as support the client's endurance in meeting this challenge. True healing comes from within. It cannot be bestowed or imposed from without. Each individual's psyche is undergoing its own process of change.

In working with adults, there are moments in the *verbal* process when it may be therapeutically advisable to draw parallels between current life issues and the client's Sandplay creations. For example, a therapist may remark as the client is discussing a specific problem, "That reminds me of the witch you placed in your last Sandplay tray." Threading the verbal and nonverbal together at the right moment can promote further understanding. Sensitively judging the right time to make this type of observation while not hindering the client's nonverbal, unconscious process is the art of Sandplay therapy with adults.

Reflection on a Series of Trays

Additional steps can deepen the Sandplay experience for adults. At the conclusion of a Sandplay process (i.e., a series of trays), therapists often review all Sandplay trays with the client. Most adults are quite interested in viewing and reflecting on their work, and they benefit from moving this unconscious material to the conscious realm.

Timing of the review is important. Client and therapist must both feel ready to view the trays. Some therapists feel that pictures of the trays should not be viewed until years after therapy has ended (Bradway, 1994), because moving too quickly into an interpretive, cognitive realm may hinder the gradual unfolding of awareness and understanding of unconscious material that continues after therapy has ended. Other therapists do not wait as long, judging that some clients are ready to integrate unconscious material more quickly and that a timely review promotes increased consciousness and ego strength.

Clients are often deeply affected by viewing their Sandplay series. Some cry when seeing their inner struggles portrayed and convey relief that they no longer feel enslaved by these old struggles. Others, moved by the creativity emanating from their unconscious, express delight and surprise. At some point during the viewing, almost everyone laughs at the way the unconscious portrayed his or her drama. Some therapists and clients find value in reviewing a series of scenes more than once, perhaps several times, each time yielding new insights.

Adult Clients Most Likely to Benefit from Sandplay

Sandplay therapy is most effective with those clients who are open to using a nonverbal technique to explore personal aspects that may be unknown or obstructing their development. Many of these clients, seeking increased insight and meaning, need to heal early wounds that continue to derail their full functioning as adults. Clients who have difficulty expressing themselves verbally, because they feel blocked or inarticulate about their deep feelings, are often open to, and grateful for, the increased "vocabulary" Sandplay affords them. Sandplay also works well when cultural differences need to be bridged, especially when the client's primary language is different from that of the therapist.

Several Sandplay therapists have discussed the types of clients most likely to benefit from Sandplay therapy. For example, both Weinrib (1989) and Ammann (1991) identified similar types of clients: (a) those who have sustained a preverbal injury, often because of a disturbance in the primary relationship with the mother or mother-figures, which made it impossible for them to grow up with a healthy trust in the world or in their own life process; and (b) those who have a fundamentally healthy and stable ego but whose worldview is too narrow and one-sided. Perhaps they lack a clear sense of identify or feel restless or depressed, sensing that an expansion of consciousness is necessary. Confronting these issues and encountering the authentic self in the sand tray disrupts old patterns and creates movement toward psychic development and individuation.

Although these two types of clients can benefit from Sandplay, we have found that not all clients who have these needs respond to Sandplay therapy. Additional characteristics are helpful, including:

- Openness to the creative unconscious.
- Genuine interest in change.
- Courage to withstand the pain and discomfort demanded in going beyond the *persona* or social mask.
- Willingness to take psychological risks to achieve another level of development.
- Curiosity about verbally inexpressible life issues such as death, dying, abuse, trauma.
- Inclusive attitude toward dreams, spontaneous inner images, and synchronistic happenings.
- The capacity to think metaphorically.
- Recognition of the existence of another dimension of reality beyond ego consciousness.

Adult Clients Least Likely to Benefit from Sandplay

Questions a therapist might think about when considering Sandplay therapy with a particular client are:

- Is Sandplay an optimum technique for this client?
- Are severely emotionally disturbed clients candidates for Sandplay?
- Is the client overreacting to the miniature display?
- Does the content of the tray contraindicate its use?
- Is Sandplay being used as an escape mechanism?

Is Sandplay an Optimum Technique for This Client?

Creating a free and protected space is basic to the climate of this therapeutic method; therefore, Sandplay should not be used with clients who seem uncomfortable with this technique. Clients communicate discomfort one way or another, through words or body language. This discomfort may be very subtle, perhaps displayed in an almost imperceptible movement away from the tray and/or the miniatures. Other times, the resistance may be clear and open, not at all subtle, with a refusal to even touch the sand. Such resistance can suggest that the client is not prepared to grapple with tensions, problems, and inner conflicts that may emerge when using this technique. Ultimately, the therapist has to trust the client about proceeding; Sandplay should never be encouraged with adults who resist its use.

Sandplay seems to be most difficult for those clients whose belief system does not include a valuing of the unconscious, noncognitive mind. These individuals often do not appreciate the imagination, are quite concrete or literal-minded, and have an excessively mental attitude toward life and themselves. The Sandplay materials may seem childish and unrealistic to them. They may even denigrate this approach. Accessing the symbolic world through a visual-tactile mode of expression is not appealing to them, and they may be unable to move beyond a literal level of awareness.

Are Severely Emotionally Disturbed Clients Candidates for Sandplay?

There has been an ongoing discussion regarding the usefulness of Sandplay with severely disturbed clients, such as those diagnosed with schizophrenia, clinical depression, or borderline characteristics (Miller, 1979, p. 157). Some therapists are concerned that providing an array of symbols might reinforce the client's chaotic and confused inner view of the world, rather than helping the client sort options and deal with practical issues in the everyday world. However, another view, expressed by Perry (1973), contends that expressing inner chaotic, negative energy is an important step in finding and activating natural and internal healing powers.

In examining this issue, Betsy Caprio (1989), art therapist and cofounder of the Center for Sacred Psychology in Los Angeles, studied the initial sand trays of 50 adult residents in a short-term psychiatric facility and found no evidence that would contraindicate the use of the sand tray with *stabilized* depressed and schizophrenic patients. In fact, just the opposite seemed to be true: These patients appreciated the color, variety, and creativity brought into their lives by their involvement in using sand tray equipment, and they did not become more disorganized or chaotic in their thinking.

Caprio's most striking finding was the absence of extraordinarily bizarre imagery in the sand trays of this group of hospitalized patients. Many of the sand trays contained few elements that depicted illness or the hospital. Instead, the trays gave clues for the direction of further treatment when they revealed the following:

- Traumatic experiences that had not been expressed verbally.
- Developmental arrests, which gave therapists indications of where reparative work might begin.
- Specific areas of strength.

Although Caprio found no negative effects from the use of sand trays with these patients, the selection process did eliminate patients who were too distraught or violent to attend this activity. In addition, these hospitalized patients had more containment than those in out-patient settings. Some therapists have noted that miniatures and Sandplay equipment could become dangerous objects when used by aggressive patients. Therefore, until further researched, no conclusion can be reached about the use of sand trays and miniatures with extremely disturbed patients.

Is the Client Overreacting to the Miniature Display?

Once in a while, a client may appear to be overwhelmed by the array of figures on the shelves. A client may either speak about this feeling by saying that it seems too much to take in ("I can't focus on anything") or simply be unable to proceed in the activity. This reaction suggests that too much of the unconscious realm has been stimulated. In this case, the therapist would note the indecision, elicit the client's feelings, and attempt to dialogue about these. Through this intervention, the client's feeling of being flooded by unconscious material would either subside and the Sandplay activity would proceed, or a decision would be made together that this session was not an optimum time to create sand pictures.

Does the Content of the Tray Contraindicate Its Use?

The content of the tray may alert the therapist to the possibility that the client is feeling overwhelmed by this activity. Although it seldom happens, Sandplay can activate the unconscious in certain individuals to such an extent that it may be wise to stop.

Is Sandplay Being Used as an Escape Mechanism?

A very few adults use Sandplay as an avoidance or escape mechanism to use up the time and avoid having to deal with the reality of a face-to-face relationship with the therapist. In this situation, it is important that the therapist note the client's reluctance and perhaps gently express this observation to the client, saying something like "I have noticed that you are so involved in Sandplay that there is little time for a face-to-face dialogue." From this comment, a discussion might ensue that brings light to the client's reluctance to talk with the therapist.

The bottom line is: Therapists must trust their own intuitive clinical sense about whether the situation is becoming destructive and overwhelming or an important process is unfolding. When in doubt, the therapist should immediately elicit the client's feelings about participating in Sandplay as well as voice his or her concerns as the therapist. Ideally, the decision to continue or stop Sandplay is a mutual one.

UNDERSTANDING SANDPLAY PICTURES: FINDING MEANING FROM IT ALL

The sand tray can be viewed and considered from a number of different theoretical perspectives. However, most Sandplay therapists consider the following:

- *Client's personal information.* The client's age, gender, socioeconomic status, racial and/or ethnic group, spiritual beliefs, motivation for creating a tray, and other demographic information can be helpful in understanding the trays.
- *Creation of sand picture.* To have a full understanding of a sand picture, it is important to be aware of the client's process in creating the tray; for example, is it created quickly or slowly, with a great deal of thought or spontaneously, with fear or excitement.
- *Content of the tray.* The tray's content should be carefully followed and recorded (either through photographs and/or sketches), noting objects used and their symbolic meaning; placement of miniatures and position changes; movement of sand; and overall organization and content of the sand picture, including themes, stages, and phases, particularly those in an initial tray.
- *Sandplay series.* It is important to notice how clients' sand pictures evolve over time, including what symbols are used regularly and how their location in the tray has changed, how the themes have developed and changed, and variations in the organization of the scenes.
- *Sandplay story.* Some clients tell a story about the sand picture; others are stimulated by the picture and recall past or present events and feelings. Listening carefully to the symbolic content, emotional overtones, themes, and story resolution of the Sandplay story gives further insight into the client's internal process.
- *Therapist's feeling response.* When the therapist can listen to his or her own feeling response and be aware of spontaneous images, a deeper understanding of the client's process and the sand creation itself can emerge.

Keeping these considerations in mind will help in understanding Sandplay scenes of your clients; however, sand pictures can still be quite perplexing. We hope that the next sections bring clarity to your work with adults and expand your understanding of their creations. Even with increased insight, it is important to remember that much of the unconscious *is* and *will continue to be* a mystery.

Initial Trays

All Sandplay expressions are important; however, the initial scene is usually especially important. Perhaps it could be likened to a topic sentence in a paragraph where the overall theme of the unfolding drama is stated. Gloria Avrech (1997), a Jungian analyst in the Los Angeles Sandplay Society, says that an initial sand tray scene is a reflection of the Sandplayer's psyche, similar to a mirror reflecting an energy that comes from the client's deepest self. In creating an initial tray, the Sandplayer might be saying, without realizing it, "Here is a possible place for my personal myth. Here is some of what I struggle with, some of what is easy for me, some of what is hard. Here is what has happened to me and what I might become" (p. 53).

Initial trays have also been likened to initial dreams. Initial dreams are the first dreams that clients report to therapists. These dreams and initial trays are generally understood to result from similar psychological processes. However, there are significant differences; principally, an awake, conscious ego is involved in the Sandplay process (as in all forms of active imagination), whereas that is not the case in dreams. Indeed, a common problem in the Sandplay process is that the client might be *too* awake, rational, and analytical. The therapist using Sandplay should try to reduce the impact of the client's conscious ego by advising the client to relax his or her mind and body and to refrain from planning a sand tray scene in advance, unless there is a specific reason for doing so.

The first sand picture that a client creates may not be his or her *initial tray*. Estelle Weinrib (1983) warns that a first tray may be just pretty, but that the second tray may authentically connect to the unconscious. There is some controversy among practitioners concerning what qualifies as an initial tray; no clear-cut definition has appeared in the literature. The therapist must use intuition, knowledge, and judgment to decide if a tray qualifies as an initial one. However, if a client uses his or her rational mind to consciously select figures for the purpose of representing specific events or personal characteristics that the client wants the therapist to note (sometimes called a *persona* tray), this would not qualify as an initial tray. Should this occur, the wise therapist accepts what the client offers and waits for another tray. In our experience, deliberate, conscious trays continue for only a short time. Usually with the second tray, the descent into the deeper realm of the psyche begins. It seems that if a client has a good enough connection with the therapist and feels a sense of containment and safety in the therapeutic relationship, it is then possible to be at ease and let the unconscious speak in the sand.

According to Dora Kalff (1988), an initial tray can indicate:

- The client's personal problem.
- A possible solution.
- His or her relation to the unconscious.
- How the client feels about therapy.

She particularly emphasized the importance of including the therapist's initial feeling response to a tray in coming to an understanding of what is being communicated by the client. She advised therapists to identify the feelings activated as the first step when viewing any tray.

In addition to recognizing her own feelings, Friedman (1986) often asks herself these questions when viewing an initial tray:

- Where are the energy spots?
- Where are the trouble spots?
- What kinds of groupings are apparent?
- What types of problems are indicated in the tray?
- Where are the sources of strength or help in the tray?

In the case of Anna that follows, we discuss her initial tray in some detail to demonstrate how a therapist might approach and understand this important tray.

Symbolism

As in all kinds of play, the symbolic process in Sandplay is as natural as breathing and can act as a bridge into the psychic realm. Play, which taps into creativity and imagination, releases instinctive energy and leads naturally to the use of symbols. Words, themselves, are symbols, but it is easy to become enmeshed in and constrained by words, perhaps believing that words are the only way to communicate, and thereby failing to make use of other symbols. Using a variety of symbols is necessary to express feelings, gain a larger perspective, and connect to the inner world—which leads to the healing experience.

Two general categories of symbols emerging in psychological work are: Individuation and Transformation. The first category relates to the individuation process, and includes symbols of such motifs as the Great Mother, the Child, the Wise Old Man, the Hero, the Shadow, the Maiden, and the Anima (in a male) or Animus (in a female). The second category is comprised of uniting symbols that represent the instinctual guiding center of the Self; the Mandala, the Circle, the Diamond, the Squared Circle, and the Sphere are a few of the forms that represent this psychic center.

Symbols, represented by miniatures in the Sandplay process, can be used as tools of expression that enable clients to reveal unconscious aspects and subtleties of their inner thoughts and feelings that speech and gestures may fail to communicate. Because symbols connect clients to unknown aspects of themselves, they can also carry the potential for transformation and healing. Winnicott (1971) believed that symbols help access inner psychic reality. He saw them as transcending "external world phenomena and the phenomena of the individual person who is being looked at" (p. 168).

Symbols are portrayals of psychic reality "expressed in unique and individual terms while, at the same time, partaking of a universal imagery" (Samuels, 1986, p. 146). A symbol points to something so deep and complex that it cannot be reduced to a simple verbal concept; its totality is beyond conscious grasp. Symbols are numinous indicators of a client's values and worldview. "Symbols speak for the inner, energy-laden pictures of the innate potentials of the human being" (Kalff, 1980, p. 29). Although the ultimate meaning of a symbol can be inferred and intuited only within limits, symbols can reintroduce individuals to unknown aspects of the self and help them reconnect with unconscious parts of themselves. Symbols carry the potential for transformation and healing precisely because they cannot be reduced to concepts that are easily verbalized, categorized, and understood.

No conscious understanding of symbols on the part of the client is needed in Sandplay. The symbol points to some perception, understanding, or process that is beyond conscious comprehension. It does not matter whether the meaning of the symbol is understood by the conscious mind. It is more a matter of inner intuitive knowledge.

Creating a safe and protected space that intentionally encourages and supports clients in using and experiencing symbols can have at least two significant benefits. First, connecting with symbols that have personal significance for a client helps to generate insights, transformation, and eventual healing. Second, understanding the meaning of the symbols represented in the miniatures and Sandplay scenes can help a therapist understand what the client is communicating both consciously and unconsciously, which enables the therapist to be of greater help to the client.

Jung (CW V.13, paragraph 36) stated that symbols arise spontaneously from two sources: the unconscious (which instinctively produces symbols) and a person's own experience. Both of these sources are important when viewing Sandplay scenes. The therapist needs to give his or her initial attention to what the symbol in the Sandplay means personally to the client and not jump to generalizations about a particular symbol. To discover what may lie at the deeper levels in an individual's psyche, the meaning of a symbol must be understood in terms of the individual's own private symbolic language. Building on the client's personal associations, a symbol can later be amplified by looking into mythological, religious, and folk tale representations of similar material. Making connections to myth, history, fantasy, imagination, drama, and poetry can be a part of giving meaning and depth to the process.

If the therapist is able to maintain a metaphorical attitude when following the symbolic process, the client's issues, strengths, and the direction of the healing process can emerge with more clarity. It is most helpful when the therapist has gained a broad understanding of the language of the unconscious and is able to follow the process and help the client establish connections to his or her external life situation.

In actual practice, the therapist's knowledge of a miniature or symbol is not shared with a client before his or her Sandplay process has been completed. Moving the experience into the cognitive realm peremptorily may interfere with the intuitive and instinctual processes that activate healing energies. At times, adult clients do spontaneously share their associations or ideas about a particular miniature. This is important information; most Sandplay therapists would include such a client's comment in their notes to consider both at that point in therapy and also later when preparing for review sessions after the Sandplay process had been completed.

Themes in Sandplay Scenes

Because the symbolic language of the unconscious is baffling at times, therapists may feel frustrated and confused when they attempt to decipher Sandplay pictures. To better understand Sandplay scenes, some years ago we began to study the Sandplay journeys of our clients to determine if we could identify patterns or themes in their work. A *Sandplay theme* is defined as a principal visual image or set of images in a Sandplay picture. We decided to emphasize the thematic approach because our observations could be supported by research, and also because it is an organic, nondiagnostic method that is congruent with the nonintrusive process of Sandplay.

We have identified several themes (listed in Table 9.1) that clustered naturally into one of two groups: (a) themes of wounding, and (b) themes of healing or transformation. Themes of wounding appeared most often in the first Sandplay pictures of clients who were suffering from the effects of abuse, trauma, illness, loss, or death of a family member in their early development. Themes of positive transformation or healing were more prominent in early trays of clients who had either grown up in healthy, less traumatic environments, or were in the latter phases of

Table 9.1   Sandplay Themes Expressed in the Healing Process

Themes that suggest wounding:

1. Chaotic	Haphazard, fragmented, or formless arrangement (e.g., objects flung into the tray, boundaries or outer reality disregarded, items carefully placed but overall appearance is jumbled).
2. Empty	Reticence to use figures or lifeless feeling with lack of energy and curiosity (e.g., a nearly empty tray with only a dead tree placed in a corner).
3. Split	Barricades that isolate, entrap, or cage figures or groups (e.g., elephants placed end to end from the bottom to the top of the tray separate a small child from his mother, a man holding a baby is placed in a cage).
4. Threatened	Predominant or frightening material with little ego development to meet the experience (e.g., aggressive animals surrounding an unprotected child).
5 Wounded.	Figures with injuries or in the process of being injured (e.g., a bandaged man lying on a stretcher, a cowboy placed in the mouth of a dinosaur).
6. Concealed	Figures buried or hidden from view (e.g., a gun hidden behind a house, a witch buried in the sand under a tree).
7. Prone	Figures that are normally upright are intentionally placed in a reclining, fallen position (e.g., a standing figure of a pregnant woman placed face down in the sand).
8. Overwhelmed	Old problems that appear so large and powerful that they hinder possibilities of new growth (e.g., a boat moving into new water is under siege by a large army).

Themes that suggest movement towards healing and transformation:

1. Journeying	Movement along a path or around a center (e.g., a knight follows a trail, a Native American paddles a canoe down a stream).
2. Bridging	Connection between elements, joining of opposites (e.g., a ladder joins earth and tall trees, a bridge links an angel and devil).
3. Energetic	Alive, vital, intense energy is visible (e.g., organic growth present, construction machines work on a task, airplanes take off from a runway).
4. Going Deeper	Discovery of a deeper dimension (e.g., a clearing is made, a treasure unearthed, a well dug, a lake explored).
5. Birthing	Emergence of new development (e.g., a baby is born, a flower opens, a bird incubates eggs).
6. Nurturing[a]	Nourishment or help are provided to support growth and development (e.g., a mother feeding babies, supportive family groups, nurse helps a patient, presence of food).

Table 9.1   (*Continued*)

7. Spiritual[b]	Sacred elements as present, such as a supernatural beings or sacred objects.
8. Reconstructing	Sand and/or objects are creatively changed or used (e.g., sand is contoured to build a land bridge, sand is moved and stacked as an essential part of a lunar compound, a house is built from twigs picked up on client's walk to school).
9. Centered	In center of tray, elements are aesthetically balanced or a union of opposites occurs (e.g., a man and woman married, mandala centered in the tray).
10. Integrated	Congruent, organized idea encompasses entire tray; unity of expression (e.g., day at the zoo, baseball game, abstract construction unifying the whole tray).

[a] Suggested by Barbara Weller, Lauren Cunningham.
[b] Suggested by by Barbara Weller, Lauren Cunningham, Gretchen Hegeman.
Note: Not to be used or copied without permission from Rie Rogers Mitchell or Harriet S. Friedman.

therapy and were moving in the direction of healing and health. For all clients, we found that trays usually contained more themes of wounding early in therapy; as therapy progressed, themes of healing and wholeness took a central place.

Tracking the evolution of Sandplay themes over time (a) gave us clues about how the unconscious expressed itself in the Sandplay journey, and (b) helped us understand how the therapeutic work, both verbal and nonverbal, was progressing. We also found that Sandplay themes changed and developed over time. Sometimes they were amplified. For example, in an early tray, a bridging theme might be expressed by placing a bridge in the back of a tray with the ends connecting to bare ground. In a later tray, the same client might use four bridges to connect verdant lands; one of these bridges might also join the opposites, for example, a male magician and a female enchantress, who are placed at each end of the bridge. We also discovered that themes diminished or were abbreviated at times. For example, in an initial tray, the wounded theme might be expressed by a bandaged man in a life raft placed in the center of the tray amidst an opposing army. In a later tray, the bandaged man might be in a hospital bed, placed off to one side of the tray.

Some themes are likely to be present throughout a client's entire series of trays. For example, it is somewhat common for the energetic theme to be present in multiple trays with miniatures portraying work machines and/or organic growth. Other themes may be dramatically expressed and then never reappear. For example, an old woman buried beneath a rock might express the concealment theme; this theme may never appear again.

Watching themes unfold in Sandplay is much like listening through a stethoscope to monitor a patient's heartbeat. As therapists view the progression of these themes in the Sandplay scenes of their clients, they will begin to gain a sense about what is happening in the core or center of the client's psyche. We have found that these themes assist us in clarifying the Sandplay process and help us understand the language and movement of the client's unconscious, as well as gauge how the client is responding to treatment.

Key Distinctions between Adult and Child Sandplay

While some therapists recognize that using Sandplay with adults is different from its use with children (Friedman & Mitchell, 2001), others report few differences in their approach. In a 1979 workshop, Kalff (as cited in Miller, 1979) said that she did not distinguish between adults and children in her use of Sandplay; in her perception, the underlying psychodynamic principles and process were the same, so she made no adjustments in the procedure. Other therapists report that adults use Sandplay less frequently than children and that they (the therapists) engage in more "introducing, explaining, directing, questioning, associating, interpreting, and integrating" when working with adults (Miller, 1979, p. 136).

Certainly adults are psychologically and physiologically more mature, sophisticated, and able to participate more consciously in their own treatments; yet they are also more rigid and stuck, and less adaptable, except with concentrated effort over long periods of time. Children are usually more resilient, spontaneous, and plastic, gravitating to the sand more easily than adults and having the ability to change over a briefer period of time.

Although adults are typically less active, playful, and spontaneous than children, the number of adults who use Sandplay is still substantial. In an international survey of therapists who use Sandplay, Friedman and Mitchell (2001) found that most of their adult clients created at least one sand scene. Internationally certified Sandplay therapists indicated that 80% to 90% of their adult clients used Sandplay at least once, while 60% of adult clients of noncertified therapists used Sandplay. Twenty years earlier, Miller (1979) conducted a similar survey; however, he found that only 45% of adult clients treated by Sandplay therapists made a sand picture. This increasing use of Sandplay by adults may be due to greater awareness and acceptance of nonverbal approaches; certainly the field of psychotherapy has become more inclusive of *feeling* and *doing* rather than just *thinking* and *saying* over the past twenty years. Overall, more children participate in Sandplay than adults. However, because certified Sandplay therapists work more with adults than children, naturally a larger number of their adult clients create Sandplays than child clients.

Because Sandplay is an adjunctive therapeutic technique, the amount of time spent doing it varies tremendously; sand pictures are not necessarily created at every session. A few adult clients use Sandplay regularly, especially those who are therapists themselves and want to experience their own Sandplay process to use this medium effectively with clients. Nevertheless, a larger number of adult clients use Sandplay only occasionally. Sometimes weeks and even months (more rarely) go by between the making of individual sand pictures. In 1982, Miller found that trays were made by clients in approximately 38% of the sessions, or every three to four therapy sessions, on average. Recently surveyed Sandplay therapists report similar periodic use by their adult clients. But even when only a few sand trays are made over years and viewed periodically, the scenes do not seem at all random; instead, they appear to be part of a continuous therapeutic process (Friedman & Mitchell, 2001). During periods when scenes are not made, therapy proceeds as usual and includes talking about everyday problems and their relationship to early wounding experiences and developing insight into interpersonal relations, dreams, and life issues, as well as participating in other play and expressive arts therapies.

Adult sand creations are usually unlike those of children. Adults tend to use a greater area of the tray, boundaries are more clearly defined, aggressive feelings are depicted symbolically rather than acted out, and verbal comments are made rather than moving or throwing figures. To express issues of control, adults use topographical features such as mountains and streams to unify scenes rather than fences or other literal structures of control, as do children (Bowyer, 1959). When adult trays deviate from these broad norms and seem more childlike, it may be an indication that the client experienced trauma during childhood.

The constructive use of sand (i.e., moving sand to make roads, waterways, and paths) seems to depend more on individual personality traits than on age. Bowyer (1959) found that the movement of sand by individuals over seven years old indicates an ability to use inner resources creatively to enlarge or restructure the tray and, symbolically, a person's own world.

Transference Issues in the Tray

Kalff did not refer to transference in the classical sense of clients' recreating impulses and feelings with their therapists that they had experienced earlier, usually in their relationships with parental figures. Influenced by both Jung and Lowenfeld, Kalff viewed transference as "the providing of space for the realization of one's potential" (Bradway 1991, p. 25). She believed that the therapist's creation of a "free and protected space" would elicit a positive transference that might, in turn, enhance the constellation of the client's self. Over time, Kalff's views on transference evolved to include the idea that the relationship between client and therapist was sometimes directly expressed in the tray.

Recently, therapists have begun to examine trays more methodically for indications of transference. For example, a client might select a miniature that depicts the client's feelings toward the therapist. In this way, the state of the transference to the therapist is embodied in the picture.

However, little attention has been paid to the many other ways the pictures reflect or address the therapeutic relationship. Based on our observations of adult sand scenes, we have identified the following ways in which transference is typically represented:

- The content of the tray relates directly to the therapist; for example, the client selects a personal item belonging to the therapist, such as a plant or other personal item, to place in the tray.
- The client unconsciously creates a tray in which the content symbolically represents the relationship with the therapist; for example, a woman places a wounded girl on a stretcher with a nurse nearby.
- The client identifies a particular object as the therapist; for example, the client places a miniature of Glinda, the good witch from the *Wizard of Oz,* on the side of the tray, explaining, "This is you [the therapist] overseeing my land."
- The use of Sandplay is either resisted or too easily accommodated.
- The client creates a sand picture that he or she thinks will please (or displease) the therapist.
- The client directly portrays the therapist in the sand; for example, by sculpting the therapist's face.
- The placement of significant figures or the orientation of figures in the tray corresponds to where the therapist is sitting in relation to the tray, perhaps sending an unconscious message to the therapist.
- Two matching miniatures are placed together, perhaps portraying the feeling of identification with the therapist.
- A Sandplay miniature is either openly shared or hidden from the therapist's view.
- The miniatures are treated uniquely; for example, they are destroyed, stolen, envied, and/or valued.
- The therapist's Sandplay equipment—for example, the miniature collection, the quality of sand, the miniature display—is criticized, praised, or compared to another's collection.

The ways in which the client uses miniatures and participates in other aspects of the Sandplay process are underlying clues about his or her relationship to the therapist as well as personal feelings about earlier relationships with significant others.

CASE OF ANNA: PUTTING IT ALL TOGETHER

To illustrate how the healing process unfolds in a clinical case, three selected Sandplay scenes created by "Anna," a middle-aged woman, are discussed in light of the theoretical perspectives described previously. Specifically, we consider:

- Parallels between her background and imagery in the sand.
- Anna's willingness to participate in Sandplay and how this influenced her trays.
- Her approach in creating a sand scene and what that suggested to us.
- Her first tray (based on Kalff and Friedman's observations on initial trays).
- Symbolic content and possible meanings.
- Her use of wounding and healing themes over time.
- Developmental guidelines.
- Anna's comments and stories about her Sandplays.
- Therapist's feeling responses to the trays.
- Transference issues.

Rather than discussing each point separately, however, an overall view of Anna and her process are covered in what we hope is a more organic approach to understanding Anna's work in the sand.

Background Information

Anna (a pseudonym), a middle-aged, married Caucasian woman with five grown children, began therapy because of dissatisfaction with her life as a wife, mother, and secretary. She was experiencing stomach distress because of food allergies that limited her physical functioning and kept her from seeking a more satisfying job commensurate with her abilities and interests, as well as from expressing herself in her usual creative way through art.

Initially, her considerable intelligence was not apparent to me (RRM) because she appeared to be fragile, insecure, and blocked in expressing her thoughts and feelings. She seemed to be in physical pain much of the time and, as I began to know her better, I felt that the pain was an underlying symptom of her emotional distress rather than its cause.

As the work proceeded, I increasingly came to realize that Anna was a bright, insightful, and imaginative woman who had suffered from a background of repression. The fundamentalist religious environment in which she had grown up supported her natural artistic talents only to a point, valuing them to the degree that they could contribute to the church and to her own home later as a mother. Her parents supported this narrow viewpoint by not allowing her to pursue interests in music and art when she entered a religiously affiliated college. She obediently majored in homemaking. Growing up with a compliant nature in such a limiting environment created a lifetime pattern of repressed feelings and submissive responses.

Near the beginning of therapy, Anna hesitantly shared her uncertain memories of occasional sexual abuse by her step-grandfather when she was a visitor in his home from ages 10 to 14 years old. Although she tried to push this out of her mind by telling herself that she was wrong—it hadn't really happened—memories continued to haunt her throughout her adolescence and into adulthood. She never spoke with her parents about the events or her feelings during these years, nor did she receive any recognition from them that something might have happened. Their lack of awareness or possibly their refusal to acknowledge any untoward behavior contributed to her feelings of self-doubt.

Anna selected me as her therapist because she knew, through another client, that I sometimes used Sandplay and other nonverbal, creative techniques in working with children and adults. It was only a short time into treatment before it became clear that she was drawn to working in the sand. She was not at all resistant to this modality, and moved easily, without formal introduction, into creating Sandplays. She clearly enjoyed this nonverbal modality and created 18 sand pictures during the first 11 months of therapy. Sometimes she made a scene every week; other times, one or two scenes a month. After the completion of the 18 scenes, Anna moved from the sand tray into an entirely verbal process for two years and nine months.

Three of Anna's Sandplay scenes are presented here: her first tray, a middle tray, and the final tray (i.e., her 18th tray). These scenes provide a thumbnail sketch of how Sandplay can help promote and activate a healing process in an ongoing, verbal therapeutic relationship. The sand trays also show how key issues are communicated through the pictures and how the scenes serve as a touchstone to indicate how Anna is progressing in treatment.

In addition to Sandplay, I used traditional verbal therapy with an eclectic mix of Rogerian client-centered therapy, Kohutian object relations theory, and Jungian-oriented dream work. At times, Anna was able to visualize symbols that arose spontaneously in her mind's eye, and when explored, related to her situation and offered further insight; therefore, this "Anna-originated" approach was used when the occasion presented itself.

Anna's Initial Tray

In her first tray (see Figure 9.1), Anna immediately descended into the deeper realm of the psyche and communicated important clues; in this way, I knew it was an initial tray rather than a superficial or *persona* tray. Her tray was a hopeful one, while also identifying painful issues. It communicated to me that she was open to using this modality to portray her inner struggles and that she had a strong connection to her unconscious with an easy ability to use symbols and play. The issues she presented were from long ago but were clearly alive now and were the source of her current distress.

When I first looked at her completed tray, I had two immediate responses—I felt overwhelmed and sad. I wondered if these feelings might be similar to Anna's feelings as well. Later I learned that these were, indeed, major feelings she was having about her life situation.

Figure 9.1   Anna's initial tray.

Anna's process in creating a tray began in a traditional manner. At my suggestion, she first touched the sand in the dry and wet trays, remarking that they both "felt good." With her hands resting palms-down in the wet sand, she slowly began to scan the miniatures. Suddenly her gaze seemed riveted, and she immediately reached for the ceramic flames (representing fire) located on a nearby shelf and quickly placed them in a double semicircle formation near the left corner of the wet tray. Pointing to the flames, Anna said, "This is energy, like a screen."

More slowly, Anna chose two additional miniatures—a leopard poised on a branch ready to strike and a wounded man on a stretcher carried by two medics. These she placed in the sand almost simultaneously: the leopard on a small ridge near the center, menacingly overlooking the wounded soldier and medics in the front of the tray. Next, a tombstone was placed in the right corner area and five hearts (one brown, three blue, and one pink) were positioned to create a semicircle in front of the stretcher. Last, Uhura, the communications officer from *Star Trek,* was placed behind the flames, separated from the other items in the tray. Anna identified Uhura as a prisoner. Then Anna stated that she, herself, was both the wounded man (on the stretcher) and the middle blue heart. The other blue hearts were her two sisters: the brown heart, her older brother; and the pink, her younger brother. As she pointed to the tombstone, Anna said, "This is where I am right now; I'm hiding under this." She commented that the leopard was threatening but "this [the leopard] is me, too." As she scanned her picture, she said, "I'm feeling a lot of frustration. This feels really familiar; it's been inside for so long."

In this sand picture, Anna clearly displays her personal drama. Her repressed feelings and issues are hidden away under a tombstone or imprisoned behind an energy screen, where Uhura, the communications officer, is held captive, unable to express herself. Yet there is hope—represented by the first symbol Anna chose and placed in the tray—fire. As an eternal element, fire is a complex symbol that embraces a number of concepts, often coexisting, such as passion, life force, illumination, power, purification, warmth, divine anger, retribution, sacrifice, death, and transformation. However, Anna specifically states that her fire symbol represents *energy.* With this comment, she captures, possibly unknowingly, the critical notion of fire as "the agent of transmutation" (Cirlot, 1962, p. 100). Like water, fire is a symbol of transformation and regeneration, as all things derive from, and return to, fire. As such, fire is often associated with the power and energy of the sun, but it is also an ambiguous symbol because its energy can be found at the level of animal passion as well as the plane of spiritual strength, or equally at the destructive level as well as the life-giving plane (Cirlot, 1962). I wondered to myself if Anna would be able to energize her own resources to bring forth her own transformation and regeneration, or would she use this energy to again screen and repress issues and feelings?

As I viewed her tray further, I was drawn to the battle-scarred man on the stretcher, representing the early wounding that she has carried and endured for so long. I wondered if the five hearts spoke to a wounded family system as well; they are placed so near to the injured soldier that they appear to be part of the wounding. I remembered that Anna was also the mother of five children (three girls and two boys). I asked myself: Were these hearts her children, as well as her family of origin?

The crouching leopard and the intense fire suggested that Anna's issues urgently needed to be addressed to prevent further threat or injury. In myths, it is the leopard that kills off the protagonist, who is then reborn in a more positive heroic form. Yet, her scene indicated some ambivalence about exploring the immediate issues. Twice in the sand tray, each time both verbally and nonverbally, she expressed this conflict: (1) when she used the tombstone and said that she was hiding under it, and (2) when she created the fire wall and indicated that it was a screen, presumably to inhibit communication (from the communications officer). Her energy was so strong, however—the fire so intense and close—that I was concerned that it could rage out of control and subsume all attempts at communication. Perhaps this was the source of her frustration, that is, wanting to communicate long-repressed feelings and issues, while not being able to or stopping herself from doing so.

In some ways, Anna's tray is reminiscent of a child's tray. She does not use all of the available space, and her aggressive feelings are depicted directly, through the crouching leopard and the raging fire. This supports the possibility of early wounding.

In this first Sandplay, wounding themes outnumber healing themes. Five wounding themes are expressed in the tray:

1. *Emptiness*—the tray appears empty and lifeless.
2. *Splitting*—groups of figures seem isolated from one another, and the tombstone is off to one side.
3. *Threat*—the leopard is about to strike.
4. *Woundedness*—a wounded man is lying on a stretcher.
5. *Concealment*—Anna imagines herself hidden under the tombstone.

Two healing themes are present:

1. *Viable energy*—the fire and leopard.
2. *Nurturance*—two medics carrying the stretcher.

The tombstone implies that something is buried or dead. Was something in Anna seeking death? After I ruled out the possibility of suicide, I wondered if the tombstone represented buried parts of her—repressed talents and feelings of anger and guilt? Or, does it represent her diffused memory of the abuse she suffered? Repression of abilities, feelings, and memories can cause immense rage, depression, and bodily pain. Will Anna be able to emerge from the fire (her rage) and communicate her feelings in therapy? I wondered and waited to see more.

Anna's Ninth Tray

Almost four months after her initial tray, Anna created this scene (see Figure 9.2) with two central mounds, each surrounded by water. My eyes were drawn to a central bridge that connected the mounds and the nearby creatures: standing on the bridge was a small, cartoon-like armadillo/dragon figure; swimming underneath, partially hidden, was a hippopotamus and a huge crocodile; and touching the right end of the bridge is a black spider. Three additional bridges (one covered; two uncovered) spanned water to join the mounds to a landmass that followed the sides of the tray. A black panther (i.e., a leopard in the black color phase) waited on top of the covered bridge poised to strike. Inside the protected bridge, Anna placed a brown heart (similar to the one she had used in her initial

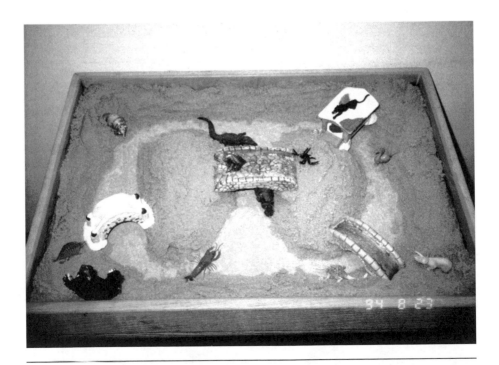

Figure 9.2   Anna's ninth tray.

tray), saying "This is how I feel—I'm this heart—like I'm hiding. Fear, discouragement, confusion, and depression are constant companions. They are major events in the day." Various primitive, somewhat menacing creatures were scattered on the land and in the water: an armadillo (in the left top corner), a green dragon (in the right top corner), a voracious bear (in the left bottom corner). I saw these creatures as representing Anna's negative feelings from which she could not free herself.

I had mixed feelings when viewing this tray. First, I focused on the bridges and felt pleased that Anna was attempting to connect and reconcile parts of herself. Then, when I saw the animals she had selected, I felt scared and wondered if Anna's attempts to free herself could stand up to the primitive threats. Finally, I relaxed a little as I realized that Anna's negative feelings were finally being expressed openly. Unconsciously, she is attempting to join these aspects, hoping to transcend her warring opposites (i.e., repressed feelings vs. consciously experienced ones) and unite them with a symbol of reconciliation (the bridge). I knew that if she were able to achieve this reconciliation, a new sense of self would transcend her divided state of self, as represented by the two mounds (Bradway, 1985). I could see how far she had come already, and I felt encouraged, for it seemed that she could trust our relationship enough to display these feelings.

In this tray, there are early indications of Anna's ability to bridge her many dark and destructive impulses and feelings. I was especially hopeful of Anna's use of the dragon/armadillo. The silent armadillo represents boundaries and the shield that protects humanity from all that is undesirable (Cooper, 1992). The fiery dragon is nearly the opposite symbol; a kind of amalgam of various animals that are particularly aggressive and dangerous, the primordial enemy with whom combat is the supreme test. According to Jung (1964), the dragon represents the shadow (i.e., the unconscious negative side of a person's nature) that must be realized and integrated in the process of obtaining the treasures of inner knowledge and self-mastery. The armadillo/dragon figure Anna placed on the central bridge symbolizes a resourceful combination of both sets of attributes, dramatically illustrating her struggle, protective silence versus fiery rage. I wondered if now she might be closer to overcoming her fears and, eventually, obtain the ultimate treasure.

In this tray, three themes of wounding are visible: splitting (e.g., the two mounds), concealment (e.g., the positioning of the heart, crocodile, and hippopotamus), and overwhelm (e.g., aggressive, powerful animals appearing so powerful that they might hinder new growth). Healing themes in the tray are: bridging (multiple bridges) and integration (an organized idea encompassing the entire tray). Fewer wounding themes are contained in this tray than in Anna's initial tray, and the bridges suggest that Anna has already begun her healing journey to overcome her repressive patterns. While she still has much to confront, she is also exposing more than ever before. She is no long hiding in the ground under the tombstone;

now she is even partially exposed under the covered bridge. She needs the courage of the dragon and the protection of the armadillo to continue to encounter her repressed feelings and experiences.

Anna's Final Tray

Six months after her ninth tray, Anna made her 18th and final sand picture (see Figure 9.3). Energetically moving the sand, she created a central island and strategically placed a bridge that permitted full access to the "mainland." Included on the island was a large green tree growing out of a rock, a swan, mermaid, bodhisattva, and monkey. Water surrounded the island, and two rivers extended to the right side of the tray. The upper waterway led in the direction of a newsstand shaded by trees next to an upright crystal. The lower waterway directly connected to two frogs sitting together on a lily pad, overlooked by a turtle. Nearby, a baby chick emerging from its shell lay within the protection of a seashell; this baby chick was the nearest miniature to where Anna was standing. On the far side of the bridge in the upper left area of the tray, a sun rested on an elevated knoll, overlooking the entire scene. Nearby were a snake and two dead

Figure 9.3   Anna's final tray.

trees, in contrast to the vibrant trees that she placed in the rest of the tray. In the lower left-hand corner, Anna carefully placed polished stones and jewels in front of another turtle.

My reaction to this tray was one of joy. From prior Sandplay pictures, I knew that Anna's internal healing energies had been activated to aid her in dealing with her life issues. In this scene, the conflicts with which she had struggled so long no longer took center stage. I was struck by the organic nature of this scene—the imperfectly fashioned island, surrounded by water, with rivers gently reaching out to a world filled with trees, new life (baby chick), spiritual support (bodhisattva), good health (monkey, credited in Asia with granting good health), and access to both land and water (i.e., the conscious and unconscious) through the mermaid, swan, frogs, and turtles. The sun, representing solar consciousness, was elevated, illuminating the entire scene. I wondered if her primitive rage, represented by the fire in her initial tray, had been transformed into a more conscious, mindful state where she now had the ability to overlook her world and to think objectively. The mermaid, bodhisattva, and monkey appeared to be looking over the bridge, across the water, to the dead trees, snake, and sun. Was this another perspective bearing the reminder that difficult issues, in some form, are present in all of our lives? Or, might the bridge span the opposites as a symbol of reconciliation? Perhaps both?

When I saw the two frogs on the lily pad, I knew that Anna was feeling supported by me as she underwent her multiple changes. Her placement of the turtle nearby helped me understand that she, like the turtle, had been able to adapt and survive through decades of difficulties. When Anna completed the scene, she observed with amazement, "Here's an island—but it's connected! This is interesting—it isn't perfectly smoothed out. This [picture] feels fluid, life-like, offering options, movement." No longer does she have to be restricted to the achievement of perfection to please the old family and religious system that does not fit or support her creative nature.

Using the thematic approach in understanding Anna's trays helped me clarify and validate her process. In Anna's first and ninth scenes, the number of wounding themes outnumbers healing themes. In this final tray, no themes of wounding are present; I see only themes of healing and wholeness (see Figure 9.4). A congruent, organized idea (i.e., her world) encompasses the entire tray (Integrated Theme) with an island in the center of the tray (Centered Theme). With the bridge joining the opposites (i.e., live tree/dead trees), a connection or reconciliation has occurred (Bridging Theme). The whole scene is alive with organic growth; vegetation is even growing out of a rock (Energetic Theme). New development is emerging as the baby chick breaks out of its egg, so close to where Anna is standing (Birthing Theme). The whole scene has a natural, spiritual quality that includes a bodhisattva on the central island (Spirituality Theme).

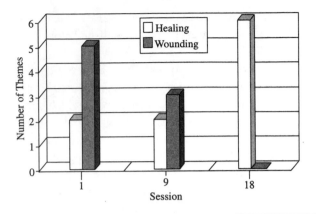

Figure 9.4   Anna's shift from wounding to healing.

Now that these healing energies have been activated by this powerful process, I knew that they would continue to support her through her therapeutic experience and, I hoped, throughout her life.

Reflection Session

Six months after this tray was created, Anna asked if I would be willing to review her trays with her. Although we were still immersed in verbal therapy, I agreed because I thought an objective look at her Sandplay process would be helpful. Reflecting on her scenes was an enriching experience for both of us.

When she viewed her final tray at this later time, Anna looked visibly moved. She commented, "It's like a celebration. This looks so eclectic, busy, hopeful, a lot of life—nowhere is it the same; it's unique. The swan feels really special to me. The turtle is carrying the treasure (the jewels)—like the specialness of who I am. I've discovered that I have a brain. The middle island is part of me, and it is connected to the whole of me. I'm such a different person now than how I was. I'm so much more whole. I'm accepting myself better, and I can rely enough on myself to spread out. I'm so much larger and have so many more options. Even if I'm afraid, I can spread out. I'm not alone. The whole tray is filled—a completeness." As I listened to her comments, it certainly seemed to me that the treasure had been found.

By this later time, Anna's outer life mirrored her final Sandplay scene. She had begun educational training as a massage therapist and enjoyed this work immensely. Later, after she had graduated and was about to open her own business, she quit her job as a secretary. She had begun to paint again. Her relationship with her husband felt easier and more satisfying; she experienced him as a more sensitive and empathetic partner, with whom she was able to share and reflect on her feelings. No longer was she given to fits of rage in trying to communicate her frustration. Her allergic symptoms had lessened significantly with the help of a medical specialist.

Sandplay was an excellent technique to use with Anna. It tapped into her natural creative ability and allowed her to express, work through, and use her sharp mind to understand what had happened to derail her so early in life and cause such wounding. Anna's Sandplay process was one of communicating, getting in touch with, understanding, and eventually integrating her negative and destructive emotions. She worked hard throughout therapy to repair the early rifts and understand her rageful feelings, eventually gaining a new awareness of herself, becoming more comfortable with her body, and giving expression to her creative self.

CONCLUSION: NOW TO BEGIN

We hope that this chapter has encouraged and inspired you to pursue and investigate the use of this modality. Sandplay can be invigorating work, offering the opportunity to add another dimension of play and variety to your clinical practice. There are many opportunities for your further development and understanding of Sandplay, including experiencing your own Sandplay process, reading, and continuing education. In our experience, the self-healing properties of the psyche activated by Sandplay can deepen therapeutic work with adults, allowing them to communicate in a nonverbal way that opens up a whole new world.

REFERENCES

Amatruda, K., & Simpson, P. H. (1997). *Sandplay: The sacred healing: A guide to the symbolic process.* Taos, NM: Trance Sand Dance Press.

Ammann, R. (1991). *Healing and transformation in sandplay: Creative processes become visible* (W. P. Rainer, Trans.). LaSalle, IL: Open Court.

Avrech, G. (1997). Initial trays: Clues to the psyche. In B. Caprio (Ed.), *Sandplay: Coming of age,* 53-63. Los Angeles: Los Angeles Sandplay Association in association with the C. G. Jung Bookstore of Los Angeles.

Bowyer, L. R. (1959). The importance of sand in the world technique: An experiment. *British Journal of Educational Psychology, 29,* 162–164.

Bradway, K. (1985). *Sandplay bridges and the transcendent function.* San Francisco: C. G. Jung Institute.

Bradway, K. (1991). Transference and countertransference in Sandplay Therapy. *Journal of Sandplay Therapy, 1*(1), 25–43.

Bradway, K. (1994). Sandplay is meant for healing. *Journal of Sandplay Therapy, 3*(2), 9–12.

Caprio, B. (1989). The sand tray: An art therapy perspective. Unpublished master's thesis, Loyola-Marymount University, Los Angeles, CA.

Cirlot, J. E. (1962). *A dictionary of symbols* (J. Sage, Trans.). London: Routledge & Kegan Paul. (Original work published 1962)

Cooper, J. C. (1992). *Symbolic and mythological animals.* London: Aquarian Press.

Friedman, H. S. (1986, March). *Sandplay: An approach to the child's unconscious.* Paper presented at the Spring lecture series, sponsored by the Hilde Kirsch Children's Center, Los Angeles.

Friedman, H. S., & Mitchell, R. R. (2001). *Survey of therapists who use Sandplay Therapy* attending the International Society of Sandplay Therapy in Zurich, Switzerland. Unpublished raw data.

Jung, C. G. (1964). *Man and his symbols.* Garden City, NY: Doubleday.

Jung, C.G. (1967). Alchemical studies (CW V.13, par.36). Princeton, NJ: Princeton University Press.

Kalff, D. (1980). *Sandplay: A psychotherapeutic approach to the psyche* (W. Ackerman, Trans.). Santa Monica, CA: Sigo Press. (Original work published 1966)

Kalff, D. (1988). *Sandplay in Switzerland.* Notes of seminar presented at Kalff's home in Zurich, Switzerland, sponsored by the University of California at Santa Cruz.

Lowenfeld, M. (1979). *The world technique.* London: Allen & Unwin.

Miller, R. R. (1979). Investigation of a psychotherapeutic tool for adults: The sand tray. *Dissertation Abstracts International, 43*(1), 257B. (UMI No. 82–07557)

Mitchell, R. R., & Friedman, H. S. (1994). *Sandplay: Past, present and future.* London: Routledge.

Perry, J. W. (1973). The creative element in madness. *Art Psychotherapy, l,* 61–65.

Samuels, A. (1986). *A critical dictionary of Jungian analysis.* London: Routledge & Kegan Paul.

Signell, K. A. (1981). The use of Sandplay with men. In K. Bradway, K. A. Signell, G. H. Spare, C. T. Stewart, L. H. Stewart, & C. Thompson (Eds.), *Sandplay studies: Origins, theory and practice,* 101-131. San Francisco: C. G. Jung Institute.

Weinrib, E. L. (1983). *Images of the self: The Sandplay therapy process.* Boston: Sigo Press.

Weinrib, E. L. (1989). *Sandplay workshop.* Workshop sponsored by Friends of C. G. Jung, Phoenix, AZ.

Winnicott, D. W. (1965). *The maturational processes and the facilitating environment: Studies in the theory of emotional development.* New York: International Universities Press.

Winnicott, D.W.(1971). Playing and reality. London: Tavistock Publication Ltd.

Chapter 10

SOMATIC CONSCIOUSNESS IN ADULT SANDPLAY THERAPY

Kate Amatruda

Sandplay seems aptly suited to elicit the mind/body connection, as it is the one form of therapy that combines the use of a container, the exploration of symbols, and all the elements: earth, air, fire, and water. The containment of the transference, which is mirrored by the physical container of the sandbox combined with the energy released by the use of the elements, seems to facilitate the opening of communication between the conscious and the unconscious, and the mind and the body. Adults often come to play therapy with ambivalence, at best. They fear the regression and descent to come, while at the same time welcoming the chance to recapitulate pieces of childhood. For some, however, instead of an excursion back in time, they journey into their bodies.

This chapter looks at cases in which the threshold between psyche and soma, mind and body, was crossed. Three types of cases are examined: those that hint at the predictive ability of the unconscious with regard to illnesses, those that unintentionally were therapeutic explorations of known illnesses and trauma, and those in which the patient came to therapy specifically to work on a life-threatening illness. Brief therapy in a hospital setting is also addressed.

The therapeutic vessel, or the transference that allows the patient to feel held and contained, is a prerequisite to enable the communication between psyche and soma to occur. "Regardless of the setting where we meet with our patients, of the types of problems that we treat, or of the treatments we use, it is the quality of the relationship between provider and client that begins and sustains the healing process" (Knight & Camic, 1998, p. 6). Dora Kalff, the originator of sandplay therapy, called this "the experience of the symbol in the free and sheltered place" or the "free and protected space" (1980, pp. 32, 39). This protection is necessary for transformation to occur, much as the infant needs the womb or the caterpillar, the chrysalis.

Kalff postulated that the "manifestation of the Self, this inner order, this pattern for wholeness, is the most important moment in the development of the personality" (1980, p. 26). The Self-ego axis then develops as the child matures. Kalff believed that a weak or neurotic ego was the function of illness, trauma, or an unsympathetic environment, particularly a disturbance in the mother-child unity at the earliest phases of development. Therefore, sandplay therapy is reparative as it gives the "Self the possibility of constellating and manifesting itself in the sandtray" (p. 29). The miniature figures can act as symbols, carrying archetypal energy for healing the Self-ego axis. "The symbol acts as a bridge: the bridging of what is familiar to that which is strange. It relates the conscious to the unconscious, the literal to the more abstract, the part to the whole" (Ryce-Menuhin, 1992, p. 22). Amplification of symbols is demonstrated in the cases presented in this chapter.

The power of earth and water has been known for ages untold by children playing in the mud or at the shore. Kalff's contribution to Lowenfeld's World Technique included integration of Jungian theory as well as the use of the elements, based in part on her interest in Tibetan Buddhism. In this system, each element correlates to an energy center in the body as well as to an emotional state. Earth is the element at the base of the spine and is associated with basic needs and ontological security. Water is the element of the lower abdomen and is correlated with attachment. Fire is held in the heart and is the element of passion, anger, and love. Air is associated with communication and lodges in the throat. Kalff also spoke of a fifth element, called *ether*, which is associated with spirit and appears at the top of the head (personal communication, October 1983).

In sandplay, the sand is real earth, not symbolic. Water may be added to the sand, allowing it to be molded and shaped. The patient may light candles or breathe onto an important sand tray, almost as if bringing it to life. It is in this "in-between place," in which the container holds the elements of transformation, that unconscious contents come to consciousness and that the cellular level of the body can communicate.

Sandplay catalyzes the psychobiological field of the unconscious of both patient and therapist. Kalff presented a case of a young boy who was referred to her because of recurrent headaches. He carefully furrowed the sand to look like a field ready for planting. "The lines were very fine," she told us. He put in a rock; Kalff found out later the boy had a brain tumor (1979). Kalff "noticed that people who were physically ill unconsciously made pictorial representations in the sand of diseased organs whose shape they did not know; or there would be some representation of the location in the body where the organ was situated" (Weinrib,

1983, p. 40). Ammann speaks of this as well; stating sandplay "can provide the grounds for the interaction of body and psyche, matter and spirit. Sandplay creates a common field within which spirit and body can mutually influence each other" (1991, p. xv). Ryce-Menuhin states that the "earth quality of the sand pulls the psyche toward body expression and this can be of inestimable value to the therapy" (1992, p. 104).

Through the use of the hands in the box of sand, cellular memories may be accessed. Jung spoke of this when he said, "Often the hands know how to solve a riddle with which the intellect has wrestled in vain" (Jung, 1981). Montecchi (1999) clarifies the role of the therapist when he states:

> If it is true that hands talk, it is also true that it is necessary to know how to listen to them. Such listening occurs not only through the ears. Within the relationship, the therapist lives, shares and listens to what the hands and the corporeality of the child express, so that this sharing and listening can activate a process of transformation. (p. 29)

PREDICTIVE ABILITY OF THE UNCONSCIOUS WITH REGARD TO THE BODY

Callie

Is it possible for a person to carry images in his or her unconscious of a cellular process of which he or she has no conscious knowledge? This mystery is explored through the sandplay therapy treatment of a 36-year-old woman whom I shall call "Callie." Although Callie came to therapy angry and grief-stricken about the suicide of her adoptive mother, a subtext of somatic awareness appeared in her sand trays. Callie's sand trays seemed to show images of the brain. When she was able to experience being mirrored and contained by the therapy, it allowed her to express the symbolic content held in the cells. Callie's symbolic representation of neurological changes preceded the diagnosis of her illness by several years.

Figure 10.1 shows Callie's 21st tray in a long series. After she made it, she said, "I wanted to make a baby but as soon as I made it, it looked like part of my brain. It is a really primitive fetus; it has a tail and little arms. Poor baby! I'm not sure why exactly, but it makes me want to cry. It has a big brain—like a fish or salamander. It is just not hooked up real well." She ended the session by talking to the baby, saying, "You will be okay." There are two women in the tray, each of whom have their backs to the baby. Callie identified these as her birth and adoptive mothers. On the edge of the sand tray is a tiny mirror. The presence of the mirror is significant because the patient must feel seen, accepted, and mirrored for somatic information to emerge.

Figure 10.1   Callie's twenty-first sandplay.

One month later, Callie made another sand tray, in which she placed several snakes and a winged horse (see Figure 10.2). In mythology, Pegasus arose when the "wise blood" of the moon goddess Medusa fell into the sea, where Poseidon reigned. There is an earlier version of Pegasus, a female winged horse, known as Aganippe. She was the "mare who destroys mercifully," which is a title of the goddess Demeter as the destroying mare of the night, or nightmare (Walker, 1983, p. 780). With the figures removed from Callie's tray, the shape of the sand is very much like that of the brain.

Later Callie was diagnosed with chronic fatigue and immune dysfunction syndrome (CFIDS), a "serious disease of immune dysfunction and neurological impairment" (Iverson, 1991, p. 5). It has been described as a virus in the brain, echoing Callie's comments about the baby in her sand tray who was not "hooked up real well." The illness causes severe neuropsychological deficits, including loss of mental acuity and memories. "CFIDS lives in the brain, and in the soul. It cripples the mind and spirit as much as it does the body" (p. 6).

Figure 10.2   Callie, one moth later.

Callie had made two imprints of her right hand at the base of the unconscious brain shape (see Figure 10.3). As she did it, she said, "These are both right hands. It's odd . . . I am left-handed, but it feels like what I need to do." Cappuchione (1989) found the following:

> My research shows that no matter which hand you normally write with, your non-dominant hand accesses abilities associated with the right brain. The nondominant hand writes from a different voice within. It expresses feelings, intuitions and wisdom far more clearly than your dominant hand. (p. 19)

Schore suggests that it is "the therapist's resonance with this right brain state, in turn, that triggers "somatic countertransference" (Lewis, 1992), and these "somatic markers" (Damasio, 1994) may be physiological responses that receive (or block) the patient's distress-inducing projective identifications" (Schore, 1997, p. 48). This ability is also known to parents of infants, suggesting that it may have an evolutionary purpose or instinctual roots. A parent often feels a sympathetic earache when the baby pulls at his or her ear, or an itchy scalp the moment his or her child comes home from school with head lice.

Therapists can amplify this innate ability by mirroring the body language, the sensory system of the language used (visual, kinesthetic, or auditory), and by matching the breathing of their patients. These techniques tend to create a state of

Figure 10.3   Callie's sandplay with the figures removed.

rapport between the patient's cells and that of the therapist, and allow the therapist to become more receptive to somatic information. Therapists can then more readily attend to any somatic sensations that arise in their own bodies, and ask themselves if they are the patient's projected sensations or their own.

Callie's handprints were in the hippocampus area of the brain. Research by neurologist Marshall Handleman has indicated that CFIDS affects the hippocampus, the region of the brain that has an important role in memory formation (Cowley, 1990).

Figure 10.4 shows the area of the hippocampus in the brain where Callie put her handprints, knowing nothing of brain structure, nor even that she had made a brain shape in the sand. In retrospect, a part of Callie knew what was happening in her brain years before she or her doctors knew on a conscious level. She later found out that the virus caused her terrible nightmares. After her diagnosis, we looked again at these images. She had remembered them exactly, almost as if they had been burned into her awareness.

It was as though her psyche knew something and needed to express it. While the literature on the predictive ability of the unconscious with regard to illness is still scant, the history of such a possibility is ancient. The Greek physician Galen

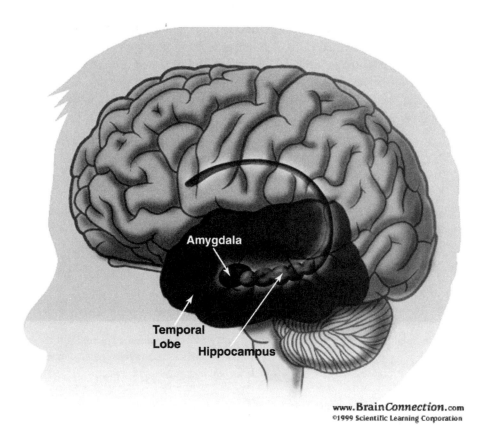

Figure 10.4   **Hippocampus area of the brain, from BrainConnection.com. Copyright 1999 Scientific Learning Company. Reprinted with permission.**

(130–200 B.C.E.) apparently used dreams not only in diagnosing illnesses, but also as guides in performing surgical operations (Dossey, 1999, p. 4). The worldview underlying this relationship between mind and matter is called *panpsychism* in contrast to the more familiar conceptualization of mind/body duality. While dualism postulates that both mind and matter are real, it assumes they are separate. Panpsychism views consciousness and matter as inseparable; "that even single cells, molecules, atoms or electrons are bundles of *sentient* energy" (deQuincey, 2000, p. 10).

What is most intriguing about Callie's work is her psyche's awareness of the neurological changes of her illness, without her ever having seen or been told of them, in fact, years before her diagnosis. She seemed to access something that is the opposite of psychosomatics; I call this phenomenon in the body *somatopsychic*. If the word *psychosomatic* describes how the psyche affects the body, *somatopsychic* describes how the body, or cellular processes, influences the psyche.

Callie exhibited a psychic awareness of what was happening in her body at the most basic level. It was as if protoplasm, the essential living matter of all cells, was imparting knowledge through Callie's hands to the sand tray.

It also is important that Callie's imagery appeared without my knowledge of her neurological diagnosis. Had I known, I would wonder if Callie were somehow sensing the imagery from me or if our joint psychobiological field was influenced by my awareness of her diagnosis. Clearly, some force was at work, enabling Callie, before her diagnosis, to symbolize with uncanny accuracy a cellular process unknown to her consciously. This speaks to Jung's idea of the *objective psyche*. Referring to the unconscious as an "autonomous psychic entity," he goes on to say, "It is and remains beyond the reach of subjective arbitrary control, in a realm where nature and her secrets can be neither improved upon nor perverted, where we can listen but may not meddle" (Jung, 1980).

Current literature tends to focus more on the predictive aspects of drawings (Bach, 1980, 1990; Furth, 2002) and dreams with regard to medical diagnoses than to how this phenomenon appears in sandplay. Siegel (2000) writes:

A patient's dreams and drawings can reveal that person's unconscious awareness of therapeutic choices and healing paths as well as the symbolic meaning of the illness. They often reveal the unknown, make it known and suggest solutions that were not available to the patient through normal awareness. (¶ 7)

In the article "Detecting Cancer in Dream Content," Horton reports the predictive quality of dreams in a 44-year-old woman that seemed to indicate the presence of a new malignancy. It is striking that Horton several times had spontaneous images of death before his patient had her dream. "While listening to her this hour, I several times had a flash to skeletons, skulls, death and the sense that I'm dealing with somebody who either is about to die or very intensely wishes for it" (1998, p. 327).

Montecchi (1999) writes of this phenomenon:

Mediated by hearing and sight, this total listening touches the *skin* of the therapist, then passes through the *stomach, heart* and *head,* and only at the end becomes thought. These three bodily areas of listening—stomach, heart and head—can be correlated with the three corresponding phases of understanding the making of the picture in the sandtray. Listening with the *stomach* corresponds to empathy, with the *heart* to countertransference and with the *head* to interpretation. (pp. 30–31)

Stephanie

Horton's experience parallels my own time with Stephanie, a woman in her late 40s. I found Stephanie's dreams and sand trays compelling, creating in me a more intense focus than is usual during sessions. Stephanie wanted to experience sandplay because she was "curious" about her symbolic side. She had heard of sandplay at a time when she had felt blocked in her life and career. She was hoping that the nonverbal approach would "jumpstart" her life. Stephanie made only seven sand trays over the course of 11 therapy sessions.

Stephanie relayed her history during our first two sessions. As she did, she was testing the therapist to see if it was safe to proceed on the sandplay journey into the unconscious. Most adult patients initiate a series of unconscious transference tests. They are asking, "Is it safe?" "Will I be judged?" "Will you be there for me?" "Where are your authentic boundaries?" and "Have you survived this journey yourself?" In fact, there is cause for concern if the patient bypasses these tests, as it may indicate the lack of sufficient ego defenses necessary for sand tray therapy to succeed. Generally, sandplay therapy is contraindicated when there is insufficient ego to contain unconscious content. As she was testing me, I was assessing her ego strength.

When Stephanie approached the sand tray during our third session, she said, "I have no idea!" She shaped a mound in the sand and placed in the center a figure of Shiva, surrounded by turtles, a butterfly (upside down), a swan, a white elephant, a lion, a unicorn, a red bird, and an opal jewel. She finished by adding two blue horses (see Figure 10.5). At the end, she stood back and said, "That's it."

Figure 10.5   Stephanie's first sandplay.

Shiva, a symbol of the cycles of creation and destruction, at the center was impressive for an initial sand tray, as were the dearth of figures reflecting ordinary life. When the initial tray is so archetypal in its content, it may indicate either poor ego boundaries with regard to unconscious content or a strong need for healing symbols to rapidly emerge. If the sandplay process is initiated when there has already been a long established therapeutic relationship, archetypal symbols may also appear in the initial sand tray. Generally, the expectation is that the symbols appearing in initial trays have some aspects of present time or past reality. As I had already assessed that Stephanie's ego was strong enough to withstand the journey into the unconscious, I found myself wondering what in her psyche needed such powerful symbols of transformation so early in the process.

I was concerned that the butterfly was upside down. Butterflies carry the archetype of transformation because of their ability to metamorphose from caterpillars. Such an important symbol, placed upside down, caused me to feel dread. I have learned to notice the sensations that occur in my body when my patients are speaking or creating sand trays. When significant material is touched in the patient's psyche, there is a resonance created in the joint psychobiological field, which manifests as a kind of "clairsentience" or knowing in the body. Stephanie's upside-down butterfly elicited such a response in my body. I felt glimmers of foreboding, but did not know why. This then compelled in me a different quality of attention toward her sand trays. Later, she had a dream about seeing a meowing cat's head on the sidewalk, to which she associated that she was not taking care of herself. This dream also made me feel uneasy.

In the fourth tray, Stephanie placed a mirror in the center of the tray. Perhaps she felt mirrored by my level of attention to her unconscious processes. Often in sandplay, the appearance of the mirror is a pivotal point in the therapy, indicating that the patient is feeling truly seen and known at the deepest levels. Shepherd (2000) speaks of this process:

> The analyst becomes an empty mirror for the analysand who comes to see her. . . . The analytic journey moves back and forth between the conscious and deep unconscious. When the process moves into the unconscious, it is often through images and feelings, rather than words alone, that the truest empathic mirroring occurs. (p. 16)

Stephanie's final tray had a blue horse standing on a slice of blue agate; she said, "It feels like something being born . . . it has a lot of energy" (see Figure 10.6).

Two weeks after her last tray, Stephanie discovered she had cervical sarcoma, a rare form of cervical cancer. She had radiation to shrink the tumor, then surgery. Almost all of her trays used the same blue agate in the center. In retrospect, the shape and center crystals in the agate look remarkably like a cervix.

Figure 10.6   Stephanie's final sandplay.

Stephanie's dreams and sand trays, combined with feeling so intensely pulled by her psyche, caused me to wonder how much "cellular" knowledge she was trying to communicate in our work together. Although cervical sarcoma has a poor prognosis, Stephanie continues to thrive, twelve years after her diagnosis.

Diagnostic dreams tend to be more emphatic than other dreams; this urgency is similar to what I experienced with Stephanie in her sand trays. Another patient had a dream in which she had ovarian cancer. She immediately took the CA125 blood test, which indicated the presence of ovarian cancer. Her surgeon said that it was the "earliest caught case" he had ever seen. In an interview, Dossey speaks of a woman who had a vivid dream that she had three white spots on her ovary. Dossey referred her to a skeptical radiologist, describing what they were looking for in the X-ray. The radiologist reported with shock that he had found the dreamer's three white spots on her left ovary (Japenga, 1999, p. 4).

A word of caution is perhaps necessary here: Until a diagnosis is made, we do not have any way of ascertaining whether an illness that appears in a dream, drawing, or sandplay will manifest on a cellular level, or remain a symbolic event. I would be extremely cautious in ever suggesting to a patient that his or her unconscious material is indicative of an illness, nor would I recommend a medical test unless it was also suggested by other factors (i.e., it was time for the patient's next mammogram; if the patient had other symptoms or concerns, etc.). There is also a paradox in the unconscious expression of somatic unawareness: If you seek it, it will not appear. Cellular consciousness arises in the presence of containment and mirroring, yet is deeply unconscious. If the patient or therapist approaches the sand tray with the conscious intention to elicit somatic material, what arises tends to be what is already known about the health.

These vignettes indicate the possibility of a place in the psyche that can access the body, specifically cellular consciousness. The somatopsychic awareness that Callie and Stephanie had of their illnesses was mirrored in the therapy, allowing for healing. Expression of imagery in symbolic play was crucial in allowing unconscious content to become conscious. Equally important was the witnessing that the therapy provided.

Sarah

When Sarah came to sandplay therapy, she surprised herself. Prominent in the lesbian community, Sarah was well-known for her brilliant and analytic work. Suddenly, at midlife, she wanted something more, but never would have imagined it was "playing in the sand with a bunch of toys!" When she did her first sand tray, Sarah had just passed her 40th birthday. In the tray, a turtle is about to embark on a long and circuitous descent, going down to a deep depression in the center of the sand tray. The path at times is broken and the turtle is in danger of losing its way. In the lower right corner of the sand tray is a young Native American man who Sarah called a "brave." He has his foot on a half-buried rose quartz egg. In his hand is a bluebird (see Figure 10.7).

Sarah's therapeutic journey progressed like that of the turtle. She shifted from a linear, ego-directed way to a more fluid, self-directed way of being in the world. Along the way, she did get depressed, much as the little turtle went down into the literal depression Sarah had made in her first sand tray. Sarah had to be "brave" to accomplish what she had in the workplace and to overcome the obstacles of sexism and homophobia. She also showed great courage and bravery in her sand trays when she explored the shadow in the form of Hitler. She sobbed over what the Nazis had done to her family and realized how she had internalized a force that was trying to kill her—to subdue her instincts and her feelings.

Like the egg, Sarah's feminine and creative sides had been deeply buried. The egg appears in countless creation myths and has myriad meanings, yet it usually has the connotation of new life, new beginnings. In Egypt, the Creator *Ptah* emerged from the chaos-egg laid by a goose (deVries, 1984, p. 158), and even astronomers talk about "Stellar eggs" when they describe new stars being born in the Eagle Nebula (Scott, 1998, p. 30). In fact, scientists now call the tiny fireball, from which all life began, the *cosmic egg*.

More than two years later, the symbolism of the egg recurred with this magnificent fish with mirror eyes and fins (see Figure 10.8). After she made it,

Figure 10.7   Sarah's first sandplay.

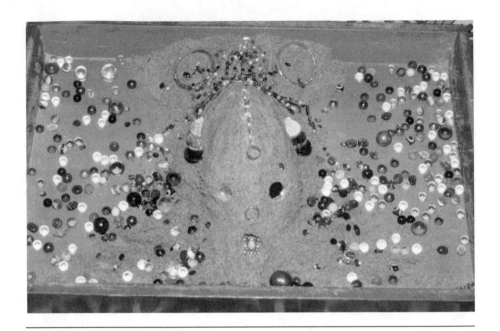

Figure 10.8   Sarah's fish with eggs.

Sarah remarked, "Eggs are everywhere! The fish is pregnant, laying millions of eggs. She is at the bottom of the ocean." Sarah may have encountered the sacred fish of folklore. According to deVries, these fish have wisdom and knowledge. They swim in healing waters and can "grant babies and lovers" (1984, p. 190).

After this sand tray, Sarah began to seriously contemplate having a child. She was in disbelief that this is where her work in the sand tray had led her. We continued to explore whether this baby was a "real" or a "symbolic" baby. Was her task to be a real mother, or to give birth to a new part of herself, more in touch with her feelings and instincts? Three years after she completed her last sand tray, she did have a baby. She also was successful in regenerating new life in her psyche.

Without the sand tray, would she have found this part of herself? Would her son have been conceived and born? It is impossible to know for sure. Yet the rose quartz egg, trod on by the masculine, and the little turtle's slow and meandering descent were clues to the psychological and symbolic process that followed. If the initial sand tray is done with a therapist with whom the patient feels safe and truly accepted on all levels, this first tray may predict the course of the therapy and the psyche's journey in the unconscious. When space created is truly "free and protected," symbols emerge from the depths of the psyche and the cells to guide the way. The therapist's task is to remain receptive and to have no preconceived outcome for the patient other than healing and wholeness.

UNINTENTIONAL THERAPEUTIC EXPLORATION OF ILLNESS AND TRAUMA

Trauma

The ability of sandplay therapy to access physiology is also relevant in the treatment of trauma, particularly as research continues to indicate a cellular component to trauma. The research of van der Kolk and Fisler, presented in "Dissociation and the Fragmentary Nature of Traumatic Memories: Overview and Exploratory Study" (1995), tends to validate anecdotal reports that memories of trauma live in the senses, and that words come later, if at all. These authors have observed that:

> [T]rauma is organized in memory on sensori-motor and affective levels . . . that "memories" of the trauma tend to, at least initially, be predominantly experienced as fragments of the sensory components of the event: as visual images, olfactory, auditory, or kinesthetic sensations, or intense waves of feelings. (¶ 20)

McClaskey (1998) expressed a similar finding:

> While our understanding of the mind-body complex may be in its infancy from a scientific perspective, it is becoming increasingly clear that the neurochemistry of emotion is a key factor that must be considered if any therapeutic intervention is to have lasting effect. All memory is encoded at the cellular level. (¶ 8)

Sandplay therapy, therefore, strives to initially disarm cognition in the service of allowing the cellular level of the unconscious to be expressed. As Jungian analyst C. A. Meier said, "For the unconscious to speak, the conscious must be silent" (1989, p. iv). In this regard, it is in some ways the opposite of imagery techniques used to treat illnesses. In imagery, adults may use "abstract conceptual skills to express the impact of cancer on their daily lives and to portray the physiological effects cancer has exerted on their bodies" (Long, 1998, p. 531).

Levine (1998) addresses the neurophysiology of how memories of trauma are accessed:

> Of particular significance in working with and understanding trauma, is a form of implicit memory that is profoundly unconscious, and forms the basis for the imprint trauma leaves on the body/mind. The relationship between implicit and explicit aspects of an experience is an important dynamic in the resolution of trauma. . . . While explicit memory is accessed primarily through cognition, implicit memory must be reached through the body. . . . This "felt sense" is made up of kinesthetic, proprioceptive, vestibular and visceral (autonomic) information channels. Afferent flow enters the brain stem as nonconscious (instinctual) information, and is then elaborated upon by the limbic (emotional) and neo-cortical

(cognitive) brain structures. Through the felt sense, interoceptive information (which forms the unconscious background of all experience) can be integrated and brought into a conscious figure. (pp. 115–121)

Words alone do not encompass the range of the terror of a trauma, nor do they have the power to discern and perhaps heal what is held in the cells from a trauma or an illness. Sandplay therapy was used to engage the psyche and the soma in the following case, a very brief sandplay process in which the patient came in for only five sessions. Yet, it appeared to address a childhood trauma caused by an illness and the family constellation that evolved in response to it. The complete case is presented here.

Lori

Lori, a woman in her early 30s, was already seeing a specialist in substance abuse who supported Lori's wish to explore the symbolic realm. We agreed at the outset to meet for five sessions. When the time for our appointment came, Lori had a cast on her right arm. She had slipped and broken her arm a few days before our initial meeting.

Lori's broken arm had both practical and symbolic implications. It meant she would be doing her sand trays with her left or nondominant hand. Use of the "other" hand seems to access unconscious content more readily, perhaps quieting the left, or verbal side of the brain, while allowing the intuitive, emotional, more fluid right side of the brain to express itself. Ammann states, "The right hemisphere (which affects the left side of the body), works with holistic, nonverbal images and plays a large role in the processing of emotional information. It seems to me to be significant that the body image is located in the right hemisphere" (1991, p. 7). Psychologically or symbolically, a broken bone might refer to the many shamanic traditions in which the breaking of the bones symbolizes that a person has been dead and has returned to life. In Siberian mythology, the soul resides in the bones. Bones in the shaman's costume represent life-substance that has been killed and then restored by the spirits of the ancestors (Eliade, 1974). Perhaps Lori's work would focus on her body, her soul, and her ancestors. Could the work in the sand facilitate her healing? A broken bone heals stronger than before the break—is this also possible for the psyche?

Lori went on to say she had come to do sandplay work with me because she knew of my experience with dying children. "I realized I had been a dying child," she told me, speaking of her severe asthma as a child, including multiple hospitalizations from the age of four. Childhood asthma has been described as "The most terrifying thing you can imagine. You become afraid to do anything, so you miss out on a lot of life. People tell you it is all in your head, which makes it much worse. Every breath you take, you fear it will be your last" (T. Barberio, personal communication, December 10, 2001).

As a young adolescent, Lori became so impaired by her asthma that she had to leave her home for a different climate where she could breathe. When her health stabilized enough to return home, her parents refused to let her come back. They were unwilling to make the changes necessary in the home so that Lori could breathe. "They chose the animals over me," she said sadly. She was fifteen years old at the time. The next years for Lori were wounding. She was homeless, on the streets, alcoholic. Slowly she began to change through sobriety and a significant relationship.

Lori went to the sand tray and sculpted the sand, initially frustrated by the clumsiness of her left hand. Soon her breathing dropped, and then she went to the shelves and picked out a bridge and the temple gate. She added a tree, a mermaid, a moon, four shells, and the green jewel. She added more shells at the top, four little angels, and then the marbles (see Figure 10.9).

She sat back, looked at the sand tray, and laughed. "Oh dear, I guess the bridge should be over the water." Indeed, the bridge did not cross over the water, but led directly into the pool. "The immersion in the 'sea' signifies the *solutio*— 'dissolution' in the physical sense of the word and at the same time . . . the solution of a problem. It is a return to the dark initial state, to the amniotic fluid of the gravid uterus" (Jung, 1985). The rite of baptism is both a spiritual rebirth and an initiation; the symbolic return to the waters and the reemergence is the

Figure 10.9   Lori's first sandplay.

first conscious birth. Lori's unconscious indicated a need to descend to the water, the element of attachment.

Tucked into the lower left corner is the mermaid, half-fish, half-woman, a being who can swim in the water. This figure probably carries Lori's transference to me as someone who knew the world of the dying as well as the living. The mermaid was placed very near to where I sat when Lori worked in the sand. The mermaid may also signify Lori's task to live in both the conscious and the unconscious worlds. Signell (1990) writes of the mermaid:

> With her supple tail, bare breasts, and her home in the ocean, the ancient symbol of the feminine, the Mermaid symbolizes a woman's connection to the Great Mother, archetype of change and changelessness, the womb of life and love, the numinous source of healing, the place of return in death. A woman knows this through her personal mother and her natural continuity with earliest childhood memories of immersion in emotion: the watery depths of oneness with the mother and within herself, the still waters, stormy seas, and rocky shores of early tenderness and sensuality that later became adult love and sexuality. (p. 162)

Lori was struck with the beauty of the tray and said of the moon, "She really takes care of me." The moon has a blue face with puffed up cheeks, looking to me like someone who cannot get enough oxygen. The blue moon is surrounded by four shells and topped by the green jewel. In her associations to the four shells and four angels, Lori said that she was four years old when she had her first severe asthma attack and needed hospitalization. She called this tray "a moment suspended in time."

The mermaid has made it to the water in Lori's second sand tray (see Figure 10.10). She sits in the center. Surrounded by natural trees, she is backed by a tree with clusters of crystal grapes on it, probably alluding to Lori's battle with alcoholism and her transformation through sobriety. For Lori, this is the tree of life. Broken and upright pillars are nearby, and the mermaid contemplates a quartz crystal in the center of the pond.

The shape of the water appears to be both butterfly and lungs. The image of the butterfly seems greatly comforting to dying children and often appears in their sand trays (Amatruda, 1984). In the mysterious hiding place of the cocoon, something happens. The caterpillar seems to die. When a butterfly emerges, it is a magical symbol of transformation.

If the shape of the water suggests lungs, then the quartz crystal would be the heart. Quartz crystals are known as "stones of light" in the healing rituals of Borneo. The shaman uses these to discover the patient's soul, and "illness is a flight of the soul and the purpose of the séance is to discover it and restore it to its place in the body" (Eliade, 1974, p. 350). Could we surmise that Lori perhaps experienced her illness and abandonment as a loss of her soul? Four intact and upright pillars surround the mermaid, maybe indicating Lori's first four years before her

Figure 10.10   Lori's second sandplay.

asthma struck. There are fifteen pillars in the sand tray, many broken or knocked down. Lori was fifteen when she tried to return home and was refused.

Lori's "dark night of the soul" appeared in her third sandplay (see Figure 10.11). It is a bleak landscape with a tiny figure on a raft. She was depressed. She had tried to contact her mother, but had failed. The last address she had was from eighteen years before. As she sculpted the mound with her left hand, she kept trying to make an overhanging or cave, but the sand kept crumbling as she added water. She said, "I am always anticipating an attack, either inner or outer. It is hard to trust." Here she is truly on her "night-sea-journey." The figure is alone, on a little raft, in a giant sea, at night. There is no cave, no shelter, no companion, no comfort.

Lori looked somehow softer when she arrived for her fourth session. She said that in the previous week, she had cried "for the first time ever" over the loss of her mother. She started her sand tray by digging in the sand and adding water. She placed a mother turtle with a baby turtle on her back, and then she poured in more water in the lower right corner. She added the seahorse, a starfish, dinosaurs, and a woolly mammoth, the ape, dolphins, her mermaid, and the fish. She put in the plants, saying, "I'm thinking it was greener back then." She scattered jewels throughout, placing a large red jewel behind the mermaid (see Figure 10.12).

She stood back and looked at the dinosaurs in what she called the "tar pits." "Oh, I am glad they are dead! I have always liked dinosaurs, but these ones are mean!" She got very happy when she looked at the jewels, and said, "I just remembered this is how diamonds are made." She went on, "I got really scared with

Figure 10.11   Lori's third sandplay.

the tar pits, until I remembered that diamonds were from there. I was really scared it would show how wounded I was."

Here we see Lori continuing her journey down to the element earth, recapitulating evolution. She starts with a pool of water, from which the turtles emerge. Turtles in Native American teaching are the oldest symbol for the planet earth and

Figure 10.12   Lori's fourth sandplay.

symbolize "the eternal mother from which our lives evolve. . . . We are born of the womb of the earth, and to her soil our bodies will return" (Sams & Carson, 1988, p. 77). Kalff used to speak of the turtle as a symbol of wholeness, of the union of the opposites. She said the body of the tortoise was square; symbolizing the earth and the feminine, while the circular shell represented the sky or masculine. She would remind us that it carried its home with it always (personal communication, October 1983). Turtle eggs are laid in the sand, then left behind to hatch. The baby turtles never see their parents, so the turtles that Lori chose never exist in nature. Bradway and McCoard (1997) state:

> So the baby turtles, abandoned by both turtle parents, use the light of both sky-parents—the sun and the moon—to direct them. . . . [The turtle is] an image that is a source of strength. It is the solid base within us that can support any burden, no matter how heavy; and it is the inner guiding spirit that goes with us on our journeys, no matter how far and no matter how deep, and eventually brings us home. (pp. 78–82)

Lori's turtles are a reparative symbol. She is finding a different solution, in which the parent does not abandon the child. The hope is that this would translate to Lori's psyche as a new ability not to abandon herself.

Lori goes to the tar pits of her psyche, to preverbal memories to find the jewels. These are the jewels hinted at by the green jewel in her first sand tray. Diamonds are the hardest jewel and one of the most rare and valuable. They are created by enormous pressure. The word comes from Sanskrit word *"dhu"* meaning "luminous being." The diamond "is an alchemical variant of the Self as an indestructible core of personality" (von Franz, 1986, p. 59). It brings light into the darkness.

Spread throughout the primeval forest, the jewels are fragments of the Self: immortal, eternal, and indestructible. Lori went back through time, to early infancy before her illness, to find her wholeness. In this tray, we see simultaneously the "greening" and the "reddening." Ammann (1991) speaks of her patient Eva's sand tray:

> The whole greening fertile picture expresses that Eva has come to the "good earth" and now can grow. Much like a seed which has fallen on fertile soil she can put down roots. Only by being born into concrete reality, by having gained a foothold on Earth, is upward, spiritually based growth made possible. (p. 74)

The red of the jewel is an important motif in a woman's psyche. In many myths and stories, the girl or woman encounters something red: Persephone ate red pomegranate seeds; Snow White ate a red apple, as did Eve; Dorothy has her ruby slippers; Rapunzel's tears cleanse the red blood from her prince's eyes; the princess with the golden ball smashes and bloodies the frog to transform him into the prince; and Little Red Riding Hood wears a red cloak. Bettelheim speaks of blood and apples as symbolic of sexuality, "The redness of the apple evokes sexual associations like the three drops of blood which led to Snow White's birth, and also menstruation, the event which marks the beginning of sexual maturity" (1976, p. 213). Red is also the color of the heart. When red appears in the sand tray, it may signal that the woman is now able to feel true Eros: warmth, intimacy, relatedness, and compassion. In finally being able to cry over the loss of her mother, Lori has found her feelings.

Lori came to her final session with her arm out of the cast. She told me, "I always dream of going somewhere, a process. I looked up *journey*. It means the search for the lost mother. I thought all week about how dinosaurs made diamonds."

Lori began her fifth and last sand tray by putting the red jewel in the center toward the front. She placed four feathers in, then three stones and a mirror. Using both hands, she raked a design in the sand around the center. Feathers on the ground indicate the flight is over. Lori is back to earth, back to her body. The four feathers indicate the healing of her trauma at age four, paralleled by her healed arm in this final session. What was broken is now whole. Feathers are so light, they dance in the air. There is no struggle for breath here (see Figure 10.13).

The mirror is perhaps her feeling truly seen in her journey and her ability to self-reflect. It may also be a sense of being connected-that each of us is only a tiny bit of reflected light in the wholeness and oneness of life. The red jewel anchors the feathers. What was hidden behind the mermaid now comes to the center.

Lori has created a mandala, the "Center of the World," where earth, sky, and underworld meet.

Figure 10.13   Lori's final sandplay.

The symbolism of the "Center of the World" is also indissolubly connected with the myth of a primordial time when communications between heaven and earth, gods and mortals, were not merely possible but easy and within reach of all mankind. Some [myths] tell of a celestial ascent performed by a hero or sovereign or sorcerer after communication was broken off . . . of returning to the origin of time, of recovering the mythical and paradisal moment before the "fall," that is, before the break in communication between heaven and earth. (Eliade, 1974, pp. 492–493)

Lori was not yet finished. She stood back, looked, and then added a house, a well, and her magical tree. She breathed, "Yes, that is better. It would be great to have that in my backyard. What I have now is rusted cars, washing machines, stuff for postmodern sculptures." Lori has found her center, her wholeness, and her connection to the divine. Yet, we cannot live just there; we must return to ordinary life. Adding elements of everyday life reflected the ego, whereas the mandala was a manifestation of the Self. We need both parts of the Self-ego axis to thrive.

I contacted Lori two years after the completion of her process in the sand. She had found her mother. She told me, "I tracked my mother down and found the entire clan! I am reengaging with them. It is pleasant, not negative. I have a multitude of feelings." She continues in her sobriety and in her relationship. She and her lover have moved. They share a little house by the beach. Plants replace the "postmodern junk," and perhaps feathers fall to the ground in Lori's backyard. She also reported that she no longer needs to take oral medications for her asthma. She said, "Sandplay helped me resolve a lot of things. With the dinosaurs, something inside me changed. It was the most profound feeling. Things changed—I can trust myself."

LIFE-THREATENING ILLNESS

Images of disease and healing, and death and transformation often appear in the sandplay work of people who are seriously ill. This section discusses two types of therapy with those who have life-threatening illnesses: long-term therapy and brief, in-hospital sandplay therapy.

Sand trays shift as a person approaches death. The themes and figures become more archetypal, and the scenes depicted have less and less to do with the everyday world. Almost as the emerging butterfly sheds the cocoon; the psyche seems to shed ordinary concerns and things of the world as death approaches.

Marianna

Marianna came to therapy already quite ill. She had non-Hodgkin's lymphoma, a cancer of the lymph system. Although she had tried alternative treatments such as bodywork, psychic healing, acupuncture, and naturopathic medicine, her cancer continued to spread. At her first session, she was bloated with fluid because her lymph system was not draining. She felt betrayed by her body and by her "failure" to heal herself. Somehow, she had incorporated the idea that she had created her cancer, and she could not understand why she could not cure herself. She was depressed and angry.

Marianna was in her early 40s. Married, she had worked her entire adult life to support herself and her husband, who either would not or could not work. Marianna had dropped out of graduate school so that her husband could stay enrolled, yet he never finished his studies. She never went back to school, and she stayed stuck in a low-paying job for 20 years. She felt that she had created her cancer because she was "supposed" to be making music. There is a disturbing trend in the "new age" that either a person is to blame for having contracted a disease, or that the right imagery will cure the illness. This belief seems to be an attempt by the ego to control the mysteries of life and death, and can be very destructive to those who are ill.

Marianna kept stating that she was not angry, and instead kept trying to "rise above" negative feelings. One of her healers had told her that bad feelings contributed to cancer, so Marianna desperately kept her emotions away from her consciousness. In terms of the elements, what Marianna had done when she

Figure 10.14   Marianna's first sandplay.

attempted to spiritualize her illness was to add ether to fire, a dangerous and explosive combination. The healing that sandplay therapy offers is the opportunity to "descend," to allow the heart element of fire to go through water to the earth. Marianna needed to go down. Her spiritual solution felt like a bypass with anger smoldering under a fragile facade. Yet, to descend meant looking at her shadow, getting angry, and grieving the losses she had experienced in her life. Embarking on this journey would take courage.

In the rear left of Marianna's initial sand tray (see Figure 10.14) were a cornhusk, a red rose, and a peacock that looks like a rainbow. Moving toward the center were two brass animals. One was a foo dog, or temple guardian; the other was a bull with its head down, ready to charge. In the rear left is Kuan Shih Yin, which translates as "She-Who-Hearkens-to-the-Cries-of-the-World". Kuan Yin is a great Bodhisattva, one who is dedicated to helping other sentient beings. She is the goddess of love and compassion, and she hears all our tears. Nearby were a yellow chrysanthemum and a second temple guardian dog. Kuan Yin formed the apex of a triangle pointing up, with the temple guardians making the base of the triangle.

In the center of Marianna's tray is a baby spilling out of a container, surrounded by three totem poles (see Figure 10.15). The vessel was knocked over; the baby is all alone. The baby also appears to be in the center of a triangle. Beside the baby was a sad-looking, seated woman, with a pink butterfly hovering

Figure 10.15   Close-up of Marianna's first sandplay.

above her. The butterfly floating above the woman further reinforced the feeling that Marianna's energies had risen; she had ascended as a defense against her despair. She had "slipped out of her cocoon," perhaps an indication of her spiritual bypass.

The metamorphosis of butterflies offers comfort to those who are in the process of transformation, especially for those facing death. Kübler-Ross (personal communication, April 1981) spoke of visiting the Maidanek concentration camp just after the liberation in 1945. She saw images of butterflies scratched into walls by children as they awaited death. In ancient Greece, people believed human souls in search of a new incarnation became butterflies and used the word *psyche* for both butterfly and soul. In Zaire, people believe that the butterfly symbolizes the soul and that humans shed their bodies as butterflies shed their cocoons. Butterflies, like human beings, need a "free and protected space" to transform. In folklore, a "dead man's soul is sometimes seen fluttering over the body as a butterfly" (de-Vries, 1984, p. 72).

In Marianna's sand tray, surrounding the sad-looking woman were a tiger, an Inuit figure holding a fish, and an Aztec shaman. There was a large plant with pink flowers. On the edge, carefully balanced on a pillow, was a white bird perched precariously on the rim, neither in nor out of the sand tray. The lack of containment of the white bird reminded me of the baby spilled out of the container in the center of her picture. Marianna was feeling neither held nor contained. She was not sure whether this white bird was a crane or a stork (see Figure 10.16).

Cranes are long-lived and mate for life. They can symbolize happiness, steadfastness, and love. They dance and sing. The sandhill crane is the oldest known currently existing bird species; thus, cranes witnessed our birth as a species. (Johnsgard, 1998, p. 28) Cranes are thought to be messengers of the gods and symbolic of the ability to enter into higher states of consciousness. Indeed, from very early times, there was an Indo–European belief that souls could take the form of birds. In Egyptian theology, a great white bird called the *ba* emerged from the body as the person took his or her last breath. The *ba* moved freely in space, following the bark of the sun god across the sky. In Celtic mythology, the crane is a form of *Pwyll,* the king of the underworld and, therefore, can herald death (Cooper, 1978, p. 44). Its longevity is mythic, and there is evidence that the ancient Japanese believed either that the dead turned into birds, or that birds carried them to another world. In Chinese mythology, cranes and dragons carry souls to Western paradise and immortality (p. 44). I wondered if the bird represented Marianna's spirit on the edge. Would she go or would she stay? As the container was not able to hold the baby, would her body be able to hold her soul? Perhaps Marianna's ambivalence was also presented in her confusion about the bird. In mythology, storks bring us into life, while cranes take us out.

Figure 10.16   Close-up of the edge of Marianna's first sandplay.

Susan Bach (1980) has studied the symbolism of the bird in the spontaneous drawings of ill children:

> Laurens van der Post sees the bird as "the inspiration, the intuition, the thought that comes unbidden into the awareness of man." This I feel somehow joins up with my own comprehension, of why the bird may in all times, cultures and countries have been taken as a symbol of the soul, its far-seeingness, its ability to see beyond where human eyes can reach, and that it knows of its destination. (p. 107)

Marianna was working very hard physically, emotionally, and spiritually; however, within four months, it was clear that her cancer was spreading. In one sand tray, an old wizard turned his back on her while a giant octopus uncoiled its tentacles, pushing through stone. Buried under a mountain of rock was a wooden box containing images of Hindu gods. "There is something in the box, but I don't know what it is," Marianna told me (see Figure 10.17). This sand tray marked the beginning of her descent. This was a painful time. My countertransference to Marianna was very strong. I was very moved by her courage and her willingness to face her pain. She had so much life and spirit, and I was absolutely powerless to

Figure 10.17   Marianna, four months later.

do anything but witness. I sat, I was sad, and I was silent. Kiepenheuer (1990) speaks of his work with dying children:

> Initially, I suffered from my helplessness in dealing with these children when I believed I ought to do something: and from my speechlessness when I thought it necessary to say something. It was only later that I learned from the children themselves that what mattered was quite different: that is, to be there, to listen and follow them emotionally. (pp. 143–144)

I needed Kuan Yin, the Bodhisattva of Compassion, at my side, to receive Marianna's and my tears.

Marianna and I worked together for about four years. During that time, she was heroic, frightened, insightful, angry, and scared. Toward the end of our work together, she made the sand tray shown in Figure 10.18.

The photograph of this sand tray appears very faded, almost as if the images were fading as she was fading. I also see it as a picture filled with light, as she got closer to the light. In this sand tray, a child on a fish was headed toward Aphrodite, the Goddess of Love. An Indian priestess was holding a drum at her heart, beating the heartbeat of the universe. The crane was golden now, watching. The central paperweight, tear-shaped, appeared filled with light. A pair of angels, one black and one white, watched over the child riding a fish in the center. Marianna placed the child on a six-pointed star.

Figure 10.18   Marianna, near the end.

The six-pointed star . . . could be a sign of the spiritual potential of the individual, for it included two interlaced triangles, masculine (Δ) and feminine (∇) which, in alchemy, were called the Sign of Solomon. The six-pointed star was considered an equivalent of the human soul, the conjunction of masculine and feminine, and of fire and water—both pairs being opposites. (Weinrib, 1983, p. 104)

Jung writes of this shape as a *"complexio oppositorum:* Δ, fire ∇ and water ✿ a mandala built on three, an unconscious acknowledgment of the trinity that includes the shadow" (1989). Kalff spoke of the "thousand-petaled lotus" that would bloom in the center of intersecting triangles, symbolizing the simultaneous ascent and descent of the fire in the heart (1983).

King Solomon was said to have exorcised demons and summoned angels with the symbol of the Star of David (Biedermann, 1994, p. 173). King Solomon described a star consisting of two triangles intertwined, surrounded by a circle at the center in which is the name of God. Called the Second Pentacle of Mars, "this pentacle serveth with great success against all kinds of diseases, if it is applied unto the afflicted part." In the symbol, surrounding the center is a sentence "In Him was life, and the life was the light of man" (Mathers, 1981, p. 71).

Marianna seemed to have found the light in the center of the intersecting triangles. In his book *Psyche and Death,* Herzog speaks of the initiatory rituals of the Ceram tribe. The initiand faces the darkness and gains the knowledge that light shines out of Death upon Life. According to the Ceram, "only the man prepared in his soul to pass through the Gate of Death becomes a living human being" (1983, p. 209).

There was very little in this sand tray that referred to the body. Susan Bach (1980) states:

> The nearer a person is to death, the less relevant it seems to be of which illness he may die. The situation (inner or outer), the nearness of such a crucial event seems to be of overriding importance . . . I would almost go so far as to say, if the illness is still depicted, there is hope for the medical profession to bring some help. (p. 98)

Jung (1989) has emphasized that the unconscious psyche pays little attention to the end of life in the body. It acts as though the psychic life of the person, or the individuation process, will, in fact, continue. von Franz (1986) states it even more emphatically when she says, "In principle, individuation dreams do not differ in their archetypal symbolism from death dreams" (p. xiii).

Marianna's final sand tray never came out on film, although I used two cameras. She died seven years after her first sand tray. Marianna asked for this quote from the naturalist, John Muir, to be read at her memorial service: "I know not a single word fine enough for LIGHT. Its currents pour . . . Light is a heavy material word not applicable to holy, beamless, bodyless, inaudible floods of light" (cited in Marianna's memorial service, source unknown). She had asked that her memorial service be called "Going Home."

The intertwined triangles held for Marianna the place where God meets man and man meets God, the union of the Masculine and the Feminine, and the place where the thousand-petaled lotus of enlightenment blooms. It also was for Marianna a portal to the next world—a place filled with light. I hope that Marianna's heart was healed and that she was filled with light as she left this life.

Sandplay Therapy in a Hospital Setting

The first container is the body, even in utero, as the body is forming to hold the spirit. Therefore, what happens when the body, the primary container, is hurt? When we are under assault from within, from an illness, and from without, from the medical procedures designed to treat and perhaps heal our illness? How can we do sandplay when there is no "free and protected space," no office, no follow-up sessions, and when even the first container, the body, is under attack?

Hospital work is brief therapy. These cases are from a 1985 through 1987 research project on sandplay imagery with adult men with AIDS at California Pacific Medical Center in San Francisco. At the time these trays were created, AIDS was essentially a death sentence. The current treatments for HIV and AIDS did not exist. We were in a war, and in 1985, we were losing. Every man I worked with had lost many friends to the epidemic; many had seen a partner die. Many of the men that I saw were extremely ill, oftentimes dying.

While sandplay can be a powerful tool for someone who is ill, there are several conditions when it is contraindicated. I worked with the hospital staff to rule out working with those patients who were borderline or had a history of psychosis. Brief sandplay therapy is not appropriate when someone is an active drug addict or alcoholic, nor in any circumstance in which there may not be a strong enough ego to contain the unconscious material elicited.

All visits took place in the hospital. Equipment included a sand tray and zip-locked bags of figures grouped by categories. People who are hospitalized have little autonomy over their bodies, they are in pain, and they are being given medicines that often make them feel sicker. I tried to counter those feelings by giving the men total control over the sessions. They could do a sandplay, or not. They directed the photography. Session time limits were permeable, some sessions were very short; others involved multiple trays, with breaks for medication, treatment, or snacks.

I saw the men from one to four times each, never really knowing in advance how many visits we would have, because they might either become too ill to continue, or be discharged home. Each session had to be complete onto itself, with no major unresolved issues, because there might be no opportunity to finish what we had started.

As a consequence of total control over the session, the psyche of the person seemed to determine how deep each man went. Moreover, I think this is why even one session could be moving to the sandplayer; it was like painting a picture or planting a garden. I provided the materials, the trust, and the respect, and stayed out of the way. The container was each man's own psyche and my trust in them. This allowed whatever wanted to emerge in that moment to arise. I found that I was able to deeply trust the people that were doing the sandplay. In each of them was a kernel of wholeness, the archetype of the Self. For a therapist to have this deep trust, he or she must have done his or her own inner work. I had learned, through my own sandplay journey, to deeply respect the process and to trust the psyche.

Roger

Roger had just been diagnosed with AIDS. "I have known for one week and two days and I am still in shock," he told me. He had ARC (Aids-Related Complex) for three years and was hospitalized for pneumocystis when he did the sand tray shown in Figure 10.19.

He shaped the sand, making a small pond on the right side. The first figure he placed in the sand tray was a man playing a flute, and then he placed a child

Figure 10.19   Roger's sandplay.

sitting on an ox while playing a flute diagonally across from the man. He added people and a paperweight containing an ocean with whales in it. In the center of his sand tray, he placed another paperweight, this one containing a blossoming lotus within. Between the paperweights is a girl with a sword. He added two statues of Kuan Yin and one of the Buddha. Fish, turtles, butterflies, and birds were added, including two cranes in flight. He said, "It is overwhelming, but real peaceful too. The girl with the knife reminds me of me. She is fighting disease and death with her anger. I am angry at having AIDS, but sadness is more prevalent. The boy with the flute is kind of sad. These [the nativity figures] are a group traveling together. This corn woman has lots of wisdom. The owl and the bird are companions to each other." Of the snowflake and water, he said, "This is a magical lake where anything can happen." Pointing to the man curled up, Roger said, "He is sort of hiding in a corner. . . . I feel sort of identified with him." Roger then told me of his childhood, how his father drank and his mother choked him, scratched him, and hurt him with knives and a belt.

The white birds are "on the peak . . . resting . . . looking down at the valley. . . . I feel good when I see them. The man with the flute is real serene." Regarding the figures of Kuan Yin, the Bodhisattva of Compassion, Roger said, "They are like statues, they are figures of reverence." When he was done with his associations, he said simply: "It is safe here. There is no disease and so much hope. It is a magical place."

Gary

Gary had been diagnosed with AIDS for one year when he created this sand tray (see Figure 10.20). He was hospitalized with his third bout of pneumocystis. He touched the sand lightly and then made two lakes, one in the lower left and one in the center. The first figure he put in was the teepee, then he placed twin towers in the sand tray, followed by the shell, twin cranes, three Native American figures in the lower right corner, trees and flowers, a bridge, and a tori. He then put in the dolphins, many birds, frogs, a seated woman, a clown, and Garfield the cat. His last figures were a duckling and a swan. It was very hard for him to talk, as he struggled for breath, so his comments were very brief.

Gary said, "Little ponds . . . I like the blue . . . the water is very healing. . . . It is pretty; I like it. There is no violence, just a few people. It has lots of color. Color and peace and water." He fell asleep after completing his sand tray, a look of peace on his face. Gary died 15 weeks after doing his sand tray. The social worker told me that he welcomed death when it came and he felt very ready to go.

Figure 10.20   Gary's sandplay.

Neither Gary nor Roger knew each other, nor were they hospitalized at the same time, yet the trays they produced were remarkably similar. It was striking the recurrent symbols that appeared in many of the men with AIDS, many of which also were in the sand trays of Marianna. In the hospital, I had a small but very wide-ranging collection, with lots of dinosaurs, animals, people, trees, buildings, and so forth, yet many of the hospitalized men created similar trays.

As death approaches, many symbols of transformation appear, and the material produced becomes much more archetypal. The repeated symbols included:

Shells: One man told me: "It is what I am leaving behind." This association to the shell is corroborated by deVries, who identifies it as "the body, discarded by the soul" (1984, p. 419).

White birds in flight (twinned): Another man told me, "My lover has already died of AIDS, as have many of my friends. My one comfort is that I am not alone where I am going." In both Roger's and Gary's sand trays, the birds are facing toward the left. Applying the orientation system of Bach, it would appear that the cranes are migrating west, toward the setting sun (1980, p. 11).

Swans: The swan often appears as people near death. It is a symbol of transformation; the story of "The Ugly Duckling" reminds us of the change from scrawny cygnet to beautiful swan. Swans know three realms: the sky, the land, and the water. "The proverbial 'swan song' (the significant final words or performance of a great person) goes back to the prophetic talent of the swan . . . it supposedly foresees its impending death and emits extraordinary cries bemoaning its own passing" (Biedermann, 1994, p. 333).

Owls: Owls have been associated with death in mythology since ancient times; it was the bird of the goddess Hecate of the underworld and symbolized the realm of the "dead sun," or night crossing in ancient Egypt (deVries, 1984, pp. 535–354). Bach (1990) writes:

> The motif of the owl as a life-threatening bird, a figure of death, takes us back to the Sumerian goddess Lilith (2300–3000 B.C.). She is depicted with clawed owl's feet and spur. . . . She is feared as a snatcher of new-born babes and an amulet called 'Night Guardian' is still in wide-spread use today, for instance in Israel, against her lethal powers. As the screech owl *(Käuzchen)* in folklore, its unpleasant call is feared as indicating death. In China the owl is called the bird that snatches away the soul. (pp. 89–90)

Ostriches: Although known in folklore as "hiding their heads in the sand," ostriches in fact put their heads down in the sand to hear and sense vibrations of approaching predators. They are birds that cannot fly and are thought to be a symbol of "man deserted by God: because of its absent-mindedness, the ostrich leaves its eggs in the desert sand; only when it sees the evening star (divine light) does it think of them again, seek them, and hatch them by its glance" (deVries, 1984, p. 353). The prevalence of the ostrich in the sand trays of the men with AIDS thus could be interpreted in many ways: Is it symbolic of the denial of AIDS for many in the gay community, or could it be that these men are sensing the footsteps of death approaching? Did they feel abandoned, much as the turtle can also indicate abandonment? "The ostrich egg, suspended in temples, Coptic churches, mosques, and sometimes over tombs, depicts creation; life; resurrection; vigilance" (Cooper, 1978, p. 123). Perhaps the ostrich simultaneously holds the symbol of death and resurrection—of being lost, then found.

Butterflies: Butterflies appeared in almost every sand tray done by the men with AIDS.

Corn Husks: Marianna put corn husks in her initial tray, and Roger's "wise woman" was made of corn husks. Corn is the "staff of life" (deVries, 1984, p. 112); and in Native American traditions, the "ear of corn (maize) with all its seeds represents the people and all things in the universe" (Cooper, 1978, p. 43). In the Greek mysteries, the "golden ears of corn are the offspring of the marriage of the luminous sun with the virgin earth . . . . and was the central symbol in the Eleusinian Mysteries: 'There was exhibited as the great, the admirable, the most perfect object of mystic contemplation, an ear of corn that had been reaped in silence' " (p. 43). The husk is the part of the corn that is left behind, paralleling the symbolism of the shell.

Kuan Yin: She is the Bodhisattva of Compassion, who stays to hear all our tears. Legend says Kuan Yin was an Indian princess who joined a convent, having forsaken marriage. This angered her father very much. She was a Buddhist Bodhisattva, a mortal who has achieved enlightenment and earned the right to enter Nirvana. When she was on the threshold of heaven, she heard someone on earth cry, and so she stopped. She vowed she would stay on earth to ease human suffering. She will not enter Heaven until all the tears have been heard. She is also known as Quan Yin, Kannon, Avalokitesvara, Miao Shan, and Tara (Blofeld, 1977). None of the men in the AIDS study knew who she was, only that she was a figure of reverence or serenity.

Journey: Death is perceived as a journey and a great mystery to those who are close to it, as well as in many religious traditions.

Magical Lake: This symbol is a variant of the sacred pool and the water of life, from which all life begins, can be healed, and ends. Lakes also symbolize "the transition of life and death, resurrections, the underwater realm from which the sun rises and into which it sinks" (deVries, 1984, p. 289).

No one used a mirror, which had been so crucial in the sandplay processes of Callie, Lori, Sarah, and Stephanie. Perhaps this alludes to my inability to mirror the experience of being a man dying of AIDS, or perhaps it underscores the unimportance of the personal as death approaches.

Speaking of his years of treating patients until they died, Jung (1981) states:

> As a rule, the approaching end was indicated by those symbols which, in normal life also, proclaim changes of psychological condition—rebirth symbols such as change of locality, journeys, and the like. . . . Dying, therefore, has its onset long before actual death. . . . On the whole, I was astonished to see how little ado the unconscious psyche makes of death. It would seem as though death were something relatively unimportant, or perhaps our psyche does not bother about what happens to the individual.

Roger's "group traveling together" had this feeling, that the journey he was on involved some level of birth or rebirth. It was striking that he did not identify the wanderers as those of the nativity, as they were a shepherd, a king, Joseph, and Mary holding the newborn Jesus.

von Franz (1986) remarks:

> All of the dreams of people who are facing death indicate that the unconscious, that is, our instinct world, prepares consciousness not for a definite end but for a profound transformation and for a kind of continuation of the life process which, however, is unimaginable to everyday consciousness. (p. 156)

CONCLUDING THOUGHTS

These men taught me that, no matter what happens to the body, the psyche feels it will go on. The psyche can always create a safe place, a "free and protected space," no matter what is happening to the body. I find that very comforting. In summation, what I learned from these extraordinary teachers—Callie, Lori, Stephanie, Sarah, Roger, Gary, and those others not named—was that if the therapist brings no expectations to the session, trusts the psyche of the person doing sandplay absolutely, and respects the process, the experience will be healing to both therapist and sandplayer. They taught me that, given the "free and protected space," access to the elements, and mirroring, cells can communicate through sandplay therapy.

All names and identifying details have been changed to protect confidentiality. Grateful acknowledgment is given to those who worked so deeply in sandplay and allowed their work to be shared.

REFERENCES

Amatruda, K. (1984). *Psychological interventions in physical illness.* Unpublished manuscript.

Ammann, R. (1991). *Healing and transformation in sandplay.* La Salle, IL: Open Court.

Bach, S. (1980). On the archetypal motif of the bird. *Psychosomatische Medizin* [Psychosomatic Medicine], *9*(4), 95–110.

Bach, S. (1990). *Life paints its own span: On the significance of spontaneous pictures by severely ill children.* Zurich, Switzerland: Daimon Verlag.

Bettelheim, B. (1976). *The uses of enchantment: The meaning and importance of fairy tales.* New York: Alfred A. Knopf.

Biedermann, H. (1994). *Dictionary of symbolism.* New York: Meridian.

Blofeld, J. (1977). *Bodhisattva of compassion: The mystical tradition of Kuan Yin.* Boston: Shambhala.

Bradway, K., & McCoard, B. (1997). *Sandplay: Silent workshop of the psyche.* London: Routledge.

Cappuchione, L., (1989). *The well-being journal.* North Hollywood, CA: Newcastle.

Cooper, J. C. (1978). *An illustrated encyclopedia of traditional symbols.* London: Thames and Hudson.

Cowley, G. (1990, November 12). Chronic fatigue syndrome. *Newsweek,* 62–70.

Damasio, A. R. (1994). *Descartes' error.* New York: Grosset/Putnam.

deQuincey, C. (2000). Consciousness: Truth or wisdom? *IONS: Noetic Sciences Review, 51,* 8–14.

deVries, A. (1984). *Dictionary of symbols and imagery.* Amsterdam: North Holland.

Dossey, L. (1999). *Reinventing medicine.* San Francisco: HarperSanFrancisco.

Eliade, M. (1974). *Shamanism.* Princeton, NJ: Princeton University Press.

Furth, G. (2002). *The secret world of drawings: Healing through art.* Toronto: Inner City Books.

Herzog, E. (1983). *Psyche and death.* Dallas, TX: Spring.

Horton, P. (1998). Detecting cancer in dream content. *Bulletin of the Menninger Clinic, 62*(3), 326–333.

Iverson, M. (1991, Spring). CFIDS: Footprints in the sand. *CFIDS Chronicle,* 5–6.

Japenga, A. (1999, September 3–5). Can dreams diagnose illness? *USA Weekend,* 4.

Johnsgard, P. (1998). *Crane music.* Washington, DC: Smithsonian Institution Press.

Jung, C. G. (1980). *Psychology and alchemy: Collected works* (Vol. 12, 2nd ed.). Princeton, NJ: Princeton University Press.

Jung, C. G. (1981). *The structure and dynamics of the psyche: Collected works* (Vol. 8, 2nd ed.). Princeton, NJ: Princeton University Press.

Jung, C. G. (1985). *The practice of psychotherapy: The psychology of the transference. Collected works* (Vol. 16, 2nd ed.). Princeton, NJ: Princeton University Press.

Jung, C. G. (1989). *The symbolic life: Collected works* (Vol. 18). Princeton, NJ: Princeton University Press.

Jung, C. G. (1990). *Symbols of transformation: Collected works* (Vol. 5, 2nd ed.). Princeton, NJ: Princeton University Press.

Kalff, D. (1980). *Sandplay: A psychotherapeutic approach to the psyche.* Boston: Sigo Press.

Kiepenheuer, K. (1990). *Crossing the bridge: A Jungian approach to adolescence.* La Salle, IL: Open Court.

Knight, S., Camic, P. (1998). Health psychology and medicine: The art of science and healing. In P. Camic & S. Knight (Ed.), *Clinical handbook of health psychology* (pp. 3–15). Seattle, WA: Hogrefe & Huber.

Kübler-Ross, E. (1983). *On children and death.* New York: Macmillan.

Levine, P. (1998). Memory, healing, and trauma. *Alternative Health Practitioner, 4*(2), 115–121.

Lewis, P. P. (1992). The creative arts in transference/countertransference relationships. *The Arts in Psychotherapy, 19,* 317–323.

Long, J. (1998). Medical art therapy: Using imagery and visual expression in healing. In P. Camic & S. Knight (Eds.), *Clinical handbook of health psychology* (pp. 523–558). Seattle, WA: Hogrefe & Huber.

Mathers, S. L. M. (Ed.). (1981). *The key of Solomon the king.* New York: Samuel Weiser.

McClaskey, T. R. (1998). *Decoding traumatic memory patterns, the American Academy of Experts in Traumatic Stress.* Retrieved October 1, 2001, from www.aaets .org/arts/art30.htm.

Meier, C. A. (1989). *Healing dream and ritual.* Zurich, Switzerland: Daimon Verlag.

Montecchi, F. (1999). Hands that talk and analytic listening. *Journal of Sandplay Therapy, 8*(1), 25–67.

Ryce-Menuhin, J. (1992). *Jungian sandplay.* London: Routledge.

Sams, J., & Carson, D. (1988). *Medicine cards: The discovery of power through the ways of animals.* Santa Fe, NM: Bear and Company.

Schore, A. (1997). Interdisciplinary developmental research as a source of clinical models. In M. Moskowtitz, C. Monk, C. Kaye, & S. Elman, (Eds.), *The neurobiological and developmental basis for psychotherapeutic intervention* (pp. 1–71). New York: Aronson.

Scientific Learning Corporation. (1999). *Hippocampus.gif.* Retrieved December 1, 2001, from www.BrainConnection.com.

Scott, E. (1998). *Close encounters: Exploring the universe with the Hubble space telescope* (p. 30). New York: Hyperion Books for Children.

Shepherd, S. (2000). On moons and mirrors. *Journal of Sandplay Therapy, 9*(1), 9–18.

Siegel, B. (2000). *Diagnosis, prognosis and healing.* Retrieved October 1, 2001, from www.imagerynet.com/atlantis/articles/diagnosis.html.

Signell, K. (1990). *Wisdom of the heart.* London: Rider.

van der Kolk, B., & Fisler, R. (1995, October). Dissociation and the fragmentary nature of traumatic memories: Overview and exploratory study. *Journal of Traumatic Stress, 8*(4). Retrieved October 1, 2001, from www.trauma-pages.com/vanderk2.htm.

von Franz, M. L. (1986). *On dreams and death.* Boston: Shambhala.

Walker, B. (1983). *The woman's encyclopedia of myths and secrets.* San Francisco: Harper & Row.

Weinrib, E. (1983). *Images of the self.* Boston: Sigo Press.

Chapter 11

PLAY THERAPY FOR INDIVIDUALS WITH DEMENTIA

Kathleen S. Mayers

FUNCTIONS OF PLAY THERAPY FOR ADULTS WITH DEMENTIA

The term *play therapy* has not routinely been used to describe play-oriented therapeutic activities, services, or interactions for aging adults with dementia diagnoses. However, the term is an appropriate label for a wide variety of activities developed for use with demented individuals by activity therapists, nurses, mental health professionals, other providers and staff, caregivers, friends, and family members. In nursing care facilities, adult family homes, and other residences in which these individuals reside, there is a clear need for play therapy opportunities and equipment for this population.

In this geriatric subpopulation, individuals diagnosed with dementia have many needs. Facilities that house and provide care to these individuals tend to have a limited number of staff to manage their nonessential needs. Typically, such facilities struggle with staffing. In an optimal situation, the facility would have a full-time, trained staff member to provide for the "play needs" of individuals with moderate to severe dementia.

Individuals diagnosed with dementia have different needs from most populations that participate in play therapies. For a child patient, a chronic psychiatric patient, or an adult who seeks an exploring, life-enhancing, or "uncovering" form of therapeutic play interaction, the functions, goals, and strategies are quite different. The needs, functions, and benefits of play therapy for the population of individuals with dementia include the following:

- Cognitive stimulation.
- Distraction from angry and aggressive impulses.
- Recreation and entertainment.
- A means to exit from a dangerous situation.
- Physical movement, exercise, and range of motion.
- Coordination training.
- Sensory stimulation.
- Activation and arousal; decreased lethargy.
- Relaxation and quieting.
- Calming and sleep.
- Decreased wandering.
- Decreased or increased activity.
- Mood elevation.
- Decreased anxiety, restlessness, or agitation.
- Decreased repetitive movement.
- Decreased boredom.
- Decreased isolation.
- Decreased efforts to leave the facility/home.
- Human interaction.
- Touch.
- Maintenance of existing skills.
- Practice in rehearsing previously learned skilled activities.
- Enhancement of ability to recall their own identities, skills, roles, and occupations.
- Reminiscence.
- Facilitated interaction with family members.
- A focus for family interactions and verbalization.
- Enhanced quality of life.
- Optimized adaptive functioning.
- Increased relatedness with caregivers.
- Improved sleep.
- Enhanced sense of purpose.

Play therapies are incorporated in a wide variety of services currently offered by many different professionals and nonprofessionals. Recreation and occupational therapists, nurses, psychiatrists, psychologists, social workers, mental health aides and technicians, housekeepers, and food aides can complete work-related tasks more effectively with the use of these techniques while offering therapeutic benefits to individuals with dementia.

By gaining an attitude of playfulness and fun, some of the adverse behavioral features of dementia may be avoided or diminished. Family members may spontaneously devise play therapy strategies because they find that those strategies optimize positive behaviors and minimize problem behaviors. Alternatively, family members may be instructed in use of play therapy techniques to facilitate behavioral management and enhance their interactions with a loved family member who now functions at a more primitive level because of dementia.

This chapter discusses many kinds of play therapies for this population and offers examples of their use by those who interact with individuals with dementia. The strategies described fall in the general category of play therapies. Modifications of these approaches to facilitate behavioral management and enhance life experiences of these individuals are strongly encouraged. An individualized, play-therapeutic manner of communicating and interacting can create a more harmonious, enjoyable relationship with less aggression, hostility, and resistance.

HISTORICAL PERSPECTIVE AND BRIEF LITERATURE REVIEW

Play Therapy with Stimulus Objects

A *play therapy* type of intervention with individuals with dementia diagnoses was used in a pilot project in 1990 completed by this author and Myra Griffin. We explored the use of play materials originally developed for use with toddlers and learned that these tools could be effectively used (or modified for use) with individuals with severe dementia. We found great variation in interest and attention to the stimulus objects; we explained this variation on the basis of the individuals' past experience and interests. Before our study, we found only a few references in the literature to play therapy approaches for this population; Francis and Baly (1987) had described the use of plush animals with individuals with dementia; Norberg, Melin, and Asplund (1985) had described responses of Alzheimer's patients to music, touch, and objects. Video game stimulation with senior citizens had been described by Riddick, Drogin, and Spector (1987) and Weisman (1983).

Our observations and the existing literature led us to consider the possibility that such stimulation could enhance cognitive function during and after exposure to play therapy. We observed enhanced alertness and increased capability to provide responsive answers to questions. A play period using a busy box was provided. Afterwards, the individual's ability to respond to his or her name and to write his or her signature was evaluated; we found improved skills and responsiveness. Since that time, several other researchers have made the same kinds of observations; play therapies have been used to enhance cognitive arousal and capabilities.

In our pilot studies, we noted a significant interest in play materials and a clear desire to continue play and exploration. Resistance to removal of the play therapy materials was apparent; just as a young child may cling to a new toy, resist removal of the toy, and fight to retain it, individuals with dementia may also display this pattern. All of this seems logical and obvious; however, the patient with a dementia diagnosis tends to be far stronger physically than a child; this may result in a risk of harm to staff, family members, or other residents who try to take away the play therapy object. The tenacity with which the resident clings to an item is an indication of the attraction to the item and the pleasure he or she derives from the opportunity to play with and explore this object. This exploration, involving play and sensory self-stimulation, may be considered an integral element in human and animal behavior. Even dementia does not result in elimination of this drive until the very late stages in the dementing process.

Our early studies focused on the use of play therapy with stimulus objects from the perspective of gender-related issues, effect on cognitive function, and the use of objects to defuse aggressive impulses. Another research direction involved use of therapeutic singing and songwriting as tools to calm, distract, provide pleasurable experiences, and facilitate appropriate behavior in individuals with dementia.

When a resident with dementia becomes agitated or combative, his or her behavior may be motivated by factors that are not obvious. Just as an infant has few behaviors in his or her behavioral repertoire beyond crying or gross motor movements such as thrashing around, the behavioral repertoire of the dementia resident also may be quite limited. Displays of agitation, resistance, and combativeness can occur when there is no actual hostility or anger. Instead, unmet needs and physical or emotional discomfort may be the motivating factors. In assessing an agitated resident, it is imperative to check the resident, offer comfort measures, try to "read the mind" of the resident, and provide the needed element, another element that can substitute, or something else that can distract the individual. If the need is for warmth, food, drink, quiet, decreased risk of harm from others, decrease in stiff joints, or diminished physical pain and discomfort, it may become apparent to the caregiver. If the motivating factor is boredom, lethargy, listlessness, social isolation, diminished anxiety and fearfulness, or a need for entertainment and recreation, it may be more difficult for the caregiver to determine the problem. In such cases, caregivers try a variety of physical comforts (food, drink, placement in a quiet area, warming, cooling, and even medication); if none of these are successful in making the individual more comfortable, the caregiver may offer individual staff attention or distraction through objects and activities. These latter strategies can be considered to incorporate the elements of play therapies. Mayers and Block (1990) surveyed nursing homes to obtain information about the kind of stimulus objects available to residents. Nursing homes that were surveyed described the use of the following activities as helpful to residents with dementia. The total number of nursing homes responding was 154; the numbers indicated after the stimulus objects reflect the number of nursing homes reporting these items as helpful:

- Pets (119).
- Books/magazines (107).
- Balls and ball games (103).
- Teddy bears and teddy bear clothing (91).
- Dolls (89).
- Different textured fabrics (86).
- Flowers (83).
- Musical instruments (80).
- Pieces of fur and cloth (74).
- Balls of yarn (70).
- Aquarium (64).
- Busy boxes/busy apron/activity centers/nesting blocks and bags (55).
- Purses (51).
- Toys (50).
- Afghans (34).
- Doilies/towels/napkins (33).
- Junk mail (31).
- Rattles (12).
- Briefcases (7).

Nursing homes responding did not specify how they used these stimulus materials in the survey. It was apparent that at times, the stimulus objects were made available to residents. At times, they were used in interactive play with staff members or families. In the survey, nursing homes reported frequent use of balls and ball games to provide coordination training, sensory stimulation, exercise, and range of motion. Nursing homes reported use of teddy bears, which can be dressed and undressed; their clothing can be snapped and unsnapped, zipped and unzipped, buttoned and tied. Some nursing homes mentioned using balls of yarn, which residents use individually or in activity groups. Agitated and disruptive residents often sit for lengthy periods contentedly winding balls of yarn. Storytelling by higher functioning residents can also be useful in a group or individual setting.

Activity Groups

Nursing homes also responded to questions about the most effective forms of therapeutic activity groups. A list of the most effective means of entertaining and stimulating nursing home residents follows. The total number of responses was 154; the numbers in parentheses indicate the number of nursing homes that described this form of activity group as helpful to their residents with dementia:

- Music therapy-including dancing, singing, rhythm band, musical reminiscence (110).
- Sing-alongs (70).
- Reality orientation groups (55).
- Outings (43).
- Socialization groups-coffee hour discussions; discussion groups with refreshments (21).
- Television (21).
- Gardening therapy (21).

Other activities mentioned by nursing homes included cards, games and crafts, coloring pictures, simplified Bingo, matching or jackpot with large cards, tossing games, gardening therapy, reminiscence, parties and luncheons, sensory stimulation, reading, looking at books, poetry reading, and exercise. Music-oriented therapies were described as particularly effective; while other skills may be lost, the words to old songs and the ability to keep rhythm can persist in individuals with severe dementia.

Sensory stimulation groups can focus on any modality of stimulation. Aroma groups focus on olfactory stimuli (e.g., "What does this smell remind you of? Have you smelled it before? When? Where? Are the memories good or bad?"). Such aromas as vanilla, cotton candy, perfumes of the 20s, grease, hay, and horses may be effective. Residents with Alzheimer's disease may have decreased ability to smell aromas; the aromas used may need to be intense. Texture exploration, tasting groups, visual stimulation using pictures, and sounds can stimulate other senses.

Practicing previously learned skills becomes a form of play therapy for individuals with dementia. Sweeping the floor, putting on their own clothing (at times, in the wrong order or location), and pushing wheelchairs are forms of play therapies selected by residents with dementia. Just as a child plays and mimics adults by trying to push a lawnmower, vacuum or mop the floor, prepare mud pies, cook at an EZ Bake oven, or try on grown-up clothing, residents with dementia role-play the skills that they once used effectively in their younger adult days. They are not learning the skill as a child would, but returning to skills they have not used recently.

Nursing homes surveyed indicated that groups of 12 or fewer residents were optimally effective. Trying to structure the group, for example, calling it a "club" such as "Wild Flowers," "Zoot Suit Mamas," "Casanovas," or "Rat Pack," and using a routine, such as a flag salute, introduction of all members, or an exercise component, are suggested. If exercise is offered, providing verbal and visual instruction and demonstration are helpful for this population—modeling the exercise, slowly explaining it verbally, and offering kinesthetic and tactile facilitation when needed by moving the residents' limbs through the exercise. The focus could be seasonal (e.g., fall colors) or could incorporate such interests as old-time fiddlers or bird-watching.

It is of note that many specialists working with dementia residents view television as inappropriate because it can be agitating. Television shows must be carefully selected. In some facilities, the television is left on for the entertainment of the staff, but this is highly inappropriate. For the resident, being forced to sit in a day room for 12 to 15 hours a day, watching and listening to police shows, murder mysteries, soap operas, and rap music may constitute torture. At times, confused residents believe that television dramas are occurring at that moment, and they view themselves as victims of the violence, resulting in fearfulness, and aggressive and defensive combativeness. At times, their confusion takes another form, and they may begin to talk about "that man" or "that woman" and describe confused, fractured elements of a television show.

Other Strategies

Since the publication of the Play Project by Mayers and Griffin in 1990, an increasing number of accounts have been published describing development of other strategies that incorporate a play orientation and provide therapeutic benefits. Moyra Jones's Gentlecare Life Care System (1996) uses a prosthetic model, with the goal of creating a fit between the individual with dementia and the programs, living area, caregivers, and other individuals who interact with the individual with dementia. This system strives to accommodate and support existing strengths and skills and provides education to caregivers to improve their understanding of how to gently assist the individual in the areas he or she has lost and avoid agitation and frustration of the individual with dementia. She focuses on educating caregivers so they can understand the losses and deficits of the resident with dementia, comprehend how they need to facilitate the resident's functioning, and provide "prostheses" to compensate for the lost skill. Her prosthetic model offers gentle touch, appropriate stimulus objects, and soothing, nonagitating living spaces suitable for "play" and exploration.

In a study by Buettner published in 1999, a research team called "Simple Pleasures" evaluated the responses to 30 handmade recreational tools and assessed their effect on the conduct of nursing home residents with dementia diagnoses. Twenty-three of these objects were found to be valuable therapeutic tools; agitation decreased with the use of these objects. Satisfaction by family members during visits improved significantly when the stimulus items were made available. The Simple Pleasures research team found that the following stimulus objects, made by volunteers and family members, had appeal for the residents: activity apron, stuffed butterfly/fish, cart for wandering, fishing box, flowers for arranging, electronic busy box, laundry for hanging, home decorator books, latch box-doors, look-inside purse, message magnets, muffs, picture dominoes, polar fleece hot water bottles, rings on hooks game, sewing cards, squeezies, table ball game, tablecloth with activities, tetherball game, vests/sensory, and wave items. The objects were placed on an open cart. Residents could freely choose from the selection of items on the cart. The preferred object for all residents in this study was a tetherball game, which held residents' attention for as long as 20 minutes. Of note is the fact that some preferred objects were warm (e.g., a warm sensory vest; a fleecy muff; a polar fleece hot water bottle). Elderly residents with little or no movement are likely to feel chilled; the warmth of these objects may serve to provide both pleasure and decreased chilling, with a resulting decrease in agitation.

Mary Lucero, Kijek, Malone, Santos, and Hendrix (2000) developed specific play products as a means of enhancing the quality of life of individuals with dementia. Her products and potential interactions included a busy box, abacus, stacking cups, *Reader's Digests,* spinning board, pat mat, and curves and waves. The interactions with these objects were varied: The resident could thumb, page, fold, hold, read, look, and touch a *Reader's Digest;* kneading, rocking, pinching, squeezing, slapping, pointing, and touching were the interactions with the pat mat. Lucero et al. considered many features in determining the suitability of their products, including gender neutrality, sensory qualities, potential interaction capability, potential for repetitive and rhythmic motion, complexity, and so on. This approach to play therapy included providing the object to the resident, demonstrating its use, and guiding the play activity by moving the resident's hands. Results of this study indicated that using an effective method of product introduction significantly improved the resident's ability to engage in activities with the stimulus object.

The Lucero group (Lucero, Pearson, Hutchinson, Leger-Krall, & Rinalducci, 2001) also explored the use of play products on self-stimulatory wanderers. They focused their study on dementia unit residents who had a pattern of touching objects in the environment or displaying industrious activities such as repetitive cleaning. They described patterns of activities in middle- and late-stage dementia;

activities displayed by these residents often focused on use of stimulus objects. These residents often engaged in such behaviors as wandering and picking up random items, placing them in equally random areas. Residents engaged in sleeping in any bed they found, smoothing bedspreads, and pulling them back; removing shoes and socks, dentures and eyeglasses; swinging doors open and closed; pulling and releasing emergency cords; rummaging through trash cans; picking up cups and glasses and drinking their contents; carrying, twirling, and stroking a feather duster; putting small objects in their mouths; and focusing on their own clothing, rubbing pieces of the fabric. The Lucero group concluded that there is a clear need for products for self-stimulatory wanderers.

Kovach and Henschel (1996) assessed the effect of various organized therapeutic activities on residents' functioning. Music therapy, art therapy, exercise, cognitive activities (including poetry reading, current events, reminiscence, and discussion), and functional household activities (cooking, dishwashing, folding towels) were compared.

They found that participants spent more time involved in the activity when they were able to form a cognitive tie between the current activity and past activities through reminiscing. They concluded that activities may be more therapeutic if they are planned around the resident's recalled history and past likes/dislikes.

Lord and Gardner (1993) found that individuals with dementia in a group that received music therapy were more alert, happier, and had better recall of past personal history than subjects in art or puzzle completion groups. The research protocol that they used assessed dementia residents six months after the groups were formed.

Enclosed garden areas can also be of great benefit for residents of special care units; they offer opportunities to wander, look at plants, and engage in gardening activities. Mather, Nemecek, and Oliver (1999) found that use of an enclosed garden resulted in less sleep during the daytime hours during the summer and more time spent looking outdoors and attempting to get outside during the winter. They also described generally improved morale as a result of garden use.

Benjamin Sobel (2001) used the game of Bingo in an adult day care program for individuals with Alzheimer's disease to stimulate cognitive function—short-term memory, concentration, word-retrieval, and word recognition. He theorized that Bingo requires multiple thought processes and would be more effective in enhancing cognition than physical activities. Cognitive functioning on the Boston Naming Test and the Word List Recognition Task was enhanced after Bingo play, but not in individuals who engaged in only physical activities. The components of Bingo play were of particular benefit in enhancing cognitive function.

Kydd (2001) reviewed the literature on the positive effects of music therapy on individuals with dementia and described a specific case study that illustrated how music therapy can be effective in facilitating the adjustment of an individual with dementia to a care facility. Music therapy has been found to improve and en-hance many aspects of the residential living situation for residents with demen-tia. Kanamori et al. (2001) explored the use of animal-assisted therapy with residents with dementia diagnoses and found improvement on measures of cogni-tive function and diminished stress.

Snyder, Faan, et al. (2001) and Snyder, Tseng, et al. (2001) have effectively used a glider swing intervention for residents with dementia. Just as swinging on a playground swing is an enjoyable play activity for children, it can be conceptual-ized as a potentially satisfying play therapy for adults with dementia. In a similar vein, Watson, Wells, and Cox (1998) used "rocking chair therapy" to improve psy-chological well-being and balance. Decreased anxiety and depression, reduction in pain medication, and improved balance were related to the amount of rocking.

Montessori-based activities have also been used as a means of enhancing life for individuals with dementia (Judge, Camp, & Orsulic-Jeras, 2000). Use of these techniques was found to be more effective in enhancing active engagement and in-volvement in activities than regular programming that was not based on Montessori principles.

Experiences with play therapies in the population of adults with dementia have helped to understand what is effective, what elements need to be consid-ered, and what risks should be avoided to provide optimal play therapy activities. The following section discusses issues to be considered in developing an under-standing of why the dementia resident needs play therapy activities and how ther-apeutic activities can improve his or her quality of life.

CONSIDERATIONS IN THE USE OF PLAY THERAPIES WITH INDIVIDUALS WITH DEMENTIA

Practice in Maintaining and Rehearsing Skilled Activities

The individual in a care facility is no longer involved in the day-to-day activities of the past life; skilled work outside the home, work in the home, hobbies, and pastimes are no longer a large part of the individual's life. In the process of the dementing illness, the individual retains residues of these past behaviors and in-terests and derives many benefits from exposure to elements of the past. Personal satisfaction, a sense of meaning and purpose, reinforcement of his or her own identity, decreased anxiety and agitation, and cognitive stimulation may be gained by practicing previously acquired skills that are critical to that individ-ual's identity. A musician who has lost the dexterity to play can sit and hold a vi-olin case; a homemaker can work with a therapist to prepare Jello, bread, cookies, or scrambled eggs; a mechanic can sort through a box of nuts and bolts.

Providing the Impetus and Initiating Play Therapeutic Tasks

For some residents with dementia, there is a loss of the capability to determine how to use the play object. When children learn to play with complex toys, they watch other children, turn the toys over and over, push buttons, pull knobs, and poke their fingers into holes. Residents with dementia may lose the capability to determine how to use some simple mechanical objects. The creativity that occurs in children may disappear in individuals with dementia. For that reason, staff or family may need to model use of the object. This is particularly important with such tools as busy boxes with mechanical parts. The role of the play therapist in this population becomes one of "priming the pump" and teaching previously learned skills. In nursing home settings, residents often do not watch each other to determine how these objects may be used; instead, play therapists serve the role of instructor and model the use of the objects or move the individual's hands.

Gender-Related Interests in Play Materials

Interests of dementia patients, especially those in their 60s and older, tend to cluster along gender lines. One of our pilot projects assessed the gender-specific interests of dementia residents; results were very predictable. The same information can be gained by following strangers in a shopping mall or outlet and observing what they look at, what they pick up, what they touch, and how they touch it, what they smell, rub, and stroke. The females tend to be interested in fabric items, especially tactually appealing items. Clothing and footwear are of particular interest. Their stimulus-seeking behavior includes stroking and rubbing of the items. They enjoy looking at attractive and pretty items. Glittery items, simple mechanical items, colorful objects, and fragrant items have appeal. Kitchen types of implements tend to be of interest to females of this age group. Typewriters and sewing machines are commonplace items of their generation; their familiarity with these objects may result in interest in using them in play therapy. Buttons and snaps; graters, wooden spoons, meat grinders, bread boxes, mixing bowls, egg beaters, and hand beaters; seersucker, gingham, rayon, and felt-these are some of the simple textures and objects that populated the lives of these women that may still be of continuing interest to them.

For males, mechanical objects may take precedence. Operating mechanical and moving parts of more complex objects, turning items over and seeing how they work, turning knobs and dials, and manipulating hard metal objects with moving parts are intriguing. Play therapeutic opportunities may include a "builders' group," with latches, bolts, hooks, screws—objects that residents can touch, hold, and combine in various ways; they can gain a sense of male camaraderie and productivity. "Sitting with the guys" and drinking nonalcoholic beer can be a pleasurable way to spend time. In a garden area, residents can work on pots and plants, watering, and "gardening." Males also like colorful objects, pretty scenes, and soft fabrics, which can be provided in group or individual settings.

Play therapeutic opportunities might include groups and individual interactions with others. Some females (and possibly males) may benefit from baking groups, meal preparation groups, and recipe discussion groups. Stimulus objects include old baking dishes, flour, dried fruit and supplies, frosting, and nuts; residents enjoy mixing, rolling, and decorating the baked goods. They may welcome opportunities to use baking equipment from the appropriate era-the 20s, 30s, 40s, 50s, 60s, 70s—when these individuals were busy feeding families and preparing countless meals. The sensory stimulation involved in tasting the raw materials and the finished product, enjoying the textures of the items and smelling the aroma of baking are gratifying experiences. Other activities that can be provided in group or individual settings include crocheting, knitting, and embroidery; working on an old typewriter and adding machine; and trips to a clothing closet, where the resident can select a tie, belt, wallet, purse, apron, hat, and so on. Residents can talk in group and individual settings about their preferences, favorites, the item they had in the past just like this one, preferred colors, fabrics, and so on.

It is hard to know whether generations of the future will also tend to display interests along gender lines. Certainly, the movement of females out of the kitchen and into the workplace will offer many nongender-related interests; computers, CD and DVD players, video and digital cameras, palm pilots, and cell phones are appropriate for both genders.

Age and Era-Related Interests

Individuals with early-onset dementias who are 60 years of age are very different from those with dementias who are in their 90s or older. Their experiences, preferences, and histories are quite dissimilar. It is necessary to know something of the lives of these individuals in developing an effective play therapy program. Knowledge of the music that they listened to, the historical events, the foods that were available, and the clothing that they wore is relevant in providing optimally effective reminiscence, music, discussion, current events, and other groups. Vintage items, including clothing, household tools, cookware, and books, become valuable commodities for nursing homes and can be used effectively as stimulus objects. For the baby boomers now in their 50s, early dementias will affect residents who respond to rock and roll, not to war songs of the 40s. Staff in these facilities will need to tailor these programs for the era in which the residents lived their earlier lives.

Potential Interests of Dementia Residents and Effective Therapeutic Stimulus Materials

Several projects have completed naturalistic observations of dementia patients in nursing home or geriatric residential facility settings to gain an understanding of each patient's preferred stimulus object. Gender may have an effect on the interests of these individuals; the location in which an individual spent his or her early years may also be relevant. Individuals who lived in cities may have interests and retained skills different from those who lived in rural settings. Those who were raised outside the United States may not be familiar with objects from the 1930s and 1940s that were common in the states. As these individuals age, they may not have access to information and skills learned later in life; thus, second languages may no longer be used or understood, complex skills may be lost, and past interests lose their relevance and importance for the individual with dementia.

It would be helpful to try to develop a history of the individual with dementia before the disease progresses. A video or written and pictorial history of the individual through his or her life, focusing on occupation, hobbies, pastimes, necessary tasks, and particular skills would be of benefit when trying to determine optimal therapeutic activities to be offered in the future, especially after the individual loses the capability to verbalize preferences and interests.

With a stimulus object that has dials or knobs, an individual with dementia might find and rotate the dials or knobs on one occasion, but he or she might not locate the dials or knobs or determine that it can be rotated on another occasion. Using therapeutic intervention by a staff member to demonstrate use of the object (no matter how simple the object) may facilitate play with the object for a lengthier period of time. Instruction in the use of moving parts, no matter how simple the mechanism, may be needed every time the individual uses the stimulus object.

Changes in Play Interests as Dementia Progresses

As the individual proceeds through the stages of a dementia and loses intellect, judgment, reasoning, and awareness, the kind of therapeutic play interaction appropriate for the individual changes. Early in the dementing process, the individual is aware of memory lapses, but remains at home and is able to meet most of his or her needs. Repetition of stories and questions, loss of names for familiar objects, and becoming lost outside the home are common. Many effective skills are retained at this point. A day care program may be optimal. As the dementia progresses and skills are lost, it becomes necessary for play therapies to focus at an increasingly basic level to avoid frustration for the resident. Play therapy offerings must demand fewer skills and less language. Even with a very low-functioning dementia resident, there still are play-oriented therapies that can be effective. Singing a soft, gentle song to the resident, holding hands and swinging arms to music, repeating childhood songs and rhymes—these all constitute playful attitudes and activities that may meet some of the severely demented residents' needs. As dementia progresses, even if the resident with dementia sits and fingers a stimulus object for 30 to 60 seconds and does nothing else with the play therapy stimulus object, this is an improvement over sitting with a blank stare, engaging in no stimulus exploration.

The progression of dementia is based on deterioration of brain function. The process of dementia involves diminished functioning of portions of the brain because of cell loss/death. The loss of the more complex elements of behavior is based on degeneration of those areas of the brain that contribute to the specific function.

Time of Play, Place of Play, Noise, Lighting, Smells, Temperature, Illness, and Other Not-So-Trivial Issues

Even such a simple variant as the time of day at which the stimulus objects are given to the dementia resident can make an enormous difference in the reaction of the resident. Whenever possible in our studies, we used morning hours to avoid the residents' falling asleep with a stimulus object clutched tightly. However, it should be noted that cuddly, stuffed animals may facilitate sleep and can be used effectively to help residents fall asleep; they may have a calming or warming effect.

Elderly individuals have poorer vision and may not have eyeglasses, hearing aides, or other adaptive equipment. Some dementia residents refuse to use adaptive equipment or lose it. Lighting can vary from place to place in a day hall and can result in differing levels of interest and attention. Glare and difficulty seeing, competing noises and distraction, and staff or residents walking around intruding and interrupting may diminish the resident's interest in play therapeutic activities. Offensive odors, feeling too cold or hot, and feeling ill may interfere with the resident's ability to pay attention or play with certain objects at certain times. Location of play, comfort of available seating, and distractions may have a significant effect. We noted an enormous variance from session to session in the interest displayed by residents in various objects.

Objections to Play Therapy; Safety and Cleanliness

Safety and cleanliness issues can effectively destroy a successful play therapy program. In one hospital setting with dementia residents, cleanliness and hygiene issues were considered to be so important that all stimulus objects would be removed from the ward unless every item was washed on a daily basis and efforts were made to ensure that the play therapy items were not passed from one patient to another; the concern was infection. Buettner (1999) appropriately discussed successful selection of recreational materials. She stated that careful attention is needed in designing, selecting, and scrutinizing these stimulus materials. Toxicity and safety considerations are paramount. Objects that are sharp, pointed, or heavy may need to be avoided. It is typical of residents with Alzheimer's disease to explore their environments with their mouths. Keys, small cars, and plastic flowers are sucked, mouthed, and chewed and pose a risk of swallowing and aspirating. Residents with dementia may repeatedly throw items off a tray table to the floor. This represents a safety hazard for individuals walking about on the ward. Nursing staff cannot be expected to repeatedly retrieve stimulus items from the floor.

In the Mayers and Block survey (1990), nursing homes often indicated that pets provided an optimal form of interactive play therapy. However, pets present dangers—risks to both the residents and the animals. In addition, some residents may be severely allergic to fur and dander. However, animals do tend to calm residents and can offer a sense of unconditional acceptance; they are used frequently in hospital, hospice, nursing home, and residential facilities, and their use can be considered a form of play therapy. In the survey, a number of nursing homes indicated that small children who come with families to visit are very effective in creating a cheerful environment; residents enjoy interacting with children. The children climb on laps, hug, and sing to the residents and are not concerned if the verbal interaction and conversation by dementia residents make no sense. There are safety concerns with children, who must be monitored closely; it is imperative to ensure their safety. Families may not know the assault history of their family member in the nursing home facility. They are certainly unaware of the assault histories of other residents and may not realize the dangers. At times, family members may use denial and fail to recognize the seriousness of the concern or blame their family member's assault on insensitive nursing care procedures when it was a random, inexplicable, but very serious assault.

Some individuals with dementia tend to put in their mouths anything small enough to fit. They may have lost the ability to distinguish between food and non-food items. While keys, beads, and other small objects are interesting to these individuals, the risks of ingestion of the stimulus objects are serious concerns.

It is apparent that maintenance and repair of nonliving therapeutic play and stimulus items are necessary. In Buettner's Simple Pleasures research project (1999), without specific individuals designated to make items available, to maintain, repair, and replace the items, the project tended to fade. This author has had the same experience in a geriatric hospital setting. Someone needs to be designated to replace, repair, maintain, and clean the play therapy objects. If no one is assigned this role, the play therapy project is not likely to persist; stimulus objects break or disappear.

A few staff members may use the idea of play therapy as a means of facilitating their own jobs. A medication nurse may use play items as a diversionary technique while distributing medication. Housekeeping staff members may use food or play therapy items to keep residents from interfering while the facility is cleaned; it is not unusual for a dementia resident to take over the mop and bucket; the use of play type objects or even another broom or mop for the residents may permit the employee to complete cleaning floors more efficiently. An aide may use play items to facilitate bathing of patients and keep them from grabbing soap, shampoo, and creams. In these situations, the staff member is likely to maintain a small number of play objects that are particularly effective in allowing the completion of their work.

Family Objections to Play Therapy: Infantilizing Issues

Mayers and Block (1990) commented on the fact that families may respond unfavorably to Grandma playing with a doll or Grandpa twirling a dial on a busy box for hours on end. It is difficult for families to cope with the declining intellectual, physical, and emotional capacities of the family member with dementia. The last straw may be the visit to the nursing home in which the family member with dementia does not recognize family members, is unable to verbalize, and sits and plays with a child's toy. Family members may view this as demeaning and insulting. In the nursing home survey by Mayers and Block, the suggestion was made that handcrafted busy boxes and aprons may avoid distressing family members; the thought of a grandparent being reduced to playing with a young child's toy can be very upsetting. Buettner (1999) also discussed the fact that these stimulus objects must be age- and stage-appropriate. Family members are likely to view some stimulus objects and play therapy interactions as potentially infantilizing and humiliating. Even when their family member with dementia loves the game and clings to the stimulus object, battling others to retain it, it is inevitable that some family members will request that Mom not be given a teddy bear and that Dad be kept away from the activity apron because it makes him look silly to be sitting there fidgeting with a toy.

EXAMPLES OF USE OF PLAY THERAPY IN INDIVIDUAL INTERACTIONS WITH INDIVIDUALS WITH DEMENTIA

Staff members in nursing homes and other care facilities have devised unique and creative play therapy treatments and interventions to facilitate care and increase the satisfaction and quality of life for the residents. A few of these are described to increase the reader's understanding of these therapies in one-to-one situations.

1. Carol Meninger refuses to eat. Staff members have tried a variety of techniques, but she remains stubborn and inflexible. A food aide decides that she'll attempt some of the same strategies that are effective with her own young daughter. She brings a "sippy cup" with a picture on the bottom and uses the same technique she has found to be effective with her two-year-old daughter. The technique does not work every time, but Mrs. Meninger smiles when she sees the picture of the little dog on the bottom of the cup. This becomes a reward for drinking for Mrs. Meninger and she laughs playfully when she sees it.

2. Ed Zinamon is restricted to a wheelchair. He watches other residents dance, but he is grumpy and agitated, often yelling during music therapy. A staff member approaches him, takes both hands, and "dances" him around, moving the wheelchair from side to side. He smiles, flirts, laughs, and displays pleasure. He remains content and happy through the rest of the music therapy session, with no agitation or grumpiness as long as he has his dance partner.

3. Mary Starr is in her bedroom, screaming loudly and refusing a bath. She has not been bathed for five days because of her repeated and insistent refusals. It is not clear why she is refusing. Modesty, discomfort related to feeling cold, fear of the unknown, unfamiliarity with the bathing area, concern about removing her clothing, and being immersed in water may contribute to her anxiety and distress. The staff members respond to her fear by developing a play therapy regimen. They sing to her as they and she work on removing her clothing:

To the tune of London Bridges:

"Mary, take your jacket off, jacket off, jacket off. Mary, take your jacket off, pretty lady.

Mary, take your sweater off, sweater off, sweater off. Mary, take your sweater off, pretty lady.

Mary, take your pants right off, pants right off, pants right off. Mary, take your pants right off, pretty lady.

Mary, take your socks right off, socks right off, socks right off. Mary, take your socks right off, pretty lady.

Mary, take your undies off, undies off, undies off. Mary, take your undies off, pretty lady.

Mary, get right in the tub, in the tub, in the tub. Mary, get right in the tub, pretty lady.

Mary, let me wash your hair, wash your hair, wash your hair. Mary, let me wash your hair, pretty lady."

Mary, help me wash your _____, wash your _____, wash your _____. Mary, help me wash your _____, pretty lady.

Mary, let me dry your _____" and so on.

In the bathtub are floating toys and bubble bath. A bottle of scent is ready for use after the bath. A pretty flowered gown and a cup of hot chocolate are additional treats to "sweeten" the bath experience. The room is heated and the entire situation is warm, caring, playful. The staff is gentle, patient, and affectionate with her, using a playful, warm manner.

4. Mr. Procter is about to hit Mr. Slone. Two staff members intervene with stimulus objects for each man. Each staff member steers one of the men away, demonstrating the use of a busy apron or mechanical toy with moving parts. An angry, physical confrontation between the two men is successfully avoided.

5. Susan Davis is crying. She seems to be responding to loss, but it is not clear what loss she is reexperiencing. There has been no recent loss, but many losses in the past. A staff member approaches, hugs and comforts her, and starts to sings a childhood lullaby, "Hush little baby, don't you cry." Mrs. Davis stops crying and looks attentively. The staff member is holding a stuffed plush toy, which Mrs. Davis takes from her and holds in her arms. She begins to sing her own lullaby to the "baby," changing her role from that of receiver of care to that of nurturer for the doll. The calming strategy has been successful.

6. Steve Nikklin is agitated and oppositional. He has lost most of his language skills, but he still can say, "No." He responds this way to any staff request. He comprehends little of what staff say to him, but inevitably, he refuses with a loud, forceful, "NO!" His eating has been poor and he is losing weight. Staff members are trying to supplement his diet with high protein milkshakes. The food aide approaches Mr. Nikklin and sings to him, "Please, Mr. Nikklin, just say yes. The milkshake is yummy. It'll help your tummy. Please, Mr. Nikklin, yes, yes, yes." She is wearing very bright red lipstick and has a large smile. Mr. Nikklin's vision is poor, but he can see her smile and he likes her soft voice. The song entertains him. The "Yes" in the song has been repeated many times. While he does not comprehend the words, he understands her friendliness, he does not become frightened, and he willingly accepts the milkshake. He tries to verbalize pleasure, but cannot form a word. At times, when he is unsuccessful in forming a word, he becomes angry and agitated and yells out the beginning consonant of a word. He says, "Bubububububububu . . ." becoming louder and louder. The food aide is accustomed to this, but she takes his verbalization and incorporates it into a simple song, which she repeats while he is drinking, "Bubububububaby, you're my baby. Bububububububaby, you're my baby with a milkshake and it tastes so good." He seems to like this song and drinks his milkshake when she sings to him.

7. Dick Sudduth is noncompliant with nursing care and sometimes escalates to aggression. It can take up to five nursing care staff to bathe him, brush his teeth, change his soiled undergarments, and complete basic hygiene and grooming. He hits, spits, bites, and kicks. When one staff member focuses entirely on entertaining and distracting Mr. Sudduth, the task is completed more easily. Using toys, stimulus objects, or even small bites of food treats, the task is completed more easily and with less risk of injury. One of Mr. Sudduth's preferred stimulus objects is a briefcase. He is very content when he can hold or walk about with his briefcase; this reminds him of when he was a businessman in his earlier life.

CONCLUSIONS

The play therapy techniques may sound silly and infantile, but they become effective with individuals with dementia. Everyone has the capacity to become playful and silly; we engage in these kinds of behaviors with our children, our spouses, and our families. When staff members allow themselves to become playful in the work setting and use these techniques with individuals with dementia, care becomes easier, cooperation is likely to be increased, and significant benefits are provided.

It is likely that in the future, more emphasis will be placed on entertaining and interacting with these residents in playful ways to diminish agitation, aggression, and unnecessary restrictiveness in their care. Restrictiveness takes many forms for this population; it can take the form of medication (chemical restraints). It can take the form of physical restraints or placement of the individual away from others. The greater the fun for the resident, the happier he or she is, the more compliant the resident is with nursing care, the better his or her cognitive function, and the fewer the restrictions that will need to be imposed.

REFERENCES

Buettner, L. L. (1999). Simple pleasures: A multilevel sensorimotor intervention for nursing home residents with dementia. *American Journal of Alzheimer's Disease and Other Dementias, 14*(1), 41–52.

Francis, G., & Baly, A. (1986). Plush animals: Do they make a difference? *Geriatric Nursing, 7*(3), 140–142.

Jones, M. (1996). *Changing the Experience of Alzheimer's Disease.* Burnaby, BC: Moyra Jones Resources.

Judge, K. S., Camp, C. J., & Orsulic-Jeras, S. (2000). Use of Montessori-based activities for clients with dementia in adult day care: Effects on engagement. *American Journal of Alzheimer's Disease, 15*(1), 42–46.

Kanamori, M., Suzuki, M., Yamamoto, K., Kanda, M., Matsui, Y., Kojima, E., et al. (2001). A day care program and evaluation of animal-assisted therapy (AAT) for the elderly with senile dementia. *American Journal of Alzheimer's Disease and Other Dementias, 16*(4), 234–239.

Kovach, C. R., & Henschel, H. (1996). Planning activities for patients with dementia: A descriptive study of therapeutic activities on special care units. *Journal of Gerontological Nursing, 22,* 33–38.

Kydd, P. (2001). Using music therapy to help a client with Alzheimer's disease adapt to long-term care. *American Journal of Alzheimer's Disease and Other Dementias, 16*(2), 103–108.

Lord, T. R., & Gardner, J. E. (1993). Effects of music on Alzheimer patients. *Perceptual and Motor Skills, 76,* 451–455.

Lucero, M., Kijek, J., Malone, L., Santos, R., & Hendrix, K. (2000). Products for Alzheimer's patients with "null" behavior. *American Journal of Alzheimer's Disease and Other Dementias, 15*(6), 347–357.

Lucero, M., Pearson, R., Hutchinson, S., Leger-Krall, S., & Rinalducci, E. (2001). Products for Alzheimer's self-stimulatory wanderers. *American Journal of Alzheimer's Disease and Other Dementias, 16*(1), 43–50.

Mather, J. A., Nemecek, D., & Oliver, K. (1999). The effect of a walled garden on behavior of individuals with Alzheimers. *American Journal of Alzheimer's Disease and Other Dementias,* 252.

Mayers, K., & Block, C. (1990). Specialized services for demented residents in Washington state nursing homes: Report of a survey. *American Journal of Alzheimer's Care and Related Disorders and Research, 5*(4), 17–21.

Mayers, K., & Griffin M. (1990). The play project: Use of stimulus objects with demented patients. *Journal of Gerontological Nursing, 16*(1), 32–37.

Norberg, A., Melin, E., & Asplund, K. (1985). Reactions to music, touch, and object presentation in the third stage of dementia: An exploratory study. *International Journal of Nursing Studies, 23*(4), 315–323.

Riddick, C. C., Drogin, E. B., & Spector, S. G. (1987). The impact of videogame play on the emotional states of senior center participants. *Gerontologist, 27*(4), 425–427.

Snyder, M., Faan, M., Tseng, Y.-H., Brandt, C., Croghan, C., Hanson, S., et al. (2001). A glider swing intervention for people with dementia. *Geriatric Nursing, 22*(2), 86–90.

Snyder, M., Tseng, Y.-H., Brandt, C., Croghan, C., Hanson, S., Constantine, R., et al. (2001). Challenges of implementing intervention research in persons with dementia: Example of a glider swing intervention. *American Journal of Alzheimer's Disease and Other Dementias, 16*(1), 51–56.

Sobel, B. P. (2001). Bingo vs. physical intervention in stimulating short-term cognition in Alzheimer's disease patients. *American Journal of Alzheimer's Disease and Other Dementias, 16*(2), 115–120.

Watson, N. M., Wells, T. J., & Cox, C. (1998). Rocking chair therapy for dementia patients: Its effect on psychosocial well-being and balance. *American Journal of Alzheimer's Disease and Other Dementias, 13,* 308.

Weisman, S. (1983). Computer games and the frail elderly. *Gerontologist, 23,* 361–363.

Chapter 12

USING THERAPEUTIC DOLLS WITH PSYCHOGERIATRIC PATIENTS

Mally Ehrenfeld

DOLL THERAPY-BACKGROUND AND RATIONAL

Patients who suffer from psychogeriatric diseases, mainly dementia or Alzheimer's disease, exhibit similar symptoms such as depression, agitation, and distress. Many of them also fail to communicate with medical staff and family. People with dementia gradually lose rewarding roles, and their disturbed behavior often reflects their loss of meaning and purpose. *Dementia* is the loss of cognitive abilities, including impairment of memory as well as one or more of the following: aphasia, apraxia, agnosia, disturbed planning, and organizing and abstract thinking disabilities. The mental deterioration that characterizes dementia often reverses the normal development from child to adult; therefore, people with dementia are often childlike in behavior. For this reason, it seems appropriate to consider treatment methods that are usually appropriate for children.

Dolls and toys have been used as a means of diagnosis and therapy with children for many years (Jennings, 1993) because it provides them with the opportunity to act out feelings and difficulties as they are experienced (McMahon, 1992; Synovitz, 1999). Through the manipulation of dolls and other everyday life items and toys, the child can show more adequately than through words how he or she feels about himself or herself and other persons and events in his or her life. It can also help in cases of sexual abuse, when the child can point on the puppet to the exact anatomic site of abuse (Eleanor, 1993; Martin, 1987). Using toys and other everyday items is needed because most children under the age of 9 or 10 have not yet developed the abstract reasoning skills and verbal abilities to sit in the therapist's office and articulate their feelings. The therapist has to recognize the child's feelings in an indirect way by using a broad variety of materials, such as dolls, dollhouses, and toys, for better and open communication with children (Axline, 1967). Puppets are also used as an alternative technique for educators. Thus, these items can be used by nurses and health providers for health promotion (Caputo, 1993; Snart & Maguire, 1986; Spann, 1994; Synovitz, 1999).

We can infer from the world of children to the world of adult patients suffering from cognitive impairments. These adults may have considerable difficulty in trying to express themselves. For these patients, sometimes words and narratives are not an effective form of expression. These patients may need to express themselves with a mediating object, which serves as a bridge to the outside world and their interactions with people. For some patients, touching, holding, and hugging facilitate their communication with others (Landreth, 1991).

The approach to patients with dementia has changed over the years. An article in the *Washington Post* (Jones, 1997) described these changes. In the past, caregivers attempted to bring patients back to reality by orienting them to place and time. This was called *reality orientation*. Recently, it is more generally accepted that the best method of communication with a patient involves accepting his or her own personal reality. So, for example, when a 78-year-old woman suffering from dementia says she is waiting for a bus to take her to work, after which she is having lunch with a friend, the appropriate response would *not* be to explain to her that she is no longer a secretary, hasn't worked for 25 years, and that her friend is long dead. Rather, the appropriate response by way of validation therapy would be, for example, to mention how lovely her pearls look and how nicely she has dressed for the occasion.

In fact, the approach today to caring for the patient suffering from dementia is: "If it works, use it" (Raymond, 2000). There seems to be no clear documentation of when doll therapy was first introduced, but it is most likely that patients who were exposed by chance to dolls adopted them. Caregivers took note of the soothing and comforting effect that the patients drew from their interactions with dolls, and doll therapy seems to have grown from a need noticed by caregivers (both family and staff). It worked, so it was used. This is in line with the tendency to use validation therapy. If the patient identifies with and finds comfort in a doll, the caregiver should validate that need, particularly if it has a positive effect on the patients' emotional well-being.

Initially, however, doll therapy tends to be looked on with some discomfort by some of the staff and family members caring for people with dementia (Piccolli, 1998).

Some seem to feel that perhaps the use of dolls is infantilizing or demeaning. However, in general, after the initial introduction of dolls into the environment, the response is so overwhelmingly positive that caregivers are amazed at its success.

Although there has not been enough research on the benefits of doll therapy, several projects show it to be very beneficial to patients (e.g., Ehrenfeld & Bergman, 1995). According to Lloyd, McKenzie, Searle, and James (2000), the benefits of doll therapy include:

- Reduction of anxiety and agitation as an alternative to medication.
- Diversion of night wanderers into meaningful activity.
- Successful retrieval of special years, which can result in improved self-esteem.
- Retrieval, validation, and resolution of distressing memories.
- Recalled memories, which can boost sense of identity, satisfaction, comfort, and security.
- Encouragment of people who are withdrawn to become actively involved.
- Communication enhancement.
- Powerful reminiscence tool.

According to directors of nursing homes, many of the patients with Alzheimer's, and particularly the women, tend to revert to their early 20s, when they were mothers of small children (Jones, 1997). The interaction with dolls seems to comfort them, and they seem to develop relationships with the dolls. The patients become more communicative, enjoy talking about their babies, and changing their clothing and diapers. They also appear to be more relaxed and generally pleased. There is less wandering about and less disquiet.

DOLL THERAPY: CLINICAL ILLUSTRATIONS

To illustrate the effectiveness of doll therapy, it is helpful to choose some examples from clinical settings in the day-care center or nursing homes. In the first illustration, it is the patient who initiates her own connection with a doll; and in the second, the patient is exposed to doll therapy in the unit to which she is admitted. The following examples are cited from a research project conducted in Israel (Ehrenfeld & Bergman, 1995).

Mrs. M. is 69 years old, married, and has two sons. She suffers from Alzheimer's disease and has been attending a day-care center three mornings a week for the past two years. She has a history of repeated depressions, but says she has never been treated. Since becoming ill, she lives in the home of a nurse, who takes care of her. When first admitted, she still could recognize her husband and her sons. In recent months, however, she suffered a severe decline and cannot recognize anyone. She walks back and forth restlessly, failing to smile or communicate with anyone. Recently, she wandered into the nurses' office, in which a big bear doll sat. Mrs. M. grabbed the doll with both hands, embraced it, and grinned broadly (the first smile for many months). She continued to embrace the doll throughout the day, clutching it to her with a big smile on her face. She introduced the bear to others by pointing at its face and caressing it. Each day she grabbed the same doll as soon as she arrived at the center. She appeared much happier.

Mrs. S. is married with three children. Born in 1914 in Romania, she immigrated to Israel in 1935. She was admitted to the psychogeriatric department following a decline in her behavior and mental condition. Family members felt they no longer could care for her in her own home.

On admission, her physical condition was found to be satisfactory. The staff noted the lack of connection between the questions being asked and the replies being given. In addition, she was not oriented to time and place.

During the first days, Mrs. S. sat near the occupation table and refused any engagement. When the nurse seated her near some clients who were busy washing dolls, Mrs. S. began caressing the doll that lay beside her. When asked why she was caressing the doll, she replied: "They are just like my grandchildren, only they don't talk." Every morning she eagerly waited for the doll. On receiving it, she smiled broadly. Her face shone as she said, "What eyes she has, look!" During the day, she spent her time talking to the doll, laughing, singing, and dressing and "feeding" the doll.

She generalized this positive attachment to the staff and family members as well. Her physical condition improved, and she exhibited emotionally positive behavior.

Another case study was done by Godfrey (1994), who described the successful use of doll therapy with a resident whose attempts to "mother" other residents were causing problems.

IMPLEMENTATION OF A DOLL THERAPY PROGRAM

Doll therapy may be used for people suffering from dementia if they are agitated or distressed, feel the need to go home to check on the children, have communication difficulties, or if they are withdrawn. The therapy is appropriate for any patient who seems to respond to interaction with a doll. The use of a baby-like doll can stimulate memories of a rewarding life role, particularly that of parents. This is appropriate for people with dementia, as familiar roles are stored deeply in the emotional memory center of the brain. Following are several tips that should be considered when implementing doll therapy in any environment for patients with dementia. These pointers have been gathered from those with experience in the field. Research on the subject is direly needed to back up these and other ideas, which at this point are based mostly on experience.

How to Begin a Doll Therapy Program

Following are suggestions for implementing a doll therapy program:

- The doll should look like a real baby. Generally, patients tend to respond to realistic-looking dolls. It is important that the dolls have eyes that open and close, because cases have been reported of patients becoming concerned that the baby cannot sleep because its eyes are always open or is dead or cannot wake up because its eyes are always closed.
- Place a variety of dolls in a central spot in the activity room.
- Let the patients select their own dolls.
- Chair-bound patients should be brought to the table to choose dolls if they wish.
- The nurses should observe and record clients' reaction to the dolls, method of selection, type of contact, verbal and body language, and behavior of the client.
- At the end of the activity period, the dolls are collected unless the clients indicate they wish to keep the dolls.
- A patient's doll should never be changed without the patient's permission.

In addition, Landreth (1991) suggested the following ideas for doll therapy:

- Facilitate a broad range of creative and emotional expression.
- Make the therapy interesting to the patient.
- Allow both verbal and nonverbal exploration and expression in the room.
- Provide experiences for the patients in which they can feel successful without having to follow certain preordained procedures.
- Choose dolls that are well-made and durable.

Goals of a Doll Therapy Program

The patient will use the doll to:

- Establish a positive relationship with the therapist.
- Express feelings.
- Explore and reenact real-life situations and relationships.
- Test limits.
- Strengthen self-concept.
- Improve self-understanding.
- Enhance self-control.

CONCLUSION

Although research is sparse on the subject of doll therapy in adults, it appears that it can be an effective intervention for clients with dementia and seems to modify clients' behavior in a positive way. Nurses who have participated in the use of doll therapy claim the dolls can be used to awaken pleasurable affective responses. These benefits can be attributed to the fact that play comes naturally to patients in a regressive state of mind. As in children who have not fully developed their abstract reasoning, adults whose abstract reasoning is impaired can feel comfortable using dolls. Patients using dolls seem to generalize positive attachment to the staff, family, and other patients. This attitude facilitates treatment; and, as a result, improves patients' general condition and well-being.

All human beings need physical closeness and physical touch. As people age, the need to be touched often increases, especially during isolation and fear, which is common during hospitalization. Touch is a way to remain in contact with the environment. Touch also elicits pleasure, reassurance, and comfort. No doubt, dolls, which people can touch, hug, and cuddle, bring a sense of physical closeness and attachment. Doll therapy is, in fact, play therapy; and once the principle that play therapy is either therapeutic or a legitimate means to improve these people's quality of life is established, any kind of play therapy should be encouraged.

Consideration of the use of doll therapy with patients suffering from psychiatric disorders other than dementia is a subject that needs further study. Some work has been done with puppets in the care of disabled children (Murtagh, 1977), in a psychiatric hospital (Campbell, 1970), in nutrition education (Henry, Standley, & Sarason, 1994), in coping with emotional and behavioral disorders (Caputo, 1993), in prevention and health promotion (Synovitz, 1999), and in other settings and clinics. Yet, although research on the use of doll therapy in different medical fields shows potential to improve treatment results, it needs further study. It is not trivial to generalize from one area to another. It is essential to establish accurate knowledge to tailor specific treatment to unique populations. It would be most worthwhile to investigate the use of doll and puppet therapy in psychiatric clinical settings under a controlled environment and under the supervision of trained professionals.

REFERENCES

Axline, V. (1967). Dibs. In *Search of self.* New York: Ballantine.

Campbell, M. (1970). Puppetry in the subnormality hospital. In A. R. Philpott (Ed.), *Puppets and therapy* (pp. 43–50). Boston: Plays.

Caputo, R. (1993). Using puppets with students with emotional and behavioral disorders. *Intervention in School and Clinic, 29,* 26–30.

Ehrenfeld, M., & Bergman, R. (1995). The therapeutic use of dolls. *Perspectives in Psychiatric Care, 31*(4), 21–22.

Eleanor, C. I. (1993). Using puppets for assessment. In C. E. Schaefer & D. M. Cangelosi (Eds.), *Play therapy techniques* (pp. 69–81). New York: Aronson.

Godfrey, S. (1994). Doll therapy. *Australian Journal on Aging, 13,* 46.

Henry, H., Standley, J., Sarason, B., & Connie-Carpenter, A. (1994). The fun and fit friends want to be popular: Puppets in nutrition education for children. *Journal of Nutrition Education, 26*(4), 205A.

Jennings, S. (1993). *Play therapy with children: A practitioner's guide.* New York: Blackwell Scientific Publication.

Jones, T. (1997, February 20). Calming the Confusion of Alzheimer's. *The Washington Post,* p. M1.

Landreth, G. L. (1991). *Play therapy: The art of the relationship.* Munice, IN: Accelerated Development.

Lloyd, J., McKenzie, T., Searle, R., & James, N. (2000). Best practice guidelines: Evidence based practice information sheet for occupational therapists. *Is doll therapy an effective form of intervention for people with dementia?* Available from www.ot.curtin.edu.au/home/html/ebp/dolltherapy.html.

Martin, A. (1987). Encouraging youngsters to discuss their feelings. *Learning, 16,* 80–81.

McMahon, L. (1992). *Play therapy.* London: Tavistock/Routledge.

Murtagh, P. (1977). Unexpected guests at a residential multi-handicap school. In A. R. Philpott (Ed.), *Puppets and therapy* (pp. 96–98). Boston: Plays.

Piccoli, S. (1998, May/June). Doll therapy. *Australian dementia care. Vol. 5: Doll therapy.* Available from www.dementia.com.au/atc10504.htm.

Raymond, F. (2000). *Surviving Alzheimer's: A guide for families.* Forest Knolls, CA: Elder Books.

Snart, F., & Maguire, T. (1986). Using puppets to increase children's knowledge and acceptance of handicapped peers. *Canadian Journal for Exceptional Children, 3,* 57–59.

Spann, M. B. (1994). Make peace-keeping playful: How to use puppets to ease classroom conflicts. *Instructor, 103,* 24–25.

Synovitz, L. B. (1999). Using puppetry in coordinated school health program. *Journal of School Health, 69,* 145–147.

PART IV

PLAY GROUPS/HYPNO-PLAY/ CLIENT-CENTERED PLAY

Chapter 13

ADULT GROUP PLAY THERAPY

Christine Caldwell

why play taboo?

As members of the primate family, we humans embody two characteristics that enable us to engage in group play therapy, both in controlled and natural circumstances. First, we are a social species. We like to hang together in groups because it increases our survival as individuals. The benefit we derive from being together is greater than the cost of managing our social relationships. Second, we are lifelong learners. Playing has often been correlated with learning. Biologists note that species that must learn how to be adults are also species that play (Fagan, 1981), and that theories of why play exists often cite play's ability to foster and integrate learning (Bekoff & Byers, 1998; Huizinga, 1950; Levy, 1978). The noted physician Ashley Montague felt that the best way to grow old was to "grow young" by continuing to play our whole lives (1981). Because it seems natural that we like to play together in groups our whole lives, developing models for group adult play therapy seems an obvious thing to do.

Play therapy tends to specialize in working with children, largely because play is every child's medium for negotiating his or her inner and outer worlds. One of the reasons adult play therapy has not been as well developed may be because of a cultural taboo against it, seeing it as childish, frivolous, and contrary to the productive work required of us. This taboo may exist because we labor under the misperception that adult play is essentially similar to child's play.

Before we can begin to articulate any adult play therapy paradigms, we must overcome this misconception and see adult play as potentially quite different from the play of children. Yes, both child's play and adult play are seemingly purposeless and done in specially defined times and places. Both tend to feel pleasurable and involve physical and social risk-taking. Both involve twisting and stretching normal actions until they lose their usual contexts. However, several crucial differences exist, and they have to do with the underlying differences in the developmental tasks in which adults find themselves. Children have one job—to play. They play to learn, to grow, to develop capacities, to anticipate change, and to recover from upsets. We grown-ups have these jobs and more. We also need to take care of others, to go to work and be productive, to cope with loss and aging, to find meaning and purpose in our lives, to feel creative, to problem-solve, to self-reflect, to express our sexuality, to develop our spirituality, and to get ready to die. It is because of these extra developmental tasks that we need to appreciate how different adult play can and should be from the play of children.

This chapter stresses these differences so that we can design play therapy groups that meet the developmental needs of adults. It begins by reviewing group therapy theory and weaves it into play therapy dynamics. It continues by introducing a model for adult group play therapy developed by the author, called the *Moving Cycle*. It ends with a call for lifelong play as our means of continuing transformation.

GROUP THEORY AND PLAY THEORY

Abraham Maslow and other personality theorists champion our social nature by insisting that human personality develops inside social contexts and via social interests (Adler, 1927/1957). We carry inside us an inherent need and drive to belong (Maslow, 1968), to alleviate isolation (Fromm, 1956/1974), to bond with others (Sullivan, 1953/1968), and to rectify disturbed interpersonal relationships (Horney, 1945). These theorists felt that adults don't fully self-actualize until they gain a greater acceptance of others, display a deep social interest, form more deep and loving interpersonal relationships, and behave more democratically with others (Maslow, 1970). Groups form a central role in our lifelong developmental tasks.

Western psychotherapy has long valued groups as a curative experience for all types of adults. Yalom (1975) has noted that groups can instill hope, promote a sense of belonging, impart information, cultivate altruism, correct dysfunctional primary family imprints, develop social skills, facilitate socialization, model relational skills, provide emotional support and catharsis, help people bond with each other, and address issues of life's meaning and purpose. Because groups naturally follow stages such as forming, storming, norming, and performing, adults engaging in curative groups can recover an ability to come together, make and keep agreements, deal with conflict and differences, feel like an integral part of something, give and receive feedback, and get things done.

Because group dynamics occur whenever people come together, the phenomena of subgrouping, alliances, scapegoating, self-disclosure, and character strategy can be flushed up and given an opportunity to heal in a psychotherapeu- tically oriented group. In addition, Yalom (1975) and others (Corey, 2000) posit that groups consciously and unconsciously address the adult tasks of knowing oneself through the eyes of others, forming a permeable "self" membrane that allows intimate contact to occur and fulfilling the adult need for connectedness and belonging.

Being a member of a defined and consistent group gives us myriad opportuni- ties for social learning. Levy (1978) believes that play gives us the opportunity to engage in social learning without the fear of experiencing serious repercussions that might occur if we attempt to learn social skills in our normal "for real" world. Bekoff and Allen (1998) find that social play in both human and nonhu- man animals involves "play signals," which are nonverbal postures and gestures that broadcast play intentions and help start play and keep it going. Both reading and broadcasting intentions such as "what comes next is play, not aggression" builds trust. Play signals involve eye contact, body posture, facial expression, voice prosody, body level, and verbal invitation. It hones our ability to have both verbal and nonverbal acuity in social signaling. By engaging in and practicing play signals as children, we may be learning crucial nonverbal communication skills that form the substrate of an adult sense of being able to read others' in- tentions and broadcast our own. Nonverbal behavior continues to form the bulk of our communication throughout our lifespan. Adult play may be an important means of continuously refining and extending our nonverbal language skills. Adult play therapy may function to help us recover lost play signal reading and broadcasting abilities, abilities often obstructed by trauma and neglect.

Steven Siviy (in Bekoff & Byers, 1998) has found that rough-and-tumble play among rats (a highly social species) helps wire the brain's pleasure and reward centers. Lewis (2000) believes that social play wires up the social brain. The neo- cortex, the area of the brain that houses social reasoning, is largest in species that engage in social play. Stuart Brown conducted studies of murderers that found that normal play behavior was virtually absent throughout the lives of highly vio- lent, antisocial men. Play deprivation and/or major play abnormalities occurred in this population at a 90% level (1998). This finding helped to bring to light the possible effects of disturbed childhood play, but it also noted that adult play was disturbed in these men as well. The popular author Tom Robbins once quipped that it's never too late to have a happy childhood. Perhaps adult play in group set- tings can help to remediate some of the physical, emotional, and social deficits of an abnormal childhood.

Most researchers report that adults play much less than children do, but this finding may reflect a lack of understanding about the nature of adult play. In child- hood, play is largely *freestanding,* meaning that it's observable as a separate entity in time and space. In adults, play becomes more *imbedded.* This means that, as adults, we can do many purposeful, productive things *playfully,* mixing serious-ness and frivolity together into the same activity at a much greater rate than chil-dren can. Adults do engage in less freestanding play than children, but the reason for this may be that, as we age, we become more highly adept at multidevelopmen-tal tasking-able to laugh while we drive, dance while we vacuum the rug, and joke while we work out a budget. Perhaps by the time we are quite old, we could be ca-pable of playing while we do anything whatsoever. What a skill to develop!

Another reason that we may make the mistake of thinking that play is less im-portant for adults is that we don't realize that many behaviors we do as adults fre-quently are not seen as play behavior when they really are play at its best. Among these are making art, making love, and making spirit. We tend to define play as a goalless activity done in the moment just for the sake of doing it. Using this def-inition, adult sexuality is a type of play, as is all art-making, as is prayer, medita-tion, and contemplation. We feel best about these behaviors when we don't do them for reward or gain, but from an inborn drive that generates its own satisfac-tion. We feel that these activities hold a tremendous amount of meaning and pur-pose; but in the moment of doing them, they serve no immediate function.

Play behavior carries within it both *randomizing* and *organizing* elements. In other words, playing a sport in which you have to do actions with precision and timing helps you to become more organized. The rulebook for major league base-ball is more than 600 pages long, and we still manage to have fun at it and feel good about how predictable it can be. Play also messes things up, flummoxing the typi-cal way we do things or think about things, much like a good joke or a brainteaser. Certain types of play randomize our experience and may train us to deal with the unexpected (Spinka, Newberry, & Bekoff, 2001), an important adult capacity.

As adults, we have quite a bit of work to do, and play seems to function as a protective mechanism against the costs of this work—a buffer against stress, a support during life transitions, a means of forming bonds and alliances, and a jump start for creativity and problem solving. It may also counteract the pull of addiction, helping us to create our own natural pleasures so that we do not need to rely on chemically induced ones (Caldwell, 1996). Play may be a factor in addic-tion recovery as well, possibly helping to restore brain chemistry depleted by ad-dictive behaviors (Caldwell, in Heller, 2001).

Brain studies have shown that trauma tends to hijack the emotional and defen-sive centers of the brain (limbic), causing them to heat up with a high level of ac-tivity, while the rational centers of the brain (prefrontal cortex) remain effectively switched off (Perry, 1997). This traps a person in an emotionally flooded state where he or she cannot think or act effectively. What other researchers have found is that play and other creative activities tend to cause the whole brain to operate, but in a cooler, more cortically efficient way. Thinking and behavior are less con-strained, and a person feels more at choice about what he or she feels and does.

The current therapy favored for trauma recovery is called the *Resource model,* a gentle, experiential process of finding resources within self to heal. Play can be one such resource. By recovering play, we can recover sanity and health.

One of the features of adult group play is its ability to provide social resourcing for its members. Members of an adult play therapy group effectively become play-mates for one another, a recapitulation of a developmental need that can counter-act the social isolation so common in adults who seek therapy. Altruism and helping behavior also increase when we feel bonded to people, which not only pro-vides for the health of a society, but also helps people feel good about themselves.

One of the other features of adult play behavior is its capacity to facilitate em-bodiment. Embodiment locates us in our bodies, in the present moment. We gener-ate and attend to sensation, and we move in ways that both nurture and challenge lungs, muscles, and bones. Our bodies in turn generate endorphins and dopamine, our internal pleasure-inducing neurotransmitters. We experience a deep immer-sion in the present moment, a sense of focus that feels both intense and effortless. As psychologist Mihaly Csikszentmihalyi (1990, 1996) puts it, we enter a state of flow. The flow state heralds and supports creativity and has been described by CEOs and scientists as well as artists (Gardner, 1993). Again, therapy that helps adults to recover this natural state of flow can profoundly support adult develop-mental tasks.

Fred Donaldson (1993) coined the term *adulterated play.* By this, he meant that often as we assume the tasks of adulthood, the natural spontaneous play be-havior of our childhood falls away, and we become rigid and rule-bound. Our play degenerates into "adulterated" proscribed games and contests that cause us to lose resiliency, social intimacy, and creativity. He maintains that as adults we need to continue the free form, improvisational physical play that children and other social animals tend to engage in so easily. He takes his message all over the world, playing with people in war-torn areas. He feels strongly that if we stay playful so that we feel connected to others and to the world, we become less ca-pable of violence, abuse, and victimization. Perhaps adult play therapy holds this promise as well—that the benefits of adult play may have far-reaching conse-quences in the areas of social justice and human connection.

THE MOVING CYCLE: A PARADIGM FOR ADULT GROUP PLAY THERAPY

I developed the *Moving Cycle* after taking years to examine successful therapy ses-sions to see if I could discern any kind of pattern or sequence of events in them. Does healing follow a predictable course across time? People often heal with no therapeutic interventions. What natural mechanisms are going on there? After years of observation, I did indeed observe a pattern, and out of this observation came the Moving Cycle. The pattern I saw seemed to predict not the content of what a group would experience, but the process of opening, deepening, committing, completing, and integrating. I believe now that when we engage in healing and are allowed to do so from the dictates of our essential nature, we unravel illness in a sequenced fashion, undoing our injuries and recovering our health in an individualized, yet predictable, way. Our presence in a supportive group can magnify this process.

As the name implies, the process of healing involves a cycle or spiral of events. The spirilic nature of healing allows us to orient toward healing as a continuous process and reinforces the concept that there is no end point, no "arriving," but only increasingly satisfying and nurturing states of flow.

Healing, growth, and transformation seem to occur in four phases. Each phase must be successfully resolved for the next one to occur. Often we move into the next phase momentarily, then fall back to complete the last one. We can see these phases in physical healing, emotional healing, cognitive healing, and transpersonal/spiritual healing. The phases are the same, and they all involve a recovery of both freestanding and embedded play.

Awareness is the first step onto the Moving Cycle. It commences as group play therapy begins, and it also begins each session. Limited awareness moves people to come into therapy, as they tell themselves "Hey, something is going on that I want to take a look at." We draw ourselves toward healing when something that was stored in the dark needs to be exposed to the light. We gravitate toward others when we need to heal via the presence of others.

This first phase involves focusing our attention on sensations, feelings, and thoughts that were not previously acknowledged. Awareness is a kind of light; and when we create a beam of that light and shine it on some part of our existence, attention occurs. We all share a birthright of the ability to pay unconditional attention to the original details of life. Often our family or our culture trains us away from this ability as a way to perpetuate entrenched patterns. Patterns limit attention to conserve energy. If we are trained to stop attending to the raw data of reality, we are unable to participate fully in self-regulation. If we begin our play the way nature designed it, with the practice of paying attention to our physical, emotional, and cognitive experiences, we create a rich substrate of consciousness. Conscious attention in and of itself is one of the primary components of healing and transformation, the first source of fuel we need for the healing journey. Our beings love the light. Another way to put it is that we all share a common developmental task—to live a revealed life. Play can be one of the most powerful means we possess to support a self-reflective life.

Focusing our attention in the Awareness phase also involves the development of an observing or "witness self," because we acknowledge that a part of us is "attending" to another part of us that is "experiencing." Witnessing generates healing in and of itself, as it allows us to acknowledge and go through what we are feeling without fixating on it as part of our identity. It allows the statement "I am *having* this feeling (it will come and it will go), and I am *not* this feeling (it is not a permanent part of who I am)." This ability to witness ourselves allows us to disentangle our pain, which is in the moment and will come and go, from our suffering, which is a fusion of present pain with unresolved past experience (dysfunctional patterns). Healing group encounters also need this witness self. We all have a deep need to feel seen and understood, and we enter groups to be seen and understood, while, at the same time, fearing that we will be criticized instead of witnessed, controlled instead of understood. In addition, we may not know how to pay attention to someone else without projecting onto them. Play practices that cultivate high quality attention and awareness, both of oneself and of one another, form the opening phase of an adult play therapy group.

Einstein once opined that what we decide to look at determines what we see. He also noted that we couldn't solve a problem in the same state of consciousness that the problem arose in. The Zen master Thich Nhat Hanh once said that all views are wrong views, but because it is in our nature to have views, we might as well relax and get them as accurate as possible. The Awareness phase is about just such a relaxing, a surrender to whatever arises in our attentional field, coupled with a willingness to change our vantage point so that our view is different, and an understanding that any view is not ultimate truth, but a transient facet of it.

Charles Darwin (1872/1998) stated that attention or conscious concentration on almost any part of the body produces some direct physical effect on it. A felt shift (Gendlin, 1976) occurs in the Awareness phase, when we let our attention drift over or focus on the less arguable, more concrete qualities of our bodies and our experience of others' bodies. We literally let our attention play in these initial moments. We gently focus it in the present moment, on ourselves and others in the group. This free play of attention stimulates cognitive flow, emotional resiliency, and physical alertness, and moves us to the second phase of the Moving Cycle.

Owning what arises comes next. High-quality attention brings hidden things into the light, and the Owning phase is about taking these revealed feelings and thoughts and working with them directly in the group. The Owning phase follows Einstein's idea that we must change our consciousness to solve problems. Numerous therapists, most notably Stan Grof (1985), believe, as many indigenous cultures do, that all healing takes place in an altered state of consciousness. In the Owning phase, we use play elements to descend or ascend out of the patterns of relating we are used to, and this alters our consciousness until new relational solutions emerge.

In the act of Owning, we take deep personal responsibility for ourselves and for what the group presents to us. For it is within this "ability to respond" that newly revealed material from the unconscious can shift from being unowned and unrecognized to being empowered. Owning gives us the energy, the next source of fuel, to relate sincerely. It generates self-efficacy, and an internal locus of control. In this realm, we tell the deepest truths we can about our experience. We back off interpretation and rest in the primal nourishment of description. For in description, we can get as close as it gets to what is real and true. When we do that in a group, we create intimacy, belonging, and social healing.

We typically resist Owning through classical means such as projection, denial, dissociation, depression, and distraction. The task of this phase is to make the play sequence more important than any of these old urges. The Awareness phase is about a change of attention. The Owning phase is about a shift in intention. We make a commitment to the emergent moment and make it more important than the old pattern. What gets stimulated in the moment of shifting our intention is our fear of death. We tend to be identified with our patterns, and we rightly fear their death as our death. A good Owning phase will kill you. It dissolves the pattern I call *me* in some way, and in its place, puts new experiences that may feel truer, but may also feel more tender, vulnerable, and unfamiliar. When we own our experiences while in the presence of others, we let the truth do the healing. The Bible has told us that the truth will set us free. It certainly forms one of the cornerstones of personal and social liberation.

When a group plays together in an atmosphere of ownership, bodies relax, and satisfaction, the natural birthright of play, occurs. We have returned to a state of increased wholeness, together. The third phase begins as we learn to tolerate and move with this satisfaction. Marianne Williamson would call it a return to love (1992). I call it the *Appreciation* phase, for this moment requires that we appreciate, welcome, hold, and caress our new-found relatedness as if it were our own child we had just birthed, one we had known before only as someone buried deep within us and growing. After the labors of Owning, we bond with one another, and we spend time greeting and caring for one another.

Many modern therapies ignore this crucial phase, not realizing that most of us need help tolerating and basking in feelings of satisfaction and love. Most of us have been enculturated by groups such as family, society, or religion to limit our positive feelings. Even when the Owning phase has uncovered feelings of rage or grief, our revealing these feelings to others and taking responsibility for them gestates new experiences that feel whole, true, and relieving. Appreciation involves spending some time with this wholeness. The Appreciation phase brings us back to a shift of attention. Thich Nhat Hanh has written that attention is like sunlight and water for a plant. What we pay attention to will grow. If we want to grow a more whole, satisfied self, we take this time to find play behaviors that celebrate and support that self while doing the same for others.

The Appreciation phase forms the essential building block of a bonded relationship. If we can unconditionally ride whatever experience we are having, then we don't have to defend or control our relationships with others. When we stay in dialogue with ourselves, we are capable of intimate dialogue with others. The play behaviors of the Appreciation phase recover the styles of social play Fred Donaldson spoke of in *Playing by Heart* (1993).

The fourth stage is *Action*, and it aligns us with the very real truth that we have to leave the room now and go back out into our daily lives. When the Appreciation stage is completed, the group experiences inner healing. For this healing to be permanent, it must find a place in our outside environment. This means literally using our thoughts, feelings, and our bodies differently, and committing this difference via daily play behaviors. Only then can we truly change and contribute this change to the benefit of the external environment. Contributing to the world may be one of our prime directives, and the Action phase honors this directive. Personal healing has no reference point, no point at all, if it does not extend into the community. It is from personal healing that planetary healing becomes possible.

The Action phase is about transitioning into the outer world, and an intention to manifest ourselves differently within it. Perhaps we will walk in a more relaxed manner. Perhaps a reluctance to reveal ourselves has melted a bit. We need to practice this change and commit it to our behavioral repertoire or else it dissolves, as all dreams and impulses do.

The Moving Cycle, though an ordered sequence, is individual to each person and each group in each situation. We are all on many Moving Cycles in our lifetime, some which take moments to complete and still others that will complete as we lie on our deathbed. Each phase liberates a portion of our energy and applies it to our healing, our growth, and our creativity. We have tendencies or patterns of obstructing our Moving Cycles at characteristic places, tending, for example, to have difficulty with the Appreciation phase no matter what the content of the specific situation is. But this ability to focus on the process of wounding and healing, rather than getting bogged down and led astray by the content of the wound, allows us to heal more efficiently and completely. We are accessing our core nature more than the less-than-accurate reconstruction of our personal history. We are addressing our habitual withdrawals from experience, which starves our core being, more than chasing down the specifics of each withdrawal.

Clinical Features of the Moving Cycle

Using the Moving Cycle in a group play therapy setting involves several other important clinical issues. Adults tend to harbor play phobias-leftover play wounds from childhood punishment or neglect. By educating the group about the different types of play, we can help group members realize what types of play they overuse, to the exclusion of others. For instance, some members may get uncomfortable with storytelling, while others don't want to do anything physical. One member may feel comfortable with sports, while another thinks sports are horrifying.

I like to use the forming phase of groups to take each member's play history. This is often a written exercise that each member first shares with a partner and then with the whole group. It asks what their earliest play memories are and who their playmates were. It asks if any types of play were punished or ne-glected and which ones were praised. It includes remembrances of getting hurt while playing, as well as memories of spectacular play triumphs. By asking group members to remember their history with play, they can begin to appreci-ate how they came to be the players they are today. Members can identify and get help with old play wounds. By asking them to share this history with others, members find that others had different, as well as similar, experiences. An in-dividual can recruit someone who loves games to help him or her get over the fear of appearing stupid and can, in turn, help that person get over feeling clumsy in physical play.

Using the members' play histories in the Awareness phase allows the group to use the Owning phase to recover from play deficits. The deficit may show up in certain types of play, or it may arise in the context of play signaling. One of the tasks of children's play is to teach the social signals that surround play. When play is traumatized or neglected in a person's history, that person is prevented from learning the complex nonverbal signals that help keep adult play safe. Per-haps one of the most powerful examples is in the area of childhood sexual abuse. One of the theories that explains why children who were victims of sexual abuse have a high incidence of adult sexual abuse is that the original trauma prevented the child from the safe and gradual practice of normal sexual play signals that occur in flirtation. When, as an adult, this person is not reading sexual signals appropriately, he or she may fall into situations in which he or she assumes one thing and finds out that his or her partner assumed and expected another. One of the important adult group play therapy tasks, then, is to create a safe environment in the Owning phase where individuals can develop and practice play signaling skills they may not have engaged in as children.

Adults often work in groups; and sooner or later, all work groups must engage in creative problem solving. In an adult play therapy group, the Awareness phase is used to shift consciousness so that flow states can occur, and adults can sup-port the creative energy that ensues. The conscious task of facilitating creativity can often guide an adult group. Csikszentmihalyi (1990, 1996) has beautifully laid out the components of creative functioning in his writings. By engaging in play processes that recreate the necessary behaviors and states of consciousness associated with creativity, groups can facilitate the very important adult developmental task of leading a creative life.

Group play therapy for adults can also identify and reinforce transpersonal and spiritual goals. In these groups, members can pay conscious attention to increasing their connection to self, others, and higher purposes. Some may find that their prayer or meditation has been far too serious a thing and that God might just appreciate it if they lightened up. This kind of lightening up can be seen as the road to enlightenment by some. In addition, it can help us face life's transitions, especially the transitions into aging, body changes, and death and dying, with equanimity and grace.

Play behaviors may recapitulate a fundamental feature of any psychotherapy. When a session goes well, it oscillates. Whatever the symptom the client or the group comes in with, our ability to play with this symptom resides in our challenging ourselves to enter the symptom—to get curious about our anger or our headache or our conflict at work—and then to relieve that same symptom via relaxing, being comforted, breathing fully, or changing the subject. Healing requires that we know how to investigate ourselves as well as how to comfort ourselves. Both skills contribute to our healing. Play oscillates in much the same manner—between seriousness and frivolity, between strong efforts and effortless repose, between self and other. In a play therapy group, this oscillation helps members use the fundamental rhythms of play to effect the fundamental changes of healing.

take play histories from the class

CASE STUDY

The group slowly formed as members arrived, many having driven more than an hour in late afternoon rush hour traffic. A circle formed in pieces as each person grabbed a large pillow and sat down. They had been doing this every Monday evening for more than nine months. The therapist signaled the start of the group. She asked that everyone take a moment and scan their bodies, tracking sensation, energy level, emotions, and thoughts. This began the Awareness phase. The therapist announced that they would pick up on last week's theme and work on knowing what you want. She remarked that, to know what you want, you have to know what you feel.

The group commenced with everyone standing. Music was put on, and each person was asked to dance out what they were feeling. One by one, each person demonstrated with expressive movement how he or she felt while the others first watched and then tried on that featured dance. One person stomped and roared, another mimicked a rag doll, another folded her arms across her chest and frowned. People began to laugh and to speculate about one another's day.

Other Possible Awareness Phase Activities

1. Sensory awareness activities—reporting inner states to others.
2. Body image drawing—tracing your body on paper and filling in the details, both physical and psychological.
3. Taking play histories and sharing them.
4. Oscillating attention, oscillating listening outside with listening inside.
5. Character work—acting out various characters adults take on and use.
6. Pairs introducing each other—how my partner likes to play, what they are afraid of, what they want from this group.
7. Full breathing.
8. Psychodrama play—how do I get people's attention?—seduction, threat, whining, bargaining, pathos, humor.
9. Group drawing—where we are now—each person contributes a line.
10. All My Relations activity done in a circle. One person in the center calls out some characteristic (for instance, "All my relations who have brown hair"), and everyone with brown hair has to rush to a different spot. The last one left is in the middle and calls out the next characteristic.

The group continued as one person remarked that the loud roar made by another member bothered her. This other member said he resented being indirectly told to be quiet. The Owning phase begins as members deal with responses and reactions to one another. The therapist asks if it's okay to work with this as a group, and everyone says yes. First, the woman is asked to "sculpt" the man into a position that reflects how she sees him in this moment. She raises his arms over his head, asks him to open his mouth wide, and take a wide, menacing stance. The therapist asks the woman to share how she is feeling as she looks at her living sculpture. She reports feeling small and helpless and scared. The Owning phase deepens as both risk seeing and being seen by others.

Then the man sculpts the woman. He also puts her in a wide stance, with her hands on her hips and a scowl on her face. He asks her to occasionally wag her finger at him disapprovingly. He reports feeling chastised, guilty, and resentful. Both now are experimenting with social signaling and its contribution to nonverbal communication. The therapist asks the two to switch stances, giving the woman permission to roar and the man permission to disapprove. They start to laugh as they get into their new roles, and things get playful. Then the rest of the group is asked to try on these characters, and different individuals start to exaggerate the stances and give the characters names like Gertrude and Aunt Louise and Blowhard. The Owning phase completes as members build empathy and reduce projection, taking ownership of their own fears by trying on qualities in one another's bodies. The group also learns that it can tolerate negative affect and get through it safely.

Other Possible Owning Phase Activities

1. Getting to know my defenses—playing out fight, flight, freeze, and faint as an animal.
2. Relationship sculpting—how it was in my family—how it is in this group—how I want it to be.
3. Character work—victim, rescuer, persecutor triangle—role playing, playing with levels of character, guessing one another's characters.
4. Charged breathing in relationship—breathing on one's own, breathing as a group, intensifying breath to vitalize the energy in the group.

The group comes back together, and members share what it was like to play with their characters as well as take on other's characters. Time is spent talking about the energy or wisdom or resource the character holds. Participants are then asked to draw their own representation of the inner need the character is fulfilling and the outer shell of how the character acts. Members then share their drawings with each other. The therapist designs an exercise in which each person goes to one other person and reveals his or her inner need directly, asking each pair to breathe fully and let their bodies express this tender place via gesture as well as voice. The recipient is asked to say, "I hear you, I see you" and any other affirming comments they care to share. The Appreciation phase occurs as members connect with each other and find that they can express themselves truthfully and directly. Some minutes are spent with the partners talking about this experience with each other. The Appreciation phase works on the ability to tolerate positive affect while in relationship, and to increase bonding and belonging among the group members. Appreciation also strengthens the healing properties of gratitude and affirmation. The therapist reminds the group that many people believe that unexpressed appreciations are a relational toxin.

Other Possible Appreciation Phase Activities

1. What I like about you, what I like about me exercise.
2. Exercise in making others laugh.
3. Writing notes about one thing you like about each person, collected, collated, and given to each, who has to read these aloud, breathe, and make eye contact.

4. Telling a love story—passing the narrative so that each person creates the next line—processing afterwards by examining love themes.

The therapist informs the group that they have ten minutes left and asks what they would like to do to feel complete for now. She suggests that the members focus on how to apply the character work they did in the session to their daily lives. The Action phase is meant to clean up any incompletes in the group, review the session, terminate the time together, apply group discoveries to the outside world, and set goals in the outside world.

Several group members wanted to check in with the two members who had been in conflict earlier. They asked how each was feeling toward the other. They both smiled at each other, and one stuck out her tongue at the other. Everyone laughed, and for a few minutes, the group commented on the "sibling" energy between the two members in conflict. The group decided to work on sibling issues next time. The therapist asked each member to bring in a play story that involved a sibling as a way to start the next group. The group ended in a standing circle, each person pledging to play with the character he or she had found that evening. Several members stated these intentions while in their characters, "hamming it up" for the group.

Other Possible Action Phase Activities

1. Writing up ideas for daily play projects and sharing them.
2. Unison dancing.
3. Group drawing—where we are now.
4. Drawing our group time line—on butcher paper—with all significant events on it.
5. "If I were to die tomorrow, how would I play until then" exercise.
6. Parallel lines, facing each other—one minute of nonverbal play, one minute verbal completion with person facing you, then step to the side to do the same with the next person.
7. Time to speak out any incompletes.
8. Goodbye ritual—group created.

CONCLUSION

The Swiss psychologist Carl Jung once voiced the theory that the unconscious is infinite. When he said this, he meant to both challenge and reassure us. We can be assured that it isn't necessary to try for a completely conscious life—we are meant to have shadows. And we also have a responsibility to look into those shadows for the rest of our lives. As adults, we can address this task by dissolving old wounds and by cultivating lost pleasures. Play therapy can turn us in both these directions—into the healing and into the natural states of positive affect that healing makes possible.

The Moving Cycle was presented as one means of recovering natural pleasure, particularly the pleasure that we can find in one another's company. Developmental psychologists often note that wounding always takes place in the context of relationships, and that healing must do so as well. By using play therapy groups to both stimulate and redirect old wounds, we can grow younger as we grow older, more able to play with each other and with life.

REFERENCES

Adler, A. (1957). *Understanding human nature*. Greenwich, CT: Fawcett. (Original work published 1927)

Bekoff, M., & Allen, C. (1998). Intentional communication and social play: How and why animals negotiate and agree to play. In M. Bekoff & J. Byers (Eds.), *Animal play: Evolutionary, comparative, and ecological perspectives* (pp. 97–114). New York: Cambridge University Press.

Bekoff, M., & Bers, J. (1998). *Animal play: Evolutionary, comparative, and ecological perspectives*. New York: Cambridge University Press.

Caldwell, C. (1996). *Getting our bodies back: Recovery, healing and transformation through body-centered psychotherapy*. Boston: Shambhala.

Corey, G. (2000). *Theory and practice of group counseling* (5th ed.). Belmont, CA: Wadsworth/Thomson Learning.

Csikszentmihalyi, M. (1990). *Flow: The psychology of optimal experience*. New York: Harper Perennial.

Csikszentmihalyi, M. (1996). *Creativity: Flow and the psychology of discovery and exploration*. New York: Harper Perennial.

Darwin, C. (1998). *The expression of emotion in man and animals*. New York: Oxford University Press. (Original work published 1872)

Donaldson, F. O. (1993). *Playing by heart: The vision and practice of belonging*. Deerfield Beach, FL: Health Communications.

Fagan, R. (1981). *Animal play behavior*. New York: Oxford University Press.

Fromm, E. (1974). *The art of loving*. New York: Harper & Row. (Original work published 1956)

Gardner, H. (1993). *Creating minds: An anatomy of creativity seen through the lives of Freud, Einstein, Picasso, Stravinsky, Eliot, Graham, and Ghandi*. New York: Basic Books.

Gendlin, E. (1976). *Focusing,* New York: Bantam Books.

Grof, S. (1985). *Beyond the brain: Birth, death and transcendence in psychotherapy.* Albany, NY: State University of New York Press.

Heller, M. (Ed.). (2001). *The flesh of the soul: The body we work with.* New York: Peter Lang.

Horney, K. (1945). *Our inner conflicts: A constructive theory of neurosis.* New York: Norton.

Huizinga, J. (1950). *Homo ludens: A study of the play element in culture.* London: Routledge & Kegan Paul.

Levy, J. (1978). *Play behavior.* Malabar, FL: Krieger.

Lewis, K. (2000). A comparative study of primate play behavior. *Folia Primatologica, 71,* 417.

Maslow, A. H. (1968). *Toward a psychology of being* (2nd ed.). New York: Van Nostrand Reinhold.

Maslow, A. H. (1970). *Motivation and personality* (2nd ed.). New York: Harper & Row.

Montague, A. (1981). *Growing young.* New York: Bergin & Garvey.

Perry, B. (1997). Incubated in terror: Neurodevelopmental factors in the cycle of violence. In J. Osofsky (Ed.), *Children in a violent society* (pp. 124–149). New York: Guilford Press.

Spinka, M., Newberry, R., & Bekoff, M. (2001). Mammalian play: Training for the unexpected. *Quarterly Review of Biology, 76*(2), 141–168.

Sullivan, H. S. (1968). *The interpersonal theory of psychiatry.* New York: Norton. (Original work published 1953)

Williamson, M. (1992). *A return to love.* New York: Harper & Row.

Yalom, I. D. (1975). *The theory and practice of group psychotherapy* (2nd ed.). New York: Basic Books.

Chapter 14 ───────────────────────────────

USING GAMES WITH ADULTS IN A PLAY THERAPY GROUP SETTING

Jennifer Kendall

This chapter is an account of my personal experience in using games with adults in a play therapy group. While the situation described took place several years ago, I have continued to use games in my therapy with adults, both in group and individual settings.

As a second-year graduate student in psychology beginning my practicum-level clinical training, I had completed a number of classes focusing on psychodynamic theories and interventions. I had also received training in clinical interviewing, crisis intervention, and psychodiagnostic assessment. However, despite my regimen of coursework, I was (as I suspect most beginning clinicians are) ill-prepared for my first direct clinical service experience. A novice and naive therapist in 1994, I began working with traumatized adults in the underserved and economically disadvantaged area of South Central Los Angeles, equipped only with my limited training and the desire to help and do good work. Specifically, I worked with women with long-term substance abuse problems who were living in a residential treatment facility for a period of nine to twelve months. As the program was intended solely for women substance abusers, most residents had an infant or toddler living with them in the treatment facility during their recovery from addiction.

While the women were labeled as "substance abusers," every resident in the program had also experienced varying types and degrees of trauma during childhood. They were survivors of sexual abuse, physical abuse, and/or neglect. The overwhelming majority had parents or primary caregivers who were substance abusers, and many recalled being introduced to drugs by a parent or parent figure. Many were bounced from one foster home to another, and others spent years in juvenile detention facilities. Some resorted to prostitution in exchange for

317

either drugs or money. As a practicum student, I provided psychotherapy to the women on an individual basis and in groups. I also worked with their children.

For the first several months, I doggedly attempted to establish rapport and trust with traditional talk therapy, which, to say the least, brought less than satisfactory results. The majority of the clients wanted nothing to do with me whatsoever; curious clients asked me, "Where is the couch?" Clients whose caseworkers made them attend sessions often refused to speak; and essentially all the clients believed that talking to me would mean they would be labeled as "crazy." There was simply no convincing them otherwise.

After months of frustration, I began working with the children, with whom I had always felt comfortable and at ease. For me, the children were easy to relate to, as even in my early adulthood, I am an ardent lover of arts and crafts, games and toys. To apply these things therapeutically, I decided to try my hand at play therapy, but to my disappointment, I could find no games or toys in the building. My off-site supervisor encouraged me to bring my own and to ask others for donations. I enthusiastically complied and soon had so many toys from generous donors that I couldn't fit them all in my car to take to the treatment center!

Several occurrences about the same time led me to a surprising insight. The first was that I began having particular trouble communicating with a mother whose two children I worked with regularly twice a week. As she became increasingly angry toward me, I decided to include her in our sessions. On doing this, I realized the problem: All along, she had wanted to play, too. She was angry because she felt left out. And indeed I had excluded her from the fun, blindly assuming that the games and activities would not be of interest to her. I could not have been more wrong—from the moment we began to play together as a group, my relationship with the children's mother changed drastically. Suddenly she was accessible; she even began to seek me out.

The next event occurred when I brought the donated toys to the center. When the word spread that I was giving away toys, the women began to come in droves to pick out toys for their children. However, it soon became apparent that not everything they wanted was for their kids—they were also choosing for themselves. They traded, bargained, and argued with each other over who got what toy; they hugged stuffed animals and put them on their beds.

What was once a frustrating mystery was now beginning to make sense. In supervision, I reported my observations and we formulated ideas; according to psychodynamic theory, the abuse clients suffered in childhood had not only left emotional scars, but also had likely left them psychologically stagnated at the time of the trauma. The earlier the abuse, the earlier was the stagnation in their psychological development. Furthermore, they exhibited a variety of symptomotology common in abused children. If not for their chronological ages, these women certainly could have been mistaken for psychologically injured children.

Even as an adult, the survivor of childhood abuse is burdened with fundamental problems in what Erikson (1963) described in his first three phases of personality development: basic trust, autonomy, and initiative. According to Erikson, the acquisition of trust, or lack of it, is truly the foundation of the personality. It is in this stage that the infant begins to establish itself in the world, determining whether the environment is a safe and reliable place, or, conversely, unstable and unreliable. This foundation of trust, or inadequate foundation of mistrust, forms the groundwork for trust with others later as an adult.

On entering therapy, abused children may be particularly anxious or resistant because they have a background that can predispose them to feeling vulnerable. The same can be said for adults. Abuse has taught them that the world is not a safe place and that people can, and will, hurt them. Bow (1993) found that play therapy can be a powerful tool for overcoming resistance. Play seems to be the best way of establishing rapport and alliance with a child because it is an activity that is inherently interesting, enjoyable, and natural to children. I hoped this would be true for my highly resistant adults as well.

Interventions for substance abuse programs lean toward the decidedly traditional, consisting of a variety of educational and therapy groups, but limited one-on-one counseling. Not discounting the importance of these interventions, I felt strongly that something essential was missing, some crucial element was not in place. It appeared that these women were unable to experience the full benefits of group therapy because of significant problems in their interpersonal skills and social functioning. These deficits in social skills were obviously long-standing, rooted in childhood abuse and neglect.

THE GAME PLAY INTERVENTION

Reflecting on my work with the children and my observations of the client's reactions to the toys provided the framework for an intervention: Not only did the women suffer social skills deficits, but also they did not know how to play. They did not play with their children, nor did they engage socially with each other. They knew nothing of solitary play and were unable to entertain themselves or participate in something they enjoyed. Indeed, they appeared to enjoy little or nothing at all and seemed to trust no one—especially their peers. While this was possibly a consequence of long-term depression, it could also have been a consequence of their trauma-stricken childhoods. They couldn't play now because they had never had time to play—never learned to play—in the beginning of their lives. While other children enjoyed themselves with dolls, games, crafts, sports, and other fun activities, they were being molested, abandoned, assaulted, and/or moved to the next foster home. Indeed, for some of them, their major caregivers introduced them to drugs as a source of recreation. Regardless of their introduction, however, drugs became their only means to experience relaxation, excitement, escape, socialization, and fun; all of these can be and should have been experienced through play. Considering the importance of play in childhood development, was it too late for them to learn to play? And if not, could I teach them?

I began by facilitating a pilot group with eight adult women, once a week for 90 minutes a session. The group was designed to provide the group members with an opportunity to participate in different games and activities that many of them had never had a chance to do as children. It would also be a valuable and refreshing respite from the difficulties and hard work required for recovering from addiction.

It is important to note here that the women's initial reaction to the group was "no way." Almost every woman I approached told me that there was no need for her to participate because play is for children, not for adults. It took some convincing otherwise to bring together eight women who were willing to give the group a try, regardless of their feelings that the group was "silly" and possibly demeaning to them as adults. After two sessions, however, I had difficulty keeping other residents out of the group, as the women had such noisy fun that everyone in the building was quite curious as to what was going on.

After experimenting with a variety of activities, I found that games appeared to be the most successful and enjoyable way for the women to have fun as a group and experience feelings of joy and pleasure. Games also required the group to interact socially, to follow rules, to experience winning and losing, to learn to negotiate as a team, and to cooperate individually with other game participants.

The use of games in play therapy is a key aspect of social development. Reid (1993) notes the dual nature of games that is observable in both children and adults, in which enjoyment and a sense of seriousness exist side by side. This duality offers unique possibilities for psychotherapeutic intervention.

Compared to free play, games require more emotional control, intellect, and social skills, as well as often paralleling "real life." Many theorists including Piaget (1962) have suggested that repeated exposure to games plays a central role in the socialization of children, fostering skills such as rule-following, fairness, turn-taking, gracious winning and losing, and cooperative and competitive behavior (Reid, 1993). Serok and Blum (1983) describe games as mini-life situations in which the basic elements of socialization (rule conformity, acceptance of the norms of the group, and control of aggression) are integral components of the process of play. In addition, games are natural and enjoyable activities and have special significance for children and adults who have difficulty experiencing pleasure, such as the circumstances of abused individuals.

The games used in the group included both board games and interactive team-oriented games. The games the women seemed to enjoy the most are listed in the next section; however, I strongly recommend experimentation with many different games in addition to these because the dynamics and desires of each group and/or individual, of course, vary. Choosing games involves deciding if a group is best suited to play all together as a large team, be broken up into smaller teams, or play against each other individually. Initially, it may be best to begin working together as a large team and move toward competition as group members build trust in each other.

In addition, I highly recommend knowing the reading level of each of the players before choosing a game, as this can be a problem and a potential cause of embarrassment for a group member who has reading difficulties. If you know beforehand that a group member has difficulty reading, he or she can be teamed up with either yourself or someone else to be sure that everyone thoroughly enjoys the game.

RECOMMENDED GAMES

Pictionary

This well-known game requires players to draw and other players to guess what is being drawn. It includes a board, but I found that using the board is not always necessary, and the game can be played with equal satisfaction without the board. A white board or large easel of paper is helpful when playing with larger groups.

Guesstures

This game is similar to charades except it's much faster and easier; the game includes cards with words that must be acted out by the players in only a few seconds. Team members attempt to guess what the player is acting out. *Guesstures* was probably the favorite of all the games we played. The game of *Charades* can be played in a modified form if the boxed game of *Guesstures* cannot be found or is no longer available.

Taboo

This game requires players to communicate words while not saying other key words; for example, if the clue is "picnic," the player must describe the word without using other words such as "ants," "park," "July 4th," and so on. *Taboo* can be a bit more challenging than some of the others.

Uno

This card game is great for either a few people or a larger group. *Uno* requires players to match and eliminate cards, but players can sabotage other players, which can make for interesting competitive dynamics to surface.

Monopoly

This familiar board game reminds many of childhood; it can also be competitive and up to eight players at a time can play.

Pay Day

This is a favorite board game of mine. *Pay Day* can accommodate up to six players but is also fun for only two or three; the game involves making decisions about money, taking risks, and paying "bills."

Sorry

This is another fun board game, but it can be played by only four at a time. *Sorry* also has the element of "sabotage," as players can send others back to the start by landing on the same space or by using a "sorry" card.

While these are the particular games played in this group, there are literally hundreds of games available at local toy and department stores, many of which are relatively inexpensive and quite entertaining for people of all ages. I have also used games to build rapport with resistant adult clients in individual therapy; in these cases, games such as *Checkers* and *Connect Four* can be used as they are designed for only two players.

CONCLUSION

Ultimately, the power of the group was the inherent power and beauty of play itself—play can be a healing force. There is growth in joy and laughter, and change requires more than grief, sorrow, and painful introspection. Schaefer (1993) describes play as intrinsically motivating, requiring no pressure or rewards from external sources. He also characterized play as so involving and engrossing that the client may often lose awareness of time and surroundings. While he writes about children, the same can be said for adults, as, in fact, adult play is a boundless national market of sports equipment, electronic gadgets, art and craft supplies, creative board games, and so on. Brought into the therapeutic realm, the idea of using toys and play for adults may provide a shortcut to the in-jured child hidden deep within the adult person. The subtle magic of play, used in conjunction with more traditional interventions, may also provide inroads to healing that child.

REFERENCES

Bow, J. N. (1993). Overcoming resistance: Play and positive emotion. In C. Schaefer (Ed.), *The therapeutic powers of play.* Northvale, NJ: Aronson.

Erikson, E. H. (1963). *Childhood and society.* New York: Norton.

Piaget, J. (1962). *Play, dreams, and imitation in childhood.* New York: Norton.

Reid, S. (1993). Game play. In C. Schaefer (Ed.), *The therapeutic powers of play.* North-vale, NJ: Aronson.

Schaefer, C. E. (1993). *The therapeutic powers of play.* Northvale, NJ: Aronson.

Serok, S., & Blum, A. (1983). Therapeutic uses of games. *Residential Group Care and Treatment, 1*(3), 3–14.

Chapter 15

HYPNO-PLAY THERAPY

Marian Kaplun Shapiro

Hypno-play therapy is the strategic use of play therapy with selected adults in a hypnotically induced age-regressed state. This method enables these adults to work on childhood issues and traumatic events in much the same way they would have if allowed the opportunity to have good psychotherapy as children.

Hypno-play therapy is based on an optimistic developmental model supported by the concept of *resiliency*. This model presupposes the existence of age-related periods in which original learning is intended to occur. Nevertheless, human beings have an amazing degree of flexibility in their capacity to work through the damage and deficits of the past long after the original period at which development should have naturally appeared (see Kagan, 1980, pp. 140–146; Clarke & Clarke, 1976). I do not believe that all early damage is irreversible, nor do I believe that all such damage is reversible. Reconstruction cannot produce the same results as a "good enough" early development. Through the replacement of negative introjects with new positive ones, hypno-play therapy affords a direct, pragmatic approach to maximizing the resilience that we have posited.

We certainly know that age regression does not produce a literal, physical return to childhood (Silverman & Retzlaff, 1986). The body and the brain of the patient are those of an adult. And, as the neurosciences become increasingly sophisticated, we learn more and more about the effects of neglect and trauma on the development of the body, through the workings of the brain and hormonal systems (see, for example, Rothschild, 2000). Publications, both scientific and polemic, rightly stir us to consider the competing evidence around the issues of accuracy of memory, and even the complexity of the very definition of memory.

This chapter is updated from a chapter by the same name in the author's book, *Second Childhood*, and contains additional material from other of her papers.

But, in contrast to the academic researcher or the forensic hypnotherapist, our clinical work is not primarily concerned with veridicality or age consistency. We are, of course, devoted to identifying and eschewing suggestive phrasing or demand situations; after all, it is the patient's therapy, the patient's truth, the patient's life. Additionally, in this era of litigious, adversarial intrusions on the therapeutic process, as ethical clinicians we must be conversant with the studies and resulting guidelines issued by the American Psychological Association, the American Psychiatric Association, the American Medical Association (all excellently abstracted in Brown, Scheflin, & Hammond, 1988), and the American Society of Clinical Hypnosis (*Clinical Hypnosis and Memory,* 1995). In addition, we must be careful to lay out the controversies around retrieval of memory, and possible risks of *any* use of hypnosis with those who intend to pursue legal cases based on their trauma histories (see, especially, Chap. 14, Brown et al., 1988). However, we must not waver in our emphasis to our patients that we are not lawyers; the intent, as therapist, is simply participation in the patient's completion of what was incomplete for the patient. We must avow and reavow our belief in the capacity for integrity of self, which is innate in every human being.

Hypno-play therapy approaches the problem at its source rather than through its elaboration in current behavior. Especially suitable where conventional depth-oriented treatments are usually prolonged and difficult, hypno-play therapy offers the possibility of relatively rapid change of a fundamental nature. In these cases, hypnotherapy occupies a central rather than a peripheral position in the treatment plan. Its application is primarily in three areas:

1. Relatively circumscribed situations, such as specific acute traumas.
2. Intransigent characterological disorders and dissociative disorders, including multiple personality (DID; see Shapiro, 1991).
3. Long-term chronic depression that is resistant to medication.

These general categories serve as umbrellas to a variety of presenting problems: panic disorders (including agoraphobia), sexual dysfunction, work/school inhibition, marital discord, somatic complains, and so forth. Is hypno-play therapy always the answer? Certainly not. It is another technique whose benefits the eclectically minded therapist trained in hypnotherapy can consider.* Like psychotherapy, hypnosis in general and age-regression and hypno-play therapy in particular are valuable when applied by some kinds of therapists with some patients for some issues at some times. You must consider the circumstances (see Shapiro, *Second Childhood,* 1988b, Chaps. 10 and 11).

---

* Preferably, the therapist should make use of ongoing supervision when beginning to work with this technique.

The saying goes that you cannot make a plant grow by pulling on its leaves. Hypno-play therapy, applied at or just below the point of deficit, allows the patient's new behavior to emerge from a grounded, well-fertilized sense of self, normally based in very early childhood. Thus, the new behavior feels relatively natural to the patient, closer to what Winnicott (1958) terms the "true self" (pp. 290, 302–303) rather than alien to it. Hypno-play therapy may minimize the risk of suicide by making it possible to build a secure holding environment through the development of an exceptionally strong, positive transference at an early developmental level. These experiences create warmth, trust, and self-confidence, which can sustain the patient through the periods of despair. Fromm (1980) wisely exhorts us, "Give to the patient—do not take away!" (p. 426). Angyal, speaking of that despair, describes the patient as feeling "hopeless, utterly ignorant of life and how to conduct it. Seeing no future ahead of him, he hardly cares whether he lives or dies" (Angyal, 1982, p. 225). Yet, the patient must stay alive before the new ways of living have taken hold. From that search for a combination of new soil for new growth and the immediate sustenance for life in the here and now, the healing possibility of play therapy emerges as a hopeful alternative in the armamentarium of psychotherapeutic approaches.

Evolution of Hypno-Play Therapy

Long before I became aware of hypnosis as a discipline, I interned at a clinic that was, like many, somewhat short of office space. In the round robin of room assignments, I occasionally found myself scheduled to meet with an adult patient in the playroom. It was hard to miss the longing expressions of some of these adults as they eyed the toys on the shelves, or "helpfully"—and infinitely slowly—replaced a stuffed animal left on the floor by the previous occupant. It was second nature to begin to incorporate these materials in the environment into the adult "talking therapy" sessions. The more primitive the developmental level of the patient, the more useful these sessions seemed, and I began to request the playroom for particular patients. However, after the conclusion of my internship, the next few years led me to more traditional office environments, and I failed to recognize the importance of what I had accidentally learned until I began private practice. Then, due to the ages of my own children, various toys remained in a basket in a corner of the room that I had converted to office space. Thus, the rediscovery of the use of play therapy with adults was twice serendipitous; remaining in my unconscious storehouse of knowledge, it remained to be refound and reworked with the additional momentum of the power of hypnosis to fuel it.

PRACTICAL ASPECTS OF HYPNO-PLAY THERAPY

The Waiting Room

The waiting room is the ideal place in which to introduce materials that beckon the playful involvement of the patient. Looking for something to do, patients search for items to engage their interest, distractions from anxiety. If all that is available is the very magazine just read at home, the desperate will pick up even that. Why, then, settle for the ubiquitous magazine rack, when the therapist can offer temptations such as a magnetic sculpture to be teased into ever-original shapes? In my experience, even the most rigid of people cannot resist the lure of this toy. And how about crystal prisms and various kinds of kaleidoscopes? Those who peek through them must, by definition, notice—again with appropriate symbolic value—that the world looks different when viewed through various lenses, that the same components can create totally new and intriguing pictures when shaken up. In addition to the obligatory hanging plants, the office and waiting room areas can display some easily accessible seedlings whose progress can be easily monitored and appreciated both in concrete and symbolic ways. Moreover, in the bookcases of learned tomes, Freud can rub shoulders with Dr. Seuss.

The Office

You need not abandon all conventional office furnishings—the chairs, couch, lamps, tables, perhaps desk—to make allowance for improvisation. In addition to these staples, you can expand your definition of "the office" in many creative directions. As a musician, I naturally include musical instruments in my office— vehicles by which to experiment with sound, to express the unsayable in melody and rhythm. It is often advantageous to include a piano, whether full-sized or table-top keyboard; playing together with a "child," improvising songs to which words— whether serving to express repressed affect or functioning as a vehicle for humor— represent another "way in" to the often untouched, and, therefore, virgin territory from which new growth can spring. In essence, the therapist's imagination (and the physical constraints of the office itself) is the only limitation, once the therapist takes the attitude that adult/adult-child play experiences have intrinsic value.

In a visually separate area of the office, you can locate the "young corner." Adult patients will doubtless notice this area, though conventional self-restraint usually inhibits them from approaching it without invitation. Research has indicated that play therapy is generally found to be most effective in clients under the age of 12. But, as Lebo (1956) points out, that fact may well stem from experience with adolescents, who disdain and distance themselves from children's toys, although, in fact, they might enjoy them. Erikson (1951) noticed, for example, that Harvard-Radcliffe students were resistant to playing with the toys offered to them. However, once covered by a rationale and a specific task—to build a dramatic scene with children's blocks—they set forth, appearing to be "overcome by a kind of infantile excitement which . . . could be shown to have originated in *childhood traumata. . . .* " (p. 669, italics his).

First, then, the therapist accepts the adult's initial resistance to the idea of playing with children's toys, by informally dividing the child and adult areas. But, by designing both areas to be visible simultaneously, the implication is made that regression is, in fact, a separate experience that exists in the context of wholeness. The boundary between here-and-now and early work remains intact. However, through the existence of the adult toys, there is tacit approval for the translation of the feelings of childhood into current life. Respect is thus offered for the external adult and for the child within.

Most of the materials provided for the adult "child" are similar to those conventionally supplied for the chronological child in play therapy environments. When choosing items, remember that, as Stern (1985) observed, even children as young as 18 months have used such materials as dolls with symbolic intent (pp. 166–167). The "young corner" can provide table and chairs; art materials; Play Doh; children's books; a xylophone; a pounding board and hammers; a dart board; a large box of wooden blocks of various sizes, shapes, and colors; an erector set with tools; large and small balls; mitten puppets; masks; water or soap bubble guns; beads; string; hammer and pegs; cars and trucks; wooden and bendable "people" of different races, ages, and occupations; soft animals; baby dolls of both sexes; balls; a bop-bag; playfood; nursing bottles; dinnerware for little "parties"; a few simple games such as Chinese checkers; and an assortment of interesting "junk"—bottlecaps, sequins, costume jewelry, matchbox cars, and so forth. A dollhouse can be useful; however, most are solid structures that do not lend themselves to rearrangement. What is the child of a housing project to make of a Colonial edifice! Blocks, on the other hand, have the advantage of serving to build whatever house is in the patient's mind. It is nice to be able to offer water and sand as well; if the therapist finds it impractical to provide such messy materials on the premises, trips to the local playground can supplement the available resources. Art items should also be limited to those that the therapist can handle without undo anxiety about the condition of the room and the clothing of both participants.

The Use of Video

The hypnotherapist might also consider an investment in a video recorder and camera. Involvement in the hypnotherapy relationship is a full involvement, sometimes including some extent of mutual regression. Certainly, hypno-play therapy requires the therapist's near-total immersion in the hypnotic agenda with the patient. Especially, given the current lack of structured workshop training in hypno-play therapy, it is immeasurably advantageous for the therapist to be able to view the session afterward, for self-observation, and for supervision with his or her consultant and/or peers. Moreover, there are times in which watching the tape together with the patient may be of particular importance, as patients begin to integrate their early growth into adult life. One brief caution: Taping is not an end in itself. Therefore, the equipment should be as automatic and nonintrusive as the latest technology can provide. As the therapist is likely to be working without an assistant, filming can be done from only one observation point and is limited to a single camera. Therefore, the camera should be equipped with automatic focus and a wide-angle lens. Lighting should be adequate for all hours that the office is in use; the built-in light meters on most cameras inform the novice if the lighting is sufficient. The video camera can be mounted on a tripod with wheels to facilitate mobility; or, in a more expensive solution, it can be mounted on a swivel base built onto a shelf attached to a wall. A long, heavy-duty extension cord for a tripod setup extends its flexibility. Multiple external battery-powered microphones are far superior to the camera's condenser microphone; by means of V-connectors and extension cords, two or more microphones can be arranged near or attached to the therapist and the patient for optimal acoustic clarity. The camera novice need not take flight at what may sound like a plethora of paraphernalia requiring sophisticated technical specialization. Lacking other informal resources, about 15 minutes of on-site instruction from your local camera supplier should suffice to instruct the rank amateur in the successful operation of a complete video apparatus. During any therapy session, the time taken to arrange such properly situated equipment effectively is limited to about one minute, the time required to insert the tape into the video machine, attach the microphones, and press the ON button. Anyone who can operate a television set has all the qualifications needed to film in video.

Designing the Play Module

The more passive forms of play therapy do not require particular attention here because the therapist's technical problems are minimal. Increasing depth of trance can be attained through a number of conventional methods or simply by assigning deepening to the physiological response the patient is emitting (e.g., "With every sigh, you can go deeper. . . . "). When sufficient depth is reached, the play activity is introduced. In other words, at that point, while the patient is in trance, the therapist can read to the patient, recite a story or poem, sing a song, direct the patient to look at the lights reflecting from a prism, offer a stuffed animal to stroke, or whatever. If it is necessary for the patient's eyes to be open for the activity, the therapist simply makes that request ("and you can find it comfortable to open your eyes now . . ."). If the use of either of the patient's hands is necessary for participation, the hand that is not cataleptic should be used. If the use of the dominant hand is required, however, previous care should be taken to assign the nondominant hand for catalepsy. If that opportunity has gone by unattended, do not despair—simply add an instruction for the cataleptic hand to lower. That behavior could perhaps be linked to another desirable accomplishment such as that of eye-opening ("As your right hand begins to lower, you can find yourself moving even deeper into trance, your eyes finding a way to open as your hand touches your lap. . . ."). When only one arm is necessary, a levitation reversal can be effected for the same deepening result. (E.g., "As your right hand begins to lower, how interesting to notice your left hand getting lighter and lighter [in appropriate voice], that set of helium balloons [if you used that image] attaching to the wrist of the left hand, floating up, up, giving your right hand its time to rest, resting on your lap. . . .").

The following tape excerpt* illustrates the use of stuffed animals in a hypno-play module. Because it is a relatively simple procedure requiring no large-scale deviation from the typical practice of age regression, this example might serve as a good introduction for the hypnotherapist's initial entrance into this specialty.

CASE EXAMPLE: MADELEINE

Madeleine, a painter in her 20s, spent a good deal of her childhood traveling among homes in Europe because of her father's work. She identified the theme of "going away" as fundamental in her life, finding those words coming to her mind frequently. Trance was induced with the prototypical method, the patient lying down as she preferred. I suggested a screen on which some image might appear that would shed light on the identified theme. It is interesting that Madeleine's vocabulary in the conscious state (not reproduced), in contrast to her speech in trance, is exceptionally erudite and scholarly.

Patient (P.): "I'm seeing the maid, the family maid, while I was very young. Her name was Thea, and she had a very big chest, very soft, and black hair, and I mostly think about her chest, how soft it is, and being held against it-[mm]. I really want to be with her." (cries). [Note the shifts back and forth from past to present tenses.]

Therapist (T.): "You miss her."

P: "Yes, I do, and she's gone; she has to go away."

---

* Identifying aspects have been altered in all case material wherever necessary to maintain patient privacy.

T: "Why does she have to?"

P: "I don't know." (looks confused) [P. seemed very young, as if my questions made no sense.]

T: "How old are you?"

P: "I don't know. I have little white boots on." (sobs)

T: "You're really feeling so bad."

P: "I want her to come back! EE-YA!" [Child's pronunciation of Thea.] (In a very plaintive small voice) "She's much nicer than my mother."

T: "Can you make her come back?"

P: "No, she's gone forever. (In a more adult voice) I think she went to Greece. (In a younger voice again) We're staying and she's going away. I can say her name as much as I want and it doesn't help. She does everything. . . . " (Compares to mother who is demanding and restrictive.) [Notice that, as Hilgard (1977, p. 46) comments, "the observing ego . . . when present . . . need not interfere with the vividness of the regressed experience."]

T: "You're just a little girl."

P: (In older voice) "I'm feeling like you're my mother now, Marian, smaller and more tight, inside . . . not so soft." [Boundaries are blurring between Thea, mother, and me.]

T: "You'd rather have Thea; it's safer with Thea."

P: "Yes, it's really great. . . . I don't want to eat by myself."

T: "Does Thea make you do it?"

P: "No! She feeds me!" (crying quietly) "I want to say over and over—EE-Ah. EE-Ah." (In an older voice) "I think it's her last day in the house. I think I see her suitcase. She's dressed up in real clothes, not a uniform." (In a younger voice) "I want to find her. I want to go where she went." (Cries, then begins to reconstitute) [An interpretation of P.'s yearning could have been made here, or it could be saved for the conscious part of the session.]

T: "Do you know how old you are?"

P: "Somewhere less than two, but I don't know, I know from reading and asking." (Lies on the couch looking desolate.)

T: (Getting several stuffed toys and a rag doll) "I have a whole bunch of friends who'd like to hug you, your chest looks so lonely." (P. hugs all of them to her.)

P: (Looking at the doll) "I don't like her, but I'd like to get to know her."

T: "She had a hard life; that's why she wears long dresses, she doesn't want her body to show." [P. has issues about her body and sexuality. She suspected sexual abuse during childhood.]

P: (Noticing that doll has no demarcated mouth.) "And she doesn't talk."

T: "What would she be saying if she had a mouth?"

P: "AAH!" (disgusted sound)

The previous dialogue is an example of a relatively simple logistics problem: All that is needed is for the therapist to get up and fetch the toys to be used, placing them in the patient's hands. But how could you get the patient to walk over to the toy area if that were necessary while still in trance? It is possible. As the sleepwalker navigates stairs in nocturnal trance state, so can the patient in a somnambulistic condition. When the patient's eyes are open, they can see. Once the patient's eyes are open, there is no difficulty with any play activity, be it playing patty-cake, building towers of blocks, banging on a drum, painting, drawing, shooting water pistols, composing a puppet play or opera together, sculpting with clay and sand—the therapist's imagination and expertise with chronological children is the only limit. If trance should lighten, the therapist can opt to deepen it or can suggest that the patient do so, as often as necessary during the session. However, the therapist may prefer to take advantage of the patient's growing willingness to participate in play activity in a more conscious, nearer-adult mode.

As when doing play therapy with chronological children, the hypno-play therapist must have in mind a specific goal, using play to introduce and develop it, sometimes in a single session, sometimes over several sessions. In the previous example, the goal was the exploration of the patient's difficulties with loss in her adult life. The secondary issue of sexual abuse emerged as traumatic material often does, from the experience of having opened the door to memory within a safe and supportive environment. To that end, as with children, the therapist, especially aware of the recent cautions regarding potential accusations of remembered child abuse, usually takes a nondirective, permissive attitude, waiting for the patient to "experience growth under the most favorable conditions" (Axline, 1964, p. 35). Or, when relevant, the therapist can move to a more active stance, as in the following case of Barbara, especially when there is a deficit of experience in playing. In such cases with chronological children, as Irwin (1983) points out, it is appropriate that "the adult is the child's first play companion and tutor. . . ." (p. 167).

CASE EXAMPLE: BARBARA

Imagine, in the following example, that the patient is Barbara, a depressed woman in her 40s. You have observed that she has had a joyless, grey life in which initiative has been squelched; because of other evidence, you speculate that she has great anxiety about expressing anger. In this session (the transcript, because of long periods of nonverbal play, has been telescoped from two hours into one), as is typical for her, the patient does not move spontaneously toward any of the available toys. You therefore decide to use an active approach. In preplay therapy trance, Barbara has given you the feel of being about three or four years old, based on her vocabulary.

Therapist (T.): "Oh! Here's the block box. What a lot of blocks! Want to look with me?"

Patient (P.): (Looks in, passively.) [T. takes initiative, adapting vocabulary to preschool level, sounding enthusiastic enough for two.]

T: (Puts hand in box, messes around, making noise with the blocks) "What a lot of blocks! Here (taking P.'s hand), do you want to feel them?"

P: (Puts hand in box, moving it around gingerly. [T. must lead the way. Best to include as many sensory modalities as possible. (Issues related to nonerotic touch addressed in Shapiro, 1988b, *Second Childhood,* Chap. 10)]

T: "That's right. Oh, that sounds good! Can I do that with you?" (P. begins to move her hand around in the box more vigorously, nodding. T. and P. get into sync, making more and more noise with the blocks.) [Joining P. in the activity makes the activity escalate while the patient remains safe.]

T: "How about we DUMP ALL the blocks on the floor! What a big noise that will make!" (T. and P. upturn the block box with a loud crash.) "AAAH!!!" (P. smiles tentatively.) [Or, a game could be made of pitching each block out of the box, if T. feels that dumping would be too big a shock at this point. T. must still carry the ball, making most of the noise.]

T: "Ooh—look what I've got here—a door! What's that red one there?" (that P. was looking at or touching)

P: "A window!"

T: "A door and a window! And here's some people. Here's a little boy with no hair!" (laughing) [The message is: Silliness is okay.]

P: "That's funny!" (Touching the doll's head, smiling with amusement.)

Therapist and patient go on to build a house together, adding matchbox cars, a little train, whatever. They make up a story together.

P: "Here's the mommy. Where should she go?"

T: "I don't know, what do you think?"

P: "Mommy can stay outside. Here's Auntie." (Puts "Auntie" next to Mommy) "They can talk to each other." [As P. is now really participating, T. takes secondary part. Note that P. is taking care of Mommy. Mommy's fear of abandonment may be an issue.]

T: "Now Mommy will be happy." (P. gives vigorous nod.) "What will we do now?" [After this daring behavior, it is important to stress partnership with P.]

P: "Put Grandma in the house. Making cookies."

Play continues, in which the doll children have more and more fun, while Mommy and Auntie (who remains a sort of Mommy-sitter without distinct personality) remain on the sidelines. T. and P. begin to build towers with other blocks, adding to the scene. Sometimes a block falls—it is especially interesting to note that P. attempts to balance blocks with the naïveté of the small child. Modeling task-centered concentration, T. sometimes works on her own tower. At other times, shifting to a cooperative mode, T. participates in adding blocks to P.'s tower. Crashes dominate, and laughter ensues more spontaneously. As the session moves toward greater freedom of physical and verbal movement, T. introduces the risky issue of the acceptability of anger by initiating a small "playfight," with words chosen for their double value:

T: "You knocked my block off! Oh, now I'm MAD." (said in a joking voice) "I'm going to knock your block off too!" [The attempt here is to decondition P.'s fear of her own anger and of the anger of others.]

P: (Giggles) "I'll knock your whole tower down." (does)

T: "Who cares, I'll make another one! And I'm going to use this truck to deliver the poles." [The options are open to develop the fight or to end it creatively. Keeping the goals in mind and the developmental gap being addressed, either (or some other) choice is made.]

Play continues, with mini car crashes, and crescendoing sound effects until the end of that segment of the session, when both T. and P. clean up the blocks by pitching them into the box.

When the play segment, or module, is complete, the therapist takes the patient back to the "adult" area of the room where the return to the hypnotic "pleasant place" is effected (as detailed in Shapiro, *Second Childhood,* 1988, Chap. 8) and the hypnotic process is completed, with or without an embedded posthypnotic suggestion. For the previous example, you could consider such a suggestion as "You will be able to notice a new delight in familiar sounds," or "You may find yourself laughing at nothing at all," or "You may surprise yourself by enjoying the thought of something silly." One suggestion is as much as a patient can absorb. Any particularly threatening affect—in the previous example, anger—warrants a cautious approach during the embedding process. Here, for example, you would not choose to embed a suggestion about feeling angry, or feeling comfortable with anger in an out-of-office experience until an in-office conscious adult experience has been successfully negotiated.

Although trance has been formally terminated, the therapist must remember that some elements of that state remain for a few minutes. The therapist can attend to this extension of some degree of light hypnosis by being alert to the dominance of the patient's use of single-syllable words (Shapiro, 1977). While emerging into adult awareness (the length of words increasing, the vocabulary becoming more adult), the patient is encouraged to talk about the experience, to become aware of the new feelings of relaxation and pleasure in the adult body.

Some simply-stated interpretation or observation of the play therapy might be made. For Barbara, the therapist might comment, "You are very careful not to leave your mother all alone." Often there is discussion of the issue brought up here—the patient's role as the parentified child, her view of her responsibilities, her image of her mother as somehow helpless, lonely, and fragile. At the end of the session, the patient might want to walk over to the "young corner" and look at the toys again or put one or two in her hand. With Barbara, it was especially valuable to use adult "toys" or attractive objects, such as the kaleidoscopes nearby as transitions to the adult world. On nice days, I might walk Barbara to her car, examining the flowers by the side of the path—touching and smelling them en route. These walks served to smooth the transition from patient to nonpatient and to incorporate the goals of the play-therapy segments into a way of living in the world.

We have seen the therapist as adult therapist with "child" patient (Madeleine) and as parent with "child" (Barbara). A third role for the hypno-play therapist is that of peer in the play-therapy life of the child, rather than of replacement for a parental figure. With the "older" child, especially, it is common to find the patient alternating between past and present while in trance. Thus, the therapist, who, by age, is most frequently more peer than parent, almost naturally can assume the role of child-peer with such a patient.

CASE EXAMPLE: BILL

In the following example, the edited transcript is of a one-hour hypno-play therapy session with Bill, a middle-age administrator, the only Black management employee of the bank. The play segment grew out of the following comment made by Bill earlier in the session: "I don't put a lot of faith in friends or whatever." [Therapist: I'd like to hear more about that.] "I've done without them for so long. . . . It can get you slapped around . . . I'm the original chameleon . . . they want the three-piece suit side, they get the three-piece suit side."

The reference to "so long," and the use of the strong verb "slapped around," pointed toward the utility of an open-ended age regression to a time that would "shed light" on the issue. A brief excerpt from the beginning of the trance segment follows:

P: "I'm on the street with Dora Brown. She's nine."
T: "How old are you?"
P: "I'm nine also. . . . I got a lot of kidding. I like that girl Dora, but I don't know how to talk to her. In front of my house, we play truth/dare/consequences. You choose one of the categories. They set me up 'cause they know I like Dora; she doesn't live around there, a couple blocks away.

They kept asking me to ask her to go steady but I was afraid." [Switches to past tense. P. continues in past, T. continues in present. P. then returns to present.]

T: "Can you ask her?"

P: "Naw, I'm chicken."

T: "How do you feel?"

P: "Nervous, very bad. . . . I'm small, I'm not cool . . . I'm sort of—there are dress fads, my parents are a little conservative, I wear regular corduroys, Buster Brown shoes . . . the boy next door, the one the parents like . . . you're a safe bet. They're right-mm-boring! I'm the littlest." [Notice the adult awareness of the scene mixed with the child's experience.]

Connected both through affect and similarity of plot, Bill continued to talk about this and other scenes with girls and his attempt to be accepted in the school band, in which he felt humiliated and even betrayed by his peers. His small size added to the feeling of inferiority and vulnerability. Eventually, we reached adolescence, when the racial issue became more prominent:

T: "Where are you?"

P: "In Quincy (a White suburban town), with Joan and her girlfriend. They have a (summer) place; we all packed up and went. I was the only Black person there. Learned to be a very funny fellow . . . I looked at myself as the weekend entertainment . . ." [P. vacillates between present and past tenses. Continues in past tense for a while.]

T: "How old are you?" [T. remains in present tense. It would seem normal for the one Black person to feel under stress; and because stress and high blood pressure were presenting problems, T. is investigating the origin of his defense against it. Note that P. now remains in present tense for a while.]

P: "12 or 13."

T: "Do you feel tense when you're there?"

P: "Not really—I'm in control . . . I think, all the world's a stage, keep 'em laughing. Even the biggest bigot in the world, they, let their—um—tensions are gone, their resistance falls. . . ."

T: "Do you want to go on this weekend?"

P: "Oh, sure, I get to go out on the rowboats, out in the ocean . . . I listen to Bill Cosby records . . . it depends on your delivery."

T: "It works well."

P: "You betcha."

T: "So 12-year-old Billy knows how to do that, and 9-year-old Billy doesn't know that too well."

P: "It was boring to be me, to be short. To be funny, people listened to you . . . I go to school with Sol, he's an artist; Kevin's my best friend, he plays basketball. I don't have a specialty, they're unique. . . . But I am funny, then they laugh with you." [Again, the vacillation between past and present.]

T: "And no one's laughing *at* you."

P: "When you're the one making the jokes."

T: [T.'s interpretation is couched in young language.] "It really hurts to be laughed at. The little boy is very smart, he learns how to stop the pain. . . . He can't change that he's Black, and he can't change that he's short, and he got screwed about being in the band, and a lot of things he can't change. . . . Maybe he can be funny if he practices it, and then be somebody special, and people won't laugh at him any more. . . . How are you feeling right now?"

P: "Tired."

T: "Why are you tired, Billy?"

P: "It's not fun to be funny all the time . . . I'd like to be accepted just for me, not 'cause I'm funny, not 'cause I'm colored, not 'cause I'm anything, just because I'm me. [P. uses term *colored* common during his childhood, one he never uses now. Note that earlier he had called himself Black, when speaking in the past tense.]

Taking the theme of the desire to be "accepted . . . just because I'm me" as the yearning that, when thwarted, became covered by the defense against the danger of trusting, a segment of play therapy around that theme was introduced. Play therapy seemed particularly apt, as in earlier sessions Bill had spoken about his "fence walking" at his job as a "game" of "walking close to the edge without breaking my neck." Although that attitude kept him safe, he felt increasingly "isolated" from his colleagues, and, in comparing himself with others, said, "I know what it means to be a lonely person. I've been lonely 40 years of my life." In this case, I therefore adopted the role of peer, to which I felt there would be the least resistance, as many of Bill's playmates were White, and as his issues were mostly peer-oriented—White peer-oriented in particular. I began by setting the stage, moving from the past tense almost immediately, as I observed Bill slumping further into trance state:

T: [Beginning in past as if using screen. Paralleling his description of his clothes and shoes, moving into present tense.] "You know, not too long ago, I was a little girl, and I can see me nine years old—and I had braids . . . and striped shirts . . . and Indian Walk shoes . . . I hate those shoes. . . . My mommy makes me wear them 'cause they're good for my feet. . . . (P. is going deeper into trance) You know, I like you a lot, you're a good kid. I don't tell on my friends. I won't tell on you if you won't tell on me. Do you want to be my friend?" [Reference is to his experience of betrayal.]

P: "Yes." (nodding slowly)

T: "I'll teach you to play skelly checkers (a street game with bottle caps) if you don't know how. You know how?"

P: "No."

T: (Describes game) "What would you teach me?"

P: "Drums!"

T: "Would you teach me?"

P: "Sure!"

T: "We could be partners! Deal?" [A metaphor for the hypnotherapeutic relationship.]

P: "Deal."

T: [Anticipating a transition—optional. I may have been feeling unnecessarily anxious about P.'s willingness to play, given his elegant attire and usual formal presentation.] ". . . and when we come back to this room, we're really going to play skelly checkers . . . tell you a secret, I got a good move the other kids don't know . . . and you can stay in trance if you want. . . . " [T. rises and gets the skelly checkers; T. sits down on the floor; P. joins T. on the floor; T. gives P. a skelly checker] "Here, you can have one, because you're my friend."

P: "Thank you!" [T. demonstrates how to shoot the checkers, teaches P. the rules of the game. T. and P. play for a while.]

P: "They want to play to win; I want to play to play." [P. often avoided conflict and competition, so T. models both options.]

T: "Sometimes I want to play to win, sometimes I want to play to play."

P: [Nods acceptingly.]

T: "Isn't it nice to have a friend and not put on an act, just be you." [Echoing his earlier sentiments, T.'s tone indicated that T. was speaking for herself, although using the ambiguous *you*.]

P: "Yeah, not tiring."

Sessions of hypno-play therapy concluded with an almost imperceptible return to the fully conscious state. Suggestions were made directly that Bill would construct a set of skelly checkers and practice the "good move" he had been taught. Bill followed these instructions with enthusiasm, bringing the results to the next sessions.

The next weeks evoked more memories of the games of latency through adolescent years—descriptions of mumblety-peg ("I don't know why I thought of it!"), of friends of those eras, of playing board games with his father. Some emergency surgery precipitated a dream about Fisk, which allowed Bill to appreciate the lack of tension around being part of an all-Black community:

> It was a long dream, about Fisk, a real tight camaraderie-type of dream. I dreamt about being on campus, feeling the feelings of the football game. A homesy atmosphere, it hits you in the chest at football games. I felt like I was going to die—I wanted to say—if they knew what I know now they don't know how good they have it. I felt sad—it was like watching over it, going to the cafeteria, sitting with the guys. It was like I made the fucking trip! [What's the sadness about?] Leaving. My primary concerns were not what they are now, dying, being Black.

Bill also began to bring in dreams about repressed anger—a tame dog versus a vicious bear, for example. The play-therapy trance was partially recalled, as we integrated reference to skelly checkers into the conscious sessions; however, much of the specifics of the hypnotic sessions remained "kinda hazy." Unlike Bill's usual discomfort with forgetting anything, he exhibited indifference toward the forgotten details. But the power of that session emerged in his forceful new insight and focus:

> If people were circles, I'd be three-quarters of a circle. Someone else might say, "Where's the other part?" I know it isn't there. [What do you think the missing quarter is?] Being able to do what I do here anytime I choose to.

In continuing with Bill in psychotherapy, further work in both conscious and unconscious modes seems a likely constructive direction.

CONCLUSION

Surely every therapist has frequently wished that many of the adults in treatment had been taken for help when they were young. If only the problem could have been addressed then, how much simpler the solution would have been, how many years of desperation or, at the least, restriction could have been eliminated! Yet, even child therapy has its built-in limitations, especially in the more serious cases: The child usually must return for most of the week to the very home in which the issues most often arise. Family systems are complex, often involving interrelated and enmeshed conflicts, compromises, neurotic adjustments, and pathological behaviors. Family therapy, frequently the treatment of choice, is usually resisted and frequently unworkable; for example, a careful study by Kaplun and Reich (1976) "does not tend to support the belief that severely abusing parents are receptive to counseling or psychotherapy; the extreme, long-standing psychopathology, the host of coexisting problems, and the paucity of insight and motivation all tend to point against this view for most cases." In the majority of their case examples, the family simply doesn't show up. Where family therapy is, in fact, initiated, parents commonly resent the position of authority of the therapist, the outsider to whom the child's attachment grows, the one whose very success only points out their deficits the more. The therapist must walk a very narrow line to avoid making the situation worse for the child at home.

Of course, the more that can be done sooner, the better. I rejoice and am in awe of the fine family and child work that triumphs over the odds. In fact, the use of hypno-play therapy with my adult clients has made them amenable, even enthusiastic about supporting individual or family work with their own children when that has become advisable, for they have learned to identify with themselves as children, and hence have become capable of a new empathy with the children for whom they are the parents.

Most practitioners of hypnotherapy still follow Spiegel, Frischholz, Maruffi, and Spiegel (1981) in the definition of *hypnosis* as "a method of disciplined concentration which can be used adjunctively with a primary treatment strategy" (p. 239). Some, such as Frischholz (1995, p. 1), therefore, object to the term *hypnotherapy,* because they "do not believe that *hypnosis* is a form of *therapy* or *treatment* in its own right." In general, that view is valid. As Frischholz continues, "It is more important to focus on how hypnosis is used in conjunction with specific primary treatment strategies" (p. 1). Hypno-play therapy, however, is a treatment modality in and of itself, used, as described in this chapter, to forward a specific end with a specific person. When it is appropriate, it can be the best way I have encountered to meet the person at the place(s) at which the damage was done, to repair it, and to move through and past it. One hypno-play therapy patient began treatment by reporting dreams of violent, vicious animals, and of houses with holes in the floors and walls. A year later, she spoke of the existence of "a bottom" from which she recognized the emergence of an embryonic "sense of forgiveness." Perhaps most, but not all, of the holes are filled, or perhaps the paint does not quite match that of the original, leaving an uneven coloration. The animals may become more or less tame or may recede into the nonthreatening distant landscape. Each case, as each person, is different.

I do not imply that the now healthy patient does not remember the original traumas, the years of pain, the losses. Rather, for the healthy person the restrictions on the being and on the expression of self are gone, or at least greatly reduced. The physical and emotional symptoms, often the presenting problems, disappear or are mostly alleviated.

The classical analyst's "internal position" is always, at bottom, a struggle for "a new and better childhood" for the patient (Racker, 1968, p. 33). With that goal in mind, I have become a pragmatic psychotherapist as well as a theoretician, a reversal of priority from an earlier, more academic orientation. Hypno-play therapy works for many for whom traditional methods do not work at all, or for whom many years are required to produce results satisfying to the patient. Is that not the point?

REFERENCES

American Society of Clinical Hypnosis. (1995). *Clinical hypnosis and memory: Guidelines for clinicians and for forensic hypnosis.* Bloomingdale, IL: Author.

Angyal, A. (1982). *Neurosis and treatment.* New York: Da Capo Press.

Axline, V. (1964). Nondirective therapy. In M. R. Haworth (Ed.), *Child psychotherapy: Practice and theory.* New York: Basic Books.

Brown, D., Scheflin, A. W., & Hammond, D. C. (1988). *Memory, trauma, treatment, and the law.* New York: Norton.

Clarke, A. M., & Clarke, A. D. B. (1976). *Early experience: Myth and evidence.* London: Open Books.

Erikson, E. H. (1951). Sex differences in the play configurations of preadolescents. *American Journal of Orthopsychiatry, 21,* 667–692.

Frischholz, E. J. (1995, July). Editorial. *American Journal of Clinical Hypnosis, 38*(1), 1–2.

Fromm, E. (1980). Values in hypnotherapy. *Psychotherapy: Theory, research and practice, 17,* 425–430.

Hilgard, E. R. (1977). *Divided consciousness.* New York: Wiley.

Irwin, E. C. (1983). The diagnosis and therapeutic use of pretend play. In C. E. Schaeffer & K. J. O'Connor (Eds.), *Handbook of play therapy* (pp. 148–173). New York: Wiley.

Kagan, J. (1980). *Infancy: Its place in human development.* Cambridge, MA: Harvard University Press.

Kaplun, D., & Reich, R. (1976, July). The murdered child and his killers. *American Journal of Psychiatry, 133*(7), 809–813.

Lebo, D. (1956). Age and suitability for nondirective play therapy. *Journal of Genetic Psychology, 89,* 232–238.

Racker, H. (1968). *Transference and counter-transference.* New York: International Universities Press.

Rothschild, B. (2000). *The body remembers.* New York: Norton.

Shapiro, M. K. (1977). *The psychology of adult learning: The role of symbolism in the process of human being.* Unpublished doctoral dissertation, Harvard Graduate School of Education, Cambridge, Massachusetts.

Shapiro, M. K. (1988a, July). Hypno-play therapy with adults: Theory, method, and practice. *American Journal of Clinical Hypnosis, 31*(1), 1–10.

Shapiro, M. K. (1988b). *Second childhood.* New York: Norton.

Shapiro, M. K. (1991, July). Bandaging a "broken heart": Hypno-play therapy in the treatment of multiple personality disorder. *American Journal of Clinical Hypnosis, 34*(1), 1–10.

Silverman, P. S., & Retzlaff, P. D. (1986). Cognitive stage regression through hypnosis: Are earlier cognitive stages retrievable? *International Journal of Clinical and Experimental Hypnosis, 34*, 192–204.

Spiegel, D., Frischholz, E. J., Maruffi, B., & Spiegel, H. (1981). Hypnotic responsivity and the treatment of flying phobia. *American Journal of Clinical Hypnosis, 23*, 239–247.

Stern, D. (1985). *The interpersonal world of the infant.* New York: Basic Books.

Winnicott, D. W. (1958). *Collected papers: Through paediatrics to psychoanalysis.* London: Tavistock.

PLAY THERAPY FOR DISSOCIATIVE IDENTITY DISORDER IN ADULTS

Laura W. Hutchison

Dissociative identity disorder (DID) is intriguing and controversial. With all the mystique and media interest surrounding the disorder, many confusions and errors have been made both in the public and in the professional world. By looking at the established definitions and exploring the history of the disorder, I hope that clarification is received and is helpful to the readers' understanding of DID. In this chapter, I examine trends of research on this subject, changes in the definition and criteria for the disorder, key people involved, how the spirit of the times affected research and the definition of dissociative identity disorder, and the use of play therapy in treating adults with DID. Because of the frequent confusion of the definition of DID and the controversy surrounding the disorder, I begin with how DID is defined today and then how it evolved through the history of psychology. To better understand what DID is, sometimes it helps to know what it is not. Therefore, I examine other disorders that will help put the DID diagnosis in perspective. Later in the chapter, I discuss using the method of play therapy with adults diagnosed with DID. I examine the what, why, when, and how of using play therapy with this population.

DEFINITION OF TERMS

As defined in the *Diagnostic and Statistical Manual of Mental Disorders,* 4th edition (*DSM-IV*; American Psychiatric Association, 1994), DID is one of the five disorders categorized under the *dissociative disorders. Dissociative amnesia, dissociative fugue, dissociative identity disorder, depersonalization disorder,* and *dissociative disorder not otherwise specified* are the current dissociative disorders recognized by the American Psychiatric Association. The *DSM-IV* states, "The essential feature of the Dissociative Disorders is a disruption in the usually integrated functions of consciousness, memory, identity, or perception of the environment. The disturbance may be sudden or gradual, transient or chronic" (p. 477).

"Dissociative Amnesia is characterized by an inability to recall important personal information, usually of a traumatic or stressful nature, that is too extensive to be explained by ordinary forgetfulness" (*DSM-IV,* p. 477). This disorder was formerly called *psychogenic amnesia* in previous *DSM* editions. It includes various memory disturbances such as localized amnesia, selective amnesia, generalized amnesia, continuous amnesia, and systematized amnesia.

"Dissociative Fugue is characterized by sudden, unexpected travel away from home or one's customary place of work, accompanied by an inability to recall one's past and confusion about personal identity or the assumption of a new identity" (*DSM-IV,* p. 477). This disorder was formerly called *psychogenic fugue.* It is a relatively rare disease occurring in 0.2% of the general population (p. 482).

"Depersonalization Disorder is characterized by a persistent or recurrent feeling of being detached from one's mental processes or body that is accompanied by intact reality testing" (*DSM-IV,* p. 477). Sensations such as being an outside observer of yourself, being in a dream or movie, and lacking control of actions are often present. Depersonalization is common and the disorder diagnosis should be made only when symptoms are severe enough to meet all of the criteria.

"Dissociative Disorder Not Otherwise Specified is included for coding disorders in which the predominant feature is a dissociative symptom, but that do not meet the criteria for any specific Dissociative Disorder" (*DSM-IV,* p. 477). Examples of this are derealization, dissociative trance disorder, loss of consciousness not related to a medical condition, and Ganser syndrome (pp. 490–491).

With an overview of the other dissociative disorders for background, I turn back to the focus of this chapter, *dissociative identity disorder.* The *DSM-IV* states:

> Dissociative Identity Disorder (formerly Multiple Personality Disorder) is characterized by the presence of two or more distinct identities or personality states that recurrently take control of the individual's behavior accompanied by an inability to recall important personal information that is too extensive to be explained by ordinary forgetfulness. (p. 477)

To meet the diagnosis criteria, the symptoms cannot be explained by a substance (alcohol or drugs), a medical condition, or, for children, fantasy play or imaginary playmates. The *DSM-IV* further states these diagnostic features:

> Dissociative Identity Disorder reflects a failure to integrate various aspects of identity, memory, and consciousness. Each personality state may be experienced as if it has a distinct personal history, self-image, and identity, including a separate

name. Usually there is a primary identity that carries the individual's given name and is passive, dependent, guilty, and depressed. The alternate identities frequently have different names and characteristics that contrast with the primary identity (e.g., are hostile, controlling, and self-destructive). Particular identities may emerge in specific circumstances and may differ in reported age and gender, vocabulary, general knowledge, or predominant affect. Alternate identities are experienced as taking control in sequence, one at the expense of the other, and may deny knowledge of one another, be critical of one another, or appear to be in open conflict. Occasionally, one or more powerful identities allocate time to the others. Aggressive or hostile identities may at times interrupt activities or place the others in uncomfortable situations. (p. 484)

Problems with memory of personal history, past and present, are frequently the nature of the disorder. Different personalities may hold different types and amounts of memories. Some memories may be lost to all entities. Transitions between identities are often triggered by stress; switches usually occur in a matter of seconds. "The number of identities reported ranges from 2 or more than 100. Half of reported cases include individuals with 10 or fewer identities" (*DSM-IV*, p. 485). "Dissociative Identity Disorder is diagnosed three to nine times more frequently in adult females than in adult males; in childhood, the female-to-male ratio may be more even, but data are limited" (pp. 485–486). There are relatively high rates of DID reported in the United States. The prevalence of this disorder remains highly controversial, which is a topic that is covered later in the chapter. The course of DID fluctuates and tends to be chronic and recurrent.

Many researchers have attempted to define the disorder and its related terminology. Previous to the *DSM-IV*, dissociative identity disorder was labeled as *multiple personality disorder* (MPD). Therefore, literature cited before 1994 refers to DID as MPD. The change in the name of this disorder has also caused controversy. In my review of the literature, I have found that authors on DID/MPD have varying opinions about the name and make different decisions on what they choose to call it. I have not found much literature on why the name of the disorder was changed in the *DSM-IV*. I did, however, find one quote on the World Wide Web. Mahari (n.d.) writes this on his Web site:

The shift to the category of DID, as I understand it is an effort to better define, classify, understand and diagnose and treat the many varying degrees to which these alterations in consciousness indeed do exist and are experienced by many more people than was originally thought by most. (¶ 6)

Whereas with DID not only does the umbrella classification cover what was originally referred to as MPD but it also extends to a wider spectrum of the variable presentations where degrees of dissociation, splitting, and fragmentation that are experienced by many, especially the survivors of sexual abuse, ritual abuse, and satanic rituals abuse. (¶ 9)

The change appears to stem from the need for the classification to cover a broader spectrum. The change in nomenclature also puts less emphasis on separateness of self, a move that is consistent with current treatment models.

I stated earlier in this chapter that prevalence of the disorder is controversial. This was apparent in my Web search. A DID Fact Sheet from the Internet states, "Although no controlled study has been conducted in the United States, an estimate of the prevalence of DID in the U.S. population is from 1 in 500 to 1 in 5,000, or between 250,000 and 2,500,000 people" (West, n.d., p. 1). The fact that "no controlled study has been conducted" does make the determination of a consistent number of cases difficult to establish and suspect for controversy! Brennan (n.d.) writes this on the Web, "Today, over 7,000 cases have been diagnosed in North America" (¶6). Obviously, further research is needed to determine the prevalence of the disorder-research that would be tricky to conduct given the controversial nature of the disorder.

Central to the disorder of DID/MPD is dissociation. Understanding what *dissociation* means is crucial to understanding DID/MPD. Several researchers have defined *dissociation*. Turkus (1992) gives her definition, "Dissociation is the *disconnection* from full awareness of self, time, and/or external circumstances. It is a complex neuropsychological process. Dissociation exists along a continuum from normal everyday experiences to disorders that interfere with everyday functioning" (¶2). The Sidran Foundation (1994) states this on dissociation:

> Dissociation is a mental process which produces a lack of connection in a person's thoughts, memories, feelings, actions, or sense of identity. During the period of time when a person is dissociating, certain information is not associated with other information as it normally would be. ("What Is Dissociation?" section, ¶1)
>
> Most clinicians believe that dissociation exists on a continuum of severity. This continuum reflects a wide range of experiences and/or symptoms. At one end are mild Dissociative experiences common to most people, such as daydreaming, highway hypnosis, or "getting lost" in a book or movie, all involve "losing touch" with conscious awareness of one's immediate surroundings. At the other extreme is complex, chronic dissociation, such as in cases of Dissociative Identity Disorder (MPD) and other Dissociative Disorders which may result in serious impairment or inability to function. ("What Is Dissociation?" section, ¶2)

Both references discussed a continuum of severity. Putnam (1989) also writes about the dissociation continuum: "Central to the concept of the adaptive function(s) of dissociation is the idea that Dissociative phenomena exist on a continuum and become maladaptive only when they exceed certain limits in intensity or frequency, or occur in inappropriate contexts" (p. 9). Braun (1986b) created the "continuum of dissociation." This continuum begins with "normal" dissociation, moves to "dissociative episode," "dissociative disorder," "atypical dissociative disorder," "atypical multiple personality disorder," "multiple personality disorder," and ends with "polyfragmented multiple personality disorder" (p. 19). Therefore, DID/MPD is at the far end of the dissociation continuum.

The theory behind the creation of the disorder, or what makes people dissociate, is that events in life became so overwhelming or painful that the person experiencing it "checked out" or left consciousness. In some cases, another consciousness appeared and took control. If these situations occurred often enough and were reinforced in some manner (i.e., relief of trauma), dissociation became a habitual coping mechanism. This complicated coping mechanism becomes DID/MPD. What I am discussing here are the predisposing factors and precipitating events of DID/MPD, a topic covered by many researchers. Braun (1986b) states:

> Two predisposing factors are hypothesized to be necessary: 1) an inborn biological/psychological capacity to dissociate that is usually identified by excellent responsivity to hypnosis and 2) repeated exposure to an inconsistently stressed environment. The inconsistency is in the patient's receiving love and abuse for the same behavior, at unpredictable times. An abusive family environment has been the source of this inconsistent stress in the vast majority of MPD cases studied so far. However, other events such as the death of a family member, frequent geographic relocation, and cultural dislocation can also be identified as sources of stress. Both of these predisposing factors are necessary for MPD to develop. Neither alone is sufficient. (p. 7)

Braun (1986b) created the 3-P Model of multiple personality disorder—Predisposing Factors (for example, an individual's biology, psychodynamics, and family dynamics), Precipitating Event, and Perpetuating Phenomena—to explain how he believes the disorder develops in a person (p. 6). The predisposing factors are the person's inborn ability to dissociate. The precipitating event is abuse, crises, and/or stress. Perpetuating Phenomena occurs when the person continues to dissociate because of the ongoing abuse. Researchers overwhelmingly state the presence of child abuse in the history of those who have DID/MPD as the precipitating event (Braun & Sachs, 1985; Gil, 1990; Kluft, 1985a; Putnam, 1985; Spiegel, 1986; Turkus, 1992; Wilbur, 1985). However, it is important to note that not all people who suffer child abuse or trauma develop DID/MPD or dissociate. The difference in those who do develop the disorder could be that the abuse is instigated by a parent or caretaker and the abuse is inconsistent, but ongoing. As Braun (1986b) writes, "The trauma is usually associated with some form of inconsistent and unpredictable abuse. For example, a child may be severely beaten or affectionately hugged for the same behavior on different occasions" (p. 8). The confusion caused by the parent/caretaker/abuser's switching from loving moments to inducing pain in the child becomes overwhelming and the child "checks out." The fact that the abuse is ongoing promotes the child to cope in the same repeated fashion, which is to dissociate. Spiegel states:

> The repeated need to mobilize a dissociative defense tends to make its use habitual. Furthermore, it becomes incorporated into a cognitive framework. A patient preserves the integrity of his or her ego by dissociating it from the trauma, by saying, "This did not happen to me." (p. 66)

The coping mechanism then becomes a disorder.

In creating understanding of the disorder DID/MPD, the terms associated with the disorder must also be understood. Braun (1986a) defined many of the terms related to DID/MPD (pp. xii–xv):

Personality. An entity that contains: (a) a consistent and ongoing set of response patterns to given stimuli, (b) a significant confluent history, (c) a range of emotions available, and (d) a range of intensity of affect for each emotion.

Fragment. An entity that is less than a personality. Fragments have a consistent and ongoing set of response patterns to given stimuli and either a significant history or range of emotions/affect, but usually not both to the same degree.

Special-purpose fragment. An entity that is less than a fragment. It has a limited set of response patterns to stimuli and minimal life history and range of emotion/affect.

Memory trace fragment. A fragment that has only a minimal set of response patterns to stimuli, life history, and range of emotion/affect but has knowledge for a short period of time.

Alter (also called *alternate personality*). Any personality or fragment other than the host personality.

Host personality. The personality that has executive control of the body for the greatest percentage of time during a given time period.

Presenting personality. The entity that first comes in for therapy; it may be the original personality, the host personality, or a fragment.

Original personality. The entity that developed first after birth and split off or remained separate from the flow of the rest of the thought process. The original personality is often difficult to locate and work with, but this needs to be done to achieve a stable and lasting integration.

Splitting. The creation of a new entity by the splitting off or coalescing of energy which forms the nucleus of a separate personality or fragment.

Switching. Going back and forth between already existing personalities or fragments. This may be precipitated by external or internal stimuli.

Two-way amnesia. The state in which one personality or fragment does not know of the existence of another personality or fragment and vice versa.

One-way amnesia. The state in which personality/fragment A does not know anything about personality/fragment B, but B knows everything about A.

Co-presence. The simultaneous presence of two or more personalities/fragments with or without their knowing of one another's existence or current presence. Co-presence can occur with or without an influence of one upon another.

Co-consciousness. The state of being aware of the thoughts or consciousness of another personality. It can be unidirectional or bi-directional, with or without co-presence, and/or with or without an influence of one upon another.

Fusion. The act or instance of bringing together two or more personalities or fragments in order to blend their essence into a single entity.

Integration. The process of bringing together the separate thought processes (personalities or fragments) and maintaining them as one. It is a process that starts before fusion and continues after it.

One of the terms mentioned is *switching,* which is the process of dissociation when one with DID/MPD changes to an alternate personality state. The phenomenon of the switching process is a highly discussed topic in DID/MPD literature and deserves further attention in this chapter. Braun (1986a) states:

> Switching of personalities may produce diverse physical appearance such as strikingly different facial expressions, permutations in posture and body language, change in handedness, significant weight gain or loss over short periods of time, and voice changes.
>
> Alternate personalities may demonstrate the behaviors that manifest their perceptions of themselves. They may speak in different accents and even different languages; their handwriting may be different; some may be creative in different arts, others not at all; and some may be male, others female in their self-perceptions, life histories, and dress. (p. xv)

It is the switching process of DID/MPD that intrigues so many. The uniqueness of transition into a completely different personality is quite amazing. Healing Hopes (2001) defines and gives characteristics for switching on its Web site:

> Switching is defined as the process of changing from one alter to another. Switching may be stimulated by an internal perception or the need for a particular alter or by an external, environmental trigger. Individuals with DID/MPD have varying degrees of control over the process. Switching may be accompanied by physiological and/or psychological changes. (¶ 1)

The site lists these "switching characteristics":

Physiological

Headache, pressure, inside and/or at the base of the head.

Stiffness in the neck.

Ringing in the ears.

Dizziness, feeling light-headed or feeling faint (like you might lose consciousness).

Light in a room changes to suddenly brighter or dimmer.

Pupil dilation, eyes are more sensitive to light.

Pressure behind the eyes.

Blurry vision.

Eyes become watery or glassy, sometimes reddened.

Objects may appear different—i.e., a change in the perceived dimensions of an object, changes in color.

Eyes may twitch or move rapidly, or roll up into your (sic) head.

Change in temperature perception—chills, too hot.

Changes in laughter, tone of voice, quality of speech, and/or speech patterns.

Psychological

Changes in self-perception—i.e., you may feel physically shorter or taller than usual.

Feeling detached from your body and/or face.

Face looks different to you in a mirror.

Thought patterns shifts—you may think about and respond to the same subject or situation differently.

Mood swings, a change in your mood and/or feelings about the same situation change in emotional reaction to the same situation.

Difficulty concentrating, unable to think clearly.

Thoughts become louder, and/or hearing many thoughts or voices with opposing views.

Feeling an urgent need to get something done.

Change in emotional age—feeling like a child.

With professional criteria and related terms defined, some may think that diagnosing DID/MPD would be pretty clear-cut. Unfortunately, this is not true. There is much confusion surrounding the diagnosis of DID/MPD. One of the reasons behind this confusion is that people with DID/MPD elicit many symptoms that are similar to other disorders and many have secondary diagnoses to complicate proper diagnosis. Symptoms may include depression, mood swings, suicidal tendencies and self-destructive thoughts and/or behaviors, sleep disorders (insomnia, night terrors, and sleep walking), anxiety, panic attacks and phobias (flashbacks, reactions to stimuli), alcohol and drug abuse, anger and rage, shame, low self-esteem, somatic pain syndromes, relationship and intimacy difficulties, sexual dysfunction, amnesia, compulsions and rituals, psychotic-like symptoms (including auditory and visual hallucinations), and eating disorders (Sidran Foundation, 1994; Turkus, 1992). The Sidran Foundation states: "As many as 80% to 100% of people diagnosed with DID (MPD) also have a secondary diagnosis of PTSD" ("What Is Dissociative Identity Disorder?" section, ¶3). PTSD, or posttraumatic stress disorder, as a secondary diagnosis, makes sense because of the understanding that abuse is almost always a precipitating factor to DID/MPD. The confusion is so great that many people with DID/MPD spend years being misdiagnosed (The International Society for the Study of Dissociation, 1997). The Sidran Foundation writes:

> DID(MPD)/DD [Dissociative Disorder] survivors often spend years living with misdiagnoses, consequently floundering within the mental health system. They change from therapist to therapist and from medication to medication, getting treatment for symptoms but making little or no actual progress. Research has documented that on average, people with DID(MPD)/DD have spent seven years in the mental health system prior to accurate diagnosis.
>
> This is common, because the list of symptoms that cause a person with DID(MPD)/DD to seek treatment is very similar to those of many other psychiatric diagnoses. In fact, many people who are diagnosed with DID(MPD)/DD also have secondary diagnoses of depression, anxiety, or panic disorders. ("Why Are Dissociative Disorders Often Misdiagnosed?" section)

I believe that the other reason that DID/MPD has been difficult to diagnose is professionals' and laypersons' confusion with it and other disorders. I have already discussed what distinguishes DID from the other dissociative disorders, but what about the other disorders that are commonly mistaken for DID or vice versa? Although I have not found any research on this topic, I believe that people mistake the category of personality disorders with dissociative disorders, when in actuality, they are quite different. As defined in the *DSM-IV:*

> A Personality Disorder is an enduring pattern of inner experience and behavior that deviates markedly from the expectations of the individual's culture, is pervasive and inflexible, has an onset in adolescence or early adulthood, is stable over time, and leads to distress or impairment. (p. 629)

This disorder has nothing to do with multiple personalities states/alters or dissociation. Currently included in the section of personality disorders are paranoid personality disorder, schizoid personality disorder, schizotypal personality disorder, antisocial personality disorder, borderline personality disorder, histrionic personality disorder, narcissistic personality disorder, avoidant personality disorder, dependent personality disorder, obsessive-complusive personality disorder, and personality disorder not otherwise specified. The fact that personality disorders and dissociation disorders sections are not the same means they could be dually diagnosed. The other disorder that DID/MPD is frequently confused with is schizophrenia. This is a mistake stemming back from the time when schizophrenia was first labeled around the turn of the twentieth century (covered later in the chapter). The mistake of confusing the two disorders is commonly made in the popular media such as movies and television shows. By looking at the criteria for schizophrenia, you can see it is a very different disorder from DID: "Schizophrenia is a disturbance that lasts for at least 6 months and includes at least 1 month of active-phase symptoms (i.e., two [or more] of the following: delusions, hallucinations, disorganized speech, grossly disorganized or catatonic behavior, negative symptoms)" (*DSM-IV*, 1994, p. 273). Although some people with DID/MPD may experience some symptoms similar to those of schizophrenia, the disorders are not the same.

THE HISTORY

With the definitions and vocabulary laid out, the history of the disorder is now examined. Several researchers found that traces of DID date back to almost four centuries ago (Braun & Sachs, 1985; Putnam, 1985). Putnam (1989) believes that archetypes of the disorder go back in time as far as religious belief and behavior can be traced. "Images of shamans, changed into animal forms or embodying spirits, can be found in Paleolithic cave paintings and contemporary Eskimo carvings" (p. 27). Putnam (1989) also mentions other early cases and theories; for example, Paracelsus's description of a case in 1646, Eberhardt Gmelin's report of a case in 1791, Benjamin Rush's theory that the disconnection between the two hemispheres of the brain was the mechanism responsible for the doubling of consciousness, Dr. Samuel Latham Mitchell's case of Mary Reynolds in 1816, and Despine's case of Estelle in 1836 (pp. 27–28).

Around the turn of the century, interest in multiple personalities grew widely (Braun & Sachs, 1985; Kluft, 1985b; Putnam, 1985, 1989). During this time, as Putnam (1989) states, "A relatively large number of cases were reported, particularly in France and the United States. Dissociation and multiple personality became subjects of intense interest for many of the great physicians, psychologists, and philosophers of the era" (p. 29). When discussing the turn-of-the-century ascent of the disorder, Pierre Janet (1859–1947) is frequently mentioned (Putnam, 1989, p. 1). Janet was born into the French upper-middle-class and was an excellent student. He first trained as a philosopher and followed the work of Jean-Martin Charcot. Following in Charcot's footsteps, Janet's focus of interest was on hypnosis. "In 1883, Janet took a position as a professor in philosophy at the Lyceum in Le Havre, beginning upon arrival to search for patients for his doctoral thesis" (Putnam, 1989, p. 2). In 1889, Janet returned to Paris to begin his medical studies while still working with patients (p. 2). Through his work with his patients, Janet was able to report a large number of dissociation cases that brought the disorder worldwide recognition (Braun, 1986a, p. 130). Putnam (1989) states that there were many pioneers examining the disorder: "Janet however, stands first among all clinicians and researchers who have inquired into the nature of dissociation" (p. 2). Janet explained *dissociation* to mean the severing of association of one thing from another to explain certain phenomena he observed in his patients (Frischholz, 1985, p. 101). His observations led him to "speculate that consciousness flowed in many streams, which did not necessarily flow together" (p. 102).

Janet had several contemporaries who helped to support and carry out further exploration on dissociation. One of these contemporaries was Morton Prince, the founder of the *Journal of Abnormal Psychology*. Putnam (1989) writes that Prince "sought to de-emphasize the importance of amnesia, making the simultaneous activity of two or more systems within one individual the crucial factor in his model of dissociation" (p. 3). Prince is most famous for his case, "Miss Beauchamp," which he described in *Dissociation of a Personality* (1906). Frischholz (1985) writes, "Prince concluded that it was 'inconceivable' that a purely physiological explanation could account for the symptoms observed in multiple personality disorder" (p. 103).

Freud's work on consciousness had direct relationships to the exploration of dissociation and perhaps the switch in interest in the disorder. Breuer and Freud's work (1895) on hypnoid states and hysteria put emphasis on the splitting of consciousness that paralleled contemporary work on dissociation. Freud's later break with Breuer, his change of mind of the hypnoid states as a necessary feature of hysteria, and his change of focus probably affected the overall interest in dissociation, especially because of Freud's popularity at the time. Interest in hypnoid states declined in Europe following Freud's rejection of hypnosis and his adoption of free association as the therapeutic technique. In the United States, Morton Prince, William James, and their contemporaries continued to investigate these altered states and their role in psychopathology for another decade (Putnam, 1989, p. 17).

After this burst of interest, focus on the disorder and dissociation declined. Two causes are normally given when discussing the decline of interest in dissociation during the early part of the twentieth century. The first is the introduction of the term *schizophrenia* in 1910. Because of similar symptoms between DID/MPD and schizophrenia, cases of DID/MPD were seemingly misdiagnosed and, therefore, underrepresented because of the popularity of the new term (Braun, 1985; Braun & Sachs, 1985; Frischholz, 1985; Putnam, 1985). As stated earlier in the chapter, to this day, the disorders are frequently confused. I personally have heard laypeople, the public, several media sources, and (sadly enough) clinicians who confuse the two disorders.

The second reason that focus on disorder and dissociation declined was the popular belief that MPD was caused by hypnosis. During this time, hypnosis was losing credibility as a diagnostic and therapeutic tool, causing skepticism surrounding MPD (Putnam, 1985, p. 71). Braun (1985) states, "Many early practitioners began to regard multiple personality disorder as the end product of 'hypnotic suggestion.' The consequence of this view was that multiple personality disorder was not considered to be a genuine diagnostic entity worthy of scientific investigation" (p. 131).

The emergence of the diagnosis of schizophrenia and the change in popular opinion about hypnosis definitely made an impact on the study and reported cases of dissociation. Frischholz (1985) brings additional insight to the trend against DID/MPD:

> The decline of reported multiple personality disorder cases from 1910 to 1970 was probably also influenced by changes in the newly expanding field of psychology. During the 1920s through the 1950s, psychology was heavily influenced by the behaviorist view of Watson, Hull, and Skinner. As a result, many psychologists preferred to focus on fluctuations in observed behavior rather than reported alterations in conscious experience. This turning away from the study of experience may have contributed to facilitating psychologists' misdiagnosis of multiple personality disorder. (p. 104)

Putnam (1989) also discusses additional changes of the time that impacted the study of DID/MPD:

> It was late in this same period that the psychopharmacological revolution began with the introduction of Thorazine, followed by a host of other neuroleptic medications. The introduction of these potent medications began the movement away from the psychoanalytic treatment model toward the current biological/medical treatment paradigm. This paradigm places less emphasis on direct contact between patient and clinician as part of the therapeutic process. The resulting decrease in patient-clinician interaction may also have contributed to the decreased recognition of MPD patients, who often require a lengthy period of intimate therapy before revealing their amnesias and other Dissociative experiences. (p. 34)

Again, studying the spirit of the times helps bring understanding of the attention shift away from multiple personality disorder. The process of examining such trends is essential when looking at the validity of diagnoses. When specific reasons and explanations are cited, the changing numbers of cases reported can be understood by knowing the school of thought or paradigms of the time.

The 1970s created a reemergence in the interest of DID/MPD. Until then, the interest lay dormant with only a few feeble attempts to look at the disorder. Frishholz (1985) cites Taylor and Martin's 1944 article that reviewed 76 documented cases of multiple personality disorder. "That such a small number of cases could be retrieved from the world's literature strengthened the general belief that the incidence of this disorder was extremely rare" (p. 104). In 1957, the movie *Three Faces of Eve* (Johnson), based on an actual case study by Thigpen and Cleckley (1954), brought brief popular and professional attention to MPD, but did not promote enough interest to continue further inquiry. Putnam (1989) states that the movie may have even helped to keep MPD in the shadows: "*The Three Faces of Eve*, while well known, gives a misleading picture of MPD and ironically may have helped to obscure the clinical features of the disorder" (p. 35). During the 1960s, interest in MPD began a rebirth. Frischholtz (1985) states, "This renewed attention paralleled a rise in the influence of the humanistic school of psychology, which accepted a person's description of his or her conscious experience as valid scientific data" (pp. 104–105). During this time, the focus of psychology shifted to include a more holistic approach to studying humans. Researchers began to again examine the mind-body connection that is essential in exploring DID/MPD. The rise of this new school of thought put emphasis (as Frischholtz stated) on the personal experience, also essential in examining the disorder. Putnam (1989) writes, "The new era began with the publication of Ellenberger's (1970) extensively researched and enlightening history of the origins and development of dynamic psychiatry" (p. 35). In the work, Ellenberger paid "considerable attention to dissociation and multiple personality" (p. 35). The popularity of the movie *Sybil* (Schreiber, 1973), based on the book about an MPD case, also brought media attention and widespread recognition to MPD, which undoubtedly also affected the reemergence of interest in research and studies on dissociation. During the 1970s, more case reports and papers were written on the subject. Putnam (1989) states:

> During the 1970s, a foundation was laid upon which the current resurgence of interest in and knowledge of MPD rests. The dedication and hard work of a small number of clinicians, initially in an isolated and independent fashion but later with increasing cooperation and mutual support, re-established MPD as a legitimate clinical disorder. The old and forgotten knowledge from the time of Janet and Morton Prince was resurrected and much new information added. (p. 34)

Frischholtz (1985) notes, "Until the late 1970s the incidence of multiple personality disorder was considered to be quite rare. Ralph B. Allison, M.D. was one of the first mental health professionals to point out the difficulties associated with making the diagnosis of multiple personality disorder" (p. 105).

With case reports of MPD increasing, the *Diagnostic and Statistical Manual of Mental Disorders,* 3rd edition (*DSM-III;* American Psychiatric Association, 1980) made MPD a legitimate, independent diagnosis. "The first two editions of the *Diagnostic and Statistical Manual of Mental Disorders* categorized multiple personality disorder as a variety of hysterical neurosis, choosing not to accord it a separate classification" (Frischholtz, 1985, p. 104). However, the *DSM-III* included MPD as a dissociative disorder, listing these diagnostic criteria:

The existence within the individual of two or more distinct personalities, each of which is dominant at a particular time.

The personality that is dominant at any particular time determines the individual's behavior.

Each individual personality is complex and integrated with its own unique behavior patterns and social relationships. (p. 259)

The criteria changed when the third edition of the *DSM* was revised (*DSM-III-R;* American Psychiatric Association, 1987). In the new edition, the criteria was slimmed down:

The existence within the person of two or more distinct personalities or personality states (each with its own relatively enduring pattern of perceiving, relating to, and thinking about the environment and self).

At least two of these personalities or personality states recurrently take full control of the person's behavior. (p. 272)

Along with the inclusion of MPD in the *DSM* in the 1980s, much professional work (research, case studies, conferences, and literature) was being done on the subject during this time. In fact, much of the research cited in this chapter was connected in the 1980s as interest in the subject blossomed. Among the books about MPD at the time was *Childhood Antecedents of Multiple Personality Disorder,* in which Kluft, the editor (1985b), states:

Aspects of Multiple Personality in Childhood, the symposium that gave rise to this monograph, was presented at the 137th Annual Meeting of the American Psychiatric Association in Los Angeles. This symposium was the first ever organized to discuss multiple personality in childhood and to explore its antecedent causes. It was a coming together of clinicians and researchers to share current knowledge and establish a database as a foundation for future work in this area. The original symposium's contributions have been augmented by additional studies, published for the first time in this monograph. (p. xi)

Research during this period was added to help create the body of knowledge as it exists today. Current research on DID/MPD includes studies about implicit and explicit memory (Eich, Macaulay, Loewenstein, & Dihle, 1997), as well as the continued search to prove or disprove (depending on which camp one sides with) the validity of the disorder (Goodwin, 1985; McHugh, n.d.; Ontario Consultants on Religious Tolerance, 2001; Shuman, 1996).

CURRENT TREATMENT BELIEFS

The history and research brings the field to its current treatment methods of the disorder. Researchers state that it is common for those diagnosed with DID/MPD to need three to five years of intensive therapy (Turkus, 1992). Duration depends on the competency level of the therapist, as well as the severity of DID/MPD and whether there are additional diagnoses. The International Society of the Study of Dissociation (1997) states:

> Opinions diverge on the length of treatment. Early anecdotal reports on treatment outcome showed that over 2–3 years of intensive outpatient psychotherapy, patients could reach a relatively stable condition in which they did not experience a sense of internal separateness. However, most therapists now see 3–5 years following the diagnosis of DID as a minimum length of treatment, with many of the more complex patients requiring 6 or more years of outpatient psychotherapy, often with brief inpatient stays during crises. The length of treatment varies with the complexity of the patient's Dissociative pathology, usually lengthening with severe Axis II pathology or other significant comorbid mental disorders. (III., B., ¶3)

Diagnostic tools have been created to help alleviate problems in diagnosing DID/MPD. Currently, there are such tools as the Dissociative Experience Scale (DES), Dissociation Questionnaire, Questionnaire of Experiences of Dissociation, and informal and structured interviews to identify the disorder. The goal of treatment is another source of controversy surrounding DID/MPD; however, most agree that integration, or at least movement away from separateness, is the suggested direction of therapy.

Clinicians write frequently about steps for the therapeutic process. Braun highlights these steps, as "13 Basic Psychotherapy Considerations of MPD" (1986b, p. 9):

1. Developing trust.
2. Making and sharing the diagnosis.
3. Communicating with each personality state.
4. Contracting.
5. Gathering history.
6. Working with each personality state's problems.
7. Undertaking special procedures.
8. Developing interpersonality communication.
9. Achieving resolution/integration.
10. Developing new behaviors and coping skills.
11. Networking and using social support systems.
12. Solidifying gains.
12. Following up.

Turkus (1992) writes about stabilization, mapping of the personality system, revisiting and reworking the trauma, and reclaiming self-worth and personal power. The emphasis on the importance of creating firm boundaries with clients with DID/MPD is also recurrent in the literature.

Many different modalities of treatment have been suggested in conjunction with individual psychotherapy. These additional treatments include group therapy, expressive therapies (art, poetry, movement, psychodrama, music), family therapy, psychoeducation, pharmacotherapy, inpatient treatment, hypnotherapy, occupational therapy, and play therapy. Additional current resources about DID/MPD are included at the end of the chapter as an appendix. Why and how play therapy is used as a treatment modality with adult clients diagnosed with DID is the focus of the rest of this chapter.

WHAT IS PLAY THERAPY?

Schaefer (Gardner, 1993) writes: "Play therapy can be defined as an interpersonal process wherein a trained therapist systematically applies the curative powers of play to help clients resolve their psychological difficulties" (p. 3). Similarly, O'Connor (2000) states:

> Play therapy consists of a cluster of treatment modalities that involve the systematic use of a theoretical model to establish an interpersonal process wherein trained play therapists use the therapeutic powers of play to help clients prevent or resolve psychosocial difficulties and achieve optimal growth and development and

the re-establishment of the child's ability to engage in play behavior as it is classically defined. (p. 7)

Landreth (1991) writes:

Play therapy is defined as a dynamic interpersonal relationship between a child and a therapist trained in play therapy procedures who provides selected play materials and facilitates the development of a safe relationship for the child to fully express and explore self (feelings, thoughts, experiences, and behaviors) through the child's natural medium of communication, play. (p. 14)

Moustakas (1953) states:

Play therapy may be thought of as a set of attitudes in and through which children may feel free enough to express themselves fully, in their own way, so that eventually they may achieve feelings of security, adequacy, and worthiness through emotional insight. The belief is that these attitudes are communicable. They can be transmitted from one person to another. (p. 2)

Moustakas (1959) also gives a definition of play therapy as a way to explain the process to parents:

Play therapy is a relationship between the child and therapist in the setting of a playroom, where the child is encouraged to express himself freely, to release pent-up emotions and repressed feelings, and to work through his fear and anger in terms of his real potentials and abilities. (p. 256)

Axline (1947) states:

Play therapy is based upon the fact that play is the child's natural medium of self-expression. It is an opportunity which is given to the child to "play out" his feelings and problems just as, in certain types of adult therapy, an individual "talks out" his difficulties. (p. 9)

The Association for Play Therapy (n.d.) defines *play therapy* on the homepage of their Web site as "The systematic use of a theoretical model to establish an interpersonal process wherein trained play therapists use the therapeutic powers of play to help clients prevent or resolve psychosocial difficulties and achieve optimal growth and development." Overall, *play therapy* can be defined as a therapeutic modality that uses the benefits of play to facilitate treatment with an emphasis on the relationship between therapist and client. By using this method, the therapist can get to know and gain understanding of the client by communicating with play.

Although I borrow from other schools of thought when appropriate, my emphasis in treatment is that of humanistic because my background and education is based in humanistic psychology. I have found this approach very beneficial in my work with a client diagnosed with DID. In humanistic psychology, there is a large emphasis on seeing and honoring clients as they are in the present and giving them insights on how they interact in the world. "The therapist respects the child for who he is at that time, at that moment, not for who he should be or who he might become" (Moustakas, 1953, p. 5). This type of treatment is centered on the client, and the therapeutic process is directed by the client. The approach is largely a nondirective method—meaning that the therapist is not pushing the client in any one direction. Rather, the client takes responsibility for the direction of the sessions.

> Nondirective therapy grants the individual the permissiveness to be himself; it accepts that self completely, without evaluation or pressure to change; it recognizes and clarifies the expressed emotionalized attitudes by a reflection of what the client has expressed; and, by the very process of nondirective therapy, it offers the individual the opportunity to be himself, to learn to know himself, to chart his own course openly and aboveboard—to rotate the kaleidoscope, so to speak, so that he may form a more satisfactory design for living. (Axline, 1947, p. 15)

Humanistic psychology incorporates a client-centered stance on treatment, believing that the client has all the knowledge needed to invoke development and growth. Landreth (1991) writes about principles of child-centered play therapy; however, I believe the same principles can be applied to clients of all ages:

> The child-centered philosophy is just that, an encompassing philosophy for living one's life in relationships with children—not a cloak of techniques to put on upon entering the playroom, but a way of being based on a deep commitment to certain beliefs about children and their innate capacity for growth. Child-centered play therapy is a complete therapeutic system, not just the application of a few rapport building techniques, and is based on the belief in the capacity and resiliency of children. Children are the best source of information about themselves. They are quite capable of appropriately directing their own growth and are granted the freedom to be themselves in the process of playing out feelings and experiences. The child creates his or her own history in the playroom, and the therapist respects the direction determined by the child. The child-centered therapist is concerned with developing the kind of relationship which facilitates inner emotional growth and children's belief in themselves. Child-centered play therapy is an attitude, a philosophy, and a way of being. (p. 55)

Moustakas (1953) states this about the child-centered approach: "The child-centered philosophy is thus not mainly concerned with techniques and skills but rather with the kind of relationship which enables children to grow emotionally and to gain faith in themselves as feeling individuals" (p. 2). Closely related to the humanistic and child/client-centered approaches are aspects of Gestalt therapy. Oaklander (2000) states this about Gestalt play therapy with children:

> The therapist is cognizant of the fact that, despite differences in age, experience, and education, she is not superior to the client; both are equally entitled. It is a relationship where two people come together in a dialogical stance. The therapist meets the child however he or she presents the self, without judgment, and with respect and honor. The therapist does not play a role. She is congruent and genuine, while at the same time respecting her own limits and boundaries, never losing herself to the child, but willing to be affected by the child. The therapist holds no expectations, yet maintains an attitude that supports the full, healthy potential of the child. The therapist is involved, contactful, and often interactive. She creates an environment of safety and never pushes the child beyond his or her capabilities or consent. The relationship itself is therapeutic; often, it provides an experience for the child that is new and unique. (pp. 28–29)

In summary, my definition and understanding of play therapy is the following: *Play therapy* uses the natural communication of play in the therapeutic relationship to accept, respect, and understand clients, which promotes self-directed, positive growth and insight.

WHY SHOULD PLAY THERAPY BE USED AS A TREATMENT METHOD FOR ADULT CLIENTS WITH DID?

With my definition of play therapy now established, I turn to the reasons I believe play therapy should be used in treating adults with DID. One reason stems from my humanistic viewpoint that all clients should be accepted just as they are. I believe that every client that walks through my office door needs to be heard and understood. This goes the same for different parts and aspects of each client, dissociative or not. What better way to listen to the voice of a child than in a child's environment? What better way to listen and understand the essence of a child alter, than in play? In much of the literature on DID, there is much discussion on the importance of knowing and understanding the different parts of a person diagnosed with DID. The more information the therapist and client can gain about the alters, the better understanding they will have of the whole person and the way the disorder has manifested itself. Munro (2000) gives this information on the Healing Hopes Web site to people with DID/MPD about knowing their different parts:

> It is important to get to know parts inside because they are a part of you and they affect how you are, how you feel, and how you act. Getting to know parts inside

can also enrich your life. You may find yourself seeing things from a different point of view, or gaining insights for the reasons you or parts inside act a certain way. Parts inside hold your history, your experiences, and some of your emotions and thus they are a vital part of you and shouldn't be ignored—to ignore them is to ignore yourself. ("Why Should I Get To Know Parts Inside?" section)

The prevalence of child alters in those who have DID is quite high because, it is speculated, the mechanism of dissociating began at a young age. Therefore, if dissociation began at a young age—usually because of outstanding abuse, crises, and/or trauma—why not be able to examine the root of the disorder and the related issues with child alters? By paying attention to who each alter is, the client and therapist gain valuable knowledge on why the alter was created in the first place. This information can help the client understand why he or she dissociated and perhaps work toward less dissociation in the future because of the self-knowledge gained. Each part of the person has an important story to tell. The stories of each of the alters help piece together the puzzle of DID in adults. Conducting play therapy with a child alter allows that part of the whole to feel comfortable and able to share his or her story. If the therapist treats the alter as an adult, he or she might miss understanding that important piece of the DID puzzle for the client.

Talking and dealing with trauma is difficult. For children and child alters, it is extremely difficult—mainly because many of them do not have the language to explain what happened or the cognitive abilities to understand the circumstance. They do not have the words to explain their experience or identity. However, they can show the therapist through their play.

> Due to the secretive nature of posttraumatic play, direct observation by therapists of posttraumatic play is most likely to occur only in a play therapy experience and then only after therapeutic conditions of acceptance and great safety are felt by the child. Play therapy seems to offer the most promise for effecting change and trauma resolution for traumatized children. There have also been promising reports in the literature describing the use of play therapy with child alters of adults with multiple personality disorders. (Landreth, Homeyer, Glover, & Sweeney, 1996, pp. 79–80)

Why not use the technique of play therapy to take advantage of the communication powers it has to offer with adult clients? Doing so gives valuable insight to both therapist and client. The child alter is able to communicate his or her story through the activities, such as fantasy play and art, in the playroom.

The nondirective nature of play therapy is also an advantage in working with adults diagnosed with DID. With all the controversy surrounding the disorder of DID and speculation that alters are created by therapists, it is of utmost importance not to create something that is not there. The nondirective nature of play therapy gives an avenue for the therapist to listen to the client and gives the client a chance to be heard and understood as he or she is. The client is directing the sessions and putting information in front of himself or herself as well as the therapist. And the therapist reflects back what was already communicated by the client. This fits in the framework of the Guidelines for Treatment set up by the International Society for the Study of Dissociation (1997):

> Whenever possible, treatment should move the patient toward a sense of integrated functioning. Although the therapist often addresses the parts of the mind as if they were separate, the therapeutic work needs to bring about an increased sense of connectedness or relatedness among the different alternate personalities. Thus, it is counterproductive to urge the patient to create additional alternate personalities, to urge alternate personalities to adopt names when they have none, or to urge that alternate personalities function in a more elaborated and autonomous way than they already are functioning in the patient. It is counterproductive to tell patients to ignore or get rid of alternate personalities. Also, the therapist should not play favorites among the alternate personalities or exclude unlikable or disruptive personalities from the therapy, although such steps may be necessary for a period of time at some stages in the treatment of some patients. (III., A., ¶2)

Therefore, the passiveness of nondirective play therapy makes this a good method for treating adults with DID.

However, there are several more directive approaches that can be delicately woven into play therapy to institute growth and development in adults with DID. Authors writing about play therapy outline many creative activities for play therapy—activities that promote insight, understanding, and movement toward growth in areas such as feelings, motivation to change, decreasing stress, skill learning, coping skills, dealing with loss, family issues, and self-esteem (Hobbay & Ollier, 1999). Schaefer (Gardner, 1993) lists overcoming resistance, communication, mastery, creative thinking, catharsis, abreaction, role play, fantasy, metaphoric teaching, attachment formation, relationship enhancement, enjoyment, mastering developmental fears, and game play as therapeutic factors of play therapy. If these activities promote therapeutic success in children, why not use their powers in therapy with adult clients that have child alters? Klein and Landreth (2001) state this about using play therapy with child alters of adults with DID:

> Often these child alters have many of the same difficulties expressing themselves verbally that children have. Therefore, these child alters could derive much of the same benefit from play therapy that children do. Children with emotional disturbances can best be treated using play therapy, since children have difficulty responding to traditional verbal therapies used by adults. Play is a natural

expression for children and is acted out effortlessly. Therefore, expressions of the child alter of the adult client will more readily be facilitated. (p. 323)

Landreth (1991) writes this about using play therapy with adults:

> Since the focus is on the play activity and not the person(s) involved, the adult becomes absorbed in the activity of play itself and thus engages in a kind of awareness that is not possible through mere verbalization. Through play the adult has a conversation with self that is a very personal experience because direct involvement is called for. The dollhouse, sandbox, paints, and Bobo are very facilitative materials for adults. Some therapists have reported exciting results allowing adults to choose toys freely in the playroom. (p. 36)

There is absolutely no reason that adults cannot learn and grow from the experience of play just as children can—especially if there were outstanding reasons and events that kept the person from learning those lessons usually learned in play as a child. Frank (1982) states:

> It may be said that adult living is largely play, but we no longer recognize it as such since the adult has largely ceased to recognize his past and is committed to the more or less specific and often rigidly patterned "make-believe" fantasies and symbolic goals of his social-cultural group, unable to play other games freely, or take on new roles as the child does. (p. 24)

The promotion of development through play is another excellent reason to incorporate play therapy into treatment of adults with DID. Play therapy with the child alter of an adult with DID can bring development and growth by allowing the person to have an experience that he or she may have never fully had before. With a childhood littered by abuse and trauma, it would make sense that these individuals would not have experienced the healthy and enriching world of play. Benefits of play therapy include gross and fine motor skill development, hand-eye coordination, cognitive and language development, and social skill development. These skills may never have had the chance to develop in adults with DID. The lack of the skills could be negatively impacting their lives and personal growth. Play is essential for the emotional growth of the individual as a whole. "Play is an important element in the development of many life skills, such as rule learning and problem solving. Children who acquire skills through play can build them into habits and roles. It assists in the development of interests, values, and motivation" (Taylor, Menarchek-Fetkovich, & Day, 2000, p. 114). I would change that statement to say, "*Anyone* who acquires skills through play can build them into habits and roles." A sense of mastery and accomplishment can be gained through the activity in play therapy. These are powerful lessons to individuals whose lives have been scattered with powerlessness and lack of control.

In examining the type and kind of play the child alter of an adult with DID is exhibiting, the therapist can gain further information about the client. By observing the play of the child alter, the therapist is able to determine what stage of play the child alter of an adult with DID is in. There are several "play epochs" that individuals progress through in their development. These epochs are sensorimotor (0 to 2 years); symbolic and simple constructive (2 to 4 years); dramatic, complex constructive, and pregame (4 to 7 years); and game and recreation (7 to 12 years) (Taylor et al., 2000, p. 117):

> To determine how children's play behaviors are progressing, it is necessary to be able to systematically evaluate their play patterns. Depending on a variety of factors, the exhibited play behaviors may be within the expected range of functioning or may be precocious, delayed, or deviant in nature. (p. 115)

The understanding of what play epoch the child alter fits into can give the therapist and the client insight on how and when the individual's development was affected. Work in the playroom can be done to promote growth in deficient areas and to teach the adult how to play in ways he or she was not able to learn before.

As I have outlined, there are many reasons that play therapy can be helpful in working with adults diagnosed with DID. The importance of accepting and getting to know the alters, the complexity in communicating traumatic events, the nondirective nature of play therapy, the known benefits of play therapy, and the developmental impact of play therapy make this method a viable option for treatment of DID in adults.

WHEN SHOULD PLAY THERAPY BE USED WITH ADULTS WITH DID?

I use play therapy with my client who is diagnosed with DID when she chooses to do so. This follows in the vein of the nondirective approach. The setup in my office makes it easy to create the self-directive decision-making scenario. My office is at the end of a hallway, and the playroom is on the other side of the hallway. When the appointment time begins, I allow the client to choose the room she would like to use that day. I have found that the child alter always decides to use the playroom and is excited to be in that environment. I have never forced a decision or set up the playroom in a directive manner. Each session has been nondirective, yet extremely revealing, as her process naturally unfolds. The use of the playroom and play therapy is just one part of many that are incorporated into this client's therapy. I did not add the method of play therapy into treatment until I felt a solid base of trust was established with the host personality.

WHERE SHOULD THE PLAY THERAPY SESSIONS
WITH ADULTS WITH DID TAKE PLACE?

The obvious choice would be in a playroom that is established for play therapy. Typically, play therapy toys and materials include a sandbox or sand tray, plastic figures (such as people and animals), dolls, dollhouse(s), cars and trucks, puppets, medical equipment, telephones, simple board games, soft balls, play dough or clay, crayons and markers, paper, dress-up clothes, and an inflatable punching bag. Some variety is necessary to include toys that facilitate different types of play, such as aggressive or nurturing, role-playing or fantasy play, and creative or rule-based. However, it is not necessary to have every type of toy because items may be created throughout the play therapy session. If a proper play therapy room is not available, a "regular" office can easily be converted into a room for play by having a ready-made playroom-in-bag/box available for such occasions consisting of a few of these articles. It is important to create a warm and inviting atmosphere. "The atmosphere in the playroom is of critical importance because that is what impacts the child first. The playroom should have an atmosphere of its own which conveys warmth and a clear message 'This is a place for children'" (Landreth, 1991, p. 109). Safety and confidentiality should always be a concern, so it is important to take into consideration how soundproof the room is, eliminate any items that could be dangerous, and make sure there is ample room to move around with the toys that are available. When creating a playroom, never include something that you do not want broken—accidents happen. There also may be purposeful behavior that may have extreme therapeutic value when discussed in the session. Boundaries and limits should always be set for appropriate playroom behavior; however, those boundaries and limits could be broken at any time by the client through acting-out behaviors. Consistency of what toys are available and where the toys are placed is also very important. The consistency gives the client a sense of safety and predictability that leads to a feeling of control over the environment—a feeling that may not be a norm for a person diagnosed with DID. Because of this rule, it is not acceptable for the client to take any of the playroom materials with him or her on leaving the session. Ensure the client that, by leaving the toys in the room, they will always be available when he or she comes to session.

HOW TO USE PLAY THERAPY WITH ADULTS
DIAGNOSED WITH DID

I have covered all the surrounding issues regarding using play therapy with adults diagnosed with DID—what the disorder is (and is not), the history of DID/MPD, and why I believe the method of play therapy is appropriate and useful in treating DID. I now turn to how to do play therapy with adults diagnosed with DID. As stated earlier, I believe it is important to establish a solid rapport with the host client before using play therapy as a treatment option. If play therapy is rushed into before a solid relationship is formed, that client may not feel comfortable using a nontraditional treatment option for adults. As with almost everything in therapy, timing is everything. When it seems that the time is right, discuss the option of play therapy with the client. With the client that I see, I discussed play therapy with both the host personality and the child alter. As part of this discussion, I explained what play therapy is and some of the things she might expect as an outcome of the play therapy. It is also important to discuss whether the client would be comfortable with recording the play therapy session either by tape or video recorder. If so, make sure proper documentation is made and permission forms are signed before taping the sessions.

With every playroom client, the first time we enter the playroom, I set the ground rules and explain play therapy. I start off by reading the book *The Child's First Book about Play Therapy,* by Marc A. Nemiroff and Jane Annunziata (1990) to the client. This book, written for children entering play therapy, explains the basis and possible expectations of play therapy. After reading the book, I explain the ground rules, such as confidentiality, time boundaries, and rules of the play room. I have very few rules: (a) The client cannot hurt himself or herself, (b) The client cannot purposely hurt me (the therapist), (c) The client cannot purposely damage toys, and (d) All toys must remain in the playroom. I repeat a statement that I learned from VanFleet (1994): "(Child's name), this is a very special room. You can do almost anything you want to do in this playroom. If there's something you cannot do, I'll let you know" (p. 15). Going over the rules and my expectations gives the client some structure and boundaries, crucial for creating safety in the relationship and process. At that point, it is up to the client to determine the direction the session should go. Allowing this to occur, I have seen several aspects unfold.

One experience I witnessed in using nondirective play therapy with an adult client diagnosed with DID was her profound reactions to childhood stimuli. Several of the items in the playroom evoked memories for the child alter. For example, certain smells in the playroom reminded her of her days in elementary school. Another example was her strong reaction to the sandbox in the playroom. Merely seeing the sandbox triggered clouded memories of a painful event that occurred in a sandbox sometime in early childhood. Both the child alter and the host personality had this reaction—both carried blurry recollections of the traumatic event. As she was recalling these memories, I reflected on her statements and asked her to put feeling words to what she was experiencing. I also emphasized to the client that she was recalling a memory, and that, here in the present, she was safe from danger. This experience allowed her to safely examine her fear and anxiety in recalling the memory. She was able to release some feelings related to that event.

> When children are unsuccessful in their attempts to deal with anxiety, the resulting tension produces disturbances in behavior. Through an acting out process, release play therapy helps the child release the anxiety that the child was unable to express fully in the original situation. Feelings that are unexpressed produce symptomatic behavior. The more the child acts out the feelings, the more the feelings are released. (Klein & Landreth, 2001, p. 326)

A large part of working with these triggers is reinforcing the difference of past and present, now and then. At the point when the client can determine the difference between past and present situations, the client can then gain power and understanding over the object or issue by restructuring.

> In play therapy, children may master a fearing object by taking on the role of one who does not fear it. They may act in ways that suggest they are not afraid. By "pretending" and practicing, the child may overcome the feared stimuli. (Knell, 2000. p. 7)

Mastery of fears helps the client gain control over his or her life. Clients can examine their own feelings and thoughts surrounding particular issues that are important to them and their recovery. They may conclude that their perceptions of certain things are skewed and they would be better off with a more realistic perspective. Play therapy can help people identify and modify maladaptive thoughts and gain control in their lives (Knell, 2000, pp. 6–7).

There are several ways to help facilitate growth and movement from these triggers and/or fears. Many of these techniques are more directive therapy approaches. They help the client think of alternative endings to situations the client believes he or she has no control over. One of these techniques is called *Mutual Storytelling:*

> In this technique, the therapist, on hearing a story, surmises its psychodynamic meaning, selects one or two important themes, and then creates a story of his own, using the same characters in a similar setting. However, the therapist's story differs from that of the child in that he introduces healthier resolutions and maturer adaptations. (Gardner, 1993, p. 199)

Another similar technique works with a drawing that the client created in a way that puts the client in control of what is occurring in the picture. I used this technique with a picture my client drew of an abusive situation she endured as a child. To protect herself in the picture, she ripped off the part of the picture where the perpetrator was drawn and tore it to shreds, leaving only herself on the page, finally safe. Alternate endings can also be created when the client is engaging in fantasy play or working with the sand tray. Clients often reenact situations that they lived through in their play to gain better understanding and insight to these situations. At this point, the therapist can ask questions to help facilitate the process. Often, these reenactments are repeated frequently when they are particularly distressing to a client. One way to break the repetitive cycle is to devise an alternative ending that puts the client in control of the situation. For example, if the plastic monsters in the sand tray are always beating up the people and burying them under the sand, it may be suggested that the people beat up and bury the monsters instead. As simple as it seems, the client may have never thought of turning the tables. Another more directed technique is to use books written on issues concerning the child alter. Bibliotherapy is becoming increasingly popular; there are thousands of books written for children and their related issues, which could easily be used with adults with DID. Other possible interventions are systematic desensitization, emotive imagery, contingency management, positive reinforcement (such as chart systems), shaping, stimulus fading, extinction, modeling, cognitive change strategies, and positive self-statements (Knell, 2000). I have outlined only a few techniques that could be used in play therapy with adult clients diagnosed with DID; however, almost any technique written for use with children in play therapy could be used and have the same therapeutic effects on adults as it had on children.

Client reactions can also be triggered by items in the playroom that may be causing them current stress. Household items, such as cleaning utensils, telephones, and dishes, may bring conversations about handling daily stresses. I have found that the child alter I work with gets very frustrated with certain items and situations that she encounters as a child in an adult's body. In these situations, I help her arrive at better ways to cope. Without this avenue to explore these items, she may not have felt comfortable in explaining her deficits in manipulating these daily functions.

Another process I have seen unfold is anger work. It seems natural that a person who underwent abuse and trauma would be angry about what happened and angry with the person who caused the pain. In many incidents, the abused person was never "allowed" to be angry with the other person. Allowing the anger to be released in the safety of the playroom can be extremely powerful and moving for the client. "Physical activities allow for kinetic dissipation of energy and the playroom provides safe objects onto which anger may be displaced" (Klein & Landreth, 2001, p. 330). The DID client that I work with has used the playroom in this manner with both the host personality and the child alter. Strong feelings, loud words, and physical aggression directed toward the bop bag allowed her an outlet for many years of pent-up anger that she never felt safe to release.

SUMMARY

The goal of this chapter was to help clarify and increase understanding of the diagnosis of dissociative identity disorder (DID) by looking at it through history, controversy, and the present. I explained the process of using the powerful technique of play therapy as part of treating adults with DID. I provided current definitions of DID and terms related to the disorder, explored the history and impact of the spirit of the times on the disorder, and discussed current trends in research (that reflected the history of the disorder). Current beliefs and guidelines for the treatment of DID/MPD were summarized. I concluded with examining the what, why, when, where, and how of using play therapy with adults diagnosed with DID.

APPENDIX

Helpful Resources about DID/MPD

Autobiographies:

Casey, J. (1992). *The flock: The autobiography of a multiple personality.* New York: Fawcett Columbine.
Chase, T. (1987). *When rabbit howls.* New York: Jove.
Sizemore, C. (1977). *I'm Eve.* Garden City, NJ: Doubleday.

Television:

Mind of a Murderer (PBS video, 120 minutes). Documentary of Kenneth Bianchi, who attempted to use DID as his defense.
The Brain: Part 8: States of Consciousness (1984), PBS video, 58 minutes.
The Unexplained: Multiple Personality Disorder (March 11, 1999), A&E video.

Web sites:

www.dissociation.com
www.healinghopes.org
www.issd.org
www.lunacat.net-mpd/did-literature
www.mentalhealth.about.com
www.multiple-personality.com
www.needid.bizland.com
www.rossinst.com
www.sidran.org
www.toddletime.com

REFERENCES

American Psychiatric Association. (1980). *Diagnostic and statistical manual of mental disorders* (3rd ed.). Washington, DC: Author.

American Psychiatric Association. (1987). *Diagnostic and statistical manual of mental disorders* (3rd ed., rev.). Washington, DC: Author.

American Psychiatric Association. (1994). *Diagnostic and statistical manual of mental disorders* (4th ed.). Washington, DC: Author.

Association for Play Therapy. (n.d.). *Play therapy.* Retrieved December 17, 2001, from www.a4pt.org.

Axline, V. (1947). *Play therapy.* Boston: Houghton Mifflin.

Braun, B. (1985). The transgenerational incidence of dissociation and multiple personality disorder: A preliminary report. In R. Kluft (Ed.), *Childhood antecedents of multiple personality* (pp. 128–150). Washington, DC: American Psychiatric Press.

Braun, B. (1986a). Introduction. In B. G. Braun (Ed.), *Treatment of multiple personality disorder* (pp. xi–xxi). Washington, DC: American Psychiatric Association.

Braun, B. (1986b). Issues in the psychotherapy of multiple personality disorder. In B. G. Braun (Ed.), *Treatment of multiple personality disorder* (pp. 3-28). Washington, DC: American Psychiatric Press.

Braun, B., & Sachs, R. (1985). The development of multiple personality disorder: Predisposing, precipitating, and perpetuating factors. In R. Kluft (Ed.), *Childhood antecedents of multiple personality* (pp. 38–64). Washington, DC: American Psychiatric Press.

Brennan, M. (n.d.). *Dissociative disorder.* Retrieved December 4, 2001, from www.personal.umd.umich.edu/~marcyb/106/psych/brennan.html.

Breuer, J., & Freud, S. (1895). *Studies on hysteria.* London: Hogarth Press.

Eich, E., Macaulay, D., Loewenstein, E., & Dihle, P. (1997). Memory, amnesia, and dissociative identity disorder. *Psychological Science, 8,* 417–422.

Ellenberger, H. (1970). *The discovery of the unconscious.* New York: Basic Books.

Frank, L. (1982). Play in personality development. In G. Landreth (Ed.), *Play therapy: Dynamics of the process of counseling with children* (pp. 19–32). Springfield, IL: Charles C Thomas.

Frischholz, E. (1985). The relationship among dissociation, hypnosis, and child abuse in the development of multiple personality disorder. In R. Kluft (Ed.), *Childhood antecedents of multiple personality* (pp. 100–136). Washington, DC: American Psychiatric Press.

Gardner, R. (1993). Mutual storytelling. In C. Schaefer & D. Cangelosi (Eds.), *Play therapy techniques* (pp. 3, 199–209). Northvale, NJ: Aronson.

Gil, E. (1990). *United we stand: A book for people with multiple personalities.* Walnut Creek, CA: Launch Press.

Goodwin, J. (1985). Credibility problems in multiple personality disorder patients and abused children. In R. Kluft (Ed.), *Childhood antecedents of multiple personality* (pp. 2–19). Washington, DC: American Psychiatric Press.

Healing Hopes. (2001). *Switching*. Retrieved December 4, 2001, from www.healing-hopes.org.library/switch.html.

Hobbay, A., & Ollier, K. (1999). *Creative therapy with children and adolescents*. Atascadero, CA: Impact.

International Society for the Study of Dissociation. (1997). *Guidelines for treating dissociative identity disorder (multiple personality disorder) in adults*. Retrieved December 4, 2001, from www.issd.org/indexpage/isdguide.htm.

Johnson, N. (Producer/Director). (1957). *The Three Faces of Eve* [Motion picture]. Century City, CA: 20th Century Fox.

Klein, J., & Landreth, G. (2001). Play therapy with dissociative identity disorder clients with child alters. In G. Landreth (Ed.), *Innovations in play therapy* (pp. 323–333). Philadelphia: Brunner-Routledge.

Kluft, R. (1985a). Childhood multiple personality disorder: Predictors, clinical findings, and treatment results. In R. Kluft (Ed.), *Childhood antecedents of multiple personality* (pp. 168–196). Washington, DC: American Psychiatric Press.

Kluft, R. (1985b). Introduction: Multiple personality disorder in the 1980s. In R. Kluft (Ed.), *Childhood antecedents of multiple personality* (pp. viii–xiv). Washington, DC: American Psychiatric Press.

Knell, S. (2000). Cognitive-behavioral play therapy for childhood fears and phobia. In H. G. Kaduson & C. Schaefer (Eds.), *Short-term play therapy for children* (pp. 3–27). New York: Guilford Press.

Landreth, G. (1991). *Play therapy: The art of the relationship*. Muncie, IN: Accelerated Development.

Landreth, G., Homeyer, L., Glover, G., & Sweeney, D. (1996). *Play therapy interventions with children's problems*. Northvale, NJ: Aronson.

Mahari, A. (n.d.). *DID/MPD defined in my own words (non-professional definition)*. Retrieved December 4, 2001, from home.golden.net/~soul/didmpd.htmpl.

McHugh, P. (n.d.) *Multiple personality disorder (dissociative identity disorder)*. Retrieved December 4, 2001, from www.psycom.net/mchugh.html.

Moustakas, C. (1953). *Children in play therapy*. New York: Ballentine.

Moustakas, C. (1959). *Psychotherapy with children*. New York: Harper & Row.

Munro, K. (2000). *DID, MPD, or multiplicity: How to respond to parts inside with a focus on kids*. Retrieved December 5, 2001, from www.healinghopes.org/library/parts.html.

Nemiroff, M., & Annunziata, J. (1990). *The child's first book about play therapy*. Washington, DC: American Psychological Association.

Oaklander, V. (2000). Short-term gestalt play therapy for grieving children. In H. G. Kaduson & C. Schaefer (Eds.), *Short-term play therapy for children* (pp. 28–52). New York: Guilford Press.

O'Connor, K. (2000). *The play therapy primer*. New York: Wiley.

Ontario Consultants on Religious Tolerance. (2001). *Nature and history of the MPD/DID controversy*. Retrieved December 4, 2001, from www.religioustolerance.org/mpd_did2.htm.

Putnam, F. (1985). Dissociation as a response to extreme trauma. In R. Kluft (Ed.), *Childhood antecedents of multiple personality* (pp. 65–97). Washington, DC: American Psychiatric Press.

Putnam, F. (1989). *Diagnosis and treatment of multiple personality disorder.* New York: Guilford Press.

Schreiber, F. (1973). *Sybil.* New York: Henry Regenry.

Shuman, D. (1996). Commentary on "multiple personality and moral responsibility." Retrieved December 4, 2001 from http://muse.jhu.edu/demo/philosophy_psychiatry _and_psychology/3.1shuman.html.

Sidran Foundation. (1994). *What is Dissociative identity disorder?* Retrieved December 4, 2001, from www.sidran.org/didbr.html.

Spiegel, D. (1986). Dissociation, double binds, and posttraumatic stress in multiple personality disorder. In B. G. Braun (Ed.), *Treatment of multiple personality disorder* (pp. 64–75). Washington, DC: American Psychiatric Press.

Taylor, K., Menarchek-Fetkovich, M., & Day, C. (2000). The play history interview. In K. Gitlin-Weiner, A. Sandgrund, & C. Schaefer (Eds.), *Play diagnosis and assessment* (2nd ed., pp. 114–138). New York: Wiley.

Thigpen, C., & Cleckley, H. (1954). A case of multiple personality. *Journal of Abnormal and Social Psychology, 49,* 135–151.

Turkus, J. (1992). *The spectrum of Dissociative disorders: An overview of diagnosis and treatment.* Retrieved December 4, 2001, from www.voiceofwomen.com /centerarticle.html.

VanFleet, R. (1994). *Filial therapy: Strengthening parent-child relationships through play.* Sarasota, FL: Professional Resource.

West, C. (n.d.). *Dissociative Identity Disorder (DID) fact sheet.* Retrieved December 4, 2001, from cameronwest.com/did1.html.

Wilbur, C. (1985). The effect of child abuse on the psyche. In R. Kluft (Ed.), *Childhood antecedents of multiple personality* (pp. 22–35). Washington, DC: American Psychiatric Press.

Epilogue

"Play takes place in the overlap of two areas of playing, that of the patient and that of the therapist. Psychotherapy has to do with two people playing together. The corollary . . . is that where playing is not possible, then the work of the therapist is directed towards bringing the patient from a state of not being able to play into a state of being able to play."

—D. W. Winnicott (1971)
Playing & Reality
New York: Basic Books, p. 38

Author Index ─────────────────────────

Subject Index